INTERNATIONAL LAW GOVERNING COMMUNICATIONS AND INFORMATION
A Collection Of
Basic Documents

Prepared by:
Edward W. Ploman,
International Institute of Communications

Greenwood Press
Westport, Ct.

Library of Congress Cataloging in Publication Data:

Main entry under title:

International law governing communications and information.

   1.   Communication and traffic—Law and legislation.
2. Communication, International.   3.   Freedom of information.   I.   Ploman, Edward W., 1926- .
K4240.I55   341.7'57   81-7036
ISBN 0-313-23277-6 (lib. bdg.)   AACR2

Library of Congress Catalog Card Number: 81-7036
ISBN: 0-313-23277-6

First published 1982

Published in the United States and Canada by
Greenwood Press, a division of Congressional
Information Service, Inc., Westport, Connecticut

English language edition, except the United States and Canada,
published by Frances Pinter (Publishers) Limited

Printed in the United States of America

TABLE OF CONTENTS

341.757
An 8 P

LIST OF INSTRUMENTS

The following list of instruments includes all the texts that have been quoted, in full or in part. The following abbreviations have been used:

UNGA: United Nations General Assembly
UNECOSOC: United Nations Economic and Social Council

D

INTRODUCTION

1. General background; approach adopted

The present image of law and regulation in the field of communications and information is one of change and confusion. Neither national legislation nor international law provide for a coherent body of law which may be defined as 'communications and information law'. Such law as exists is pluralistic and uncoordinated. It is dispersed among a variety of legal regimes that are of diverse origin and development, that regulate different although inter-related and overlapping processes and products, and that are adopted by or within the framework of organizations with different objectives and mandates.

The development of the legal regimes that are applicable to communications and information has been subject to three main influences:

  i. the transformation of international relations and the international system since 1945,
 ii. changes in attitudes towards the communications/information complex,
iii. the introduction of new communications technology and services.

Communications represent an area of international relations where modern, functional international law first developed: telecommunications and postal law and intellectual property rights belong to the oldest forms of functional international law, dating back to the middle of last century. The original concepts were formulated and adopted by a limited number of mainly European states. Consequently, these branches of international law have in recent years been subject to considerable stress through the need of adapting to the changing international situation, symbolized in the process of de-colonization. Other branches of relevant law such as outer space law have from the beginning developed in the present wider international context.

Such branches of international communications law as telecommunications regulation and copyright have thus been under continuous but separate evolution since the second half of the last century. Other early agreements concerned the content of international information flows in the sense of promoting the exchange of information in specified areas, or in rules added after the First World War of prohibiting certain kinds of content (war propaganda, obscenity).

In modern international law as it has developed since 1945, the new bases for standard-setting and regulation in the field of communications and information have mainly been associated with human rights, under the headings of freedom of information and free flow of information (Charter of the United Nations, Universal Declaration of Human Rights, Unesco Constitution). Subsequently, scientific and technological developments have required international agreement and regulation in new areas such as outer space and informatics. The increasing politicization of information issues and the changes in attitudes towards communications have also resulted in a growing attention to policy formation and law in this field, particularly with regard to the mass media. In the last few years, critique of traditional concepts and practices has been expressed through new concepts such as the new international information order and the right to communicate. Such concepts are revealing in that they represent a double movement: conceptually they represent attempts to go beyond traditional notions towards a more holistic, global view of the communications/information complex; in terms of objectives and possible guides for policy and regulation, they represent attempts to change current patterns of communication and information flows, nationally and internationally.

The expressions 'communication(s)' and 'information', particularly when used in conjunction, are now given wide, often vague and not rarely inconsistent interpretation. One problem therefore concerns the definition of the subject matter, the need to set the limits for what should and can be included under 'communications and information law'. A reasonable, although not entirely satisfactory approach has been suggested in terms of international transactions being seen as movements of information, of physical objects, of people and of money. According to this approach

- communication concerns the movements of information and ideas
- transportation concerns the movements of physical objects
- travel concerns the movements of people
- finance or financial transactions concern the movements of money

For the purpose of this collection the focus is on communications and on transportation in so far as it concerns the movement of information on physical support (printed, recorded products). The term 'communications' is used as referring to formalized systems and not, except by implication, to interpersonal, face to face communication.

A further difficulty has been the search for a conceptual structure that would be reasonably logical and at the same time practical. In the absence of a generally agreed approach to the international legal regimes applicable to communications and information, a special framework had to be developed. Whenever appropriate, traditionally used categories have been taken as a basis even though they are not consistent nor adequate in other respects. The conceptual framework also had to be flexible enough to provide a reasonably coherent approach to related and overlapping subject areas, and to relate legal regimes to law-making organizations. At the same time, the conceptual structure had to accommodate emerging legal regimes such as those governing transborder data flows as well as such recent issue areas as the new international information order and the right to communicate. In order to provide the context for the instruments that specifically regulate communications and information, the collection includes general documents of international law that are relevant to the conduct of communications and establish the intergovernmental law-making process and organizational structure.

The collection therefore includes three categories of international law:

- general international law which is applicable in the field of communications and information as in all other areas
- legal rules and agreements in a wide range of areas which include references to the conduct of communications and information for the achievement of stated goals (e.g. international understanding, disarmament, social and economic progress)
- the bulk of the texts represents currently valid rules in the various branches of law that deal explicitly and directly with communications and information. Of the categories used for this collection

some refer to clearly established or recognized branches of international law such as telecommunications law, space law and intellectual property rights; others like information law are a composite covering a number of related subject and issue areas.

Since this collection has to comprise texts from a wide range of legal branches which sometimes provide regulations in painstaking detail, it has not been possible to include all relevant texts in full and still keep the collection within manageable size. The selection has been based on the following criteria:

- instruments of general international law: a selection of the most important provisions which contain principles and rules applicable to all international behaviour and relations, and to the organizational structure and law-making process
- instruments dealing with subject matters other than communications: general principles and the specific references to the role of communication and information
- instruments explicitly and specifically governing communication and information activities; in the case of instruments that provide for detailed technical regulation, provisions have been included that refer to basic principles or have general validity.

Each section has been supplied with an introduction intended to provide guidance and point to important features of the instruments included. Within each section the instruments are set out in chronological order.

2.   Remarks on the sources of international law and the validity of different instruments

International legal rules and agreements are expressed in an almost bewildering diversity of texts with different status and validity: treaties, conventions, covenants, declarations, resolutions, acts, protocols. This diversity is striking in the area of communications and information where it reflects the number and variety of both issues and law-making organizations.

There seems to be general agreement that law is binding only if laid down in an appropriate manner, i.e. if it proceeds from a recognized source. The most authoritative statement concerning the sources of international law is to be found in Article 38 of the Statute of the International Court of Justice. In this article the law-creating processes are enumerated and ordered in an hierarchical manner:

1. international conventions
2. international customary law
3. general principles of law recognized by civilized nations

As a strictly subsidiary means for the determination of rules of international law are also mentioned judicial decisions and academic writings.

  i.   The place of treaties is of crucial importance in international law. Treaties are used by states as the major instrument to establish legally binding agreements, whether simple bilateral arrangements or complex multilateral expression of international law. The fundamental principle of treaty law is that treaties are binding upon the parties to them and must be performed in good faith (*pacta servanda sunt*).

The form of the instrument by which the common will of the parties is expressed is immaterial. Thus, treaties are known by a variety of names ranging from conventions, agreements, pacts, general acts and charters to statutes, covenants or protocols. Whatever their titles, their subject matter or the number of signatories, treaties conform to the same definition: an international agreement concluded between states in written form and governed by international law. An authoritative reflection of current rules and practices is embodied in the Vienna Convention on the Law of Treaties 1969.

Among these binding instruments figure agreements of universal or quasi-universal adherence such as the constituent documents of modern international organizations to which virtually all countries belong, e.g. the Charter of the United Nations, the Constitution of Unesco or the International Telecommunication Convention. Others are multilateral agreements laying down legal rules accepted by a majority or a large number of states such as the Outer Space Treaty of 1967. Others bind only a limited number of states, often on a regional level, such as the European or American Conventions on Human Rights. The majority of treaties, however, consist of bilateral agreements regulating relations at the highest political level as the Franco–German Treaty of Co-operation to instruments regulating minor matters such as the building of a customs shed.

The focus of this collection is on multilateral conventions including the constituent instruments of relevant international organizations and the principles laid down in important regional agreements. A wide range of bilateral agreements have been concluded in the communications and information field, but these have not been included in the present collection.

In contrast to treaties, expressions of international agreement which are formulated in declarations, resolutions and recommendations are not legally binding upon states. Yet, they contain legal significance and have a legal function. Such instruments play a crucial role in the development of international law. A significant example is the declaration of legal principles governing outer space activities adopted by the UN General Assembly in 1963 which provided the basis for the 1967 Outer Space Treaty. Moreover, declarations and resolutions can have great power in terms of standard-setting and moral persuasion; one of the most famous examples is the Universal Declaration of Human Rights.

If such declarations and resolutions are adopted by a majority verging on unanimity or virtually without opposition, they may contribute to or be evidence of the formation of international customary law. It has also been argued that while UN General Assembly resolutions do not have binding force, the principle of good faith would not permit a state to disregard a recommendation which it has formally approved by a positive vote. It should be noted that a resolution which is not binding upon states may have binding force on the internal order of the concerned international institution.

The importance of an international legal instrument also depends on the acceptance it has gained; in principle, the wider the acceptance, the greater its importance. To some extent, the status of an international instrument is even defined in relation to the hierarchy of the law-making organizations; thus, a text adopted by the UN General Assembly is, by some countries, seen as carrying more weight than texts adopted by the specialized agencies.

ii.   International customary law is a dynamic source of law which is both complex and controversial. The essence of custom as stated in Article 38 of the Statutes of the International Court of Justice is that it should constitute 'evidence of a general practice accepted as law'. For a rule of international customary law to come into existence, no particular form is required, nor must the rule have existed for any particular length of time. It totally depends on general acceptance as a rule of law. Thus, it is generally felt that there are two basic elements in the make-up of custom. There are the material facts, i.e. the actual, observable behaviour of states, and the psychological, subjective element, i.e. the belief that certain behaviour is 'law'.

Often, customary law is seen as appropriate when novel problems arise with unpredictable implications. States may prefer to regulate these problems on the basis of customary law which is less precise, more fluid and easier to change than formal treaty law.

Customary international law has been exemplified by such principles as sovereignty, recognition, consent, good faith, freedom of the seas, international responsibility and self-defence.

iii.   As a third source of international law, Article 38 includes a provision on the 'general principles of law recognized by civilized nations'. Not surprisingly, there is little agreement as to the precise definition and significance of these general principles of law. In practical terms, their significance would vary according to the level of international integration on which they are invoked.

According to one school of thought, general principles of law are not so much a source of law as a method of using existing sources, i.e. extension of existing rules by analogy and reasoning, application of rules which have not yet crystallized into definite custom, etc.

iv.   Finally, Article 38, includes 'judicial decisions and the teachings of the most highly qualified publicists of the various nations' as a strictly 'subsidiary means for the determination of rules of law'. These sources are obviously open to interpretation and in any case do not play any role in the context of this collection where the focus is on positive law in terms of existing legal instruments.

The international legal texts that comprise this collection have been selected so as to include:
− all major binding instruments applicable to communications and information
− other important documents of a non-binding character: resolutions, declarations etc. adopted by major organizations, including relevant draft treaty texts that have not yet been agreed
− texts adopted by the international organizations particularly those within the UN system and the most important texts adopted by regional organizations.

PART ONE
GENERAL INTERNATIONAL LAW

This first part comprises a selection of major international legal instruments containing general principles of international law that regulate or set standards for the conduct of states. They are thus applicable in the field of communications and information as they are in other areas. Also included in this section are international instruments governing a variety of subject matters which comprise rules specifically referring to the role of communications and information to achieve stated objectives; as examples may be mentioned the international conventions on the elimination of racial discrimination and on the suppression of apartheid. Moreover, a number of documents setting out objectives in such areas as social progress and development include references to the role of communications for their realization.

The documentation in this section has been ordered according to organizational origin: it comprises, first, relevant instruments adopted or sponsored by the UN and agencies within the UN system; this is followed by instruments adopted by regional and other organizations outside of the UN system.

I. INSTRUMENTS ADOPTED OR SPONSORED BY THE UNITED NATIONS

Similar to the structure of the following sections, the material has been divided into two main groups: instruments of a binding nature and non-binding declarations, recommendations or resolutions. Given the wide range of subject matters of relevance to communications and information, the texts in the second group have been divided into four categories: human rights, including political independence and decolonization; security and disarmament; peace and international understanding; social progress and development.

The focus is on the decisions of the General Assembly. Other UN bodies particularly those involved in development activities also contribute to evolving communication policies, e.g. the Economic and Social Council (ECOSOC), United Nations Development Programme (UNDP) and the United Nations Regional Commissions for Africa (ECA), Asia and the Pacific (ESCAP) and Latin America (ECLA). Resolutions of these bodies have generally not been included.

1. The Charter of the United Nations and related instruments

The Charter of the United Nations adopted in 1945 is generally regarded as a key source of modern international law. The Articles that have been included in this collection comprise the purposes and principles of the UN, the basic provisions on the most important UN organs and on international economic and social co-operation. In this section is also included Article 38 of the Statutes of the International Court of Justice concerning the sources of international law.

Evidence of the consensus among Member States of the UN on the significance and meaning of the Charter can be found in the Declaration on Principles of International Law concerning Friendly Relations and Co-operation among States in accordance with the Charter of the United Nations, adopted by the General Assembly in 1970. In view of its importance, the extensive preamble of the Declaration has been included in this section.

Documents

i. Charter of the United Nations, 1945
   - Preamble
   - Articles 1-2, 4, 7, 9-10, 13, 23.1, 33-34, 52, 55-64, 68-71, 92-103, 108
ii. Statute of the International Court of Justice 1945
   - Article 38
iii. Declaration on Principles of International Law concerning Friendly Relations and Co-operation among States in accordance with the Charter of the United Nations, General Assembly Resolution 2625 (XXV) 1970
   - Preamble

CHARTER OF THE UNITED NATIONS, 1945

WE THE PEOPLES OF THE UNITED NATIONS DETERMINED

to save succeeding generations from the scourge of war, which twice in our lifetime has brought untold sorrow to mankind, and

to reaffirm faith in fundamental human rights, in the dignity and worth of the human person, in the equal rights of men and women and of nations large and small, and

to establish conditions under which justice and respect for the obligations arising from treaties and other sources of international law can be maintained, and

to promote social progress and better standards of life in larger freedom,

AND FOR THESE ENDS

to practise tolerance and live together in peace with one another as good neighbours, and

to unite our strength to maintain international peace and security, and

to ensure, by the acceptance of principles and the institution of methods, that armed force shall not be used, save in the common interest, and

to employ international machinery for the promotion of the economic and social advancement of all peoples,

HAVE RESOLVED TO COMBINE OUR EFFORTS TO ACCOMPLISH THESE AIMS

Accordingly, our respective Governments, through representatives assembled in the City of San Francisco, who have exhibited their full powers found to be in good and due form, have agreed to the present Charter of the United Nations and do hereby establish an international organization to be known as the United Nations.

Chapter I. Purposes and Principles

Article 1

The Purposes of the United Nations are:

1. To maintain international peace and security, and to that end: to take effective collective measures for the prevention and removal of threats to the peace, and for the suppression of acts of aggression or other breaches of the peace, and to bring about by peaceful means, and in conformity with the principles of justice and international law, adjustment or settlement of international disputes or situations which might lead to a breach of the peace;

2. To develop friendly relations among nations based on respect for the principle of equal rights and self-determination of peoples, and to take other appropriate measures to strengthen universal peace;

3. To achieve international co-operation in solving international problems of an economic, social, cultural, or humanitarian character, and in promoting and encouraging respect for human rights and for fundamental freedoms for all without distinction as to race, sex, language, or religion; and

4. To be a centre for harmonizing the actions of nations in the attainment of these common ends.

Article 2

The Organization and its Members, in pursuit of the Purposes stated in Article 1, shall act in accordance with the following Principles:

1. The Organization is based on the principle of the sovereign equality of all its Members.

2. All Members, in order to ensure all of them the rights and benefits resulting from

membership, shall fulfil in good faith the obligations assumed by them in accordance with the present Charter.

3. All Members shall settle their international disputes by peaceful means in such a manner that international peace and security, and justice, are not endangered.

4. All Members shall refrain in their international relations from the threat or use of force against the territorial integrity or political independence of any State, or in any other manner inconsistent with the Purposes of the United Nations.

5. All Members shall give the United Nations every assistance in any action it takes in accordance with the present Charter, and shall refrain from giving assistance to any State against which the United Nations is taking preventive or enforcement action.

6. The Organization shall ensure that States which are not Members of the United Nations act in accordance with these Principles so far as may be necessary for the maintenance of international peace and security.

7. Nothing contained in the present Charter shall authorize the United Nations to intervene in matters which are essentially within the domestic jurisdiction of any State or shall require the Members to submit such matters to settlement under the present Charter; but this principle shall not prejudice the application of enforcement measures under Chapter VII.

*   *   *

Chapter II. Membership

Article 4

1. Membership in the United Nations is open to all other peace-loving States which accept the obligations contained in the present Charter and, in the judgment of the Organization, are able and willing to carry out these obligations.

2. The admission of any such State to membership in the United Nations will be effected by a decision of the General Assembly upon the recommendation of the Security Council.

*   *   *

Chapter III. Organs

Article 7

1. There are established as the principal organs of the United Nations: a General Assembly, a Security Council, an Economic and Social Council, a Trusteeship Council, an International Court of Justice, and a Secretariat.

2. Such subsidiary organs as may be found necessary may be established in accordance with the present Charter.

*   *   *

Chapter IV. The General Assembly

Article 9

1. The General Assembly shall consist of all the Members of the United Nations.

2. Each Member shall have not more than five representatives in the General Assembly.

Article 10

The General Assembly may discuss any questions or any matters within the scope of the present Charter or relating to the powers and functions of any organs provided for in the present Charter, and, except as provided in Article 12, may make recommendations to the Members of the United Nations or to the Security Council or to both on any such questions or matters.

* * *

Article 13

1. The General Assembly shall initiate studies and make recommendations for the purpose of:
(a) promoting international co-operation in the political field and encouraging the progressive development of international law and its codification;
(b) promoting international co-operation in the economic, social, cultural, educational, and health fields, and assisting in the realization of human rights and fundamental freedoms for all without distinction as to race, sex, language, or religion.
2. The further responsibilities, functions, and powers of the General Assembly with respect to matters mentioned in paragraph 1 (b) above are set forth in Chapters IX and X.

* * *

Chapter V. The Security Council

Article 23

1. The Security Council shall consist of *fifteen* Members of the United Nations. The Republic of China, France, the Union of Soviet Socialist Republics, the United Kingdom of Great Britain and Northern Ireland, and the United States of America shall be permanent members of the Security Council. The General Assembly shall elect *ten* other Members of the United Nations to be non-permanent members of the Security Council, due regard being specially paid, in the first instance, to the contribution of Members of the United Nations to the maintenance of international peace and security and to the other purposes of the Organization, and also to equitable geographical distribution.

* * *

Chapter VI. Pacific Settlement of Disputes

Article 33

1. The parties to any dispute, the continuance of which is likely to endanger the maintenance of international peace and security, shall first of all, seek a solution by negotiation, enquiry, mediation, conciliation, arbitration, judicial settlement, resort to regional agencies or arrangements, or other peaceful means of their own choice.
2. The Security Council shall, when it deems necessary, call upon the parties to settle their dispute by such means.

Article 34

The Security Council may investigate any dispute, or any situation which might lead to international friction or give rise to a dispute, in order to determine whether the continuance of the dispute or situation is likely to endanger the maintenance of international peace and security.

* * *

Chapter VIII. Regional Arrangements

Article 52

1. Nothing in the present Charter precludes the existence of regional arrangements or agencies for dealing with such matters relating to the maintenance of international peace and security as are appropriate for regional action, provided that such arrangements or agencies and their activities are consistent with the Purposes and Principles of the United Nations.

2. The Members of the United Nations entering into such arrangements or constituting such agencies shall make every effort to achieve pacific settlement of local disputes through such regional arrangements or by such regional agencies before referring them to the Security Council.

3. The Security Council shall encourage the development of pacific settlement of local disputes through such regional arrangements or by such regional agencies either on the initiative of the States concerned or by reference from the Security Council.

4. This Article in no way impairs the application of Articles 34 and 35.

*   *   *

Chapter IX. International Economic and Social Co-operation

Article 55

With a view to the creation of conditions of stability and well-being which are necessary for peaceful and friendly relations among nations based on respect for the principle of equal rights and self-determination of peoples, the United Nations shall promote:

(a)   higher standards of living, full employment, and conditions of economic and social progress and development;

(b)   solutions of international economic, social, health, and related problems; and international cultural and educational co-operation; and

(c)   universal respect for, and observance of, human rights and fundamental freedoms for all without distinction as to race, sex, language, or religion.

Article 56

All Members pledge themselves to take joint and separate action in cooperation with the Organization for the achievement of the purposes set forth in Article 55.

Article 57

1. The various specialized agencies, established by inter-governmental agreement and having wide international responsibilities, as defined in their basic instruments, in economic, social, cultural, educational, health, and related fields, shall be brought into relationship with the United Nations in accordance with the provisions of Article 63.

2. Such agencies thus brought into relationship with the United Nations are hereinafter referred to as specialized agencies.

Article 58

The Organization shall make recommendations for the co-ordination of the policies and activities of the specialized agencies.

Article 59

The Organization shall, where appropriate, initiate negotiations among the States concerned for the creation of any new specialized agencies required for the accomplishment of the purposes set forth in Article 55.

Article 60

Responsibility for the discharge of the functions of the Organization set forth in this Chapter shall be vested in the General Assembly and, under the authority of the General Assembly, in the Economic and Social Council, which shall have for this purpose the powers set forth in Chapter X.

Chapter X. The Economic and Social Council

Article 61

1. The Economic and Social Council shall consist of twenty-seven Members of the United Nations elected by the General Assembly.

* * *

Article 62

1. The Economic and Social Council may make or initiate studies and reports with respect to international economic, social, cultural, educational, health, and related matters and may make recommendations with respect to any such matters to the General Assembly, to the Members of the United Nations, and to the specialized agencies concerned.

2. It may make recommendations for the purpose of promoting respect for, and observance of, human rights and fundamental freedoms for all.

3. It may prepare draft conventions for submission to the General Assembly, with respect to matters falling within its competence.

4. It may call, in accordance with the rules prescribed by the United Nations, international conferences on matters falling within its competence.

Article 63

1. The Economic and Social Council may enter into agreements with any of the agencies referred to in Article 56, defining the terms on which the agency concerned shall be brought into relationship with the United Nations. Such agreements shall be subject to approval by the General Assembly.

2. It may co-ordinate the activities of the specialized agencies through consultation with and recommendations to such agencies and through recommendations to the General Assembly and to the Members of the United Nations.

Article 64

1. The Economic and Social Council may take appropriate steps to obtain regular reports from the specialized agencies. It may make arrangements with the Members of the United Nations and with the specialized agencies to obtain reports on the steps taken to give effect to its own recommendations and to recommendations on matters falling within its competence made by the General Assembly.

* * *

Article 68

The Economic and Social Council shall set up commissions in economic and social fields and for the promotion of human rights, and such other commissions as may be required for the performance of its functions.

Article 69

The Economic and Social Council shall invite any Member of the United Nations to participate, without vote, in its deliberations on any matter of particular concern to that Member.

Article 70

The Economic and Social Council may make arrangements for representatives of the specialized agencies to participate, without vote, in its deliberations and in those of the commissions established by it and for its representatives to participate in the deliberations of the specialized agencies.

Article 71

The Economic and Social Council may make suitable arrangements for consultation with non-governmental organizations which are concerned with matters within its competence.

Such arrangements may be made with international organizations and, where appropriate, with national organizations after consultation with the Members of the United Nations concerned.

*   *   *

Chapter XIV. The International Court of Justice

Article 92

The International Court of Justice shall be the principal judicial organ of the United Nations. It shall function in accordance with the annexed Statute, which is based upon the Statute of the Permanent Court of International Justice and forms an integral part of the present Charter.

Article 93

1. All Members of the United Nations are *ipso facto* parties to the Statute of the International Court of Justice.

2. A State which is not a Member of the United Nations may become a party to the Statute of the International Court of Justice on conditions to be determined in each case by the General Assembly upon the recommendation of the Security Council.

Article 94

1. Each Member of the United Nations undertakes to comply with the decision of the International Court of Justice in any case to which it is a party.

2. If any party to a case fails to perform the obligations incumbent upon it under a judgment rendered by the Court, the other party may have recourse to the Security Council, which may, if it deems necessary, make recommendations or decide upon measures to be taken to give effect to the judgment.

Article 95

Nothing in the present Charter shall prevent Members of the United Nations from entrusting the solution of their differences to other tribunals by virtue of agreements already in existence or which may be concluded in the future.

Article 96

1. The General Assembly or the Security Council may request the International Court of Justice to give an advisory opinion on any legal question.

2. Other organs of the United Nations and specialized agencies, which may at any time be so authorized by the General Assembly, may also request advisory opinions of the Court on legal questions arising within the scope of their activities.

Chapter XV. The Secretariat

Article 97

The Secretariat shall comprise a Secretary-General and such staff as the Organization may require. The Secretary-General shall be appointed by the General Assembly upon the recommendation of the Security Council. He shall be the chief administrative officer of the Organization.

Article 98

The Secretary-General shall act in that capacity in all meetings of the General Assembly, of the Security Council, of the Economic and Social Council, and of the Trusteeship Council, and shall perform such other functions as are entrusted to him by these organs. The Secretary-General shall make an annual report to the General Assembly on the work of the Organization.

Article 99

The Secretary-General may bring to the attention of the Security Council any matter which in his opinion may threaten the maintenance of international peace and security.

Article 100

1. In the performance of their duties the Secretary-General and the staff shall not seek or receive instructions from any government or from any other authority external to the Organization. They shall refrain from any action which might reflect on their position as international officials responsible only to the Organization.

2. Each Member of the United Nations undertakes to respect the exclusively international character of the responsibilities of the Secretary-General and the staff and not to seek to influence them in the discharge of their responsibilities.

Article 101

1. The staff shall be appointed by the Secretary-General under regulations established by the General Assembly.

2. Appropriate staffs shall be permanently assigned to the Economic and Social Council, the Trusteeship Council, and, as required, to other organs of the United Nations. These staffs shall form a part of the Secretariat.

3. The paramount consideration in the employment of the staff and in the determination of the conditions of service shall be the necessity of securing the highest standards of efficiency, competence, and integrity. Due regard shall be paid to the importance of recruiting the staff on as wide a geographical basis as possible.

Chapter XVI. Miscellaneous Provisions

Article 102

1. Every treaty and every international agreement entered into by any Member of the United Nations after the present Charter comes into force shall as soon as possible be registered with the Secretariat and published by it.

2. No party to any such treaty or international agreement which has not been

registered in accordance with the provisions of paragraph 1 of this Article may invoke that treaty or agreement before any organ of the United Nations.

Article 103

In the event of a conflict between the obligations of the Members of the United Nations under the present Charter and their obligations under any other international agreement, their obligations under the present Charter shall prevail.

*   *   *

Chapter XVIII. Amendments

Article 108

Amendments to the present Charter shall come into force for all Members of the United Nations when they have been adopted by a vote of two-thirds of the members of the General Assembly and ratified in accordance with their respective constitutional processes by two-thirds of the Members of the United Nations, including all the permanent members of the Security Council.

STATUTE OF THE INTERNATIONAL COURT OF JUSTICE, 1945

Article 38

1. The Court, whose function is to decide in accordance with international law such disputes as are submitted to it, shall apply:

(a)   international conventions, whether general or particular, establishing rules expressly recognized by the contesting States:
(b)   international custom, as evidence of a general practice accepted as law;
(c)   the general principles of law recognized by civilized nations;
(d)   subject to the provisions of Article 59, judicial decisions and the teachings of the most highly qualified publicists of the various nations, as subsidiary means for the determination of rules of law.

2. This provision shall not prejudice the power of the Court to decide a case *ex aequo et bono,* if the parties agree thereto.

DECLARATION ON PRINCIPLES OF INTERNATIONAL LAW CONCERNING FRIENDLY RELATIONS AND CO-OPERATION AMONG STATES IN ACCORDANCE WITH THE CHARTER OF THE UNITED NATIONS

General Assembly Resolution, 2625 (xxv), 1970

Preamble

The General Assembly,

Reaffirming the terms of the Charter that the maintenance of international peace and security and the development of friendly relations and co-operation between nations are among the fundamental purposes of the United Nations,

Recalling that the peoples of the United Nations are determined to practise tolerance and live together in peace with one another as good neighbours,

Bearing in mind the importance of maintaining and strengthening international peace founded upon freedom, equality, justice and respect for fundamental human rights and of developing friendly relations among nations irrespective of their political, economic and social systems or the levels of their development,

Bearing in mind also the paramount importance of the Charter of the United Nations in the promotion of the rule of law among nations,

Considering that the faithful observance of the principles of international law concerning friendly relations and co-operation among States and the fulfilment in good faith of the obligations assumed by States, in accordance with the Charter, is of the greatest importance for the maintenance of international peace and security and for the implementation of the other purposes of the United Nations,

Noting that the great political, economic and social changes and scientific progress which have taken place in the world since the adoption of the Charter of the United Nations give increased importance to these principles and to the need for their more effective application in the conduct of States wherever carried on,

Recalling the established principle that outer space, including the moon and other celestial bodies, is not subject to national appropriation by claim of sovereignty, by means of use or occupation, or by any other means, and mindful of the fact that consideration is being given in the United Nations to the question of establishing other appropriate provisions similarly inspired,

Convinced that the strict observance by States of the obligation not to intervene in the affairs of any other State is an essential condition to ensure that nations live together in peace with one another, since the practice of any form of intervention not only violates the spirit and letter of the Charter, but also leads to the creation of situations which threaten international peace and security,

Recalling the duty of the States to refrain in their international relations from military, political, economic or any other form of coercion aimed against the political independence or territorial integrity of any State,

Considering it essential that all States shall refrain in their international relations from the threat or use of force against the territorial integrity or political independence of any State, or in any other manner inconsistent with the purposes of the United Nations,

Considering it equally essential that all States shall settle their international disputes by peaceful means in accordance with the Charter,

Reaffirming, in accordance with the Charter, the basic importance of sovereign equality and stressing that the purposes of the United Nations can be implemented only if States enjoy sovereign equality and comply fully with the requirements of this principle in their international relations,

Convinced that the subjection of peoples to alien subjugation, domination and exploitation constitutes a major obstacle to the promotion of international peace and security,

Convinced that the principle of equal rights and self-determination of peoples constitutes a significant contribution to contemporary international law, and that its effective application is of paramount importance for the promotion of friendly relations among States, based on respect for the principle of sovereign equality,

Convinced in consequence that any attempt aimed at the partial or total disruption of the national unity and territorial integrity of a State or country or at its political independence is incompatible with the purposes and principles of the Charter,

Considering the provisions of the Charter as a whole and taking into account the role of relevant resolutions adopted by the competent organs of the United Nations relating to the content of the principles,

Considering that the progressive development and codification of the following principles:

(a) The principle that States shall refrain in their international relations from the threat or use of force against the territorial integrity or political independence of any State, or in any other manner inconsistent with the purposes of the United Nations;

(b) The principle that States shall settle their international disputes by peaceful means in such a manner that international peace and security and justice are not endangered;

(c) The duty not to intervene in matters within the domestic jurisdiction of any State, in accordance with the Charter;

(d) The duty of States to co-operate with one another in accordance with the Charter;

(e) The principle of equal rights and self-determination of peoples;

(f) The principle of sovereign equality of States;

(g) The principle that States shall fulfil in good faith the obligations assumed by them in accordance with the Charter; so as to secure their more effective application within the international community would promote the realization of the purposes of the United Nations;

*   *   *

2. Basic instruments on human rights

The references to human rights included in the Charter of the United Nations (see Preamble, Articles 1, 55, 56, 62 and 68) have provided the basis for the elaboration of international law in this area. In 1948, the General Assembly adopted the Universal Declaration of Human Rights which despite its non-binding character has served as a bench-mark for the promotion of human rights. The two International Covenants on human rights adopted in 1966, to a large extent represent a codification in binding form of the provisions set out in the Declaration. Included in this section are the relevant parts of the other treaties dealing with human rights which specifically refer to the conduct of communications and information.

Documents

(a) General instruments concerning human rights
  i. Universal Declaration of Human Rights, 1948
      – Full text (see in particular Articles 19, 29)
  ii. International Covenant on Economic, Social and Cultural Rights, 1966
      – Preamble
      – Articles 1-16 (see in particular Articles 13, 15)
  iii. International Covenant on Civil and Political Rights, 1966
      – Preamble
      – Articles 1-29, 40 (see in particular Articles 17, 19, 20)

(b) Other treaties
  iv. Convention on the Prevention and Punishment of the Crime of Genocide, 1948
      – Preamble
      – Articles I–VI (See in particular Article III)
  v. International Convention on the Elimination of All Forms of Racial Discrimination, 1966
      – Preamble
      – Articles 1–8 (See in particular Articles 4, 5, 7)

UNIVERSAL DECLARATION OF HUMAN RIGHTS, 1948

Whereas recognition of the inherent dignity and of the equal and inalienable rights of all members of the human family is the foundation of freedom, justice and peace in the world,

Whereas disregard and contempt for human rights have resulted in barbarous acts which have outraged the conscience of mankind, and the advent of a world in which human beings shall enjoy freedom of speech and belief and freedom from fear and want has been proclaimed as the highest aspiration of the common people,

Whereas it is essential, if man is not to be compelled to have recourse, as a last resort, to rebellion against tyranny and oppression, that human rights should be protected by the rule of law,

Whereas it is essential to promote the development of friendly relations between nations,

Whereas the peoples of the United Nations have in the Charter reaffirmed their faith in fundamental human rights, in the dignity and worth of the human person and in the equal rights of men and women and have determined to promote social progress and better standards of life in larger freedom,

Whereas Member States have pledged themselves to achieve, in cooperation with the United Nations, the promotion of universal respect for and observance of human rights and fundamental freedoms,

Whereas a common understanding of these rights and freedoms is of the greatest importance for the full realization of this pledge.

Now, therefore,
The General Assembly
proclaims
This universal declaration of human rights as a common standard of achievement for all peoples and all nations, to the end that every individual and every organ of society, keeping this Declaration constantly in mind, shall strive by teaching and education to promote respect for these rights and freedoms and by progressive measures, national and international, to secure their universal and effective recognition and observance, both among the peoples of Member States themselves and among the peoples of territories under their jurisdiction.

Article 1.

All human beings are born free and equal in dignity and rights. They are endowed with reason and conscience and should act towards one another in a spirit of brotherhood.

Article 2

Everyone is entitled to all the rights and freedoms set forth in this Declaration, without distinction of any kind, such as race, colour, sex, language, religion, political or other opinion, national or social origin, property, birth or other status.

Furthermore, no distinction shall be made on the basis of the political, jurisdictional or international status of the country or territory to which a person belongs, whether it be independent, trust, non-self-governing or under any other limitation of sovereignty.

Article 3

Everyone has the right to life, liberty and security of person.

Article 4

No one shall be held in slavery or servitude; slavery and the slave trade shall be prohibited in all their forms.

Article 5

No one shall be subjected to torture or to cruel, inhuman or degrading treatment or punishment.

Article 6

Everyone has the right to recognition everywhere as a person before the law.

Article 7

All are equal before the law and are entitled without any discrimination to equal protection of the law. All are entitled to equal protection against any discrimination in violation of this Declaration and against any incitement to such discrimination.

Article 8

Everyone has the right to an effective remedy by the competent national tribunals for acts violating the fundamental rights granted him by the constitution or by law.

Article 9

No one shall be subjected to arbitrary arrest, detention or exile.

Article 10

Everyone is entitled in full equality to a fair and public hearing by an independent and impartial tribunal, in the determination of his rights and obligations and of any criminal charge against him.

Article 11

1. Everyone charged with a penal offence has the right to be presumed innocent until proved guilty according to law in a public trial at which he has had all the guarantees necessary for his defence.

2. No one shall be held guilty of any penal offence on account of any act or omission which did not constitute a penal offence, under national or international law, at the time when it was committed. Nor shall a heavier penalty be imposed than the one that was applicable at the time the penal offence was committed.

Article 12

No one shall be subjected to arbitrary interference with his privacy, family, home or correspondence, nor to attacks upon his honour and reputation. Everyone has the right to the protection of the law against such interference or attacks.

Article 13

1. Everyone has the right to freedom of movement and residence within the borders of each state.

2. Everyone has the right to leave any country, including his own, and to return to his country.

Article 14

1. Everyone has the right to seek and to enjoy in other countries asylum from persecution.

2. This right may not be invoked in the case of prosecutions genuinely arising from non-political crimes or from acts contrary to the purposes and principles of the United Nations.

Article 15

1. Everyone has the right to a nationality.

2. No one shall be arbitrarily deprived of his nationality nor denied the right to change his nationality.

Article 16

1. Men and women of full age, without any limitation due to race, nationality or religion, have the right to marry and to found a family. They are entitled to equal rights as to marriage, during marriage and at its dissolution.

2. Marriage shall be entered into only with the free and full consent of the intending spouses.

3. The family is the natural and fundamental group unit of society and is entitled to protection by society and the State.

Article 17

1. Everyone has the right to own property alone as well as in association with others.

2. No one shall be arbitrarily deprived of his property.

Article 18

Everyone has the right to freedom of thought, conscience and religion; this right includes freedom to change his religion or belief, and freedom, either alone or in community with others and in public or private, to manifest his religion or belief in teaching, practice, worship and observance.

Article 19

Everyone has the right to freedom of opinion and expression; this right includes freedom to hold opinions without interference and to seek, receive and impart information and ideas through any media and regardless of frontiers.

Article 20

1. Everyone has the right to freedom of peaceful assembly and association.

2. No one may be compelled to belong to an association.

Article 21

1. Everyone has the right to take part in the government of his country, directly or through freely chosen representatives.

2. Everyone has the right of equal access to public service in his country.

3. The will of the people shall be the basis of the authority of government; this will shall be expressed in periodic and genuine elections which shall be by universal and equal suffrage and shall be held by secret vote or by equivalent free voting procedures.

Article 22

Everyone, as a member of society, has the right to social security and is entitled to realization, through national effort and international co-operation and in accordance with the organization and resources of each State, of the economic, social and cultural rights indispensable for his dignity and the free development of his personality.

Article 23

1. Everyone has the right to work, to free choice of employment, to just and favourable conditions of work and to protection against unemployment.

2. Everyone, without any discrimination, has the right to equal pay for equal work.

3. Everyone who works has the right to just and favorable remuneration ensuring

for himself and his family an existence worthy of human dignity, and supplemented, if necessary, by other means of social protection.

4. Everyone has the right to form and to join trade unions for the protection of his interests.

Article 24

Everyone has the right to rest and leisure, including reasonable limitation of working hours and periodic holidays with pay.

Article 25

1. Everyone has the right to a standard of living adequate for the health and well-being of himself and of his family, including food, clothing, housing and medical care and necessary social services, and the right to security in the event of unemployment, sickness, disability, widowhood, old age or other lack of livelihood in circumstances beyond his control.

2. Motherhood and childhood are entitled to special care and assistance. All children, whether born in or out of wedlock, shall enjoy the same social protection.

Article 26

1. Everyone has the right to education. Education shall be free, at least in elementary and fundamental stages. Elementary education shall be compulsory. Technical and professional education shall be made generally available and higher education shall be equally accessible to all on the basis of merit.

2. Education shall be directed to the full development of the human personality and to the strengthening of respect for human rights and fundamental freedoms. It shall promote understanding, tolerance and friendship among all nations, racial or religious groups, and shall further the activities of the United Nations for the maintenance of peace.

3. Parents have a prior right to choose the kind of education that shall be given their children.

Article 27

1. Everyone has the right freely to participate in the cultural life of the community, to enjoy the arts and to share in scientific advancement and its benefits.

2. Everyone has the right to the protection of the moral and material interests resulting from any scientific, literary or artistic production of which he is the author.

Article 28

Everyone is entitled to a social and international order in which the rights and freedoms set forth in this Declaration can be fully realized.

Article 29

1. Everyone has duties to the community in which alone the free and full development of his personality is possible.

2. In the exercise of his rights and freedoms, everyone shall be subject only to such limitations as are determined by law solely for the purpose of securing due recognition and respect for the rights and freedoms of others and of meeting the just requirements of morality, public order and the general welfare in a democratic society.

3. These rights and freedoms may in no case be exercised contrary to the purposes and principles of the United Nations.

Article 30

Nothing in the Declaration may be interpreted as implying for any State, group or person any right to engage in any activity or to perform any act aimed at the destruction of any of the rights and freedoms set forth herein.

INTERNATIONAL COVENANT ON ECONOMIC, SOCIAL AND CULTURAL RIGHTS, 1966

The States Parties to the present Covenant,
Considering that, in accordance with the principles proclaimed in the Charter of the United Nations, recognition of the inherent dignity and of the equal and inalienable rights of all members of the human family is the foundation of freedom, justice and peace in the world,

Recognizing that these rights derive from the inherent dignity of the human person,

Recognizing that, in accordance with the Universal Declaration of Human Rights, the ideal of free human beings enjoying freedom from fear and want can only be achieved if conditions are created whereby everyone may enjoy his economic, social and cultural rights, as well as his civil and political rights,

Considering the obligation of States under the Charter of the United Nations to promote universal respect for, and observance of, human rights and freedoms,

Realizing that the individual, having duties to other individuals and to the community to which he belongs, is under a responsibility to strive for the promotion and observance of the rights recognized in the present Covenant,

Agree upon the following articles:

Article 1

1. All peoples have the right of self-determination. By virtue of that right they freely determine their political status and freely pursue their economic, social and cultural development.

2. All peoples may, for their own ends, freely dispose of their natural wealth and resources without prejudice to any obligations arising out of international economic co-operation, based upon the principle of mutual benefit, and international law. In no case may a people be deprived of its own means of subsistence.

3. The States Parties to the present Covenant, including those having responsibility for the administration of Non-Self-Governing and Trust Territories, shall promote the realization of the right of self-determination, and shall respect that right, in conformity with the provisions of the Charter of the United Nations.

Article 2

1. Each State Party to the present Covenant undertakes to take steps, individually and through international assistance and co-operation, especially economic and technical, to the maximum of its available resources, with a view to achieving progressively the full realization of the rights recognized in the present Covenant by all appropriate means, including particularly the adoption of legislative measures.

2. The States Parties to the present Covenant undertake to guarantee that the rights enunciated in the present Covenant will be exercised without discrimination of any kind as to race, colour, sex, language, religion, political or other opinion, national or social origin, property, birth or other status.

3. Developing countries, with due regard to human rights and their national economy, may determine to what extent they would guarantee the economic rights recognized in the present Covenant to non-nationals.

Article 3

The States Parties to the present Covenant undertake to ensure the equal right of men and women to the enjoyment of all economic, social and cultural rights set forth in the present Covenant.

Article 4

The States Parties to the present Covenant recognize that, in the enjoyment of those rights provided by the State in conformity with the present Covenant, the State may subject such rights only to such limitations as are determined by law only in so far as this may be compatible with the nature of these rights and solely for the purpose of promoting the general welfare in a democratic society.

Article 5

1. Nothing in the present Covenant may be interpreted as implying for any State, group or person any right to engage in any activity or to perform any act aimed at the destruction of any of the rights or freedoms recognized herein, or at their limitation to a greater extent than is provided for in the present Covenant.

2. No restriction upon or derogation from any of the fundamental human rights recognized or existing in any country in virtue of law, conventions, regulations or custom shall be admitted on the pretext that. the present Covenant does not recognize such rights or that it recognizes them to a lesser extent.

Article 6

1. The States Parties to the present Covenant recognize the right to work, which includes the right of everyone to the opportunity to gain his living by work which he freely chooses or accepts, and will take appropriate steps to safeguard this right.

2. The steps to be taken by a State Party to the present Covenant to achieve the full realization of this right shall include technical and vocational guidance and training programmes, policies and techniques to achieve steady economic, social and cultural development and full and productive employment under conditions safeguarding fundamental political and economic freedoms to the individual.

Article 7

The States Parties to the present Covenant recognize the right of everyone to the enjoyment of just and favourable conditions of work, which ensure, in particular:

(a)   Remuneration which provides all workers, as a minimum, with:
   i.   Fair wages and equal remuneration for work of equal value without distinction of any kind, in particular women being guaranteed conditions of work not inferior to those enjoyed by men, with equal pay for equal work;
   ii. A decent living for themselves and their families in accordance with the provisions of the present Covenant;
(b)   Safe and healthy working conditions;
(c)   Equal opportunity for everyone to be promoted in his employment to an appropriate higher level, subject to no considerations other than those of seniority and competence;
(d)   Rest, leisure and reasonable limitation of working hours and periodic holidays with pay, as well as remuneration for public holidays.

Article 8

1. The States Parties to the present Covenant undertake to ensure:

(a)   The right of everyone to form trade unions and join the trade union of his choice, subject only to the rules of the organization concerned, for the promotion and protection of his economic and social interests. No restrictions may be placed on the exercise of this right other than those prescribed by law and which are necessary in a democratic society in the interests of national security or public order or for the protection of the rights and freedoms of others;

(b) The right of trade unions to establish national federations or confederations and the right of the latter to form or join international trade union organizations;

(c) The right of trade unions to function freely subject to no limitations other than those prescribed by law and which are necessary in a democratic society in the interests of national security or public order or for the protection of the rights and freedoms of others;

(d) The right to strike, provided that it is exercised in conformity with the laws of the particular country.

2. This article shall not prevent the imposition of lawful restrictions on the exercise of these rights by members of the armed forces or of the police or of the administration of the State.

3. Nothing in this article shall authorize States Parties to the International Labour Organisation Convention of 1948 concerning Freedom of Association and Protection of the Right to Organize to take legislative measures which would prejudice, or apply the law in such a manner as would prejudice, the guarantees provided for in that Convention.

Article 9

The States Parties to the present Covenant recognize the right of everyone to social security, including social insurance.

Article 10

The States Parties to the present Covenant recognize that:

1. The widest possible protection and assistance should be accorded to the family, which is the natural and fundamental group unit of society, particularly for its establishment and while it is responsible for the care and education of dependent children. Marriage must be entered into with the free consent of the intending spouses.

2. Special protection should be accorded to mothers during a reasonable period before and after childbirth. During such period working mothers should be accorded paid leave or leave with adequate social security benefits.

3. Special measures of protection and assistance should be taken on behalf of all children and young persons without any discrimination for reasons of parentage or other conditions. Children and young persons should be protected from economic and social exploitation. Their employment in work harmful to their morals or health or dangerous to life or likely to hamper their normal development should be punishable by law. States should also set age limits below which the paid employment of child labour should be prohibited and punishable by law.

Article 11

1. The States Parties to the present Covenant recognize the right of everyone to an adequate standard of living for himself and his family, including adequate food, clothing and housing, and to the continuous improvement of living conditions. The States Parties will take appropriate steps to ensure the realization of its right, recognizing to this effect the essential importance of international co-operation based on free consent.

2. The States Parties to the present Covenant, recognizing the fundamental right of everyone to be free from hunger, shall take, individually and through international co-operation, the measures, including specific programmes, which are needed:

(a) To improve methods of production, conservation and distribution of food by making full use of technical and scientific knowledge, by disseminating knowledge of the principles of nutrition and by developing or reforming agrarian systems in such a way as to achieve the most efficient development and utilization of natural resources;

(b) Taking into account the problems of both food-importing and food-exporting countries, to ensure an equitable distribution of world food supplies in relation to need.

Article 12

1. The States Parties to the present Covenant recognize the right of everyone to the enjoyment of the highest attainable standard of physical and mental health.

2. The steps to be taken by the States Parties to the present Covenant to achieve the full realization of this right shall include those necessary for:

(a) the provision for the reduction of the stillbirth-rate and of infant mortality and for the healthy development of the child;

(b) The improvement of all aspects of environmental and industrial hygiene;

(c) The prevention, treatment and control of epidemic, endemic, occupational and other diseases;

(d) The creation of conditions which would assure to all medical service and medical attention in the event of sickness.

Article 13

1. The States Parties to the present Covenant recognize the right of everyone to education. They agree that education shall be directed to the full development of the human personality and the sense of its dignity, and shall strengthen the respect for human rights and fundamental freedoms. They further agree that education shall enable all persons to participate effectively in a free society, promote understanding, tolerance and friendship among all nations and all racial, ethnic or religious groups, and further the activities of the United Nations for the maintenance of peace.

2. The States Parties to the present Covenant recognize that, with a view to achieving the full realizaton of this right:

(a) Primary education shall be compulsory and available free to all;

(b) Secondary education in its different forms, including technical and vocational secondary education, shall be made generally available and accessible to all by every appropriate means, and in particular by the progressive introduction of free education;

(c) Higher education shall be made equally accessible to all, on the basis of capacity, by every appropriate means, and in particular by the progressive introduction of free education;

(d) Fundamental education shall be encouraged or intensified as far as possible for those persons who have not received or completed the whole period of their primary education;

(e) The development of a system of schools at all levels shall be actively pursued, an adequate fellowship system shall be established, and the material conditions of teaching staff shall be continuously improved.

3. The States Parties to the present Covenant undertake to have respect for the liberty of parents and, when applicable, legal guardians, to choose for their children schools, other than those established by the public authorities, which conform to such minimum education standards as may be laid down or approved by the State and to ensure the religious and moral education of their children in conformity with their own convictions.

4. No part of this article shall be construed so as to interfere with the liberty of individuals and bodies to establish and direct educational institutions, subject always

to the observance of the principles set forth in paragraph 1 of this article and to the requirement that the education given in such institutions shall conform to such minimum standards as may be laid down by the State.

Article 14

Each State Party to the present Covenant which, at the time of becoming a Party, has not been able to secure in its metropolitan territory or other territories under its jurisdiction compulsory primary education, free of charge, undertakes, within two years, to work out and adopt a detailed plan of action for the progressive implementation, within a reasonable number of years, to be fixed in the plan, of the principle of compulsory education free of charge for all.

Article 15

1. The States Parties to the present Covenant recognize the right of everyone:

(a) To take part in cultural life;
(b) To enjoy the benefits of scientific progress and its applications;
(c) To benefit from the protection of the moral and material interests resulting from any scientific, literary or artistic production of which he is the author.

2. The steps to be taken by the States Parties to the present Covenant to achieve the full realization of this right shall include those necessary for the conservation, the development and the diffusion of science and culture.

3. The States Parties to the present Covenant undertake to respect the freedom indispensable for scientific research and creative activity.

4. The States Parties to the present Covenant recognize the benefits to be derived from the encouragement and development of international contacts and co-operation in the scientific and cultural fields.

Article 16

1. The States Parties to the present Covenant undertake to submit in conformity with this part of the Covenant reports on the measures which they have adopted and the progress made in achieving the observance of the rights recognized herein.

2.
(a) All reports shall be submitted to the Secretary-General of the United Nations, who shall transmit copies to the Economic and Social Council for consideration in accordance with the provisions of the present Covenant.
(b) The Secretary-General of the United Nations shall also transmit to the specialized agencies copies of the reports, or any relevant parts therefrom, from States Parties to the present Covenant which are also members of these specialized agencies in so far as these reports, or parts therefrom, relate to any matters which fall within the responsibilities of the said agencies in accordance with their constitutional instruments.

* * *

INTERNATIONAL COVENANT ON CIVIL AND POLITICAL RIGHTS, 1966

Preamble

The States Parties to the present Covenant,
Considering that, in accordance with the principles proclaimed in the Charter of the United Nations, recognition of the inherent dignity and of the equal and inalienable rights of all members of the human family is the foundation of freedom, justice and peace in the world,

Recognizing that these rights derive from the inherent dignity of the human person,

Recognizing that, in accordance with the Universal Declaration of Human Rights, the ideal of free human beings enjoying civil and political freedom and freedom from fear and want can only be achieved if conditions are created whereby everyone may enjoy his civil and political rights, as well as his economic, social and cultural rights,

Considering the obligation of States under the Charter of the United Nations to promote universal respect for, and observance of, human rights and freedoms,

Realizing that the individual, having duties to other individuals and to the community to which he belongs, is under a responsibility to strive for the promotion and observance of the rights recognized in the present Covenant,

Agree upon the following articles:

Article 1

1. All peoples have the right of self-determination. By virtue of that right they freely determine their political status and freely pursue their economic, social and cultural development.

2. All peoples may, for their own ends, freely dispose of their natural wealth and resources without prejudice to any obligations arising out of international economic co-operation, based upon the principle of mutual benefit, and international law. In no case may a people be deprived of its own means of subsistence.

3. The States Parties to the present Covenant, including those having responsibility for the administration of Non-Self-Governing and Trust Territories, shall promote the realization of the right of self-determination, and shall respect that right, in conformity with the provisions of the Charter of the United Nations.

Article 2

1. Each State Party to the present Covenant undertakes to respect and to ensure to all individuals within its territory and subject to its jurisdiction the rights recognized in the present Covenant, without distinction of any kind, such as race, colour, sex, language, religion, political or other opinion, national or social origin, property, birth or other status.

2. Where not already provided for by existing legislative or other measures, each State Party to the present Covenant undertakes to take the necessary steps, in accordance with its constitutional processes and with the provisions of the present Covenant, to adopt such legislative or other measures as may be necessary to give effect to the rights recognized in the present Covenant.

3. Each State Party to the present Covenant undertakes:

(a) To ensure that any person whose rights or freedoms as herein recognized are violated shall have an effective remedy, notwithstanding that the violation has been committed by persons acting in an official capacity;

(b) To ensure that any person claiming such a remedy shall have his right thereto determined by competent judicial, administrative or legislative authorities, or by any other competent authority provided for by the legal system of the State, and to develop the possibilities of judicial remedy;

(c) To ensure that the competent authorities shall enforce such remedies when granted.

Article 3

The States Parties to the present Covenant undertake to ensure the equal right of men and women to the enjoyment of all civil and political rights set forth in the present Covenant.

Article 4

1. In time of public emergency which threatens the life of the nation and the existence of which is officially proclaimed, the States Parties to the present Covenant may take measures derogating from their obligations under the present Covenant to the extent strictly required by the exigencies of the situation, provided that such measures are not inconsistent with their other obligations under international law and do not involve discrimination solely on the ground of race, colour, sex, language, religion or social origin.

2. No derogation from Articles 6, 7, 8 (paragraphs 1 and 2), 11, 15, 16 and 18 may be made under this provision.

3. Any State Party to the present Covenant availing itself of the right of derogation shall immediately inform the other States Parties to the present Covenant, through the intermediary of the Secretary-General of the United Nations of the provisions from which it has derogated and of the reasons by which it was actuated. A further communication shall be made, through the same intermediary on the date on which it terminates such derogation.

Article 5

1. Nothing in the present Covenant may be interpreted as implying for any State, group or person any right to engage in any activity or perform any act aimed at the destruction of any of the rights and freedoms recognized herein or at their limitation to a greater extent than is provided for in the present Covenant.

2. There shall be no restriction upon or derogation from any of the fundamental human rights recognized or existing in any State Party to the present Covenant pursuant to law, conventions, regulations or custom on the pretext that the present Covenant does not recognize such rights or that it recognizes them to a lesser extent.

Article 6

1. Every human being has the inherent right to life. This right shall be protected by law. No one shall be arbitrarily deprived of his life.

2. In countries which have not abolished the death penalty, sentence of death may be imposed only for the most serious crimes in accordance with the law in force at the time of the commission of the crime and not contrary to the provisions of the present Covenant and to the Convention on the Prevention and Punishment of the Crime of Genocide. This penalty can only be carried out pursuant to a final judgment rendered by a competent court.

3. When deprivation of life constitutes the crime of genocide, it is understood that nothing in this article shall authorize any State Party to the present Covenant to derogate in any way from any obligation assumed under the provisions of the Convention on the Prevention and Punishment of the Crime of Genocide.

4. Anyone sentenced to death shall have the right to seek pardon or commutation of the sentence. Amnesty, pardon or commutation of the sentence of death may be granted in all cases.

5. Sentence of death shall not be imposed for crimes committed by persons below eighteen years of age and shall not be carried out on pregnant women.

6. Nothing in this article shall be invoked to delay or to prevent the abolition of capital punishment by any State Party to the present Covenant.

Article 7

No one shall be subjected to torture or to cruel, inhuman or degrading treatment or punishment. In particular, no one shall be subjected without his free consent to medical or scientific experimentation.

Article 8

1. No one shall be held in slavery; slavery and the slave-trade in all their forms shall be prohibited.

2. No one shall be held in servitude.

3.
(a) No one shall be required to perform forced or compulsory labour;
(b) Paragraph 3 (a) shall not be held to preclude, in countries where imprisonment with hard labour may be imposed as a punishment for a crime, the performance of hard labour in pursuance of a sentence to such punishment by a competent court;
(c) For the purpose of this paragraph the term 'forced or compulsory labour' shall not include:
    i.   Any work or service, not referred to in sub-paragraph (b), normally required of a person who is under detention in consequence of a lawful order of a court, or of a person during conditional release from such detention;
    ii. Any service of a military character and, in countries where conscientious objection is recognized, any national service required by law of conscientious objectors;
    iii. Any service exacted in cases of emergency or calamity threatening the life or well-being of the community;
    iv. Any work or service which forms part of normal civil obligations.

Article 9

1. Everyone has the right to liberty and security of person. No one shall be subjected to arbitrary arrest or detention. No one shall be deprived of his liberty except on such grounds and in accordance with such procedure as are established by law.

2. Anyone who is arrested shall be informed, at the time of arrest, of the reasons for his arrest and shall be promptly informed of any charges against him.

3. Anyone arrested or detained on a criminal charge shall be brought promptly before a judge or other officer authorized by law to exercise judicial power and shall be entitled to trial within a reasonable time or to release. It shall not be the general rule that persons awaiting trial shall be detained in custody, but release may be subject to guarantees to appear for trial, at any other stage of the judicial proceedings, and, should occasion arise, for execution of the judgement.

4. Anyone who is deprived of his liberty by arrest or detention shall be entitled to take proceedings before a court, in order that that court may decide without delay on the lawfulness of his detention and order his release if the detention is not lawful.

5. Anyone who has been the victim of unlawful arrest or detention shall have an enforceable right to compensation.

Article 10

1. All persons deprived of their liberty shall be treated with humanity and with respect for the inherent dignity of the human person.

2.
(a) Accused persons shall, save in exceptional circumstances, be segregated from convicted persons and shall be subject to separate treatment appropriate to their status as unconvicted persons;
(b) Accused juvenile persons shall be separated from adults and brought as speedily as possible for adjudication.

3. The penitentiary system shall comprise treatment of prisoners the essential aim

of which shall be their reformation and social rehabilitation. Juvenile offenders shall be segregated from adults and be accorded treatment appropriate to their age and legal status.

Article 11

No one shall be imprisoned merely on the ground of inability to fulfil a contractual obligation.

Article 12

1. Everyone lawfully within the territory of a State shall, within that territory, have the right to liberty of movement and freedom to choose his residence.

2. Everyone shall be free to leave any country, including his own.

3. The above-mentioned rights shall not be subject to any restrictions except those which are provided by law, are necessary to protect national security, public order (ordre public), public health or morals or the rights and freedoms of others, and are consistent with the other rights recognized in the present Covenant.

4. No one shall be arbitrarily deprived of the right to enter his own country.

Article 13

An alien lawfully in the territory of a State Party to the present Covenant may be expelled therefrom only in pursuance of a decision reached in accordance with law and shall, except where compelling reasons of national security otherwise require, be allowed to submit the reasons against his expulsion and to have his case reviewed by, and be represented for the purpose before, the competent authority or a person or persons especially designated by the competent authority.

Article 14

1. All persons shall be equal before the courts and tribunals. In the determination of any criminal charge against him, or of his rights and obligations in a suit at law, everyone shall be entitled to a fair and public hearing by a competent, independent and impartial tribunal established by law. The Press and the public may be excluded from all or part of a trial for reasons of morals, public order (ordre public) or national security in a democratic society, or when the interest of the private lives of the parties so requires, or to the extent strictly necessary in the opinion of the court in special circumstances where publicity would prejudice the interests of justice; but any judgement rendered in a criminal case or in a suit at law shall be made public except where the interest of juvenile persons otherwise requires or the proceedings concern matrimonial disputes or the guardianship of children.

2. Everyone charged with a criminal offence shall have the right to be presumed innocent until proved guilty according to law.

3. In the determination of any criminal charge against him, everyone shall be entitled to the following minimum guarantees, in full equality:

(a) To be informed promptly and in detail in a language which he understands of the nature and cause of the charge against him;

(b) To have adequate time and facilities for the preparation of his defence and to communicate with counsel of his own choosing;

(c) To be tried without undue delay;

(d) To be tried in his presence, and to defend himself in person or through legal assistance of his own choosing; to be informed, if he does not have legal assistance, of this right; and to have legal assistance assigned to him, in any case where the interests of justice so require, and without payment by him in any such case if he does not have sufficient means to pay for it;

(e) to examine, or have examined, the witnesses against him and to obtain the attendance and examination of witnesses on his behalf under the same conditions
as witnesses against him;

(f) To have the free assistance of an interpreter if he cannot understand or speak
the language used in court;

(g) Not to be compelled to testify against himself or to confess guilt.

4. In the case of juvenile persons, the procedure shall be such as will take account of
their age and the desirability of promoting their rehabilitation.

5. Everyone convicted of a crime shall have the right to his conviction and sentence
being reviewed by a higher tribunal according to law.

6. When a person has by a final decision been convicted of a criminal offence and
when subsequently his conviction has been reversed or he has been pardoned on the
ground that a new or newly discovered fact shows conclusively that there has been a
miscarriage of justice, the person who has suffered punishment as a result of such
conviction shall be compensated according to law, unless it is proved that the non-
disclosure of the unknown fact in time is wholly or partly attributable to him.

7. No one shall be liable to be tried or punished again for an offence for which he
has already been finally convicted or acquitted in accordance with the law and penal
procedure of each country.

Article 15

1. No one shall be held guilty of any criminal offence on account of any act or omission which did not constitute a criminal offence, under national or international law,
at the time when it was committed. Nor shall a heavier penalty be imposed than the
one that was applicable at the time when the criminal offence was committed. If,
subsequent to the commission of the offence, provision is made by law for the imposition of a lighter penalty, the offender shall benefit thereby.

2. Nothing in this article shall prejudice the trial and punishment of any person for
any act or omission which, at the time when it was committed, was criminal according to the general principles of law recognized by the community of nations.

Article 16

Everyone shall have the right to recognition everywhere as a person before the law.

Article 17

1. No one shall be subjected to arbitrary or unlawful interference with his privacy,
family, home or correspondence, nor to unlawful attacks on his honour and reputation.

2. Everyone has the right to the protection of the law against such interference or attacks.

Article 18

1. Everyone shall have the right to freedom of thought, conscience and religion.
This right shall include freedom to have or to adopt a religion or belief of his choice,
and freedom, either individually or in community with others and in public or
private, to manifest his religion or belief in worship, observance, practice and
teaching.

2. No one shall be subject to coercion which would impair his freedom to have or to
adopt a religion or belief of his choice.

3. Freedom to manifest one's religion or beliefs may be subject only to such limitations as are prescribed by law and are necessary to protect public safety, order,
health, or morals or the fundamental rights and freedoms of others.

4. The States Parties to the present Covenant undertake to have respect for the liberty of parents and, when applicable, legal guardians to ensure the religious and moral education of their children in conformity with their own convictions.

Article 19

1. Everyone shall have the right to hold opinions without interference.

2. Everyone shall have the right to freedom of expression; this right shall include freedom to seek, receive and impart information and ideas of all kinds, regardless of frontiers, either orally, in writing or in print, in the form of art, or through any other media of his choice.

3. The exercise of the rights provided for in paragraph 2 of this Article carries with it special duties and responsibilities. It may therefore be subject to certain restrictions, but these shall only be such as are provided by law and are necessary:

(a) For respect of the rights or reputations of others;
(b) For the protection of national security or of public order (ordre public), or of public health or morals.

Article 20

1. Any propaganda for war shall be prohibited by law.

2. Any advocacy of national, racial or religious hatred that constitutes incitement to discrimination, hostility or violence shall be prohibited by law.

Article 21

The right of peaceful assembly shall be recognized. No restrictions may be placed on the exercise of this right other than those imposed in conformity with the law and which are necessary in a democratic society in the interests of national security or public safety, public order (ordre public), the protection of public health or morals or the protection of the rights and freedoms of others.

Article 22

1. Everyone shall have the right to freedom of association with others, including the right to form and join trade unions for the protection of his interests.

2. No restrictions may be placed on the exercise of this right other than those which are prescribed by law and which are necessary in a democratic society in the interests of national security or public safety, public order (ordre public), the protection of public health or morals or the protection of the rights and freedoms of others. This Article shall not prevent the imposition of lawful restrictions on members of the armed forces and of the police in their exercise of this right.

3. Nothing in this article shall authorize States Parties to the International Labour Organisation Convention of 1948 concerning Freedom of Association and Protection of the Right to Organize to take legislative measures which would prejudice, or to apply the law in such a manner as to prejudice, the guarantees provided for in that Convention.

Article 23

1. The family is the natural and fundamental group unit of society and is entitled to protection by society and the State.

2. The right of men and women of marriageable age to marry and to found a family shall be recognized.

3. No marriage shall be entered into without the free and full consent of the intending spouses.

4. States Parties to the present Covenant shall take appropriate steps to ensure equality of rights and responsibilities of spouses as to marriage, during marriage and at its dissolution. In the case of dissolution, provision shall be made for the necessary protection of any children.

Article 24

1. Every child shall have, without any discrimination as to race, colour, sex, language, religion, national or social origin, property or birth, the right to such measures of protection as are required by his status as a minor, on the part of his family, society and the State.

2. Every child shall be registered immediately after birth and shall have a name.

3. Every child has the right to acquire a nationality.

Article 25

Every citizen shall have the right and the opportunity, without any of the distinctions mentioned in Article 2 and without unreasonable restrictions:

(a) To take part in the conduct of public affairs, directly or through freely chosen representatives;

(b) To vote and to be elected at genuine periodic elections which shall be by universal and equal suffrage and shall be held by secret ballot, guaranteeing the free expression of the will of the electors;

(c) To have access, on general terms of equality, to public service in his country.

Article 26

All persons are equal before the law and are entitled without any discrimination to the equal protection of the law. In this respect, the law shall prohibit any discrimination and guarantee to all persons equal and effective protection against discrimination on any ground such as race, colour, sex, language, religion, political or other opinion, national or social origin, property, birth or other status.

Article 27

In those States in which ethnic, religious or linguistic minorities exist, persons belonging to such minorities shall not be denied the right, in community with the other members of their group, to enjoy their own culture, to profess and practise their own religion, or to use their own language.

Article 28

1. There shall be established a Human Rights Committee (hereafter referred to in the present Covenant as the Committee). It shall consist of eighteen members and shall carry out the functions hereinafter provided.

2. The Committee shall be composed of nationals of the States Parties to the present Covenant who shall be persons of high moral character and recognized competence in the field of human rights, consideration being given to the usefulness of the participation of some persons having legal experience.

3. The members of the Committee shall be elected and shall serve in their personal capacity.

Article 29

1. The members of the Committee shall be elected by secret ballot from a list of persons possessing the qualifications prescribed in Article 28 and nominated for the purpose by the States Parties to the present Covenant.

2. Each State Party to the present Covenant may nominate not more than two persons. These persons shall be nationals of the nominating State.

3. A person shall be eligible for renomination.

*   *   *

Article 40

1. The States Parties to the present Covenant undertake to submit reports on the measures they have adopted which give effect to the rights recognized herein and on the progress made in the enjoyment of those rights:

(a) Within one year of the entry into force of the present Covenant for the States Parties concerned;

(b) Thereafter whenever the Committee so requests.

2. All reports shall be submitted to the Secretary-General of the United Nations, who shall transmit them to the Committee for consideration. Reports shall indicate the factors and difficulties, if any, affecting the implementation of the present Covenant.

3. The Secretary-General of the United Nations may, after consultation with the Committee, transmit to the specialized agencies concerned copies of such parts of the reports as may fall within their field of competence.

4. The Committee shall study the reports submitted by the States Parties to the present Covenant. It shall transmit its reports, and such general comments as it may consider appropriate, to the States Parties. The Committee may also transmit to the Economic and Social Council these comments along with the copies of the reports it has received from States Parties to the present Covenant.

5. The States Parties to the present Covenant may submit to the Committee observations on any comments that may be made in accordance with paragraph 4 of this Article.

*   *   *

CONVENTION ON THE PREVENTION AND PUNISHMENT OF THE CRIME OF GENOCIDE, 1948

The Contracting Parties,

Having considered the declaration made by the General Assembly of the United Nations in its resolution 96(I) dated 11 December 1946 that genocide is a crime under international law, contrary to the spirit and aims of the United Nations and condemned by the civilized world;

Recognizing that at all periods of history genocide has inflicted great losses on humanity; and

Being convinced that, in order to liberate mankind from such an odious scourge, international co-operation is required,

Hereby agree as hereinafter provided:

Article I

The Contracting Parties confirm that genocide, whether committed in time of peace or in time of war, is a crime under international law which they undertake to prevent and to punish.

Article II

In the present Convention, genocide means any of the following acts committed with intent to destroy, in whole or in part, a national, ethnical, racial or religious group, as such:

(a) Killing members of the group;
(b) Causing serious bodily or mental harm to members of the group;
(c) Deliberately inflicting on the group conditions of life calculated to bring about its physical destruction in whole or in part;
(d) Imposing measures intended to prevent births within the group;
(e) Forcibly transferring children of the group to another group.

Article III

The following acts shall be punishable:

(a) Genocide;
(b) Conspiracy to commit genocide;
(c) Direct and public incitement to commit genocide;
(d) Attempt to commit genocide;
(e) Complicity in genocide.

Article IV

Persons committing genocide or any of the other acts enumerated in Article III shall be punished, whether they are constitutionally responsible rulers, public officials or private individuals.

Article V

The Contracting Parties undertake to enact, in accordance with their respective Constitutions, the necessary legislation to give effect to the provisions of the present Convention and, in particular, to provide effective penalties for persons guilty of genocide or of any of the other acts enumerated in Article III.

Article VI

Persons charged with genocide or any of the other acts enumerated in Article III shall be tried by a competent tribunal of the State in the territory as may have jurisdiction with respect to those Contracting Parties which shall have accepted its jurisdiction.

*   *   *

INTERNATIONAL CONVENTION ON THE ELIMINATION OF ALL FORMS OF RACIAL DISCRIMINATION, 1966

The States Parties to this Convention,
Considering that the Charter of the United Nations is based on the principles of the dignity and equality inherent in all human beings, and that all Member States have pledged themselves to take joint and separate action, in co-operation with the Organization, for the achievement of one of the purposes of the United Nations which is to promote and encourage universal respect for and observance of human rights and fundamental freedoms for all, without distinction as to race, sex, language or religion,
Considering that the Universal Declaration of Human Rights proclaims that all human beings are born free and equal in dignity and rights and that everyone is entitled to all the rights and freedoms set out therein, without distinction of any kind, in particular as to race, colour or national origin,
Considering that all human beings are equal before the law and are entitled to equal protection of the law against any discrimination and against any incitement to discrimination,

Considering that the United Nations has condemned colonialism and all practices of segregation and discrimination associated therewith, in whatever form and wherever they exist, and that the Declaration on the Granting of Independence to Colonial Countries and Peoples of 14 December 1960 (General Assembly resolution 1514 (XV)) has affirmed and solemnly proclaimed the necessity of bringing them to a speedy and unconditional end,

Considering that the United Nations Declaration on the Elimination of All Forms of Racial Discrimination of 20 November 1963 (General Assembly resolution 1940 (XVIII)) solemnly affirms the necessity of speedily eliminating racial discrimination throughout the world in all its forms and manifestations and of securing understanding of and respect for the dignity of the human person,

Convinced that any doctrine of superiority based on racial differentiation is scientifically false, morally condemnable, socially unjust and dangerous, and that there is no justification for racial discrimination, in theory or in practice, anywhere,

Reaffirming that discrimination between human beings on the grounds of race, colour or ethnic origin is an obstacle to friendly and peaceful relations among nations and is capable of disturbing peace and security among peoples and the harmony of persons living side by side even within one and the same State,

Convinced that the existence of racial barriers is repugnant to the ideals of any human society,

Alarmed by manifestations of racial discrimination still in evidence in some areas of the world and by governmental policies based on racial superiority or hatred, such as policies of *apartheid*, segregation or separation,

Resolved to adopt all necessary measures for speedily eliminating racial discrimination in all its forms and manifestations, and to prevent and combat racist doctrines and practices in order to promote understanding between races and to build an international community free from all forms of racial segregation and racial discrimination,

Bearing in mind the Convention concerning Discrimination in respect of Employment and Occupation adopted by the International Labour Organization in 1958, and the Convention against Discrimination in Education adopted by the United Nations Educational, Scientific and Cultural Organization in 1960,

Desiring to implement the principles embodied in the United Nations Declaration on the Elimination of All Forms of Racial Discrimination and to secure the earliest adoption of practical measures to that end,

Have agreed as follows:

Article 1

1. In this Convention, the term 'racial discrimination' shall mean any distinction, exclusion, restriction or preference based on race, colour, descent, or national or ethnic origin which has the purpose or effect of nullifying or impairing the recognition, enjoyment or exercise, on an equal footing, of human rights and fundamental freedoms in the political, economic, social, cultural or any other field of public life.

2. This Convention shall not apply to distinctions, exclusions, restrictions or preferences made by a State Party to this Convention between citizens and non-citizens.

3. Nothing in this Convention may be interpreted as affecting in any way the legal provisions of States Parties concerning nationality, citizenship or naturalization, provided that such provisions do not discriminate against any particular nationality.

4. Special measures taken for the sole purpose of securing adequate advancement of certain racial or ethnic groups or individuals requiring such protection as may be necessary in order to ensure such groups or individuals equal enjoyment or exercise of human rights and fundamental freedoms shall not be deemed racial discrimination, provided, however, that such measures do not, as a consequence, lead to the maintenance of separate rights for different racial groups and that they shall not be continued after the objectives for which they were taken have been achieved.

Article 2

1. States Parties condemn racial discrimination and undertake to pursue by all appropriate means and without delay a policy of eliminating racial discrimination in all its forms and promoting understanding among all races, and, to this end:

(a) Each State Party undertakes to engage in no act or practice of racial discrimination against persons, groups of persons or institutions and to ensure that all public authorities and public institutions, national and local, shall act in conformity with this obligation;

(b) Each State Party shall take effective measures to review governmental, national and local policies, and to amend, rescind or nullify any laws and regulations which have the effect of creating or perpetuating racial discrimination wherever it exists;

(d) Each State Party shall prohibit and bring to an end, by all appropriate means, including legislation as required by circumstances, racial discrimination by any persons, group or organization;

(e) Each State Party undertakes to encourage, where appropriate, integrationist multi-racial organizations and movements and other means of eliminating barriers between races, and to discourage anything which tends to strengthen racial division.

2. States Parties shall, when the circumstances so warrant, take, in the social, economic, cultural and other fields, special and concrete measures to ensure the adequate development and protection of certain racial groups or individuals belonging to them, for the purpose of guaranteeing them the full and equal enjoyment of human rights and fundamental freedoms. These measures shall in no case entail as a consequence the maintenance of unequal or separate rights for different racial groups after the objectives for which they were taken have been achieved.

Article 3

States Parties particularly condemn racial segregation and *apartheid* and undertake to prevent, prohibit and eradicate all practices of this nature in territories under their jurisdiction.

Article 4

States Parties condemn all propaganda and all organizations which are based on ideas or theories of superiority of one race or group of persons of one colour or ethnic origin, or which attempt to justify or promote racial hatred and discrimination in any form, and undertake to adopt immediate and positive measures designed to eradicate all incitement to, or acts of, such discrimination and, to this end, with due regard to the principles embodied in the Universal Declaration of Human Rights and the rights expressly set forth in Article 5 of this Convention, *inter alia:*

(a) Shall declare an offence punishable by law all dissemination of ideas based on racial superiority or hatred, incitement to racial discrimination, as well as all acts of violence or incitement to such acts against any race or group of persons of another colour or ethnic origin, and also the provisions of any assistance to racist activities, including the financing thereof;

(b) Shall declare illegal and prohibit organizations, and also organized and all other propaganda activities, which promote and incite racial discrimination, and shall recognize participation in such organizations or activities as an offence punishable by law;

(c) Shall not permit public authorities or public institutions, national or local, to promote or incite racial discrimination.

Article 5

In compliance with the fundamental obligations laid down in Article 2 of this Convention, States Parties undertake to prohibit and to eliminate racial discrimination in all its forms and to guarantee the right of everyone, without distinction as to race, colour, or national or ethnic origin, to equality before the law, notably in the enjoyment of the following rights:

(a) The right to equal treatment before the tribunals and all other organs administering justice;
(b) The right to security of person and protection by the State against violence or bodily harm, whether inflicted by government officials or by individual, group or institution;
(c) Political rights, in particular the rights to participate in elections – to vote and to stand for election – on the basis of universal and equal suffrage, to take part in the Government as well as in the conduct of public affairs at any level and to have equal access to public service;
(d) Other civil rights, in particular:
    i. The right to freedom of movement and residence within the border of the State;
    ii. The right to leave any country, including one's own, and to return to one's country;
    iii. The right to nationality;
    iv. The right to marriage and choice of spouse;
    v. The right to own property alone as well as in association with others;
    vi. The right to inherit;
    vii. The right to freedom of thought, conscience and religion;
    viii. The right to freedom of opinion and expression;
    ix. The right to freedom of peaceful assembly and association;
(e) Economic, social and cultural rights, in particular:
    i. The rights to work, to free choice of employment, to just and favourable conditions of work, to protection against unemployment, to equal pay for equal work, to just and favourable remuneration;
    ii. The right to form and join trade unions;
    iii. The right to housing;
    iv. The right to public health, medical care, social security and social services;
    v. The right to education and training;
    vi. The right to equal participation in cultural activities;
(f) The right of access to any place or service intended for use by the general public, such as transport, hotels, restaurants, cafés, theatres and parks.

Article 6

States Parties shall assure to everyone within their jurisdiction effective protection and remedies, through the competent national tribunals and other State institutions, against any acts of racial discrimination which violate his human rights and fundamental freedoms contrary to this Convention, as well as the right to seek from such tribunals just and adequate reparation or satisfaction for any damage suffered as a result of such discrimination.

Article 7

States Parties undertake to adopt immediate and effective measures, particularly in fields of teaching, education, culture and information, with a view to combating prejudices which lead to racial discrimination and to promoting understanding, tolerance and friendship among nations and racial or ethnical groups, as well as to propagating the purposes and principles of the Charter of the United Nations, the Universal Declaration of Human Rights, the United Nations Declaration on the Elimination of All Forms of Racial Discrimination, and this Convention.

Article 8

1. There shall be established a Committee on the Elimination of Racial Discrimina-

tion (hereinafter referred to as the Committee) consisting of eighteen experts of high moral standing and acknowledged impartiality elected by States Parties from among their nationals, who shall serve in their personal capacity, consideration being given to equitable geographical distribution and to the representation of the different forms of civilization as well as of the principal legal systems.

2. The members of the Committee shall be elected by secret ballot from a list of persons nominated by the States Parties. Each State Party may nominate one person from among its own nationals.

*   *   *

3.   Declarations and resolutions

(a) Human rights
Following the basic human rights instruments contained in the previous section, the texts in this section concern decolonization and the elimination of various forms of discrimination with mention of the role of communications to achieve these objectives. In view of its importance as a further elaboration of human rights the Proclamation adopted by the UN-sponsored International Conference on Human rights in 1968 has also been included. Throughout the years, the General Assembly has continuously paid attention to various aspects of human rights which is reflected in numerous resolutions dealing with decolonization, discrimination, racism and apartheid.

Documents

i.   Universal Declaration of Human Rights, 1948
    – see previous section for text in full
ii. (a) Declaration on the Granting of Independence to Colonial Countries and Peoples, General Assembly Resolution 151 (XV), 1960
        – Full text
    (b) Programme of action for the full implementation of the Declaration on the Granting of Independence to Colonial Countries and Peoples, General Assembly Resolution 2621 (XXV), 1970
        – Preamble
        – Points 4, 7, 8
    (c) Dissemination of information on decolonisation, General Assembly Resolution 2879 (XXVI), 1971
        – Full text
iii. Declaration on the Elimination of Discrimination Against Women, General Assembly Resolution 2263 (XXII), 1967
    – Preamble
    – Articles 1–3, 9
iv. Draft International Convention on the Elimination of All Forms of Religious Intolerance, Economic and Social Council Resolution 1233 (XLII), 1967
    – Full text
v.   The Proclamation of Tehran, 1968
    – Full text
vi. Declaration of the Rights of the Child, General Assembly Resolution 1386 (XIV), 1959
    – Full text

DECLARATION ON THE GRANTING OF INDEPENDENCE TO COLONIAL COUNTRIES AND PEOPLES

General Assembly Resolution 151 (XV), 1960

The General Assembly,

Mindful of the determination proclaimed by the peoples of the world in the Charter of the United Nations to reaffirm faith in fundamental human rights, in the dignity and worth of the human person, in the equal rights of men and women and of nations large and small and to promote social progress and better standards of life in larger freedom,

Conscious of the need for the creation of conditions of stability and well-being and peaceful and friendly relations based on respect for the principles of equal rights and self-determination of all peoples, and of universal respect for, and observance of, human rights and fundamental freedoms for all without distinction as to race, sex, language or religion,

Recognizing the passionate yearning for freedom in all dependent peoples and the decisive role of such peoples in the attainment of their independence,

Aware of the increasing conflicts resulting from the denial of or impediments in the way of the freedom of such peoples, which constitute a serious threat to world peace,

Considering the important role of the United Nations in assisting the movement for independence in Trust and Non-Self-Governing Territories,

Recognizing that the peoples of the world ardently desire the end of colonialism in all its manifestations,

Convinced that the continued existence of colonialism prevents the development of international and economic co-operation, impedes the social, cultural and economic development of dependent peoples and militates against the United Nations ideal of universal peace,

Affirming that peoples may, for their own ends, freely dispose of their natural wealth and resources without prejudice to any obligations arising out of international economic co-operation, based upon the principle of mutual benefit, and international law,

Believing that the process of liberation is irresistible and that, in order to avoid serious crises, an end must be put to colonialism and all practices of segregation and discrimination associated therewith,

Welcoming the emergence in recent years of a large number of dependent territories into freedom and independence, and recognizing the increasingly powerful trends towards freedom in such territories which have not yet attained independence,

Convinced that all peoples have an inalienable right to complete freedom, the exercise of their sovereignty and the integrity of their national territory, *Solemnly proclaims* the necessity of bringing to a speedy and unconditional end colonialism in all its forms and manifestations;

And to this end

Declares that:

1. The subjection of peoples to alien subjugation, domination and exploitation constitutes a denial of fundamental human rights, is contrary to the Charter of the United Nations and is an impediment to the promotion of World peace and co-operation.

2. All peoples have the right to self-determination; by virtue of that right they freely determine their political status and freely pursue their economic, social and cultural development.

3. Inadequacy of political, economic, social or educational preparedness should never serve as a pretext for delaying independence.

4. All armed action or repressive measures of all kinds directed against dependent peoples shall cease in order to enable them to exercise peacefully and freely their right to complete independence, and the integrity of their national territory shall be respected.

5. Immediate steps shall be taken, in Trust and Non-Self-Governing Territories or all other territories which have not yet attained independence, to transfer all powers to the peoples of those territories, without any conditions or reservations, in accordance with their freely expressed will and desire, without any distinction as to race, creed or colour, in order to enable them to enjoy complete independence and freedom.

6. Any attempt aimed at the partial or total disruption of the national unity and the territorial integrity of a country is incompatible with the purposes and principles of the Charter of the United Nations.

7. All States shall observe faithfully and strictly the provisions of the Charter of the United Nations, the Universal Declaration of Human Rights and the present Declaration on the basis of equality, non-interference in the internal affairs of all States, and respect for the sovereign rights of all peoples and their territorial integrity.

PROGRAMME OF ACTION FOR THE FULL IMPLEMENTATION OF THE DECLARATION ON THE GRANTING OF INDEPENDENCE TO COLONIAL COUNTRIES AND PEOPLES

General Assembly Resolution 2621 (XXV), 1970

The General Assembly,
Having decided to hold a special commemorative session on the occasion of the tenth anniversary of the Declaration on the Granting of Independence to Colonial Countries and Peoples,
   Considering that, by arousing world public opinion and promoting practical action for the speedy liquidation of colonialism in all its forms and manifestations, the Declaration has played and will continue to play an important role in assisting the peoples under colonial domination in their struggle for freedom and independence,
   Conscious of the fact that, although many colonial countries and peoples have achieved freedom and independence in the last ten years, the system of colonialism continues to exist in many areas of the world,
   Reaffirming that all peoples have the right to self-determination and independence and that the subjection of the peoples to alien domination constitutes a serious impediment to the maintenance of international peace and security and the development of peaceful relations among nations,
   Adopts the following programme of action to assist in the full implementation of the Declaration on the Granting of Independence to Colonial Countries and Peoples:

* * *

4. Member States shall wage a vigorous and sustained campaign against activities and practices of foreign economic, financial and other interests operating in colonial Territories for the benefit and on behalf of colonial Powers and their allies, as these constitute a major obstacle to the achievement of the goals embodied in resolution 1514 (XV). Member States shall consider the adoption of necessary steps to have their nationals and companies under this jurisdiction discontinue such activities and practices and these steps should also aim at preventing the systematic influx of foreign immigrants into colonial Territories, which disrupts the integrity and sociopolitical and cultural unity of the peoples under colonial domination.

* * *

7. All States shall undertake measures aimed at enhancing public awareness of the need for active assistance in the achievement of complete decolonisation.

8. The United Nations as well as all States shall intensify their efforts in the field of public information in the area of decolonization through all media, including publications, radio and television. Of special importance will be programmes relating to United Nations activities on decolonization, the situation in colonial Territories and the struggle being waged by colonial peoples and the national liberation movements.

DISSEMINATION OF INFORMATION ON DECOLONIZATION

General Assembly Resolution 2879 (XXVI), 1971

The General Assembly,
Having examined the chapters of the report of the Special Committee on the Situation with regard to the Implementation of the Declaration on the Granting of Independence to Colonial Countries and Peoples relating to the question of publicity for the work of the United Nations in the field of decolonization,

Recalling its resolution 1514 (XV) of 14 December 1960, containing the Declaration on the Granting of Independence to Colonial Countries and Peoples, and its resolution 2621 (XXV) of 12 October 1970, containing the programme of action for the full implementation of the Declaration,

Conscious of the urgent need to intensify widespread and continuous dissemination of information on the work of the United Nations in the field of decolonization, on the situation in the colonial Territories and on the continuing struggle for liberation being waged by the colonial peoples and the activities of their national liberation movements,

Taking into account the suggestions of the Special Committee as well as the views of the Office of Public Information on the implementation of these suggestions, as reflected in the relevant chapters of the report of the Special Committee,

Taking into account the recommendations of the Fifth Committee relating to the report of the Secretary-General on the review and reappraisal of United Nations information policies and activities, and noting the report of the Secretary-General on the joint meeting of the Special Committee on the Situation with regard to the Implementation of the Declaration on the Granting of Independence to Colonial Countries and Peoples, the Special Committee on *Apartheid* and the United Nations Council for Namibia,

Recognizing the importance of publicity as an instrument for furthering the aims and purposes of the Declaration and the need for the Office of Public Information to intensify its efforts to acquaint world public opinion with all aspects of the problems of decolonization,

1. *Approves* the chapters of the report of the Special Committee on the Situation with regard to the Implementation of the Declaration on the Granting of Independence to Colonial Countries and Peoples relating to the question of publicity for the work of the United Nations in the field of decolonization;

2. *Affirms* the vital importance of urgently effecting the widest possible dissemination of information on the evils and dangers of colonialism, the continuing struggle for liberation being waged by the colonial peoples, particularly in southern Africa, and the efforts being made by the international community to eliminate the remaining vestiges of colonialism in all its forms and manifestations;

3. *Requests* the Secretary-General, having regard to the suggestions of the Special Committee, to continue to take concrete measures through all the media at his disposal, including publications, radio and television, to give widespread and con-

tinuous publicity to the work of the United Nations in the field of decolonization, to the situation in the colonial Territories and to the continuing struggle for liberation being waged by the colonial peoples and, *inter alia:*

(a) To intensify the activities of the information centres located in southern Africa, including the establishment of an additional information centre where appropriate;

(b) To maintain a close working relationship with the Organization of African Unity by holding periodic consultations and a systematic exchange of the relevant information with that organization;

(c) To enlist, from the non-governmental organizations in consultative status with the Economic and Social Council and from those non-governmental organizations having a special interest in the field of decolonization, support in the dissemination of the relevant information;

(d) To continue to publish, in consultation with the Special Committee, selected issues of the periodical *Objective: Justice* and the bulletin "United Nations and Southern Africa" in other languages besides English and French;

4. *Requests* Member States, in particular the administering Powers, to co-operate fully with the Secretary-General in the discharge of the tasks entrusted to him under paragraph 3 above;

5. *Invites* all States, the specialized agencies and other organizations within the United Nations system and non-governmental organizations in consultation status with the Economic and Social Council, as well as other non-governmental organizations having a special interest in the field of decolonization, to undertake, in co-operation with the Secretary-General and within their respective spheres of competence, the large-scale dissemination of the information referred to in paragraph 2 above;

6. *Requests* the Secretary-General, in consultation with the Special Committee, to collect and prepare on a continuous basis for redissemination by the Office of Public Information, basic material, studies and articles relating to various aspects of the problems of decolonization;

7. *Requests* the Secretary-General to report to the Special Committee on the implementation of the present resolution;

8. *Requests* the Special Committee to continue to examine the question at its next session and to report thereon to the General Assembly at its twenty-seventh session.

DECLARATION ON THE ELIMINATION OF DISCRIMINATION AGAINST WOMEN

General Assembly Resolution 2263 (XXII), 1967

The General Assembly,
Considering that the peoples of the United Nations have, in the Charter, reaffirmed their faith in fundamental human rights, in the dignity and worth of the human person and in the equal rights of men and women,

Considering that the Universal Declaration of Human Rights asserts the principle of non-discrimination and proclaims that all human beings are born free and equal in dignity and rights and that everyone is entitled to all the rights and freedoms set forth therein, without distinction of any kind, including any distinction as to sex,

Taking into account the resolutions, declarations, conventions and recommendations of the United Nations and the specialized agencies designed to eliminate all forms of discrimination and to promote equal rights for men and women,

Concerned that, despite the Charter of the United Nations, the Universal Declaration of Human Rights, the International Covenants on Human Rights and other instruments of the United Nations and the specialized agencies and despite the progress made in the matter of equality of rights, there continues to exist considerable discrimination against women,

Considering that discrimination against women is incompatible with human dignity and with the welfare of the family and of society, prevents their participation, on equal terms with men, in the political, social, economic and cultural life of their countries and is an obstacle to the full development of the potentialities of women in the service of their countries and of humanity,

Bearing in mind the great contribution made by women to social, political, economic and cultural life and the part they play in the family and particularly in the rearing of children,

Convinced that the full and complete development of a country, the welfare of the world and the cause of peace require the maximum participation of women as well as men in all fields,

Considering that it is necessary to ensure the universal recognition in law and in fact of the principle of equality of men and women,

Solemnly proclaims this Declaration:

Article 1

Discrimination against women, denying or limiting as it does their equality of rights with men, is fundamentally unjust and constitutes an offence against human dignity.

Article 2

All appropriate measures shall be taken to abolish existing laws, customs, regulations and practices which are discriminatory against women, and to establish adequate legal protection for equal rights of men and women, in particular:

(a) The principle of equality of rights shall be embodied in the constitution or otherwise guaranteed by law;
(b) The international instruments of the United Nations and the specialized agencies relating to the elimination of discrimination against women shall be ratified or acceded to and fully implemented as soon as practicable.

Article 3

All appropriate measures shall be taken to educate public opinion and to direct national aspirations towards the eradication of prejudice and the abolition of customary and all other practices which are based on the idea of the inferiority of women.

* * *

Article 9

All appropriate measures shall be taken to ensure to girls and women, married or unmarried, equal rights with men in education at all levels, and in particular:

(a) Equal conditions of access to, and study in, educational institutions of all types, including universities and vocational, technical and professional schools;
(b) The same choice of curricula, the same examinations, teaching staff with qualifications of the same standard, and school premises and equipment of the same quality, whether the institutions are coeducational or not;
(c) Equal opportunities to benefit from scholarships and other study grants;
(d) Equal opportunities for access to programmes of continuing education, including adult literacy programmes;
(e) Access to educational information to help in ensuring the health and well-being of families.

DRAFT INTERNATIONAL CONVENTION ON THE ELIMINATION
OF ALL FORMS OF RELIGIOUS INTOLERANCE, 1967

Economic and Social Council Resolution 1233 (XLII), 1967

Preamble

The States Parties to the present Convention,
Considering that one of the basic principles of the Charter of the United Nations is that of the dignity and equality inherent in all human beings, and that all States Members have pledged themselves to take joint and separate action in co-operation with the Organization to promote and encourage universal respect for and observance of human rights and fundamental freedoms for all, without distinction as to race, sex, language or religion,

Considering that the Universal Declaration of Human Rights proclaims the principle of non-discrimination and the right to freedom of thought, conscience, religion and belief,

Considering that the disregard and infringement of human rights and fundamental freedoms, and in particular of the right of freedom of thought, conscience, religion and belief, have brought great suffering to mankind,

Considering that religion or belief, for anyone who professes either, is a fundamental element in his conception of life, and that freedom to practise religion as well as to manifest a belief should be fully respected and guaranteed,

Considering it essential that Governments, organizations and private persons should strive to promote through education, and by other means, understanding, tolerance and respect in matters relating to freedom of religion and belief,

Noting with satisfaction the coming into force of conventions concerning discrimination, *inter alia,* on the ground of religion, such as the Convention concerning Discrimination in Respect of Employment and Occupation adopted by the International Labour Organization in 1958, the Convention against Discrimination in Education adopted by the United Nations Educational, Scientific and Cultural Organization in 1960, and the United Nations Convention on the Prevention and Punishment of the Crime of Genocide, adopted in 1948,

Concerned by manifestations of intolerance in such matters still in evidence in some areas of the world,

Resolved to adopt all necessary measures for eliminating speedily such intolerance in all its forms and manifestations and to prevent and combat discrimination on the ground of religion or belief,

Have agreed as follows:

Article I

For the purpose of this Convention:

(a)   The expression 'religion or belief' shall include theistic, nontheistic and atheistic beliefs;

(b)   The expression 'discrimination on the ground of religion or belief' shall mean any distinction, exclusion, restriction or preference based on religion or belief which has the purpose or effect of nullifying or impairing the recognition, enjoyment or exercise, on equal footing, of human rights and fundamental freedoms in the political, economic, social, cultural or any other field of public life;

(c)   The expression 'religious intolerance' shall mean intolerance in matters of religion or belief;

(d)   Neither the establishment of a religion nor the recognition of a religion or belief by a State nor the separation of Church from State shall by itself be considered religious intolerance or discrimination on the ground of religion or belief; provided that this paragraph shall not be construed as permitting violation of specific provisions of the Convention.

Article II

States Parties recognize that the religion or belief of an individual is a matter for his own conscience and must be respected accordingly. They condemn all forms of religious intolerance and all discrimination on the ground of religion or belief and undertake to promote and implement policies which are designed to protect freedom of thought, conscience, religion or belief, to secure religious tolerance and to eliminate all discrimination on the ground of religion or belief.

Article III

1. States Parties undertake to ensure to everyone within their jurisdiction the right to freedom of thought, conscience, religion or belief. This right shall include:

(a) Freedom to adhere or not to adhere to any religion or belief and to change his religion or belief in accordance with the dictates of his conscience without being subjected either to any of the limitations referred to in Article XII or to any coercion likely to impair his freedom of choice or decision in the matter, provided that this sub-paragraph shall not be interpreted as extending to manifestations of religion or belief;

(b) Freedom to manifest his religion or belief either alone or in community with others, and in public or in private, without being subjected to any discrimination on the ground of religion or belief;

(c) Freedom to express opinions on questions concerning a religion or belief.

2. States Parties shall in particular ensure to everyone within their jurisdiction:

(a) Freedom to worship, to hold assemblies related to religion or belief and to establish and maintain places of worship or assembly for these purposes;

(b) Freedom to teach, to disseminate and to learn his religion or belief and its sacred languages or traditions, to write, print and publish religious books and texts, and to train personnel intending to devote themselves to its practices or observances;

(c) Freedom to practise his religion or belief by establishing and maintaining charitable and educational institutions and by expressing in public life the implications of religion or belief;

(d) Freedom to observe the rituals, dietary and other practices of his religion or belief and to produce or if necessary import the objects, foods and other articles and facilities customarily used in its observances and practices;

(e) Freedom to make pilgrimages and other journeys in connexion with his religion or belief, whether inside or outside his country;

(f) Equal legal protection for the places of worship or assembly, the rites, ceremonies and activities, and the places of disposal of the dead associated with his religion or belief;

(g) Freedom to organize and maintain local, regional, national and international associations in connexion with his religion or belief, to participate in the activities, and to communicate with his coreligionists and believers;

(h) Freedom from compulsion to take an oath of religious nature.

Article IV

1. States Parties undertake to respect the right of parents and, where applicable, legal guardians, to bring up in the religion or belief of their choice their children or wards who are as yet incapable of exercising the freedom of choice guaranteed under article III, paragraph 1 (a).

2. The exercise of this right carries with it the duty of parents and legal guardians to inculcate in their children or wards tolerance for the religion or belief of others, and to protect them from any precepts or practices based on religious intolerance or discrimination on the ground of religion or belief.

3. In the case of a child who has been deprived of his parents, their expressed or presumed wishes shall be duly taken into account.

4. In applying the provisions of this article, the best interests of the child shall be the guiding principle for those who are responsible for his upbringing and education.

Article V

States Parties shall ensure to everyone freedom to enjoy and to exercise political, civic, economic, social and cultural rights without discrimination on the ground of religion or belief.

Article VI

States Parties undertake to adopt immediate and effective measures, particularly in the fields of teaching, education, culture and information, with a view to combating prejudices as, for example, anti-Semitism and other manifestations which lead to religious intolerance and to discrimination on the ground of religion or belief, and to promoting and encouraging in the interest of universal peace, understanding, tolerance, co-operation and friendship among nations, groups and individuals, irrespective of differences in religion or belief, in accordance with the purposes and principles of the Charter of the United Nations, the Universal Declaration of Human Rights and this Convention.

Article VII

1. In compliance with the fundamental obligations laid down in article II, States Parties shall take effective measures to prevent and eliminate discrimination on the ground of religion or belief, including the enactment or abrogation of laws or regulations where necessary to prohibit such discrimination by any person, group or organization.

2. States Parties undertake not to pursue any policy or enact or retain laws or regulations restricting or impeding freedom of conscience, religion or belief or the free and open exercise thereof, nor discriminate against any person, group or organization on account of membership or non-membership in, practice or non-practice of, or adherence or non-adherence to any religion or belief.

Article VIII

States Parties undertake to ensure to everyone equality before the law without any discrimination in the exercise of the right to freedom of thought, conscience, religion or belief, and the right to equal protection of the law against any discrimination on the ground of religion or belief.

Article IX

States Parties shall ensure equal protection of the law against promotion of or incitement to religious intolerance or discrimination on the ground of religion or belief. Any act of violence against the adherents of any religion or belief or against the means used for its practice, any incitement to such acts or incitement to hatred likely to result in acts of violence against any religion or belief or its adherents, shall be considered as offences punishable by law. Membership in an organization based on religion or belief does not remove the responsibility for the abovementioned acts.

Article X

States Parties shall ensure to everyone within their jurisdiction effective protection and remedies, through the competent national tribunals and other State institutions, against any acts, including acts of discrimination on the ground of religion or belief, which violate his human rights and fundamental freedoms contrary to this

Convention, as well as the right to seek from such tribunals just and adequate reparation or satisfaction for any damage suffered as a result of such acts.

Article XI

Nothing in this Convention shall be interpreted as giving to any person, group, organization or institution the right to engage in activities aimed at prejudicing national security, friendly relations between nations or the purposes and principles of the United Nations.

Article XII

Nothing in this Convention shall be construed to preclude a State Party from prescribing by law such limitations as are necessary to protect public safety, order, health or morals, or the individual rights and freedoms of others, or the general welfare in a democratic society.

PROCLAMATION OF TEHERAN, 1968

The International Conference on Human Rights,
Having met at Teheran from April 22 to May 13, 1968 to review the progress made in the twenty years since the adoption of the Universal Declaration of Human Rights and to formulate a programme for the future,
Having considered the problems relating to the activities of the United Nations for the promotion and encouragement of respect for human rights and fundamental freedoms,
Bearing in mind the resolutions adopted by the Conference,
Noting that the observance of the International Year for Human Rights takes place at a time when the world is undergoing a process of unprecedented change,
Having regard to the new opportunities made available by the rapid progress of science and technology,
Believing that, in an age when conflict and violence prevail in many parts of the world, the fact of human interdependence and the need for human solidarity are more evident than ever before,
Recognizing that peace is the universal aspiration of mankind and that peace and justice are indispensable to the full realization of human rights and fundamental freedoms,
Solemnly proclaims that:

1. It is imperative that the members of the international community fulfil their solemn obligations to promote and encourage respect for human rights and fundamental freedoms for all without distinctions of any kind such as race, colour, sex, language, religion, political or other opinions;

2. The Universal Declaration of Human Rights states a common understanding of the peoples of the world concerning the inalienable and inviolable rights of all members of the human family and constitutes an obligation for the members of the international community;

3. The International Covenant on Civil and Political Rights, the International Covenant on Economic, Social and Cultural Rights, the Declaration on the Granting of Independence to Colonial Countries and Peoples, the International Convention on the Elimination of All Forms of Racial Discrimination, as well as other conventions and declarations in the field of human rights adopted under the auspices of the United Nations, the specialized agencies and the regional inter-governmental organizations, have created new standards and obligations to which States should conform;

4. Since the adoption of the Universal Declaration of Human Rights the United Nations has made substantial progress in defining standards for the enjoyment and protection of human rights and fundamental freedoms. During this period many impor-

tant international instruments were adopted but much remains to be done in regard to the implementation of those rights and freedoms;

5. The primary aim of the United Nations in the sphere of human rights is the achievement by each individual of the maximum freedom and dignity. For the realization of this objective, the laws of every country should grant each individual, irrespective of race, language, religion or political belief, freedom of expression, of information, of conscience and of religion, as well as the right to participate in the political, economic, cultural and social life of his country;

6. States should reaffirm their determination effectively to enforce the principles enshrined in the Charter of the United Nations and in other international instruments that concern human rights and fundamental freedoms;

7. Gross denials of human rights under the repugnant policy of *apartheid* is a matter of the gravest concern to the international community. This policy of *apartheid*, condemned as a crime against humanity, continues seriously to disturb international peace and security. It is therefore imperative for the international community to use every possible means to eradicate this evil. The struggle against *apartheid* is recognized as legitimate;

8. The peoples of the world must be made fully aware of the evils of racial discrimination and must join in combating them. The implementation of this principle of non-discrimination, embodied in the Charter of the United Nations, the Universal Declaration of Human Rights, and other international instruments in the field of human rights, constitutes a most urgent task of mankind, at the international as well as at the national level. All ideologies based on racial superiority and intolerance must be condemned and resisted;

9. Eight years after the General Assembly's Declaration on the Granting of Independence to Colonial Countries and Peoples the problems of colonialism continue to preoccupy the international community. It is a matter of urgency that all Member States should co-operate with the appropriate organs of the United Nations so that effective measures can be taken to ensure that the Declaration is fully implemented;

10. Massive denials of human rights, arising out of aggression or any armed conflict with their tragic consequences, and resulting in untold human misery, engender reactions which could engulf the world in ever growing hostilities. It is the obligation of the international community to co-operate in eradicating such scourges;

11. Gross denials of human rights arising from discrimination on grounds of race, religion, belief or expressions of opinion outrage the conscience of mankind and endanger the foundations of freedom, justice and peace in the world;

12. The widening gap between the economically developed and developing countries impedes the realization of human rights in the international community. The failure of the Development Decade to reach its modest objectives makes it all the more imperative for every nation, according to its capacities, to make the maximum possible effort to close this gap;

13. Since human rights and fundamental freedoms are indivisible, the full realization of civil and political rights without the enjoyment of economic, social and cultural rights, is impossible. The achievement of lasting progress in the implementation of human rights is dependent upon sound and effective national and international policies of economic and social development;

14. The existence of over seven hundred million illiterates throughout the world is an enormous obstacle to all efforts at realizing the aims and purposes of the Charter of the United Nations and the provisions of the Universal Declaration of Human Rights. International action aimed at eradicating illiteracy from the face of the earth and promoting education at all levels requires urgent attention;

15. The discrimination of which women are still victims in various regions of the world must be eliminated. An inferior status for women is contrary to the Charter of

the United Nations as well as the provisions of the Universal Declaration of Human Rights. The full implementation of the Declaration on the Elimination of All Forms of Discrimination Against Women is a necessity for the progress of mankind;

16. The protection of the family and of the child remains the concern of the international community. Parents have a basic human right to determine freely and responsibly the number and the spacing of their children;

17. The aspirations of the younger generation for a better world, in which human rights and fundamental freedoms are fully implemented, must be given the highest encouragement. It is imperative that youth participate in shaping the future of mankind;

18. While recent scientific discoveries and technological advances have opened vast prospects for economic, social and cultural progress, such developments may nevertheless endanger the rights and freedoms of individuals and will require continuing attention;

19. Disarmament would release immense human and material resources now devoted to military purposes. These resources should be used for the promotion of human rights and fundamental freedoms. General and complete disarmament is one of the highest aspirations of all peoples;

Therefore,

The International Conference on Human Rights,

1. *Affirming* its faith in the principles of the Universal Declaration of Human Rights and other international instruments in this field,

2. *Urges* all peoples and governments to dedicate themselves to the principles enshrined in the Universal Declaration of Human Rights and to redouble their efforts to provide for all human beings a life consonant with freedom and dignity and conducive to physical, mental, social and spiritual welfare.

DECLARATION OF THE RIGHTS OF THE CHILD

General Assembly Resolution 1386 (XIV), 1959

Preamble

Whereas the peoples of the United Nations have, in the Charter, reaffirmed their faith in fundamental human rights and in the dignity and worth of the human person, and have determined to promote social progress and better standards of life in larger freedom,

Whereas the United Nations has, in the Universal Declaration of Human Rights, proclaimed that everyone is entitled to all the rights and freedoms set forth therein, without distinction of any kind, such as race, colour, sex, language, religion, political or other opinion, national or social origin, property, birth or other status,

Whereas the child by reason of his physical and mental immaturity, needs special safeguards and care, including appropriate legal protection, before as well as after birth,

Whereas the need for such special safeguards has been stated in the Geneva Declaration of the Rights of the Child of 1924, and recognized in the Universal Declaration of Human Rights and in the statutes of specialized agencies and international organizations concerned with the welfare of children,

Whereas mankind owes to the child the best it has to give,

Now therefore,

The General Assembly

Proclaims this Declaration of the Rights of the Child to the end that he may have a happy childhood and enjoy for his own good and for the good of society the rights and freedoms herein set forth, and calls upon parents, upon men and women as individuals, and upon voluntary organizations, local authorities and national Governments to recognize these rights and strive for their observance by legislative and other measures progressively taken in accordance with the following principles:

Principle 1

The child shall enjoy all the rights set forth in this Declaration. Every child, without any exception whatsoever, shall be entitled to these rights, without distinction or discrimination on account of race, colour, sex, language, religion, political or other opinion, national or social origin, property, birth or other status, whether of himself or of his family.

Principle 2

The child shall enjoy special protection, and shall be given opportunities and facilities, by law and by other means, to enable him to develop physically, mentally, morally, spiritually and socially in a healthy and normal manner and in conditions of freedom and dignity. In the enactment of laws for this purpose, the best interests of the child shall be the paramount considerations.

Principle 3

The child shall be entitled from his birth to a name and a nationality.

Principle 4

The child shall enjoy the benefits of social security. He shall be entitled to grow and develop in health; to this end, special care and protection shall be provided both to him and to his mother, including adequate pre-natal and post-natal care. The child shall have the right to adequate nutrition, housing, recreation and medical services.

Principle 5

The child who is physically, mentally or socially handicapped shall be given the special treatment, education and care required by his particular condition.

Principle 6

The child, for the full and harmonious development of his personality, needs love and understanding. He shall, wherever possible, grow up in the care and under the responsibility of his parents, and, in any case, in an atmosphere of affection and of moral and material security; a child of tender years shall not, save in exceptional circumstances, be separated from his mother. Society and the public authorities shall have the duty to extend particular care to children without a family and to those without adequate means of support. Payment of State and other assistance towards the maintenance of children of large families is desirable.

Principle 7

The child is entitled to receive education, which shall be free and compulsory, at least in the elementary stages. He shall be given an education which will promote his general culture, and enable him, on a basis of equal opportunity, to develop his abilities, his individual judgement, and his sense of moral and social responsibility, and to become a useful member of society.

The best interests of the child shall be the guiding principle of those responsible for his education and guidance; that responsibility lies in the first place with his parents.

The child shall have full opportunity for play and recreation, which should be directed to the same purposes as education; society and the public authorities shall endeavour to promote the enjoyment of this right.

Principle 8

The child shall in all circumstances be among the first to receive protection and relief.

Principle 9

The child shall be protected against all forms of neglect, cruelty and exploitation. He shall not be the subject of traffic, in any form.

The child shall not be admitted to employment before an appropriate minimum age; he shall in no case be caused or permitted to engage in any occupation or employment which would prejudice his health or education, or interfere with his physical, mental or moral development.

Principle 10

The child shall be protected from practices which may foster racial, religious and any other form of discrimination. He shall be brought up in a spirit of understanding, tolerance, friendship among peoples, peace and universal brotherhood, and in full consciousness that his energy and talents should be devoted to the service of his fellow men.

(b) Security and Disarmament

In this area one of the main provisions of international law concerned with communication and information is the prohibition against war propaganda which was already expressed in 1936 with regard to the use of broadcasting in the cause of peace (see Part Two, Section 4). In more general terms, the same prohibition was laid down in General Assembly Resolution 110 (II); 1947 which has served as a point of reference to the inclusion of rules against war propaganda in other international instruments of a binding and non-binding nature: see the International Covenant on Civil and Political Rights (Art. 20), the Outer Space Treaty (Preamble), the American Convention on Human Rights, (Art.13.5), the Unesco Mass Media Declaration, 1978. References to the role of communications and public opinion have also been made in other instruments that concern the strengthening of international security and disarmament.

Documents

vi. Measures to be taken against propaganda and the inciters of a new war, General Assembly Resolution 110 (II), 1947
   – Full text
vii. Declaration on the Strengthening of International Security, General Assembly Resolution 2734 (XXV), 1970
   – Full text
viii. Final Document of the Tenth Special Session of the General Assembly, Resolution S10/2, 1978
   – Preamble
   – Declaration: Points 11, 15, 18–19, 93, 99–107 (see in particular Points 15, 99, and ff)

MEASURES TO BE TAKEN AGAINST PROPAGANDA AND THE
INCITERS OF A NEW WAR

General Assembly Resolution 110 (11), 1947

Whereas in the Charter of the United Nations the peoples express their determination to save succeeding generations from the scourge of war, which twice in our lifetime has brought untold sorrow to mankind, and to practice tolerance and live together in peace with one another as good neighbours, and

Whereas the Charter also calls for the promotion of universal respect for, and observance of, fundamental freedoms which include freedom of expression, all Members having pledged themselves in Article 56 to take joint and separate action for such observance of fundamental freedoms,

The General Assembly

1. *Condemns* all forms of propaganda, in whatsoever country conducted, which is either designed or likely to provoke or encourage any threat to the peace, breach of the peace, or act of aggression;

2. *Requests* the Government of each Member to take appropriate steps within its constitutional limits:

(a) To promote, by all means of publicity and propaganda available to them, friendly relations among nations based upon the Purposes and Principles of the Charter;

(b) To encourage the dissemination of all information designed to give expression to the undoubted desire of all peoples for peace;

3. *Directs* that this resolution be communicated to the forthcoming Conference on Freedom of Information.

DECLARATION ON THE STRENGTHENING OF INTERNATIONAL SECURITY

General Assembly Resolution 2734 (XIV), 1970

The General Assembly,

Recalling the determination of the peoples of the United Nations, as proclaimed by the Charter, to save succeeding generations from the scourge of war, and to this end to live together in peace with one another as good neighbours and to unite their strength to maintain international peace and security,

Considering that in order to fulfil the purposes and principles of the United Nations Member States must strictly abide by all provisions of the Charter,

Recalling its resolution 2606 (XXIV) of 16 December 1969 in which the General Assembly, *inter alia*, expressed the desire that the twenty-fifth year of the Organization's existence should be marked by new initiatives to promote peace, security, disarmament and economic and social progress for all mankind and the conviction of the urgent need to make the United Nations more effective as an instrument for maintaining international peace and security,

Mindful of the observations, proposals and suggestions advanced during the debate at the twenty-fourth session of the General Assembly or presented subsequently by Governments of Member States concerning the attainment of this objective, and of the report submitted by the Secretary-General in conformity with paragraph 5 of resolution 2606 (XXIV),

Having in mind the Declaration on Principles of International Law concerning Friendly Relations and Co-operation among States in accordance with the Charter of the United Nations, adopted unanimously at the current session,

Conscious of its duty to examine in depth the present international situation and to study the means and recourses provided by the relevant provisions of the Charter in order to build peace, security and co-operation in the world,

1. *Solemnly reaffirms* the universal and unconditional validity of the purposes and principles of the Charter of the United Nations as the basis of relations among States irrespective of their size, geographical location, level of development or political, economic and social systems and declares that the breach of the principles cannot be justified in any circumstance whatsoever;

2. *Calls upon* all States to adhere strictly in their international relations to the pur-

poses and principles of the Charter, including the principle that States should refrain in their international relations from the threat or use of force against the territorial integrity and political independence of any State or in any other manner inconsistent with the purposes of the United Nations; the principle that States shall settle their international disputes by peaceful means in such a manner that international peace and security and justice are not endangered; the duty not to intervene in matters within the domestic jurisdiction of any State, in concordance with the Charter; the duty of States to co-operate with one another in accordance with the Charter; the principle of equal rights and self-determination of peoples; the principle of sovereign equality of States; and the principle that States shall fulfil in good faith the obligations assumed by them in concordance with the Charter;

3. *Solemnly reaffirms* that, in the event of a conflict between the obligations of the Members of the United Nations under the Charter and their obligations under any other international agreement, their obligations under the Charter shall prevail;

4. *Solemnly reaffirms* that States must fully respect the sovereignty of other States and the right of peoples to determine their own destinies, free of external intervention, coercion or constraint, especially involving the threat or use of force, overt or covert, and refrain from any attempt aimed at the partial or total disruption of the national unity and territorial integrity of any other State or country;

5. *Solemnly reaffirms* that every State has the duty to refrain from the threat or use of force against the territorial integrity and political independence of any other State, and that the territory of a State shall not be the object of military occupation resulting from the use of force in contravention of the provisions of the Charter, that the territory of a State shall not be the object of acquisition by another State resulting from the threat or use of force, that no territorial acquisition resulting from the threat or use of force shall be recognized as legal and that every State has the duty to refrain from organizing, instigating, assisting or participating in acts of civil strife or terrorist action another State;

6. *Urges* Member States to make full use and improved implementation of the means and methods provided for in the Charter for the exclusively peaceful settlement of any dispute or any situation, the continuance of which is likely to endanger the maintenance of international peace and security, including negotiation, inquiry, mediation, conciliation, arbitration, judicial settlement, resort to regional agencies or arrangements, good offices including those of the Secretary-General, or other peaceful means of their own choice, it being understood that the Security Council in dealing with such disputes or situations should also take into consideration that legal disputes should as a general rule be referred by the parties to the International Court of Justice in accordance with the provisions of the Statute of the Court;

FINAL DOCUMENT OF THE TENTH SPECIAL SESSION OF THE
GENERAL ASSEMBLY, S10/2, 1978

The General Assembly,
Alarmed by the threat to the very survival of mankind posed by the existence of nuclear weapons and the continuing arms race, and recalling the devastation inflicted by all wars,
  Convinced that disarmament and arms limitation, particularly in the nuclear field, are essential for the prevention of the danger of nuclear war and the strengthening of international peace and security and for the economic and social advancement of all peoples, thus facilitating the achievement of the new international economic order,
  Having resolved to lay the foundations of an international disarmament strategy which, through co-ordinated and persevering efforts in which the United Nations should play a more effective role, aims at general and complete disarmament under effective international control,

Adopts the following Final Document of this special session of the General Assembly devoted to disarmament:

*   *   *

II. Declaration

11. Mankind today is confronted with an unprecedented threat of self-extinction arising from the massive and competitive accumulation of the most destructive weapons ever produced. Existing arsenals of nuclear weapons alone are more than sufficient to destroy all life on earth. Failure of efforts to halt and reverse the arms race, in particular the nuclear arms race, increases the danger of the proliferation of nuclear weapons. Yet the arms race continues. Military budgets are constantly growing, with enormous consumption of human and material resources. The increase in weapons, especially nuclear weapons, far from helping to strengthen international security, on the contrary weakens it. The vast stockpiles and tremendous build-up of arms and armed forces and the competition for qualitative refinement of weapons of all kinds, to which scientific resources and technological advances are diverted, pose incalculable threat to peace. This situation both reflects and aggravates international tensions, sharpens conflicts in various regions of the world, hinders the process of detente, exacerbates the differences between opposing military alliances, jeopardizes the security of all States, heightens the sense of insecurity among all States, including the non-nuclear-weapon States, and increases the threat of nuclear war.

*   *   *

15. It is essential that not only Governments but also the peoples of the world recognize and understand the dangers in the present situation. In order that an international conscience may develop and that world public opinion may exercise a positive influence, the United Nations should increase the dissemination of information on the armaments race and disarmament with the full co-operation of Member States.

*   *   *

18. Removing the threat of a world war – a nuclear war – is the most acute and urgent task of the present day. Mankind is confronted with a choice: we must halt the arms race and proceed to disarmament or face annihilation.

19. The ultimate objective of the efforts of States in the disarmament process is general and complete disarmament under effective international control. The principal goals of disarmament are to ensure the survival of mankind and to eliminate the danger of war, in particular nuclear war, to ensure that war is no longer an instrument for settling international disputes and that the use and the threat of force are eliminated from international life, as provided for in the Charter of the United Nations. Progress towards this objective requires the conclusion and implementation of agreements on the cessation of the arms race and on genuine measures of disarmament, taking into account the need of States to protect their security.

*   *   *

93. In order to facilitate the process of disarmament, it is necessary to take measures and pursue policies to strengthen international peace and security and to build confidence among States. Commitment to confidence-building measures could significantly contribute to preparing for further progress in disarmament. For this purpose, measures such as the following and other measures yet to be agreed upon, should be undertaken:

*   *   *

99. In order to mobilize world public opinion on behalf of disarmament, the specific measures set forth below, designed to increase the dissemination of information about the armaments race and the efforts to halt and reverse it, should be adopted.

100. Governmental and non-governmental information organs and those of the United Nations and its specialized agencies should give priority to the preparation and distribution of printed and audio-visual material relating to the danger represented by the armaments race as well as to the disarmament efforts and negotiations on specific disarmament measures.

101. In particular, publicity should be given to the Final Document of the tenth special session.

102. The General Assembly proclaims the week starting 24 October, the day of the foundation of the United Nations, as a week devoted to fostering the objectives of disarmament.

103. To encourage study and research on disarmament, the United Nations Centre for Disarmament should intensify its activities in the presentation of information concerning the armaments race and disarmament. Also, the United Nations Educational, Scientific and Cultural Organization is urged to intensify its activities aimed at facilitating research and publications on disarmament, related to its fields of competence, especially in developing countries, and should disseminate the results of such research.

104. Throughout this process of disseminating information about developments in the disarmament field of all countries, there should be increased participation by non-governmental organizations concerned with the matter, through closer liaison between them and the United Nations.

105. Member States should be encouraged to ensure a better flow of information with regard to the various aspects of disarmament to avoid dissemination of false and tendentious information concerning armaments, and to concentrate on the danger of escalation of the armaments race and on the need for general and complete disarmament under effective international control.

106. With a view to contributing to a greater understanding and awareness of the problems created by the armaments race and of the need for disarmament, Governments and governmental and non-governmental international organizations are urged to take steps to develop programmes of education for disarmament and peace studies at all levels.

107. The General Assembly welcomes the initiative of the United Nations Educational, Scientific and Cultural Organization in planning to hold a world congress on disarmament education and, in this connexion, urges that organization to step up its programme aimed at the development of disarmament education as a distinct field of study through the preparation, *inter alia*, of teachers' guides, textbooks, readers and audio-visual materials. Member States should take all possible measures to encourage the incorporation of such materials in the curricula of their educational institutions.

(c) *Peace, international understanding*
A number of the documents mentioned in the previous sections are cast in a negative form in the sense of prohibiting certain behaviour or action. Other documents have a positive character by recommending certain behaviour, or promoting agreed objectives. The documents selected for this section concern the promotion of peace and international understanding and include references to the role of communications. Conversely, as will be shown in the following sections, documents which deal directly with communications and information often refer to the objectives of promoting peace and international understanding.

Documents

DECLARATION ON THE PROMOTION AMONG YOUTH OF THE IDEALS OF PEACE, MUTUAL RESPECT AND UNDERSTANDING BETWEEN PEOPLES

General Assembly Resolution 2037 (XX), 1965

The General Assembly,

Recalling that under the terms of the Charter of the United Nations the peoples have declared themselves determined to save succeeding generations from the scourge of war,

Recalling further that in the Charter the United Nations has affirmed its faith in fundamental human rights, in the dignity of the human person and in the equal rights of men and nations,

Reaffirming the principles embodied in the Universal Declaration of Human Rights, the Declaration on the Granting of Independence to Colonial Countries and Peoples, the United Nations Declaration on the Elimination of All Forms of Racial Discrimination, General Assembly resolution 110 (II) of 3 November 1947 condemning all forms of propaganda designed or likely to provoke or encourage any threat to the peace, the Declaration of the Rights of the Child,[12] and General Assembly resolution 1572 (XV) of 18 December 1960, which have a particular bearing upon the upbringing of young people in a spirit of peace, mutual respect and understanding among peoples,

Recalling that the purpose of the United Nations Educational, Scientific and Cultural Organization is to contribute to peace and security by promoting collaboration among nations through education, science and culture, and recognizing the role and contributions of that organization towards the education of young people in the spirit of international understanding, co-operation and peace,

Taking into consideration the fact that in the conflagrations which have afflicted mankind it is the young people who have had to suffer most and who have had the greatest number of victims,

Convinced that young people wish to have an assured future and that peace, freedom and justice are among the chief guarantees that their desire for happiness will be fulfilled,

Bearing in mind the important part being played by young people in every field of human endeavour and the fact that they are destined to guide the fortunes of mankind,

Bearing in mind furthermore that in this age of great scientific, technological and cultural achievements, the energies, enthusiasm and creative abilities of the young should be devoted to the material and spiritual advancement of all peoples,

Convinced that the young should know, respect and develop the cultural heritage of their own country and that of all mankind,

Convinced furthermore that the education of the young and exchanges of young people and of ideas in a spirit of peace, mutual respect and understanding between peoples can help to improve international relations and to strengthen peace and security,

Proclaims this Declaration on the Promotion among Youth of the Ideals of Peace,

Mutual Respect and Understanding between Peoples and calls upon Governments, non-governmental organizations and youth movements to recognize the principles set forth therein and to ensure their observance by means of appropriate measures:

Principle I

Young people shall be brought up in the spirit of peace, justice, freedom, mutual respect and understanding in order to promote equal rights for all human beings and all nations, economic and social progress, disarmament and the maintenance of international peace and security.

Principle II

All means of education, including as of major importance the guidance given by parents or family, instruction and information intended for the young should foster among them the ideals of peace, humanity, liberty and international solidarity and all other ideals which help to bring peoples closer together, and acquaint them with the role entrusted to the United Nations as a means of preserving and maintaining peace and promoting international understanding and co-operation.

Principle III

Young people shall be brought up in the knowledge of the dignity and equality of all men, without distinction as to race, colour, ethnic origins or beliefs, and in respect for fundamental human rights and for the right of peoples to self-determination.

Principle IV

Exchanges, travel, tourism meetings, the study of foreign languages, the twinning of towns and universities without discrimination and similar activities should be encouraged and facilitated among young people of all countries in order to bring them together in educational, cultural and sporting activities in the spirit of this Declaration.

Principle V

National and international associations of young people should be encouraged to promote the purposes of the United Nations, particularly international peace and security, friendly relations among nations based on respect for the equal sovereignty of States, the final abolition of colonialism and of racial discrimination and other violations of human rights.

Youth organizations in accordance with this Declaration should take all appropriate measures within their respective fields of activity in order to make their contribution without any discrimination to the work of educating the young generation in accordance with these ideals.

Such organizations, in conformity with the principle of freedom of association, should promote the free exchange of ideas in the spirit of the principles of this Declaration and of the purposes of the United Nations set forth in the Charter.

All youth organizations should conform to the principles set forth in this Declaration.

Principle VI

A major aim in educating the young shall be to develop all their faculties and to train them to acquire higher moral qualities, to be deeply attached to the noble ideals of peace, liberty, the dignity and equality of all men, and imbued with respect and love for humanity and its creative achievements. To this end the family has an important role to play.

Young people must become conscious of their responsibilities in the world they will be called upon to manage and should be inspired with confidence in a future of happiness for mankind.

DECLARATION ON THE PREPARATION OF SOCIETIES FOR LIFE IN PEACE

General Assembly Resolution 33/73, 1978

The General Assembly

Recalling that in the Charter the peoples of the United Nations proclaimed their determination to save succeeding generations from the scourge of war and that one of the fundamental purposes of the United Nations is to maintain international peace and security,

Reaffirming that, in accordance with General Assembly resolution 95 (I) of 11 December 1946, planning, preparation, initiation or waging of a war of aggression are crimes against peace and that, pursuant to the Declaration on Principles of International Law concerning Friendly Relations and Co-operation among States in accordance with the Charter of the United Nations, of 24 October 1970, and the Definition of Aggression of 14 December 1974, a war of aggression constitutes a crime against the peace,

Reaffirming the right of individuals, States and all mankind to life in peace,

Aware that, since wars begin in the minds of men, it is in the minds of men that the defences of peace must be constructed,

Recognizing that peace among nations is mankind's paramount value, held in the highest esteem by all principal political, social and religious movements,

Guided by the lofty goal of preparing societies for and creating conditions of their common existence and co-operation in peace, equality, mutual confidence and understanding,

Recognizing the essential role of Governments, as well as governmental and non-governmental organizations, both national and international, the mass media, educational processes and teaching methods, in promoting the ideals of peace and understanding among nations,

Convinced that, in the era of modern scientific and technological progress, mankind's resources, energy and creative talents should be directed to the peaceful economic, social and cultural development of all countries, should promote the implementation of the new international economic order and should serve the raising of the living standards of all nations,

Stressing with utmost concern that the arms race, in particular in the nuclear field, and the development of new types and systems of weapons, based on modern scientific principles and achievements, threaten world peace,

Recalling that, in the Final Document of the Tenth Special Session of the General Assembly, the States Members of the United Nations solemnly reaffirmed their determination to make further collective efforts aimed at strengthening peace and international security and eliminating the threat of war, and agreed that, in order to facilitate the process of disarmament, it was necessary to take measures and pursue policies to strengthen international peace and security and to build confidence among States,

Reaffirming the principles contained in the Declaration on the Granting of Independence to Colonial Countries and Peoples, of 14 December 1960, the Declaration on the Strengthening of International Security, of 16 December 1970 and the Declaration on the Deepening and Consolidation of International Détente, of 19 December 1977,

Recalling the Declaration on the Promotion among Youth of the Ideals of Peace, Mutual Respect and Understanding between Peoples, of 7 December 1965,

Further recalling the Universal Declaration of Human Rights, of 10 December 1948, as well as the International Covenant on Civil and Political Rights, of 16 December 1966, and bearing in mind that the latter states, *inter alia*, that any propaganda for war shall be prohibited by law,

I

Solemnly invites all States to guide themselves in their activities by the recognition of the supreme importance and necessity of establishing, maintaining and strengthening a just and durable peace for present and future generations and, in particular, to observe the following principles:

1. Every nation and every human being, regardless of race, conscience, language or sex, has the inherent right to life in peace. Respect for that right, as well as for the other human rights, is in the common interest of all mankind and an indispensable condition of advancement of all nations, large and small, in all fields.

2. A war of aggression, its planning, preparation or initiation are crimes against peace and are prohibited by international law.

3. In accordance with the purposes and principles of the United Nations, States have the duty to refrain from propaganda for wars of aggression.

4. Every State, acting in the spirit of friendship and good-neighbourly relations, has the duty to promote all-round, mutually advantageous and equitable political, economic, social and cultural co-operation with other States, notwithstanding their socio-economic systems, with a view to securing their common existence and co-operation in peace, in conditions of mutual understanding of and respect for the identity and diversity of all peoples, and the duty to take up actions conducive to the furtherance of the ideals of peace, humanism and freedom.

5. Every State has the duty to respect the right of all peoples to self-determination, independence, equality, sovereignty, the territorial integrity of States and the inviolability of their frontiers, including the right to determine the road of their development, without interference or intervention in their internal affairs.

6. A basic instrument of the maintenance of peace is the elimination of the threat inherent in the arms race, as well as efforts towards general and complete disarmament, under effective international control, including partial measures with that end in view, in accordance with the principles agreed upon within the United Nations and relevant international agreements.

7. Every State has the duty to discourage all manifestations and practices of colonialism, as well as racism, racial discrimination and *apartheid*, as contrary to the right of peoples to self-determination and to other human rights and fundamental freedoms.

8. Every State has the duty to discourage advocacy of hatred and prejudice against other peoples as contrary to the principles of peaceful coexistence and friendly co-operation.

II

Calls upon all States, in order to implement the above principles:

(a) To act perseveringly and consistently, with due regard for the constitutional rights and the role of the family, the institutions and the organizations concerned:

i.   To ensure that their policies relevant to the implementation of the present Declaration, including educational processes and teaching methods as well as media information activities, incorporate contents compatible with the task of the preparation for life in peace of entire societies and, in particular, the young generations;

ii.   Therefore, to discourage and eliminate incitement to racial hatred, national or other discrimination, injustice or advocacy of violence and war;

(b)   To develop various forms of bilateral and multilateral co-operation, also in international, governmental and non-governmental organizations, with a view to enhancing preparation of societies to live in peace and, in particular, exchanging experiences on projects pursued with that end in view;

III

1. *Recommends* that the governmental and nongovernmental organizations concerned should initiate appropriate action towards the implementation of the present Declaration;

2. *States* that a full implementation of the principles enshrined in the present Declaration calls for concerted action on the part of Governments, the United Nations and the specialized agencies, in particular the United Nations Educational, Scientific and Cultural Organization, as well as other interested international and national organizations, both governmental and non-governmental;

3. Requests the Secretary-General to follow the progress made in the implementation of the present Declaration and to submit periodic reports thereon to the General Assembly, the first such report to be submitted not later than at its thirty-sixth session.

(d)   *Social Progress and Economic Development*
These documents on social progress and development include general provisions applicable to communications and information or refer directly to the role of communications. The documents concerning the establishment of a new International Economic Order have been included in view of their close link to the demands for a new international information order which is dealt with in Part Two, Section 8.

Documents

xi.   (a)   Declaration on Social Progress and Development, General Assembly Resolution 2542 (XXIV), 1969
          −   Articles 1–3, 5–6, 10–15, 18, 21–22, 24–25
xii. (a)   Declaration on the Establishment of a New International Economic Order, General Assembly Resolution 3201 (S-VI), 1974
          −   Full text
      (b)   Charter of the Economic Rights and Duties of States, General Assembly Resolution 3281 (XXIX), 1974
          −   Preamble
          −   Chapters I, II: Articles 1–17

DECLARATION ON SOCIAL PROGRESS AND DEVELOPMENT

General Assembly Resolution 2542, (XXIV), 1969

Part I Principles

Article 1

All peoples and all human beings, without distinction as to race, colour, sex, language, religion, nationality, ethnic origin, family or social status, or political or other conviction, shall have the right to live in dignity and freedom and to enjoy the fruits of social progress and should, on their part, contribute to it.

Article 2

Social progress and development shall be founded on respect for the dignity and value of the human person and shall ensure the promotion of human rights and social justice, which requires:

(a) The immediate and final elimination of all forms of inequality, exploitation of peoples and individuals, colonialism and racism, including nazism and *apartheid*, and all other policies and ideologies opposed to the purposes and principles of the United Nations;

(b) The recognition and effective implementation of civil and political rights as well as of economic, social and cultural rights without any discrimination.

Article 3

The following are considered primary conditions of social progress and development:

(a) National independence based on the right of peoples to self-determination;

(b) The principle of non-interference in the internal affairs of States;

(c) Respect for the sovereignty and territorial integrity of States;

(d) Permanent sovereignty of each nation over its natural wealth and resources;

(e) The right and responsibility of each State and, as far as they are concerned, each nation and people to determine freely its own objectives of social development, to set its own priorities and to decide in conformity with the principles of the Charter of the United Nations the means and methods of their achievement without any external interference;

(f) Peaceful coexistence, peace, friendly relations and co-operation among States irrespective of differences in their social, economic or political systems.

* * *

Article 5

Social progress and development require the full utilization of human resources, including, in particular:

(a) The encouragement of creative initiative under conditions of enlightened public opinion;

(b) The dissemination of national and international information for the purpose of making individuals aware of changes occurring in society as a whole;

(c) The active participation of all elements of society, individually or through associations, in defining and in achieving the common goals of development with full respect for the fundamental freedoms embodied in the Universal Declaration of Human Rights;

(d) The assurance to disadvantaged or marginal sectors of the population of equal opportunities for social and economic advancement in order to achieve an effectively integrated society.

Article 6

Social development requires the assurance to everyone of the right to work and the free choice of employment.

Social progress and development require the participation of all members of society in productive and socially useful labour and the establishment, in conformity with human rights and fundamental freedoms and with the principles of justice and the social function of property, of forms of ownership of land and of the means of production which preclude any kind of exploitation of man, ensure equal rights to property for all and create conditions leading to genuine equality among people.

* * *

Part II Objectives

Social progress and development shall aim at the continuous raising of the material and spiritual standards of living of all members of society, with respect for and in compliance with human rights and fundamental freedoms, through the attainment of the following main goals:

Article 10

(a) The assurance at all levels of the right to work and the right of everyone to form trade unions and workers' associations and to bargain collectively; promotion of full productive employment and elimination of unemployment and under-employment; establishment of equitable and favourable conditions of work for all, including the improvement of health and safety conditions; assurance of just remuneration for labour without any discrimination as well as a sufficiently high minimum wage to ensure a decent standard of living; the protection of the consumer;

(b) The elimination of hunger and malnutrition and the guarantee of the right to proper nutrition;

(c) The elimination of poverty; the assurance of a steady improvement in levels of living and of a just and equitable distribution of income;

(d) The achievement of the highest standards of health and the provision of health protection for the entire population, if possible free of charge;

(e) The eradication of illiteracy and the assurance of the right to universal access to culture, to free compulsory education at the elementary level and to free education at all levels; the raising of the general level of life-long education;

(f) The provision for all, particularly persons in low income groups and large families, of adequate housing and community services.

Social progress and development shall aim equally at the progressive attainment of the following main goals:

Article 11

(a) The provision of comprehensive social security schemes and social welfare services; the establishment and improvement of social security and insurance schemes for all persons who, because of illness, disability or old age, are temporarily or permanently unable to earn a living, with a view to ensuring a proper standard of living for such persons and for their families and dependants;

(b) The protection of the rights of the mother and child; concern for the upbringing and health of children; the provision of measures to safeguard the health and welfare of women and particularly of working mothers during pregnancy and the infancy of their children, as well as of mothers whose earnings are the sole source of livelihood for the family; the granting to women of pregnancy and maternity leave and allowances without loss of employment or wages;

(c) The protection of the rights and the assuring of the welfare of children, the aged and the disabled; the provision of protection for the physically or mentally disadvantaged;

(d) The education of youth in, and promotion among them of, the ideals of justice and peace, mutual respect and understanding among peoples; the promotion of full participation of youth in the process of national development;

(e) The provision of social defence measures and the elimination of conditions leading to crime and delinquency, especially juvenile delinquency;

(f) The guarantee that all individuals, without discrimination of any kind, are made aware of their rights and obligations and receive the necessary aid in the exercise and safeguarding of their rights.

Social progress and development shall further aim at achieving the following main objectives:

Article 12

(a) The creation of conditions for rapid and sustained social and economic development, particularly in the developing countries; change in international economic relations; new and effective methods of international co-operation in which equality of opportunity should be as much a prerogative of nations as of individuals within a nation;

(b) The elimination of all forms of discrimination and exploitation and all other practices and ideologies contrary to the purposes and principles of the Charter of the United Nations;

(c) The elimination of all forms of foreign economic exploitation, particularly that practised by international monopolies, in order to enable the people of every country to enjoy in full the benefits of their national resources.

Social progress and development shall finally aim at the attainment of the following main goals:

Article 13

(a) Equitable sharing of scientific and technological advances by developed and developing countries, and a steady increase in the use of science and technology for the benefit of the social development of society;

(b) The establishment of a harmonious balance between scientific, technological and material progress and the intellectual, spiritual, cultural and moral advancement of humanity;

(c) The protection and improvement of the human environment.

Part III Means and Methods

On the basis of the principles set forth in this Declaration, the achievement of the objectives of social progress and development requires the mobilization of the necessary resources by national and international action, with particular attention to such means and methods as:

Article 14

(a) Planning for social progress and development, as an integrated part of balanced over-all development planning;

(b) The establishment, where necessary, of national systems for framing and carrying out social policies and programmes, and the promotion by the countries concerned of planned regional development, taking into account differing regional conditions and needs, particularly the development of regions which are less favoured or under-developed by comparison with the rest of the country;

(c) The promotion of basic and applied social research, particularly comparative international research applied to the planning and execution of social development programmes.

Article 15

(a) The adoption of measures to ensure the effective participation, as appropriate, of all the elements of society in the preparation and execution of national plans and programmes of economic and social development;

(b) The adoption of measures for an increasing rate of popular participation in the economic, social, cultural and political life of countries through national governmental bodies, non-governmental organizations, co-operatives, rural associations, workers' and employers' organizations and women's and youth organizations, by such methods as national and regional plans for social and economic progress and community development, with a view to achieving a fully integrated national society, accelerating the process of social mobility and consolidating the democratic system;

(c) Mobilization of public opinion, at both national and international levels, in support of the principles and objectives of social progress and development;

(d) The dissemination of social information, at the national and the international level, to make people aware of changing circumstances in society as a whole, and to educate the consumer.

*   *   *

Article 18

(a) The adoption of appropriate legislative, administrative and other measures ensuring to everyone not only political and civil rights, but also the full realization of economic, social and cultural rights without any discrimination;

(b) The promotion of democratically based social and institutional reforms and motivation for change basic to the elimination of all forms of discrimination and exploitation and conducive to high rates of economic and social progress, to include land reform, in which the ownership and use of land will be made to serve best the objectives of social justice and economic development;

(c) The adoption of measures to boost and diversify agricultural production through, *inter alia*, the implementation of democratic agrarian reforms, to ensure an adequate and well-balanced supply of food, its equitable distribution among the whole population and the improvement of nutritional standards;

(d) The adoption of measures to introduce, with the participation of the Government, low-cost housing programmes in both rural and urban areas;

(e) Development and expansion of the system of transportation and communications, particularly in developing countries.

*   *   *

Article 21

(a) The training of national personnel and cadres, including administrative, executive, professional and technical personnel needed for social development and for over-all development plans and policies;

(b) The adoption of measures to accelerate the extension and improvement of general, vocational and technical education and of training and retraining, which should be provided free at all levels;

(c) Raising the general level of education; development and expansion of national information media, and their rational and full use towards continuing education of the whole population and towards encouraging its participation in social development activities; the constructive use of leisure, particularly that of children and adolescents;

(d) The formulation of national and international policies and measures to avoid the "brain drain" and obviate its adverse effects.

Article 22

(a) The development and co-ordination of policies and measures designed to strengthen the essential functions of the family as a basic unit of society;

(b) The formulation and establishment, as needed, of programmes in the field of population, within the framework of national demographic policies and as part of the welfare medical services, including education, training of personnel and the provision to families of the knowledge and means necessary to enable them to exercise their right to determine freely and responsibly the number and spacing of their children;

(c) The establishment of appropriate child-care facilities in the interest of children and working parents.

The achievement of the objectives of social progress and development finally requires the implementation of the following means and methods:

* * *

Article 24

(a) Intensification of international co-operation with a view to ensuring the international exchange of information, knowledge and experience concerning social progress and development;

(b) The broadest possible international technical, scientific and cultural co-operation and reciprocal utilization of the experience of countries with different economic and social systems and different levels of development, on the basis of mutual advantage and strict observance of and respect for national sovereignty;

(c) Increased utilization of science and technology for social and economic development; arrangements for the transfer and exchange of technology, including know-how and patents, to the developing countries.

Article 25

(a) The establishment of legal and administrative measures for the protection and improvement of the human environment at both national and international levels;

(b) The use and exploitation, in accordance with the appropriate international régimes, of the resources of areas of the environment such as outer space and the sea-bed and ocean floor and the subsoil thereof, beyond the limits of national jurisdiction, in order to supplement national resources available for the achievement of economic and social progress and development in every country, irrespective of its geographical location, special consideration being given to the interests and needs of the developing countries.

* * *

DECLARATION ON THE ESTABLISHMENT OF A NEW INTERNATIONAL ECONOMIC ORDER

General Assembly Resolution 3201 (S-VI) 1974

The General Assembly
Adopts the following Declaration:

Declaration on the Establishment of a New International Economic Order

We, the Members of the United Nations,
Having convened a special session of the General Assembly to study for the first time the problems of raw materials and development, devoted to the consideration of the

most important economic problems facing the world community,

Bearing in mind the spirit, purposes and principles of the Charter of the United Nations to promote the economic advancement and social progress of all peoples,

Solemnly proclaim our united determination to work urgently for THE ESTABLISHMENT OF A NEW INTERNATIONAL ECONOMIC ORDER based on equity, sovereign equality, interdependence, common interest and cooperation among all States, irrespective of their economic and social systems which shall correct inequalities and redress existing injustices, make it possible to eliminate the widening gap between the developed and the developing countries and ensure steadily accelerating economic and social development and peace and justice for present and future generations, and, to that end, declare:

1. The greatest and most significant achievement during the last decades has been the independence from colonial and alien domination of a large number of peoples and nations which has enabled them to become members of the community of free peoples. Technological progress has also been made in all spheres of economic activities in the last three decades, thus providing a solid potential for improving the well-being of all peoples. However, the remaining vestiges of alien and colonial domination, foreign occupation, racial discrimination, *apartheid* and neo-colonialism in all its forms continue to be among the greatest obstacles to the full emancipation and progress of the developing countries and all the peoples involved. The benefits of technological progress are not shared equitably by all members of the international community. The developing countries, which constitute 70 per cent of the world's population, account for only 30 per cent of the world's income. It has proved impossible to achieve an even and balanced development of the international community under the existing international economic order. The gap between the developed and the developing countries continues to widen in a system which was established at a time when most of the developing countries did not even exist as independent States and which perpetuates inequality.

2. The present international economic order is in direct conflict with current developments in international political and economic relations. Since 1970, the world economy has experienced a series of grave crises which have had severe repercussions, especially on the developing countries because of their generally greater vulnerability to external economic impulses. The developing world has become a powerful factor that makes its influence felt in all fields of international activity. These irreversible changes in the relationship of forces in the world necessitate the active, full and equal participation of the developing countries in the formulation and application of all decisions that concern the international community.

3. All these changes have thrust into prominence the reality of interdependence of all the members of the world community. Current events have brought into sharp focus the realization that the interests of the developed countries and those of the developing countries can no longer be isolated from each other, that there is a close interrelationship between the prosperity of the developed countries and the growth and development of the developing countries, and that the prosperity of the international community as a whole depends upon the prosperity of its constituent parts. International co-operation for development is the shared goal and common duty of all countries. Thus the political, economic and social well-being of present and future generations depends more than ever on co-operation between all the members of the international community on the basis of sovereign equality and the removal of the disequilibrium that exists between them.

4. The new international economic order should be founded on full respect for the following principles:

(a)   Sovereign equality of States, self-determination of all peoples, inadmissibility of the acquisition of territories by force, territorial integrity and noninterference in the internal affairs of other States;

(b)   The broadest co-operation of all the States members of the international community, based on equity, whereby the prevailing disparities in the world may be banished and prosperity secured for all;

(c) Full and effective participation on the basis of equality of all countries in the solving of world economic problems in the common interest of all countries, bearing in mind the necessity to ensure the accelerated development of all the developing countries, while devoting particular attention to the adoption of special measures in favour of the least developed, land-locked and island developing countries as well as those developing countries most seriously affected by economic crises and natural calamities, without losing sight of the interests of other developing countries;

(d) The right of every country to adopt the economic and social system that it deems the most appropriate for its own development and not to be subjected to discrimination of any kind as a result;

(e) Full permanent sovereignty of every State over its natural resources and all economic activities. In order to safeguard these resources, each State is entitled to exercise effective control over them and their exploitation with means suitable to its own situation, including the right to nationalization or transfer of ownership to its nationals, this right being an expression of the full permanent sovereignty of the State. No State may be subjected to economic, political or any other type of coercion to prevent the free and full exercise of this inalienable right;

(f) The right of all States, territories and peoples under foreign occupation, alien and colonial domination or *apartheid* to restitution and full compensation for the exploitation and depletion of, and damages to, the natural resources and all other resources of those States, territories and peoples;

(g) Regulation and supervision of the activities of transnational corporations by taking measures in the interest of the national economies of the countries where such transnational corporations operate on the basis of the full sovereignty of those countries;

(h) The right of the developing countries and the peoples of territories under colonial and racial domination and foreign occupation to achieve their liberation and to regain effective control over their natural resources and economic activities;

(i) The extending of assistance to developing countries, peoples and territories which are under colonial and alien domination, foreign occupation, racial discrimination or *apartheid* or are subjected to economic, political or any other type of coercive measures to obtain from them the subordination of the exercise of their sovereign rights and to secure from them advantages of any kind, and to neocolonialism in all its forms, and which have established or are endeavouring to establish effective control over their natural resources and economic activities that have been or are still under foreign control;

(j) Just and equitable relationship between the prices of raw materials, primary commodities, manufactured and semi-manufactured goods exported by developing countries and the prices of raw materials, primary commodities, manufactures, capital goods and equipment imported by them with the aim of bringing about sustained improvement in their unsatisfactory terms of trade and the expansion of the world economy;

(k) Extension of active assistance to developing countries by the whole international community, free of any political or military conditions;

(l) Ensuring that one of the main aims of the reformed international monetary system shall be the promotion of the development of the developing countries and the adequate flow of real resources to them;

(m) Improving the competitiveness of natural materials facing competition from synthetic substitutes;

(n) Preferential and non-reciprocal treatment for developing countries, wherever feasible, in all fields of international economic co-operation whenever possible;

(o) Securing favourable conditions for the transfer of financial resources to developing countries;
(p) Giving to the developing countries access to the achievements of modern science and technology, and promoting the transfer of technology and the creation of indigenous technology for the benefit of the developing countries in forms and in accordance with procedures which are suited to their economies;
(q) The need for all States to put an end to the waste of natural resources, including food products;
(r) The need for developing countries to concentrate all their resources for the cause of development;
(s) The strengthening, through individual and collective actions, of mutual economic, trade, financial and technical co-operation among the developing countries, mainly on a preferential basis;
(t) Facilitating the role which producers' associations may play within the framework of international co-operation and, in pursuance of their aims, *inter alia* assisting in the promotion of sustained growth of the world economy and accelerating the development of developing countries.

5. The unanimous adoption of the International Development Strategy for the Second United Nations Development Decade was an important step in the promotion of international economic co-operation on a just and equitable basis. The accelerated implementation of obligations and commitments assumed by the international community within the framework of the Strategy, particularly those concerning imperative development needs of developing countries, would contribute significantly to the fulfilment of the aims and objectives of the present Declaration.

6. The United Nations as a universal organization should be capable of dealing with problems of international economic co-operation in a comprehensive manner and ensuring equally the interests of all countries. It must have an even greater role in the establishment of a new international economic order. The Charter of Economic Rights and Duties of States, for the preparation of which the present Declaration will provide an additional source of inspiration, will constitute a significant contribution in this respect. All the States Members of the United Nations are therefore called upon to exert maximum efforts with a view to securing the implementation of the present Declaration, which is one of the principal guarantees for the creation of better conditions for all peoples to reach a life worthy of human dignity.

7. The present Declaration on the Establishment of a New International Economic Order shall be one of the most important bases of economic relations between all peoples and all nations.

CHARTER OF ECONOMIC RIGHTS AND DUTIES OF STATES

General Assembly Resolution 3281 (XXIX), 1974

Preamble

The General Assembly,
Reaffirming the fundamental purposes of the United Nations, in particular the maintenance of international peace and security, the development of friendly relations among nations and the achievement of international co-operation in solving international problems in the economic and social fields,
Affirming the need for strengthening international co-operation in these fields,
Reaffirming further the need for strengthening international co-operation for development,

Declaring that it is a fundamental purpose of the present Charter to promote the establishment of the new international economic order, based on equity, sovereign equality, interdependence, common interest and co-operation among all States, irrespective of their economic and social systems,

Desirous of contributing to the creation of conditions for:

(a) The attainment of wider prosperity among all countries and of higher standards of living for all peoples,

(b) The promotion by the entire international community of the economic and social progress of all countries, especially developing countries,

(c) The encouragement of co-operation, on the basis of mutual advantage and equitable benefits for all peace-loving States which are willing to carry out the provisions of the present Charter, in the economic, trade, scientific and technical fields, regardless of political, economic or social systems,

(d) The overcoming of main obstacles in the way of the economic development of the developing countries,

(e) The acceleration of the economic growth of developing countries with a view to bridging the economic gap between developing and developed countries,

(f) The protection, preservation and enhancement of the environment,

Mindful of the need to establish and maintain a just and equitable economic and social order through:

(a) The achievement of more rational and equitable international economic relations and the encouragement of structural changes in the world economy,

(b) The creation of conditions which permit the further expansion of trade and intensification of economic co-operation among all nations,

(c) The strengthening of the economic independence of developing countries,

(d) The establishment and promotion of international economic relations, taking into account the agreed differences in development of the developing countries and their specific needs,

Determined to promote collective economic security for development, in particular of the developing countries, with strict respect for the sovereign equality of each State and through the co-operation of the entire international community,

Considering that genuine co-operation among States, based on joint consideration of and concerted action regarding international economic problems, is essential for fulfilling the international community's common desire to achieve a just and rational development of all parts of the world,

Stressing the importance of ensuring appropriate conditions for the conduct of normal economic relations among all States, irrespective of differences in social and economic systems, and for the full respect of the rights of all peoples, as well as strengthening instruments of international economic co-operation as a means for the consolidation of peace for the benefit of all,

Convinced of the need to develop a system of international economic relations on the basis of sovereign equality, mutual and equitable benefit and the close interrelationship of the interests of all States,

Reiterating that the responsibility for the development of every country rests primarily upon itself but that concomitant and effective international co-operation is an essential factor for the full achievement of its own development goals,

Firmly convinced of the urgent need to evolve a substantially improved system of international economic relations,

Solemnly adopts the present Charter of Economic Rights and Duties of States.

Chapter I. Fundamentals of International Economic Relations

Economic as well as political and other relations among States shall be governed, *inter alia,* by the following principles:

(a) Sovereignty, territorial integrity and political independence of States;

(b)   Sovereign equality of all States;
(c)   Non-aggression;
(d)   Non-intervention;
(e)   Mutual and equitable benefit;
(f)   Peaceful coexistence;
(g)   Equal rights and self-determination of peoples;
(h)   Peaceful settlement of disputes;
(i)   Remedying of injustices which have been brought about by force and which deprive a nation of the natural means necessary for its normal development;
(j)   Fulfilment in good faith of international obligations;
(k)   Respect for human rights and fundamental freedoms;
(l)   No attempt to seek hegemony and spheres of influence;
(m)   Promotion of international social justice;
(n)   International co-operation for development;
(o)   Free access to and from the sea by land-locked countries within the framework of the above principles.

Chapter II. Economic Rights and Duties of States

Article I

Every State has the sovereign and inalienable right to choose its economic system as well as its political, social and cultural systems in accordance with the will of its people, without outside interference, coercion or threat in any form whatsoever.

Article 2

1. Every State has and shall freely exercise full permanent sovereignty, including possession, use and disposal, over all its wealth, natural resources and economic activities.

2. Each State has the right:

(a)   To regulate and exercise authority over foreign investment within its national jurisdiction in accordance with its laws and regulations and in conformity with its national objectives and priorities. No State shall be compelled to grant preferential treatment to foreign investment;
(b)   To regulate and supervise the activities of transnational corporations within its national jurisdiction and take measures to ensure that such activities comply with its laws, rules and regulations and conform with its economic and social policies. Transnational corporations shall not intervene in the internal affairs of a host State. Every State should, with full regard for its sovereign rights, co-operate with other States in the exercise of the right set forth in this sub-paragraph;
(c)   To nationalize, expropriate or transfer ownership of foreign property, in which case appropriate compensation should be paid by the State adopting such measures, taking into account its relevant laws and regulations and all circumstances that the State considers pertinent. In any case where the question of compensation gives rise to a controversy, it shall be settled under the domestic law of the nationalizing State and by its tribunals, unless it is freely and mutually agreed by all States concerned that other peaceful means be sought on the basis of the sovereign equality of States and in accordance with the principle of free choice of means.

Article 3

In the exploitation of natural resources shared by two or more countries, each State must co-operate on the basis of a system of information and prior consultations in order to achieve optimum use of such resources without causing damage to the legitimate interest of others.

Article 4

Every State has the right to engage in international trade and other forms of economic co-operation irrespective of any differences in political, economic and social systems. No State shall be subjected to discrimination of any kind based solely on such differences. In the pursuit of international trade and other forms of economic co-operation, every State is free to choose the forms of organization of its foreign economic relations and to enter into bilateral and multilateral arrangements consistent with its international obligations and with the needs of international economic co-operation.

Article 5

All States have the right to associate in organizations of primary commodity producers in order to develop their national economies, to achieve stable financing for their development and, in pursuance of their aims, to assist in the promotion of sustained growth of the world economy, in particular accelerating the development of developing countries. Correspondingly, all States have the duty to respect that right by refraining from applying economic and political measures that would limit it.

Article 6

It is the duty of States to contribute to the development of international trade of goods, particularly by means of arrangements and by the conclusion of long-term multilateral commodity agreements, where appropriate, and taking into account the interests of producers and consumers. All States share the responsibility to promote the regular flow and access of all commercial goods traded at stable, remunerative and equitable prices, thus contributing to the equitable development of the world economy, taking into account, in particular, the interests of developing countries.

Article 7

Every State has the primary responsibility to promote the economic, social and cultural development of its people. To this end, each State has the right and the responsibility to choose its means and goals of development, fully to mobilize and use its resources, to implement progressive economic and social reforms and to ensure the full participation of its people in the process and benefits of development. All States have the duty, individually and collectively, to co-operate in eliminating obstacles that hinder such mobilization and use.

Article 8

States should co-operate in facilitating more rational and equitable international economic relations and in encouraging structural changes in the context of a balanced world economy in harmony with the needs and interests of all countries, especially developing countries, and should take appropriate measures to this end.

Article 9

All States have the responsibility to co-operate in the economic, social, cultural, scientific and technological fields for the promotion of economic and social progress throughout the world, especially that of the developing countries.

Article 10

All States are juridically equal and, as equal members of the international community, have the right to participate fully and effectively in the international decision-making process in the solution of world economic, financial and monetary problems, *inter alia*, through the appropriate international organizations in accordance with their existing and evolving rules, and to share equitably in the benefits resulting therefrom.

Article 11

All States should co-operate to strengthen and continuously improve the efficiency of international organizations in implementing measures to stimulate the general economic progress of all countries, and therefore should co-operate to adapt them, when appropriate, to the changing needs of international economic co-operation.

Article 12

1. States have the right, in agreement with the parties concerned, to participate in subregional, regional and interregional co-operation in the pursuit of their economic and social development. All States engaged in such co-operation have the duty to ensure that the policies of those groupings to which they belong correspond to the provisions of the present Charter and are outward-looking, consistent with their international obligations and with the needs of international obligations and with the needs of international economic co-operation, and have full regard for the legitimate interests of third countries, especially developing countries.

2. In the case of groupings to which the States concerned have transferred or may transfer certain competences as regards matters that come within the scope of the present Charter, its provisions shall also apply to those groupings in regard to such matters, consistent with the responsibilities of such States as members of such groupings. Those States shall co-operate in the observance by the groupings of the provisions of this Charter.

Article 13

1. Every State has the right to benefit from the advances and developments in science and technology for the acceleration of its economic and social development.

2. All States should promote international scientific and technological co-operation and the transfer of technology, with proper regard for all legitimate interests including, *inter alia*, the rights and duties of holders, suppliers and recipients of technology. In particular, all States should facilitate the access of developing countries to the achievements of modern science and technology, the transfer of technology and the creation of indigenous technology for the benefit of the developing countries in forms and in accordance with procedures which are suited to their economies and their needs.

3. Accordingly, developed countries should co-operate with the developing countries in the establishment, strengthening and development of their scientific and technological infrastructures and their scientific research and technological activities so as to help to expand and transform the economies of developing countries.

4. All States should co-operate in research with a view to evolving further internationally accepted guidelines or regulations for the transfer of technology, taking fully into account the interests of developing countries.

Article 14

Every State has the duty to co-operate in promoting a steady and increasing expansion and liberalization of world trade and an improvement in the welfare and living standards of all peoples, in particular those of developing countries. Accordingly, all States should co-operate, *inter alia*, towards the progressive dismantling of obstacles to trade and the improvement of the international framework for the conduct of world trade and, to these ends, co-ordinated efforts shall be made to solve in an equitable way the trade problems of all countries, taking into account the specific trade problems of the developing countries. In this connexion, States shall take measures aimed at securing additional benefits for the international trade of developing countries so as to achieve a substantial increase in their foreign exchange earnings, the diversification of their exports, the acceleration of the rate of growth of their trade, taking into account their development needs, an improvement in the possibilities for these countries to participate in the expansion of world trade and a balance more favourable to developing countries in the sharing of the advantages resulting from this expansion, through, in the largest possible measure, a substantial improvement in the conditions of access for the products of interest to the developing countries and, wherever appropriate, measures designed to attain stable equitable and remunerative prices for primary products.

Article 15

All States have the duty to promote the achievement of general and complete disarmament under effective international control and to utilize the resources released by effective disarmament measures for the economic and social development of countries, allocating a substantial portion of such resources as additional means for the development needs of developing countries.

Article 16

1. It is the right and duty of all States, individually and collectively, to eliminate colonialism, *apartheid*, racial discrimination, neo-colonialism and all forms of foreign aggression, occupation and domination, and the economic and social consequences thereof, as a prerequisite for development. States which practise such coercive policies are economically responsible to the countries, territories and peoples affected for the restitution and full compensation for the exploitation and depletion of, and damages to, the natural and all other resources of those countries, territories and peoples. It is the duty of all States to extend assistance to them.

2. No State has the right to promote or encourage investments that may constitute an obstacle to the liberation of a territory occupied by force.

Article 17

International co-operation for development is the shared goal and common duty of all States. Every State should co-operate with the efforts of developing countries to accelerate their economic and social development by providing favourable external conditions and by extending active assistance to them, consistent with their development needs and objectives, with strict respect for the sovereign equality of States and free of any conditions derogating from their sovereignty.

*   *   *

II. TEXTS ADOPTED BY SPECIALIZED AGENCIES WITHIN THE UNITED NATIONS SYSTEM

At the founding of the modern international system, the decision was for a decentralized arrangement. The United Nations system therefore represents a network of organs, specialized agencies, programmes, funds and various other elements. Each specialized agency is legally based on a special international treaty which sets out its mandate, functions and organization. Co-ordination within the UN system is governed by the Charter of the United Nations, the constitutions of the Specialized Agencies, and the agreements which have been concluded between the UN and Specialized Agencies. The pertinent articles of the Charter, which outline the juridical framework of the relations between the UN and the Specialized Agencies are Articles 17, 57, 58, 60 and 63 (see Section I). The agreements between the UN and the Specialized Agencies recognize the status and competence of each Agency as well as the co-ordinating function of the UN by way of consultation and recommendation.

In this section are included the Unesco Constitution and texts adopted by the Unesco General Conference which deal with the promotion of human rights, peace and disarmament and the new international economic order; since these subject matters have become the subject of resolutions at each General Conference, a selection of recent resolutions has been made. Apart from the relevant parts of the declaration on the aims of the International Labour Organization, the instruments adopted within the framework of other Specialized Agencies concern specific branches of law applicable to communications and information and have therefore been included in the corresponding sections.

1. Unesco: Constitution and relevant resolutions

Documents

Treaties
    i. The Constitution of the United Nations Educational, Scientific and Cultural Organization, 1945
        – Preamble
        – Articles I – XIII

Declaration and resolutions
    (a) Promotion of peace and human rights
    ii. Unesco's contribution to peace and its tasks with respect to the promotion of human rights and the elimination of colonialism and racialism, General Conference Resolution 11.1, 1974
        – Parts I, III
    iii. Declaration on Race and Racial Prejudice, General Conference Resolutions 3/1.1/2, 1978
        – Full Text (see in particular Articles 5–7)

CONSTITUTION OF THE UNITED NATIONS EDUCATIONAL, SCIENTIFIC AND CULTURAL ORGANIZATION, 1945 (WITH AMENDMENTS)

The governments of the States Parties to this Constitution on behalf of their peoples, declare:

That since wars begin in the minds of men, it is in the minds of men that the defences of peace must be constructed:

That ignorance of each other's ways and lives has been a common cause, throughout the history of mankind, of that suspicion and mistrust between the peoples of the world through which their differences have all too often broken into war;

That the great and terrible war which has now ended was a war made possible by the denial of the democratic principles of the dignity, equality and mutual respect of men and by the propagation, in their place, through ignorance and prejudice, of the doctrine of the inequality of men and races;

That the wide diffusion of culture, and the education of humanity for justice and liberty and peace are indispensable to the dignity of man and constitute a sacred duty which all the nations must fulfil in a spirit of mutual assistance and concern;

That a peace based exclusively upon the political and economic arrangements of governments would not be a peace which could secure the unanimous, lasting and sincere support of the peoples of the world, and that the peace must therefore be founded, if it is not to fail, upon the intellectual and moral solidarity of mankind.

For these reasons, the States Parties to this Constitution, believing in full and equal opportunities for education for all, in the unrestricted pursuit of objective truth, and in the free exchange of ideas and knowledge, are agreed and determined to develop and to increase the means of communication between their peoples and to employ these means for the purposes of mutual understanding and a truer and more perfect knowledge of each other's lives;

In consequence whereof they do hereby create the United Nations Educational, Scientific and Cultural Organization for the purpose of advancing, through the educational and scientific and cultural relations of the peoples of the world, the objectives of international peace and of the common welfare of mankind for which the United Nations Organization was established and which its Charter proclaims.

Article I. Purposes and functions

1. The purpose of the Organization is to contribute to peace and security by promoting collaboration among the nations through education, science and culture in order to further universal respect for justice, for the rule of law and for the human rights and fundamental freedoms which are affirmed for the peoples of the world, without distinction of race, sex, language or religion by the Charter of the United Nations.

2. To realize this purpose the Organization will:

(a) Collaborate in the work of advancing the mutual knowledge and understanding of peoples, through all means of mass communication and to that end recommend such international agreements as may be necessary to promote the free flow of ideas by word and image;

(b) Give fresh impulse to popular education and to the spread of culture;

by collaborating with Members, at their request, in the development of educational activities;

by instituting collaboration among the nations to advance the ideal of equality of educational opportunity without regard to race, sex or any distinctions, economic or social;

by suggesting educational methods best suited to prepare the children of the world for the responsibilities of freedom;

(c) Maintain, increase and diffuse knowledge;

by assuring the conservation and protection of the world's inheritance of books, works of art and monuments of history and science, and recommending to the nations concerned the necessary international conventions;

by encouraging co-operation among the nations in all branches of intellectual activity, including the international exchange of persons active in the fields of education, science and culture and exchange of publications, objects of artistic and scientific interest and other materials of information;

by initiating methods of international co-operation calculated to give the people of all countries access to the printed and published materials produced by any of them.

3. With a view to preserving the independence, integrity and fruitful diversity of the cultures and educational systems of the States members of this Organization, the Organization is prohibited from intervening in matters which are essentially within their domestic jurisdiction.

Article II. Membership

1. Membership of the United Nations Organization shall carry with it the right to membership of the United Nations Educational, Scientific and Cultural Organization.

2. Subject to the conditions of the Agreement between this Organization and the United Nations Organization, approved pursuant to Article X of this Constitution, States not members of the United Nations Organization may be admitted to membership of the Organization, upon recommendation of the Executive Board, by a two-thirds majority vote of the General Conference.

3. Territories or groups of territories which are not responsible for the conduct of their international relations may be admitted as Associate Members by the General Conference by a two-thirds majority of Members present and voting, upon application made on behalf of such territory or group of territories by the Member or other authority having responsibility for their international relations. The nature and extent of the rights and obligations of Associate Members shall be determined by the General Conference.

4. Members of the Organization which are suspended from the exercise of the rights and privileges of membership of the United Nations Organization shall, upon the re-

quest of the latter, be suspended from the rights and privileges of this Organization.

5. Members of the Organization which are expelled from the United Nations Organization shall automatically cease to be members of this Organization.

6. Any Member State or Associate Member of the Organization may withdraw from the Organization by notice addressed to the Director-General. Such notice shall take effect on 31 December of the year following that during which the notice was given. No such withdrawal shall affect the financial obligations owed to the Organization on the date withdrawal takes effect. Notice of withdrawal by an Associate Member shall be given on its behalf by the Member State or other authority having responsibility for its international relations.

Article III. Organs

The Organization shall include a General Conference, an Executive Board and a Secretariat.

Article IV. The General Conference

A. *Composition*
1. The General Conference shall consist of the representatives of the States members of the Organization. The government of each Member State shall appoint not more than five delegates, who shall be selected after consultation with the National Commission, if established, or with educational, scientific and cultural bodies.

B. *Functions*
2. The General Conference shall determine the policies and the main lines of work of the Organization. It shall take decisions on programmes submitted to it by the Executive Board.

3. The General Conference shall, when it deems desirable and in accordance with the regulations to be made by it, summon international conferences of States on education, the sciences and humanities or the dissemination of knowledge; non-governmental conferences on the same subjects may be summoned by the General Conference or by the Executive Board in accordance with such regulations.

4. The General Conference shall, in adopting proposals for submission to the Member States, distinguish between recommendations and international conventions submitted for their approval. In the former case a majority shall be required. Each of the Member States shall submit recommendations or conventions to its competent authorities within a period of one year from the close of the session of the General Conference at which they were adopted.

5. Subject to the provisions of Article V, paragraph 5.c, the General Conference shall advise the United Nations Organization on the educational, scientific and cultural aspects of matters of concern to the latter; in accordance with the terms and procedure agreed upon between the appropriate authorities of the two Organizations.

6. The General Conference shall receive and consider the reports submitted periodically by Member States as provided by Article VIII.

7. The General Conference shall elect the members of the Executive Board and, on the recommendation of the Board, shall appoint the Director-General.

C. *Voting*
8. *(a)* Each Member State shall have one vote in the General Conference. Decisions shall be made by a simple majority except in cases in which a two-thirds majority is required by the provisions of this Constitution, or of the Rules of Procedure of the General Conference. A majority shall be a majority of the Members present and voting.

(b) A Member State shall have no vote in the General Conference if the total amount of contributions due from it exceeds the total amount of contributions payable by it for the current year and the immediately preceding calendar year. The General Conference may nevertheless permit such a Member State to vote, if it is satisfied that the failure to pay is due to

(c) Conditions beyond the control of the Member Nation.

D. *Procedure*

9. *(a)* The General Conference shall meet in ordinary session every two years. It may meet in extraordinary session if it decides to do so itself or if summoned by the Executive Board, or on the demand of at least one-third of the Member States.

(b) At each session the location of its next ordinary session shall be designated by the General Conference. The location of an extraordinary session shall be decided by the General Conference if the session is summoned by it, or otherwise by the Executive Board.

10. The General Conference shall adopt its own rules of procedure. It shall at each session elect a President and other officers.

11. The General Conference shall set up special and technical committees and such other subordinate bodies as may be necessary for its purposes.

12. The General Conference shall cause arrangements to be made for public access to meetings, subject to such regulations as it shall prescribe.

E. *Observers*

13. The General Conference, on the recommendation of the Executive Board and by a two-thirds majority may, subject to its rules of procedure, invite as observers at specified sessions of the Conference or of its Commissions representatives of international organizations, such as those referred to in Article XI, paragraph 4.

14. When consultative arrangements have been approved by the Executive Board for such international non-governmental or semi-governmental organizations in the manner provided in Article XI, paragraph 4, those organizations shall be invited to send observers to sessions of the General Conference and its Commissions.

Article V. Executive Board

A. *Composition*

1. The Executive Board shall be elected by the General Conference from among the delegates appointed by the Member States and shall consist of thirty-four members, each of whom shall represent the Government of the State of which he is a national. The President of the General Conference shall sit *ex officio* in an advisory capacity on the Executive Board.

2. In electing the members of the Executive Board the General Conference shall endeavour to include persons competent in the arts, the humanities, the sciences, education and the diffusion of ideas, and qualified by their experience and capacity to fulfil the administrative and executive duties of the Board. It shall also have regard to the diversity of cultures and a balanced geographical distribution. Not more than one national of any Member State shall serve on the Board at any one time, the President of the Conference excepted.

*   *   *

B. *Functions*

5. *(a)* The Executive Board shall prepare the agenda for the General Conference. It shall examine the programme of work for the Organization and corresponding budget estimates submitted to it by the Director-General in accordance with

paragraph 3 of Article VI and shall submit them with such recommendations as it considers desirable to the General Conference.

(b) The Executive Board, acting under the authority of the General Conference, shall be responsible for the execution of the programme adopted by the Conference. In accordance with the decisions of the General Conference and having regard to circumstances arising between two ordinary sessions, the Executive Board shall take all necessary measures to ensure the effective and rational execution of the programme by the Director-General.

(c) Between ordinary sessions of the General Conference, the Board may discharge the functions of adviser to the United Nations, set forth in Article IV, paragraph 5, whenever the problem upon which advice is sought has already been dealt with in principle by the Conference, or when the solution is implicit in decisions of the Conference.

* * *

Article VI. Secretariat

1. The Secretariat shall consist of a Director-General and such staff as may be required.

2. The Director-General shall be nominated by the Executive Board and appointed by the General Conference for a period of six years, under such conditions as the Conference may approve, and shall be eligible for reappointment. He shall be the chief administrative officer of the Organization.

3. *(a)* The Director-General, or a deputy designated by him shall participate, without the right to vote, in all meetings of the General Conference, of the Executive Board, and of the Committees of the Organization. He shall formulate proposals for appropriate action by the Conference and the Board, and shall prepare for submission to the Board a draft programme of work for the Organization with corresponding budget estimates.

(b) The Director-General shall prepare and communicate to Member States and to the Executive Board periodical reports on the activities of the Organization. The General Conference shall determine the periods to be covered by these reports.

4. The Director-General shall appoint the staff of the Secretariat in accordance with staff regulations to be approved by the General Conference. Subject to the paramount consideration of securing the highest standards of integrity, efficiency and technical competence, appointment to the staff shall be on as wide a geographical basis as possible.

5. The responsibilities of the Director-General and of the staff shall be exclusively international in character. In the discharge of their duties they shall not seek or receive instructions from any government or from any authority external to the Organization. They shall refrain from any action which might prejudice their position as international officials. Each State member of the Organization undertakes to respect the international character of the responsibilities of the Director-General and the staff, and not to seek to influence them in the discharge of their duties.

6. Nothing in this Article shall preclude the Organization from entering into special arrangements with the United Nations Organization for common services and staff and for the interchange of personnel.

Article VII. National Co-operating Bodies

1. Each Member State shall make such arrangements as suit its particular conditions for the purpose of associating its principal bodies interested in education, scientific and cultural matters with the work of the Organization, preferably by the formation of a National Commission broadly representative of the government and such bodies.

2. National Commissions or National Co-operating Bodies, where they exist, shall act in an advisory capacity to their respective delegations to the General Conference and to their governments in matters relating to the Organization and shall function as agencies of liaison in all matters of interest to it.

3. The Organization may, on the request of a Member State, delegate, either temporarily or permanently, a member of its Secretariat to serve on the National Commission of that State, in order to assist in the development of its work.

Article VIII. Reports by Member States

Each Member State shall report periodically to the Organization, in a manner to be determined by the General Conference, on its laws, regulations and statistics relating to educational, scientific and cultural life and institutions, and on the action taken upon the recommendations and conventions referred to in Article IV, paragraph 4.

Article IX. Budget

1. The Budget shall be administered by the Organization.
2. The General Conference shall approve and give final effect to the budget and to the apportionment of financial responsibility among the States members of the Organization subject to such arrangement with the United Nations as may be provided in the agreement to be entered into pursuant to Article X.
3. The Director-General, with the approval of the Executive Board, may receive gifts, bequests, and subventions directly from governments, public and private institutions, associations and private persons.

Article X. Relations with the United Nations Organization

This Organization shall be brought into relation with the United Nations Organization, as soon as practicable, as one of the Specialized Agencies referred to in Article 57 of the Charter of the United Nations. This relationship shall be effected through an agreement with the United Nations Organization under Article 63 of the Charter, which agreement shall be subject to the approval of the General Conference of this Organization. The agreement shall provide for effective co-operation between the two Organizations in the pursuit of their common purposes, and at the same time shall recognize the autonomy of this Organization, within the fields of its competence as defined in this Constitution. Such agreement may, among other matters, provide for the approval and financing of the budget of the Organization by the General Assembly of the United Nations.

Article XI. Relations with other Specialized International Organizations and Agencies

1. This Organization may co-operate with other specialized intergovernmental organizations and agencies whose interests and activities are related to its purposes. To this end the Director-General, acting under the general authority of the Executive Board, may establish effective working relationships with such organizations and agencies and establish such joint committees as may be necessary to assure effective co-operation. Any formal arrangements entered into with such organizations or agencies shall be subject to the approval of the Executive Board.

2. Whenever the General Conference of this Organization and the competent authorities of any other specialized intergovernmental organizations or agencies whose purposes and functions lie within the competence of this Organization, deem it desirable to effect a transfer of their resources and activities to this Organization, the Director-General, subject to the approval of the Conference, may enter into mutually acceptable arrangements for this purpose.

3. This Organization may make appropriate arrangements with other intergovernmental organizations for reciprocal representation at meetings.

4. The United Nations Educational, Scientific and Cultural Organization may make suitable arrangements for consultation and co-operation with non-governmental international organizations concerned with matters within its competence, and may invite them to undertake specific tasks. Such co-operation may also include appropriate participation by representatives of such organizations on advisory committees set up by the General Conference.

Article XII. Legal Status of the Organization

The provisions of Articles 104 and 105 of the Charter of the United Nations Organization concerning the legal status of that Organization, its privileges and immunities, shall apply in the same way to this Organization.

Article XIII. Amendments

1. Proposals for amendments to this Constitution shall become effective upon receiving the approval of the General Conference by a two-thirds majority; provided, however, that those amendments which involve fundamental alterations in the aims of the Organization or new obligations for the Member States shall require subsequent acceptance on the part of two-thirds of the Member States before they come into force. The draft texts of proposed amendments shall be communicated by the Director-General to the Member States at least six months in advance of their consideration by the General Conference.

2. The General Conference shall have power to adopt by a two-thirds majority rules of procedure for carrying out the provisions of this Article.

UNESCO'S CONTRIBUTION TO PEACE AND ITS TASKS WITH RESPECT TO THE PROMOTION OF HUMAN RIGHTS AND THE ELIMINATION OF COLONIALISM AND RACISM

General Conference Resolution 11.1, 1974

The General Conference

I

1. *Takes note* of the Director-General's Report on Unesco's contribution to peace and its tasks with respect to the elimination of colonialism and racism, and application of the resolutions relating to the African peoples fighting for their liberation;

2. *Declares* that Unesco should take a more active part in the struggle against all forms and manifestations of fascism, neo-colonialism and all other forms of oppression and tyranny, racism and apartheid caused by imperialism, and should intensify its action to preserve peace, achieve *détente* at a still deeper level and strengthen international understanding so as to make this process irreversible;

3. *Declares* that Unesco must intensify its action in this field;

4. *Invites* all Member States to lend Unesco effective support in its activities on behalf of world peace, international understanding and the promotion of human rights;

5. *Calls upon* Member States:

(a) to co-operate actively, by all means at their disposal, in achieving *détente*, striving to make the process irreversible, and regarding it as an important prerequisite for the further development of all Unesco's activities, in order to promote social progress:

(b)   to take the necessary steps to extend co-operation in the fields of Unesco's competence, which is an important factor in the strengthening of understanding between peoples and the improvement of relations between States;

6. *Invites* the Director-General to prepare a long-term programme of measures whereby Unesco can contribute to the strengthening of peace and to further international *détente*, providing for:

(a)   measures relating to Unesco's contribution, within its fields of competence, to the strengthening of peace and the extension and furthering of *détente*, and measures to promote security and co-operation on all continents;

(b)   research on problems relating to peace, the security of nations and the protection of human rights;

(c)   conferences and symposia on the role of education, science, culture and information in developing international co-operation in the interests of peace and the promotion of human rights;

(d)   the elaboration of effective measures to apply international recommendations concerning the education of young people and adults in the spirit of peace and mutual understanding among peoples;

(e)   the systematic publication by Unesco of material showing the importance of international *détente* based on national independence, equality among nations, freedom and justice and the need to extend this process to all parts of the world and make it irreversible, with a view to the development of education, science, culture and information and social progress;

(f)   the extension of co-operation with non-governmental organizations concerned with the preservation of peace, the development of international co-operation and the promotion of human rights in Unesco's fields of competence and in accordance with its Constitution;

7. *Declares* that in conformity with the fundamental principles laid down in the Charter of the United Nations, the Constitution of Unesco and the Universal Declaration of Human Rights, genuine international co-operation requires:

(a)   the equal rights and self-determination of peoples, which implies the principle of non-intervention in affairs falling essentially within the internal jurisdiction of a State;

(b)   unconditional recognition of and respect for the dignity of the individual and equality among men;

(c)   respect for the specific identity and cultural aspiration of each and every people;

(d)   a realization of the growing interdependence of countries and of the need for the establishment of a new international economic order;

(e)   a recognition of the priority need to do everything possible to put right the injustice of which the most disadvantaged countries, groups and individuals are the victims;

*   *   *

III

14. *Strongly condemns* all forms and varieties of racialism, fascism and apartheid, and all other ideologies which inspire national or racial hatred and violations of human rights and fundamental freedoms;

15. *Invites* all Member States to make wider use of the information media and organs for reaching the general public to intensify the struggle against racialism and apartheid and other violations of human rights and fundamental freedoms;

16. *Calls on* the Member States:

(a) to inform the public on the abominable practices of racial segregation;

(b) to publicize among the public at large the text of the International Convention for the Suppression and Punishment of the Crime of Apartheid (resolution 3068 (XXVIII) adopted by the United Nations General Assembly on 30 November 1973) by means of the mass media;

(c) to devote increased attention in teaching programmes and textbooks to the education of youth with regard to the condemnation of apartheid;

(d) to intensify the boycott in sports, culture and all other activities of Unesco of those countries whose governments adopt a racist policy;

17. *Requests* the Director-General:

(a) to take the necessary steps to ensure the international dissemination of the text of this Convention;

(b) to continue, with the Executive Board, to take the utmost care to ensure that no non-governmental organization having working relations with Unesco participates in any way in the policy of apartheid and racial discrimination practised in the Republic of South Africa and Southern Rhodesia, and to report to the Executive Board;

(c) to offer the liberation movements recognized by the Organization of African Unity in these countries every means to play a full part in Unesco's activities;

(d) *to ensure* that Unesco's dealings with banks and businesses are subject to the same rules concerning economic sanctions against these countries as are applied by the Secretary-General of the United Nations in pursuance of the relevant resolutions of the General Assembly;

18. *Invites* the Executive Board:

(a) *to continue* to refuse to allow any non-governmental organization participating in any way at all in the policy of apartheid and racial discrimination practised in the Republic of South Africa and Southern Rhodesia to participate in Unesco's activities;

(b) *to ensure* that no subventions are granted to non-governmental organizations which support the policy of the Government of the Republic of South Africa or of the illegal Government of Southern Rhodesia;

DECLARATION ON RACE AND RACIAL PREJUDICE

General Conference Resolution 3/1.1/2, 1978

Preamble

The General Conference of the United Nations Educational, Scientific and Cultural Organization, meeting at Paris at its twentieth session, from 24 October to 28 November 1978,

Whereas it is stated in the Preamble to the Constitution of Unesco, adopted on 16 November 1945, that 'the great and terrible war which has now ended was a war made possible by the denial of the democratic principles of the dignity, equality and mutual respect of men, and by the propagation, in their place, through ignorance and prejudice, of the doctrine of the inequality of men and races', and whereas, according to Article I of the said Constitution, the purpose of Unesco 'is to contribute to peace and security by promoting collaboration among the nations through education, science and culture in order to further universal respect for justice, for the rule of law and for the human rights and fundamental freedoms . . . which are affirmed for the peoples of the world, without distinction of race, sex, language or religion, by the Charter of the United Nations',

Recognizing that, more than three decades after the founding of Unesco, these principles are just as significant as they were when they were embodied in its Constitution,

Mindful of the process of decolonization and other historical changes which have led most of the peoples formerly under foreign rule to recover their sovereignty, making the international community a universal and diversified whole and creating new opportunities of eradicating the scourge of racism and of putting an end to its odious manifestations in all aspects of social and political life, both nationally and internationally,

Convinced that the essential unity of the human race and consequently the fundamental equality of all human beings and all peoples, recognized in the loftiest expressions of philosophy, morality and religion, reflect an ideal towards which ethics and science are converging today,

Convinced that all peoples and all human groups, whatever their composition or ethnic origin, contribute according to their own genius to the progress of the civilizations and cultures which, in their plurality and as a result of their interpretation, constitute the common heritage of mankind,

Confirming its attachment to the principles proclaimed in the United Nations Charter and the Universal Declaration of Human Rights and its determination to promote the implementation of the International Covenants on Human Rights as well as the Declaration on the Establishment of a New International Economic Order,

Determined also to promote the implementation of the United Nations Declaration and the International Convention on the Elimination of all Forms of Racial Discrimination,

Noting the International Convention on the Prevention and Punishment of the Crime of Genocide, the International Convention on the Suppression and Punishment of the Crime of Apartheid and the Convention on the Non-Applicability of Statutory Limitation to War Crimes and Crimes against Humanity,

Recalling also the international instruments already adopted by Unesco, including in particular the Convention and Recommendation against Discrimination in Education, the Recommendation concerning the Status of Teachers, the Declaration of the Principles of International Cultural Co-operation, the Recommendation concerning Education for International Cultural Co-operation, the Recommendation concerning Education for International Understanding, Co-operation and Peace and Education relating to Human Rights and Fundamental Freedoms, the Recommendation on the Status of Scientific Researchers, and the Recommendation on participation by the people at large in cultural life and their contribution to it,

Bearing in mind the four statements on the race question adopted by experts meeting at Unesco,

Reaffirming its desire to play a vigorous and constructive part in the implementation of the programme of the Decade for Action to Combat Racism and Racial Discrimination, as defined by the General Assembly of the United Nations at its twenty-eighth session,

Noting with the gravest concern that racism, racial discrimination, colonialism and apartheid continue to afflict the world in ever-changing forms, as a result both of the continuation of legislative provisions and government and administrative practices contrary to the principles of human rights and also of the continued existence of political and social structures, and of relationships and attitudes, characterized by injustice and contempt for human beings and leading to the exclusion, humiliation and exploitation, or to the forced assimilation, of the members of disadvantaged groups,

Expressing its indignation at these offences against human dignity, *deploring* the obstacles they place in the way of mutual understanding between peoples and *alarmed* at the danger of their seriously disturbing international peace and security,

Adopts and solemnly proclaims this Declaration on Race and Racial Prejudice:

Article 1

1. All human beings belong to a single species and are descended from a common stock. They are born equal in dignity and rights and all form an integral part of humanity.

2. All individuals and groups have the right to be different, to consider themselves as different and to be regarded as such. However, the diversity of life styles and the right to be different may not, in any circumstances, serve as a pretext for racial prejudice; they may not justify either in law or in fact any discriminatory practice whatsoever, nor provide a ground for the policy of apartheid, which is the extreme form of racism.

3. Identity of origin in no way affects the fact that human beings can and may live differently, nor does it preclude the existence of differences based on cultural, environmental and historical diversity nor the right to maintain cultural identity.

4. All peoples of the world possess equal faculties for attaining the highest level in intellectual, technical, social, economic, cultural and political development.

5. The differences between the achievements of the different peoples are entirely attributable to geographical, historical, political, economic, social and cultural factors. Such differences can in no case serve as a pretext for any rank-ordered classification of nations or peoples.

Article 2

1. Any theory which involves the claim that racial or ethnic groups are inherently superior or inferior, thus implying that some would be entitled to dominate or eliminate others, presumed to be inferior, or which bases value judgements on racial differentiation, has no scientific foundation and is contrary to the moral and ethical principles of humanity.

2. Racism includes racist ideologies, prejudiced attitudes, discriminatory behaviour, structural arrangements and institutionalized practices resulting in racial inequality as well as the fallacious notion that discriminatory relations between groups are morally and scientifically justifiable; it is reflected in discriminatory provisions in legislation or regulations and discriminatory practices as well as in anti-social beliefs and acts; it hinders the development of its victims, perverts those who practise it, divides nations internally, impedes international co-operation and gives rise to political tensions between peoples; it is contrary to the fundamental principles of international law and, consequently, seriously disturbs international peace and security.

3. Racial prejudice, historically linked with inequalities in power, reinforced by economic and social differences between individuals and groups, and still seeking today to justify such inequalities, is totally without justification.

Article 3

Any distinction, exclusion, restriction or preference based on race, colour, ethnic or national origin or religious intolerance motivated by racist considerations, which destroys or compromises the sovereign equality of States and the right of peoples of self-determination, or which limits in an arbitrary or discriminatory manner the right of every human being and group to full development is incompatible with the requirements of an international order which is just and guarantees respect for human rights; the right to full development implies equal access to the means of personal and collective advancement and fulfillment in a climate of respect for the values of civilizations and cultures, both national and world-wide.

Article 4

1. Any restriction on the complete self-fulfilment of human beings and free communication between them which is based on racial or ethnic considerations is contrary to the principle of equality in dignity and rights; it cannot be admitted.

2. One of the most serious violations of this principle is represented by apartheid, which, like genocide, is a crime against humanity, and gravely disturbs international peace and security.

3. Other policies and practices of racial segregation and discrimination constitute crimes against the conscience and dignity of mankind and may lead to political tensions and gravely endanger international peace and security.

Article 5

1. Culture, as a product of all human beings and a common heritage of mankind, and education in its broadest sense, offer men and women increasingly effective means of adaptation, enabling them not only to affirm that they are born equal in dignity and rights, but also to recognize that they should respect the right of all groups to their own cultural identity and the development of their distinctive cultural life within the national and international context, it being understood that it rests with each group to decide in complete freedom on the maintenance and, if appropriate, the adaptation or enrichment of the values which it regards as essential to its identity.

2. States, in accordance with their constitutional principles and procedures, as well as all other competent authorities and the entire teaching profession, have a responsibility to see that the education resources of all countries are used to combat racism, more especially by ensuring that curricula and textbooks include scientific and ethical considerations concerning human unity and diversity and that no invidious distinctions are made with regard to any people; by training teachers to achieve these ends; by making the resources of the educational system available to all groups of the population without racial restriction or discrimination; and by taking appropriate steps to remedy the handicaps from which certain racial or ethnic groups suffer with regard to their level of education and standard of living and in particular to prevent such handicaps from being passed on to children.

3. The mass media and those who control or serve them, as well as all organized groups within national communities, are urged – with due regard to the principles embodied in the Universal Declaration of Human Rights, particularly the principle of freedom of expression – to promote understanding, tolerance and friendship among individuals and groups and to contribute to the eradication of racism, racial discrimination and racial prejudice, in particular by refraining from presenting a stereotyped, partial, unilateral or tendentious picture of individuals and of various human groups. Communication between racial and ethnic groups must be a reciprocal process, enabling them to express themselves and to be fully heard without let or hindrance. The mass media should therefore be freely receptive to ideas of individuals and groups which facilitate such communication.

Article 6

1. The State has prime responsibility for ensuring human rights and fundamental freedoms on an entirely equal footing in dignity and rights for all individuals and all groups.

2. So far as its competence extends and in accordance with its constitutional principles and procedures, the State should take all appropriate steps, *inter alia* by legislation, particularly in the spheres of education, culture and communication, to prevent, prohibit and eradicate racism, racist propaganda, racial segregation and

apartheid and to encourage the dissemination of knowledge and the findings of appropriate research in natural and social sciences on the causes and prevention of racial prejudice and racist attitudes, with due regard to the principles embodied in the Universal Declaration of Human Rights and in the International Covenant on Civil and Political Rights.

3. Since laws proscribing racial discrimination are not in themselves sufficient, it is also incumbent on States to supplement them by administrative machinery for the systematic investigation of instances of racial discrimination, by a comprehensive framework of legal remedies against acts of racial discrimination, by broadly based education and research programmes designed to combat racial prejudice and racial discrimination and by programmes of positive political, social, educational and cultural measures calculated to promote genuine mutual respect among groups. Where circumstances warrant, special programmes should be undertaken to promote the advancement of disadvantaged groups and, in the case of nationals, to ensure their effective participation in the decision-making processes of the community.

Article 7

In addition to political, economic and social measures, law is one of the principal means of ensuring equality in dignity and rights among individuals, and of curbing any propaganda, any form of organization or any practice which is based on ideas or theories referring to the alleged superiority of racial or ethnic groups or which seeks to justify or encourage racial hatred and discrimination in any form. States should adopt such legislation as is appropriate to this end and see that it is given effect and applied by all their services, with due regard to the principles embodied in the Universal Declaration of Human Rights. Such legislation should form part of a political, economic and social framework conducive to its implementation. Individuals and other legal entities, both public and private, must conform with such legislation and use all appropriate means to help the population as a whole to understand and apply it.

Article 8

1. Individuals, being entitled to an economic, social, cultural and legal order, on the national and international planes, such as to allow them to exercise all their capabilities on a basis of entire equality of rights and opportunities, have corresponding duties towards their fellows, towards the society in which they live and towards the international community. They are accordingly under an obligation to promote harmony among the peoples, to combat racism and racial prejudice and to assist by every means available to them in eradicating racial discrimination in all its forms.

2. In the field of racial prejudice and racist attitudes and practices, specialists in natural and social sciences and cultural studies, as well as scientific organizations and associations, are called upon to undertake objective research on a wide interdisciplinary basis; all States should encourage them to this end.

3. It is, in particular, incumbent upon such specialists to ensure, by all means available to them, that their research findings are not misinterpreted, and also that they assist the public in understanding such findings.

Article 9

1. The principle of the equality in dignity and rights of all human beings and all peoples, irrespective of race, colour and origin, is a generally accepted and recognized principle of international law. Consequently any form of racial discrimination

practised by a State constitutes a violation of international law giving rise to its international responsibility.

2. Special measures must be taken to ensure equality in dignity and rights for individuals and groups wherever necessary, while ensuring that they are not such as to appear racially discriminatory. In this respect, particular attention should be paid to racial or ethnic groups which are socially or economically disadvantaged, so as to afford them, on a completely equal footing and without discrimination or restriction, the protection of the laws and regulations and the advantages of the social measures in force, in particular in regard to housing, employment and health; to respect the authenticity of their culture and values; and to facilitate their social and occupational advancement, especially through education.

3. Population groups of foreign origin, particularly migrant workers and their families who contribute to the development of the host country, should benefit from appropriate measures designed to afford them security and respect for their dignity and cultural values and to facilitate their adaptation to the host environment and their professional advancement with a view to their subsequent reintegration in their country of origin and their contribution to its development; steps should be taken to make it possible for their children to be taught their mother tongue.

4. Existing disequilibria in international economic relations contribute to the exacerbation of racism and racial prejudice; all States should consequently endeavour to contribute to the restructuring of the international economy on a more equitable basis.

Article 10

International organizations, whether universal or regional, governmental or non-governmental, are called upon to co-operate and assist, so far as their respective fields of competence and means allow, in the full and complete implementation of the principles set out in this Declaration, thus contributing to the legitimate struggle of all men, born equal in dignity and rights, against the tyranny and oppression of racism, racial segregation, apartheid and genocide, so that all the peoples of the world may be forever delivered from these scourges.

CREATION OF A CLIMATE OF PUBLIC OPINION CONDUCIVE TO THE HALTING OF THE ARMS RACE AND THE TRANSITION TO DISARMAMENT

General Conference Resolution 11.1, 1980

The General Conference,
Mindful that the purpose of Unesco, in accordance with Article I of its constitution, is 'to contribute to peace and security by promoting collaboration among the nations through education, science and culture in order to further universal respect for justice, for the rule of law and for the human rights and fundamental freedoms which are affirmed for the peoples of the world, without distinction of race, sex, language or religion, by the Charter of the United Nations',
Convinced that Unesco's activity, based on the purposes and functions set out in its Constitution, will continue to influence world public opinion in favour of promoting the ideals of peace, mutual respect and understanding between peoples,
Emphasizing in this connection that the arms race, the dimensions of which are growing and which is imperilling the future of all mankind, remains one of the chief obstacles to the strengthening of peace,
Recognizing the terrible dangers to which a nuclear war would expose mankind,

Noting the obligation of all States to refrain in their international relations from the threat or use of force against the sovereignty, territorial integrity or political independence of any State and from any other action inconsistent with the purposes and principles of the Charter of the United Nations, and convinced that the implementation of those principles is indispensable for generating a climate conducive to the halting of the arms race,

Drawing attention to the fact that the development process and the establishment of a new international economic order are seriously inhibited by the growing expenditure of human and material resources on the arms race,

Recalling that the problem of disarmament constitutes one of the major preoccupations of our century, and *further recalling* the decisions adopted in this field by the United Nations General Assembly,

Realizing that the dangers threatening mankind call for redoubled efforts to solve the problems of halting the arms race and of the transition to disarmament,

Noting with satisfaction that the United Nations has proclaimed the 1980s a Second Disarmament Decade,

Welcoming the decision to hold a special session of the United Nations General Assembly devoted to disarmament in 1982,

Recognizing further that disarmament could afford possibilities of improving the lives of the people of the world and of promoting the solution of a multitude of urgent socio-economic problems,

Noting that the Final Document of the Tenth Special Session of the General Assembly urged governments and governmental and non-governmental international organizations to take steps to develop programmes of education for disarmament and peace studies at all levels with a view to contributing to a greater understanding and awareness of the problems created by the armaments race and of the need for disarmament, and that it specifically urged Unesco to step up its programme aimed at the development of disarmament education as a distinct field of study through the preparation, *inter alia*, of teachers' guides, textbooks, readers and audio-visual materials,

Noting with satisfaction the substantial and constructive efforts that Unesco has made within its fields of competence to promote understanding of the problem of disarmament, as reflected in the Director-General's report on the implementation of resolution 11.1 adopted by the General Conference at its twentieth session,

Considering that, in the present international situation, Unesco should continue and make more effective its efforts to generate a climate of public opinion conducive to the halting of the arms race and the transition to disarmament,

Noting in particular that Unesco's action to promote public education, research and information activities, in consultation with the competent United Nations bodies and the non-governmental organizations concerned, with a view to contributing, within its spheres of competence, to international peace, disarmament and security and to respect for human rights, can constitute a substantial contribution to international efforts in this field,

Taking note with interest of the Final Document of the World Congress on Disarmament Education (Paris, 9–13 June 1980),

Recalling in this connection that the United Nations General Assembly, at its Tenth Special Session devoted to disarmament, drew particular attention to the potential influence of world public opinion for halting the arms race and achieving disarmament, and welcomed Unesco's contribution to understanding of these problems whose urgency brooks no delay,

I

1. *Calls upon* all those active in Unesco's spheres of competence to participate in the Organization's efforts to generate a climate of public opinion conducive to the halting of the arms race and the transition to disarmament;

2. *Invites* Member States:

(a)   to continue to encourage the development of the activities in Unesco's fields of competence set out in the relevant paragraphs of the Final Document adopted by the United Nations General Assembly at its Tenth Special Session, and to publicize the results of such efforts;

(b)   to take note of the Final Document of the World Congress on Disarmament Education;

(c)   to encourage public and private scientific research institutions which could usefully contribute to a better understanding of the problems relating to disarmament;

(d)   to take the necessary steps to make adequate information available on matters concerning disarmament, in order to make meaningful and informed disarmament education possible;

(e)   to respond actively to the call of the General Assembly at its special session to observe the week beginning 24 October as a week devoted to fostering the objectives of disarmament;

* * *

UNESCO'S CONTRIBUTION TO THE ESTABLISHMENT OF A NEW INTERNATIONAL ECONOMIC ORDER

General Conference Resolution 9.1, 1978

The General Conference,

Conscious of the important role of Unesco in creating an appropriate moral climate and new attitude on the part of all concerned with the advancement of development, peace and the cultural integrity of peoples,

Recalling resolutions 3201 and 3202 (S-VI), adopted by the United Nations General Assembly containing the Declaration and Programme of Action on the Establishment of a New International Economic Order, resolution 3281 (XXIX) of 12 December 1974, containing the Charter of Economic Rights and Duties of States, and resolution 3362 (S-VII),

Recalling resolution 9.11, adopted by the General Conference at its nineteenth session, and resolution 12.1, adopted by the General Conference at its eighteenth session, concerning Unesco's contribution to the establishment of a new international economic order,

Bearing in mind the main lines of action contained in the book *Moving Towards Change* and *taking into account* the Medium-Term Plan (19C/4), the Draft Adjustments to the Medium-Term Plan (20C/4) and the Draft Programme and Budget for 1979–1980 (20C/5),

Noting the report of the Director-General on the implementation of 19C/Resolution 9.11,

Emphasizing that the efforts made to apply the resolutions concerning the establishment of a new international economic order have not produced the practical effects expected, even though it has been possible to identify the main problems,

Considering that the gap between developed and developing countries in the socio-economic fields of education, science, culture and communication represents a substantial manifestation of the inequalities between individuals, groups and nations,

Considering that the concept of 'basic human needs', presented as one of the foundations of development strategy, cannot replace the concrete concepts and principles on which a new international economic order should be built,

Having regard to the role that international co-operation based on the principles of equality, solidarity and justice can play in the positive transformation of international relations as a whole,

Aware of Unesco's important role in the promotion and application of the principles on which a new international economic order should be based, in the realization of its objectives and in the launching of actions leading to its establishment,

Considering that the establishment of a new international economic order is inseparable from the elimination of all factors jeopardizing international peace and security, such as the arms race, colonialism, neo-colonialism, imperialism, apartheid, all forms of foreign occupation, domination and racial, cultural or political oppression,

1. *Invites* Member States:

(a) to intensify the efforts made to implement the resolutions of the United Nations concerning the establishment of a new international economic order, particularly in the fields of education, science, culture and information, mustering for this purpose their intellectual and material resources, developing international co-operation and understanding among nations, and extending to the economic field the process of the elimination of colonialism and neo-colonialism in all their forms and manifestations;

(b) to associate in this effort both governmental bodies and non-governmental organizations and associations and to take measures conducive to the creation of a climate of opinion favourable to the attainment of the objectives of a new international economic order through the development of international co-operation;

(c) to develop, particularly among the developing countries themselves, mutual co-operation and exchanges of experience designed to solve the problems raised by the establishment of a new international economic order, making sure that such co-operation is in accordance with principles which safeguard genuine sovereignty and respect for the legitimate rights of the parties concerned;

(d) to support the efforts of developing countries to train managerial staff and to establish the necessary institutional infrastructures, while respecting their specific circumstances and needs, their national and cultural identity and their sovereign right to take in full independence the decisions governing their development;

2. *Invites* the Director-General:

(a) to continue his efforts to promote increased participation by the Organization in the establishment of a new international economic order, particularly through such means as studies designed to deepen awareness of the concepts and principles on which a new international economic order should be based;

(b) to intensify the action needed to inform and arouse public opinion, particularly among young people, graduates and workers, and, to this end, promote the organization of symposia, meetings and conferences at the national, regional and international levels;

(c) to devote special attention, in the implementation of the biennial programme and the Medium-Term Plan, as well as in the preparation of the Medium-Term Plan for 1983–1989, to activities which can make a direct contribution to the attainment of these objectives;

(d) to develop and encourage programmes of mutual co-operation among Member States designed to facilitate the attainment of the objectives of the new international economic order;

(e) to encourage co-operation among developing countries, in particular for the implementation of endogenous development programmes;

(f) to implement as rapidly and as fully as possible the recommendations adopted by the regional ministerial conferences in the fields of education, science, culture and communication, particularly when they have a direct bearing on the attainment of the objectives of the new international economic order;

(g) to submit to the United Nations General Assembly, at the special session to be held in 1980 to evaluate progress made in the solution of international economic problems and in the establishment of a new international economic order, a critical report on activities relating to the establishment of a new international economic order in Unesco's fields of competence;

(h) to reflect on the content and forms of Unesco's action and to take part, in due course, in the Organization's fields of competence, in preparatory work leading to the definition of the objectives of the Third Development Decade, having regard to the satisfactory and unsatisfactory aspects of the past two United Nations Development Decades;

(i) to consider that the concept of 'basic human needs', which is a subject of thought, among others, in the study and the working out of development strategies, is insufficient as a basis for planning and programming Unesco's action for the establishment of a new international economic order;

(j) to continue to take part, in Unesco's field of competence, in the work in progress within the United Nations system with a view to the elaboration of a code of conduct for transnational corporations, in respect of provisions relating to the establishment of a new international economic order;

(k) to prepare a series of studies designed to facilitate the participation of the Organization in the establishment of a new international economic order and the formulation of a strategy for the Third Development Decade and in similar activities of other organizations of the United Nations system;

(l) to report periodically to the Executive Board of Unesco on the implementation of this resolution and to prepare a comprehensive report for the twenty-first session of the General Conference, together with the comments and observations of the Executive Board.

DECLARATION CONCERNING THE AIMS AND PURPOSES OF THE INTERNATIONAL LABOUR ORGANIZATION, 1944

The General Conference of the International Labour Organization, meeting in its Twenty-sixth Session in Philadelphia, hereby adopts, this tenth day of May in the year nineteen hundred and forty-four, the present Declaration of the aims and purposes of the International Labour Organization and of the principles which should inspire the policy of its Members.

I

The conference reaffirms the fundamental principles on which the Organization is based and, in particular, that:

(a) labour is not a commodity;

(b) freedom of expression and of association are essential to sustained progress;

(c) poverty anywhere constitutes a danger to prosperity everywhere;

(d) the war against want requires to be carried on with unrelenting vigour within each nation, and by continuous and concerted international effort in which the representatives of workers and employers, enjoying equal status with those of Governments, join with them in free discussion and democratic decision with a view to the promotion of the common welfare.

II

Believing that experience has fully demonstrated the truth of the statement in the Constitution of the International Labour Organization that lasting peace can be established only if it is based on social justice, the Conference affirms that:

(a) all human beings, irrespective of race, creed, or sex, have the right to pursue both their material well-being and their spiritual development in conditions of freedom and dignity, of economic security, and equal opportunity;

(b) the attainment of the conditions in which this shall be possible must constitute the central aim of national and international policy;

(c) all national and international policies and measures, in particular those of an economic and financial character, should be judged in this light and accepted only in so far as they be held to promote and not to hinder the achievement of this fundamental objective;

(d) it is a responsibility of the International Labour Organization to examine and consider all international economic and financial policies and measures in the light of this fundamental objective;

(e) in discharging the tasks entrusted to it the International Labour Organization, having considered all relevant economic and financial factors, may include in its decisions and recommendations any provisions which it considers appropriate.

III

The Conference recognizes the solemn obligation of the International Labour Organization to further among the nations of the world programmes which will achieve:

(a) full employment and the raising of standards of living;

(b) the employment of workers in the occupations in which they can have the satisfaction of giving the fullest measure of their skill and attainments and make their greatest contribution to the common well-being;

(c) the provision, as a means to the attainment of this end and under adequate guarantees for all concerned, of facilities for training and the transfer of labour, including migration for employment and settlement;

(d) Policies in regard to wages and earnings, hours and other conditions of work calculated to ensure a just share of the fruits of progress to all, and a minimum living wage to all employed and in need of such protection;

(e) the effective recognition of the right of collective bargaining, the co-operation of management and labour in the continuous improvement of productive efficiency, and the collaboration of workers and employers in the preparation and application of social and economic measures;

(f) the extension of social security measures to provide a basic income to all in need of such protection and comprehensive medical care;

(g) adequate protection for the life and health of workers in all occupations;

(h) provision for child welfare and maternity protection;

(i) the provision of adequate nutrition, housing, and facilities for recreation and culture;

(j) the assurance of equality of educational and vocational opportunities.

IV

Confident that the fuller and broader utilization of the world's productive resources necessary for the achievement of the objectives set forth in this Declaration can be secured by effective international and national action, including measures to expand production and consumption, to avoid severe economic fluctuations, to promote the economic and social advancement of the less developed regions of the world, to assure greater stability in world prices of primary products, and to promote a high and steady volume of international trade, the Conference pledges the full co-operation of the International Labour Organization with such international bodies as may be entrusted with a share of the responsibility for this great task and for the promotion of the health, education, and well-being of all peoples.

V

The Conference affirms that principles set forth in this Declaration are fully applicable to all peoples everywhere and that, while the manner of their application must be determined with due regard to the stage of social and economic development reached by each people, their progressive application to peoples who are still dependent, as well as to those who have already achieved self-government, is a matter of concern to the whole civilized world.

III. INSTRUMENTS ADOPTED BY REGIONAL AND OTHER ORGANIZATIONS

The UN system is complemented by regional and other organizations, conferences or other arrangements which provide the framework for international agreements among their respective member states. The distinction between organizations of general competence (i.e. UN) and those of limited competence (i.e. specialized agencies) is also valid at this level as in the case of the Arab League and the specialized organs established under its sponsorship.

As in the case of the UN Charter, the constituent instruments of the organizations of general competence contain general principles applicable to communications and information. Such organizations have also adopted instruments in areas of relevance in this context e.g. human rights, international security and co-operation.

A number of organizations and conferences comprise a membership beyond a purely geographical definition. Of particular importance in this context are the Organization for Economic Co-operation and Development, the movement of Non-Aligned Countries and the Conference on Security and Co-operation in Europe. Instruments of general importance are included in this section; those texts dealing with specific issues of communications and information will be found in the following specialized sections.

Documents

1. Europe
  i. Statute of the Council of Europe, 1949 (revised)
     – Preamble
     – Articles 1–3, 10, 15, 23, 25(a)
  ii. European Convention on Human Rights, 1954
     – Preamble
     – Articles 1–26, 38–39, 44–53 (see in particular Art. 8–11, 13–14)

2. The Americas
  iii. Charter of the Organization of American States, 1948 (OAS) (amended)
     – Preamble
     – Articles, 1–3, 16, 30–31, 36, 39, 42, 45–51
  iv. American Declaration of the Rights and Duties of Man, 1948
     – Preamble
     – Articles I–V, X, XII, XIII, XXI–XXII
  v. American Convention on Human Rights, 1969
     – Preamble
     – Articles 1–2, 11–16, 33 (see in particular Art. 13–14)

3. Africa
  vi. Charter of the Organization of African Unity, 1963 (OAU)
     – Preamble
     – Articles 1–3

4. Asia

vii. The Association of Southeast Asian Nations Declaration, 1967 (ASEAN)
   - Full text

5. Arab Region

viii. Pact of the League of Arab States, 1945
   - Preamble
   - Articles 1–4, 7, 12, 19

6. Trans-regional organizations and conferences

ix. Convention of the Organization for Economic Co-operation and Development (OECD), 1960
   - Preamble
   - Articles 1–10

x. Conferences of the Non-Aligned Countries
   (a) The Policy of Non-Alignment and the Strengthening of its Independent Role, Political Declaration, Sixth Summit Conference of Heads of State or Government of Non-Aligned Countries, Havana, 1979
      - Points 12–13, 17–21
   (b) Decision regarding the Composition and Mandate of the Co-ordinating Bureau and Co-ordination of Action Programme, Fifth Summit Conference of Heads of State or Government of Non-Aligned Countries, Colombo,1976
      - I, Points 1–4, II–III,

xi. Conference on Security and Co-operation in Europe, Final Acts, Helsinki, 1975
   - Preamble
   - Section I

STATUTE OF THE COUNCIL OF EUROPE (REVISED)

London, 5th May, 1949

The Governments of the Kingdom of Belgium, the Kingdom of Denmark, the French Republic, the Irish Republic, the Italian Republic, the Grand Duchy of Luxembourg, the Kingdom of the Netherlands, the Kingdom of Norway, the Kingdom of Sweden and the United Kingdom of Great Britain and Northern Ireland;

Convinced that the pursuit of peace based upon justice and international co-operation is vital for the preservation of human society and civilisation;

Reaffirming their devotion to the spiritual and moral values which are the common heritage of their peoples and the true source of individual freedom, political liberty and the rule of law, principles which form the basis of all genuine democracy;

Believing that, for the maintenance and further realization of these ideals and in the interests of economic and social progress, there is a need of a closer unity between all like-minded countries of Europe;

Considering that, to respond to this need and to the expressed aspirations of their peoples in this regard, it is necessary forthwith to create an organization which will bring European States into closer association;

Have in consequence decided to set up a Council of Europe consisting of a Committee of representatives of Governments and of a Consultative Assembly, and have for this purpose adopted the following Statute: –

Chapter I. Aim of the Council of Europe

Article 1

(a) The aim of the Council of Europe is to achieve a greater unity between its Members for the purpose of safeguarding and realising the ideals and principles which are their common heritage and facilitating their economic and social progress.

(b) This aim shall be pursued through the organs of the Council by discussion of questions of common concern and by agreements and common action in economic, social, cultural, scientific, legal and administrative matters and in the maintenance and further realization of human rights and fundamental freedoms.

(c) Participation in the Council of Europe shall not affect the collaboration of its Members in the work of the United Nations and of other international organizations or unions to which they are parties.

(d) Matters relating to National Defence do not fall within the scope of the Council of Europe.

Chapter II. Membership

Article 2

The Members of the Council of Europe are the Parties to this Statute.

Article 3

Every Member of the Council of Europe must accept the principles of the rule of law and of the enjoyment by all persons within its jurisdiction of human rights and fundamental freedoms, and collaborate sincerely and effectively in the realisation of the aim of the Council as specified in Chapter 1.

* * *

Article 10

The organs of the Council of Europe are:
   i. the Committee of Ministers;
  ii. the Consultative Assembly.
  Both these organs shall be served by the Secretariat of the Council of Europe.

* * *

Article 15

(a) On the recommendation of the Consultative Assembly or on its own initiative, the Committee of Ministers shall consider the action required to further the aim of the Council of Europe, including the conclusion of conventions or agreements and the adoption by Governments of a common policy with regard to particular matters. Its conclusions shall be communicated to Members by the Secretary-General.

(b) In appropriate cases, the conclusions of the Committee may take the form of recommendations to the Governments of Members, and the Committee may request the Governments of Members to inform it of the action taken by them with regard to such recommendations.

* * *

Article 23

(a) The Consultative Assembly may discuss and make recommendations upon any matter within the aim and scope of the Council of Europe as defined in Chapter 1. It shall also discuss and may make recommendations upon any matter referred to it by the Committee of Ministers with a request for its opinion.

(b) The Assembly shall draw up its Agenda in accordance with the provisions of paragraph (a) above. In so doing, it shall have regard to the work of other European intergovernmental organisations to which some or all of the Members of the Council are parties.

(c) The President of the Assembly shall decide, in case of doubt, whether any question raised in the course of the Session is within the Agenda of the Assembly.

*   *   •

Article 25

(a) The Consultative Assembly shall consist of representatives of each Member elected by its Parliament or appointed in such manner as that Parliament shall decide, subject, however, to the right of each Member Government to make any additional appointments necessary when the Parliament is not in session and has not laid down the procedure to be following in that case. Each Representative must be a national of the Member whom he represents, but shall not at the same time be a member of the Committee of Ministers.

*   *   *

EUROPEAN CONVENTION ON HUMAN RIGHTS, 1954

The Governments signatory hereto, being Members of the Council of Europe,

Considering the Universal Declaration of Human Rights proclaimed by the General Assembly of the United Nations on 10 December 1948;

Considering that this Declaration aims at securing the universal and effective recognition and observance of the Rights therein declared;

Considering that the aim of the Council of Europe is the achievement of greater unity between its Members and that one of the methods by which that aim is to be pursued is the maintenance and further realization of Human Rights and Fundamental Freedoms;

Reaffirming their profound belief in those Fundamental Freedoms which are the foundation of justice and peace in the world and are best maintained on the one hand by an effective political democracy and on the other by a common understanding and observance of the Human Rights upon which they depend;

Being resolved as the Governments of European countries which are likeminded and have a common heritage of political traditions, ideals, freedom and the rule of law to take the first steps for the collective enforcement of certain of the Rights stated in the Universal Declaration;

Have agreed as follows:

Article 1

The High Contracting Parties shall secure to everyone within their jurisdiction the rights and freedoms defined in Section 1 of this Convention.

Section I

Article 2

1. Everyone's right to life shall be protected by law. No one shall be deprived of his

life intentionally save in the execution of a sentence of a court following his conviction of a crime for which this penalty is provided by law.

2. Deprivation of life shall not be regarded as inflicted in contravention of this Article when it results from the use of force which is no more than absolutely necessary:

(a) in defence of any person from unlawful violence;

(b) in order to effect a lawful arrest or to prevent the escape of a person lawfully detained;

(c) in action lawfully taken for the purpose of quelling a riot or insurrection.

Article 3

No one shall be subjected to torture or inhuman or degrading treatment or punishment.

Article 4

1. No one shall be held in slavery or servitude.

2. No one shall be required to perform forced or compulsory labor.

3. For the purpose of this Article the term 'forced or compulsory labour' shall not include:

(a) any work required to be done in the ordinary course of detention imposed according to the provisions of Article 5 of this Convention or during conditional release from such detention;

(b) any service of a military character or, in case of conscientious objectors in countries where they are recognized, service exacted instead of compulsory miltary service;

(c) any service exacted in case of an emergency or calamity threatening the life or well-being of the community;

(d) any work or service which forms part of normal civic obligations.

Article 5

1. Everyone has the right to liberty and security of person.

No one shall be deprived of his liberty save in the following cases and in accordance with a procedure prescribed by law;

(a) the lawful arrest or detention of a person for non-compliance with the lawful order of a court or in order to secure the fulfilment of any obligation prescribed by law;

(b) the lawful arrest or detention of a person for non-compliance with the lawful order of a court or in order to secure the fulfilment of any obligation prescribed by law;

(c) the lawful arrest or detention of a person effected for the purpose of bringing him before the competent legal authority on reasonable suspicion of having committed an offence or when it is reasonably considered necessary to prevent his committing an offence or fleeing after having done so;

(d) the detention of a minor by lawful order for the purpose of educational supervision or his lawful detention for the purpose of bringing him before the competent legal authority;

(e) the lawful detention of persons for the prevention of the spreading of infectious diseases, of persons of unsound mind, alcoholics or drug addicts, or vagrants;

(f) the lawful arrest or detention of a person to prevent his effecting an unauthorized entry into the country or of a person against whom action is being taken with a view to deportation or extradition.

2. Everyone who is arrested shall be informed promptly, in a language which he understands, of the reasons for his arrest and of any charge against him.

3. Everyone arrested or detained in accordance with the provisions of paragraph 1

(c) of the Article shall be brought promptly before a judge or other officer authorized by law to exercise judicial power and shall be entitled to trial within a reasonable time or to release pending trial. Release may be conditioned by guarantees to appear for trial.

4. Everyone who is deprived of his liberty by arrest or detention shall be entitled to take proceedings by which the lawfulness of his detention shall be decided speedily by a court and his release ordered if the detention is not lawful.

5. Everyone who has been the victim of arrest or detention in contravention of the provisions of this Article shall have an enforceable right to compensation.

Article 6

1. In the determination of his civil rights and obligations or of any criminal charge against him everyone is entitled to a fair and public hearing within a reasonable time by an independent and impartial tribunal established by law. Judgment shall be pronounced publicly but the press and public may be excluded from all or part of the trial in the interest of morals, public order or national security in a democratic society, where the interest of juveniles or the protection of the private life of the parties so require, or to the extent strictly necessary in the opinion of the court in special circumstances where publicity would prejudice the interests of justice.

2. Everyone charged with a criminal offence shall be presumed innocent until proved guilty according to law.

3. Everyone charged with a criminal offence has the following minimum rights:

(a)   to be informed promptly, in a language which he understands and in detail, of the nature and cause of the accusation against him;
(b)   to have adequate time and facilities for the preparation of his defence;
(c)   to defend himself in person or through legal assistance of his own choosing or, if he has not sufficient means to pay for legal assistance, to be given it free when the interests of justice so require;
(d)   to examine or have examined witnesses against him and to obtain the attendance and examination of witness on his behalf under the same conditions as witnesses against him;
(e)   to have the free assistance of an interpreter if he cannot understand or speak the language used in court.

Article 7

1. No one shall be held guilty of any criminal offence on account of any act or omission which did not constitute a criminal offence under national or international law at the time when it was committed. Nor shall a heavier penalty be imposed than the one that was applicable at the time the criminal offence was committed.

2. This Article shall not prejudice the trial and punishment of any person for any act or omission which, at the time when it was committed, was criminal according to the general principles of law recognized by civilized nations.

Article 8

1. Everyone has the right to respect for his private and family life, his home and his correspondence.

2. There shall be no interference by a public authority with the excercise of this right except such as is in accordance with the law and is necessary in a democratic society in the interests of national security, public safety or the economic well-being of the country, for the prevention of disorder or crime, for the protection of health or morals, or for the protection of the rights and freedoms of others.

Article 9

1. Everyone has the right to freedom of thought, conscience and religion; this right includes freedom to change his religion or belief, and freedom, either alone or in community with others and in public or private to manifest his religion or belief, in worship, teaching, practice and observance.

2. Freedom to manifest one's religion or beliefs shall be subject only to such limitations as are prescribed by law and are necessary in a democratic society in the interests of public safety, for the protection of public order, health or morals, or for the protection of the rights and freedoms of others.

Article 10

1. Everyone has the right to freedom of expression. This right shall include freedom to hold opinions and to receive and impart information and ideas without interference by public authority and regardless of frontiers. This Article shall not prevent States from requiring the licensing of broadcasting, television or cinema enterprises.

2. The exercise of these freedoms, since it carries with it duties and responsibilities, may be subject to such formalities, conditions, restrictions or penalties as are prescribed by law and are necessary in a democratic society, in the interests of national security, territorial integrity or public safety, for the prevention of disorder or crime, for the protection of health or morals, for the protection of the reputation or rights of others, for preventing the disclosure of information received in confidence, or for maintaining the authority and impartiality of the judiciary.

Article 11

1. Everyone has the right to freedom of peaceful assembly and to freedom of association with others, including the right to form and to join trade unions for the protection of his interests.

2. No restrictions shall be placed on the exercise of these rights other than such as are prescribed by law and are necessary in a democratic society in the interests of national security or public safety, for the prevention of disorder or crime, for the protection of health or morals or for the protection of the rights and freedoms of others. This Article shall not prevent the imposition of lawful restrictions on the exercise of these rights by members of the armed forces, of the police or of the administration of the State.

Article 12

Men and women of marriageable age have the right to marry and to found a family, according to the national laws governing the exercise of this right.

Article 13

Everyone whose rights and freedoms as set forth in this Convention are violated shall have an effective remedy before a national authority notwithstanding that the violation has been committed by persons acting in an official capacity.

Article 14

The enjoyment of the rights and freedoms set forth in this Convention shall be secured without discrimination on any ground such as sex, race, colour, language, religion, political or other opinion, national or social origin, association with a national minority, property, birth or other status.

Article 15

1. In time of war or other public emergency threatening the life of the nation any High Contracting Party may take measures derogating from its obligations under this Convention to the extent strictly required by the exigencies of the situation, provided that such measures are not inconsistent with its other obligations under international law.

2. No derogation from Article 2, except in respect of deaths resulting from lawful acts of war, or from Articles 3, 4 (paragraph 1) and 7 shall be made under this provision.

3. Any High Contracting Party availing itself of this right of derogation shall keep the Secretary-General of the Council of Europe fully informed of the measures which it has taken and the reasons therefor. It shall also inform the Secretary-General of the Council of Europe when such measures have ceased to operate and the provisions of the convention are again being fully executed.

Article 16

Nothing in Articles 10, 11, and 14 shall be regarded as preventing the High Contracting Parties from imposing restrictions on the political activity of aliens.

Article 17

Nothing in this Convention may be interpreted as implying for any State, group or person any right to engage in any activity or perform any act aimed at the destruction of any of the rights and freedoms set forth herein or at their limitation to a greater extent than is provided for in the Convention.

Article 18

The restrictions permitted under this Convention to the said rights and freedoms shall not be applied for any purpose other than those for which they have been prescribed.

Section II

Article 19

To ensure the observance of the engagements undertaken by the High Contracting Parties in the present Convention, there shall be set up:

1. A European Commission of Human Rights hereinafter referred to as 'the Commission';

2. A European Court of Human Rights, hereinafter referred to as 'the Court'.

Section III

Article 20

The Commission shall consist of a number of members equal to that of the High Contracting Parties. No two members of the Commission may be nationals of the same State.

Article 21

1. The members of the Commission shall be elected by the Committee of Ministers by an absolute majority of votes, from a list of names drawn up by the Bureau of the Consultative Assembly; each group of the Representatives of the High Contracting

Parties in the Consultative Assembly shall put forward three candidates, of whom two at least shall be its nationals.

2. As far as applicable, the same procedure shall be followed to complete the Commission in the event of other States subsequently becoming Parties to this convention, and in filling casual vacancies.

Article 22

1. The members of the Commission shall be elected for a period of six years. They may be re-elected. However, of the members elected at the first election, the terms of seven members shall expire at the end of three years.

2. The members whose terms are to expire at the end of the initial period of three years shall be chosen by lot by the Secretary-General of the Council of Europe immediately after the first election has been completed.

3. A member of the Commission elected to replace a member whose term of office has not expired shall hold office for the remainder of his predecessor's term.

4. The members of the Commission shall hold office until replaced. After having been replaced, they shall continue to deal with such cases as they already have under consideration.

Article 23

The members of the Commission shall sit on the Commission in their individual capacity.

Article 24

Any High Contracting Party may refer to the Commission through the Secretary-General of the Council of Europe, any alleged breach of the provisions of the Convention by another High Contracting Party.

Article 25

1. The Commission may receive petitions addressed to the Secretary-General of the Council of Europe from any person, non-governmental organization or group of individuals claiming to be the victim of a violation by one of the High Contracting Parties of the rights set forth in this Convention, provided that the High Contracting Party against which the complaint has been lodged has declared that it recognizes the competence of the Commission to receive such petitions. Those of the High Contracting Parties who have made such a declaration undertake not to hinder in any way the effective exercise of this right.

2. Such declarations may be made for a specific period.

3. The declarations shall be deposited with the Secretary-General of the Council of Europe who shall transmit copies thereof to the High Contracting Parties and publish them.

4. The Commission shall only exercise the powers provided for in this Article when at leas six High Contracting Parties are bound by declarations made in accordance with the preceding paragraphs.

Article 26

The Commission may only deal with the matter after all domestic remedies have been exhausted, according to the generally recognized rules of international law, and within a period of six months from the date on which the final decision was taken.

*　　*　　*

Section IV

Article 38

The European Court of Human Rights shall consist of a number of judges equal to that of the Members of the Council of Europe. No two judges may be nationals of the same State.

Article 39

1. The members of the Court shall be elected by the Consultative Assembly by a majority of the votes cast from a list of persons nominated by the Members of the Council of Europe; each Member shall nominate three candidates, of whom two at least shall be its nationals.

2. As far as applicable, the same procedure shall be followed to complete the Court in the event of the admission of new members of the Council of Europe, and in filling casual vacancies.

3. The candidates shall be of high moral character and must either possess the qualifications required for appointment to high judicial office or be jurisconsults of recognized competence.

*   *   *

Article 44

Only the High Contracting Parties and the Commission shall have the right to bring a case before the Court.

Article 45

The jurisdiction of the Court shall extend to all cases concerning the interpretation and application of the present Convention which the High Contracting Parties or the Commission shall refer to it in accordance with Article 48.

Article 46

1. Any of the High Contracting Parties may at any time declare that it recognizes as compulsory *ipso facto* and without special agreement the jurisdiction of the Court in all matters concerning the interpretation and application of the present Convention.

2. The declaration referred to above may be made unconditionally or on condition of reciprocity on the part of several or certain other High Contracting Parties or for a specified period.

3. These declarations shall be deposited with the Secretary-General of the Council of Europe who shall transmit copies thereof to the High Contracting Parties.

Article 47

The Court may only deal with a case after the Commission has acknowledged the failure of efforts for a friendly settlement and within the period of three months provided for in Article 32.

Article 48

The following may bring a case before the Court, provided that the High Contracting Party concerned, if there is only one, or the High Contracting Parties concerned, if there is more than one, are subject to the compulsory jurisdiction of the Court or, failing that, with the consent of the High Contracting Party concerned, if there is only one, or of the High Contracting Parties concerned if there is more than one:

(a) the Commission;
(b) a High Contracting Party whose national is alleged to be a victim;
(c) a High Contracting Party which referred the case to the Commission;
(d) a High Contracting Party against which the complaint has been lodged.

Article 49

In the event of dispute as to whether the Court has jurisdiction, the matter shall be settled by the decision of the Court.

Article 50

If the Court finds that a decision or a measure taken by a legal authority or any other authority of a High Contracting Party, is completely or partially in conflict with the obligations arising from the present Convention, and if the internal law of the said Party allows only partial reparation to be made for the consequences of this decision or measure, the decision of the Court shall, if necessary, afford just satisfaction to the injured party.

Article 51

1. Reasons shall be given for the judgment of the Court.

2. If the judgment does not represent in whole or in part the unanimous opinion of the judges, any judge shall be entitled to deliver a separate opinion.

Article 52

The judgment of the Court shall be final.

Article 53

The High Contracting Parties undertake to abide by the decision of the Court in any case to which they are parties.

* * *

CHARTER OF THE ORGANIZATION OF AMERICAN STATES, 1948 (OAS) (AMENDED)

In the Name of Their Peoples, the States Represented at the Ninth International Conference of American States,

Convinced that the historic mission of America is to offer to man a land of liberty, and a favorable environment for the development of his personality and the realization of his just aspirations;

Conscious that that mission has already inspired numerous agreements, whose essential value lies in the desire of the American peoples to live together in peace, and, through their mutual understanding and respect for the sovereignty of each one, to provide for the betterment of all, in independence, in equality and under law;

Confident that the true significance of American solidarity and good neighborliness can only mean the consolidation on this continent, within the framework of democratic institutions, of a system of individual liberty and social justice based on respect for the essential rights of man;

Persuaded that their welfare and their contribution to the progress and the civilization of the world will increasingly require intensive continental co-operation;

Resolved to perservere in the noble undertaking that humanity has conferred upon the United Nations, whose principles and purposes they solemnly reaffirm;

Convinced that juridical organization is a necessary condition for security and peace founded on moral order and on justice; and

In accordance with Resolution IX of the Inter-American Conference on Problems of War and Peace, held at Mexico City,

Have Agree upon the following.

Article 1

The American States establish by this Charter the international organization that they have developed to achieve an order of peace and justice, to promote their solidarity, to strengthen their collaboration, and to defend their sovereignty, their territorial integrity, and their independence. Within the United Nations, the Organization of American States is a regional agency.

Article 2

The organization of American States, in order to put into practice the principles on which it is founded and to fulfill its regional obligations under the Charter of the United Nations, proclaims the following essential purposes:

(a)   To strengthen the peace and security of the continent;

(b)   To prevent possible causes of difficulties and to ensure the pacific settlement of disputes that may arise among the Member States;

(c)   To provide for common action on the part of those States in the event of aggression;

(d)   To seek the solution of political, juridical, and economic problems that may arise among them; and

(e)   To promote, by co-operative action, their economic, social, and cultural development.

Chapter II. Principles

Article 3

The American States reaffirm the following principles:

(a)   International law is the standard of conduct of States in their reciprocal relations;

(b)   International order consists essentially of respect for the personality, sovereignty, and independence of States, and the faithful fulfilment of obligations derived from treaties and other sources of international law;

(c)   Good faith shall govern the relations between States;

(d)   The solidarity of the American States and the high aims which are sought through it require the political organization of those States on the basis of the effective exercise of representative democracy;

(e)   The American States condemn war of agression: victory does not give rights;

(f)   An act of aggression against one American State is an act of agression against all the other American States;

(g)   Controversies of an international character arising between two or more American States shall be settled by peaceful procedures;

(h)   Social justice and social security are bases of lasting peace;

(i)   Economic co-operation is essential to the common welfare and prosperity of the peoples of the continent;

(j)   The American States proclaim the fundamental rights of the individual without distinction as to race, nationality, creed, or sex;

*   *   *

Article 16

Each State has the right to develop its cultural, political, and economic life freely and naturally. In this free development, the State shall respect the rights of the individual and the principles of universal morality.

* * *

Article 30

The Member States pledge themselves to mobilize their own national human and material resources through suitable programs, and recognize the importance of operating within an efficient domestic structure, as fundamental conditions for their economic and social progress and for assuring effective inter-American cooperation.

Article 31

To accelerate their economic and social development, in accordance with their own methods and procedures and within the framework of the democratic principles and the institutions of the inter-American system, the member States agree to dedicate every effort to achieve the following basic goals:

(a) Rapid eradication of illiteracy and expansion of educational opportunities for all;

* * *

Article 36

The Member States shall extend among themselves the benefits of science and technology by encouraging the exchange and utilization of scientific and technical knowledge in accordance with existing treaties and national laws.

* * *

Article 39

The Member States, in order to accelerate their economic development, regional integration, and the expansion and improvement of the conditions of their commerce, shall promote improvement and coordination of transportation and communication in the developing countries and among the Member States.

* * *

Article 42

The Member States agree that technical and financial cooperation that seeks to promote regional economic integration should be based on the principle of harmonious, balanced, and efficient development, with particular attention to the relatively less-developed countries, so that it may be a decisive factor that will enable them to promote, with their own efforts, the improved development of their infrastructure programs, new lines of production, and export diversification.

* * *

Chapter IX. Educational, Scientific, and Cultural Standards

Article 45

The member States will give primary importance within their development plans to the encouragement of education, science, and culture, oriented toward the over-all improvement of the individual, and as a foundation for democracy, social justice, and progress.

Article 46

The Member States will co-operate with one another to meet their educational needs, to promote scientific research, and to encourage technological progress. They consider themselves individually and jointly bound to preserve and enrich the cultural heritage of the American peoples.

Article 47

The Member States will exert the greatest efforts, in accordance with their constitutional processes, to ensure the effective exercise of the right to education on the following bases:

(a) Elementary education, compulsory for children of school age, shall also be offered to all others who can benefit from it. When provided by the State it shall be without charge:

(b) Middle-level education shall be extended progressively to as much of the population as possible, with a view to social improvement. It shall be diversified in such a way that it meets the development needs of each country without prejudice to providing a general education; and

(c) Higher education shall be available to all, provided that, in order to maintain its high level, the corresponding regulatory or academic standards are met.

Article 48

The Member States will give special attention to the eradication of illiteracy, will strengthen adult and vocational education systems and will ensure that the benefits of culture will be available to the entire population. They will promote the use of all information media to fulfil these aims.

Article 49

The Member States will develop science and technology through educational and research institutions and through expanded information programs. They will organize their co-operation in these fields efficiently and will substantially increase exchange of knowledge, in accordance with national objectives and laws and with treaties in force.

Article 50

The Member States, with due respect for the individuality of each of them, agree to promote cultural exchange as an effective means of consolidating inter-American understanding; and they recognize that regional integration programs should be strengthened by close ties in the fields of education, science, and culture.

Part Two
Chapter X. The Organs

Article 51

The Organization of American States accomplishes its purposes by means of:

(a) The General Assembly;
(b) The Meeting of Consultation of Ministers of Foreign Affairs;
(c) The Councils;
(d) The Inter-American Juridical Committee;
(e) The Inter-American Commission on Human Rights;
(f) The General Secretariat;
(g) The Specialized Conferences; and
(h) The Specialized Organizations.

There may be established, in addition to those provided for in the Charter and in accordance with the provisions thereof, such subsidiary organs, agencies, and other entities as are considered necessary.

AMERICAN DECLARATION OF THE RIGHTS
AND DUTIES OF MAN, 1948

Preamble

All men are born free and equal, in dignity and in rights, and, being endowed by nature with reason and conscience, they should conduct themselves as brothers one to another.

The fulfillment of duty by each individual is a prerequisite to the rights of all. Rights and duties are interrelated in every social and political activity of man. While rights exalt individual liberty, duties express the dignity of that liberty.

Duties of a juridical nature presuppose others of a moral nature which support them in principle and constitute their basis.

Inasmuch as spiritual development is the supreme end of human existence and the highest expression thereof, it is the duty of man to serve that end with all his strength and resources.

Since culture is the highest social and historical expression of that spiritual development, it is the duty of man to preserve, practice and foster culture by every means within his power.

And, since moral conduct constitutes the noblest flowering of culture, it is the duty of every man always to hold it in high respect.

Chapter One. Rights

Article I

Every human being has the right to life, liberty and the security of his person.

Article II

All persons are equal before the law and have the rights and duties established in this Declaration, without distinction as to race, sex, language, creed or any other factor.

Article III

Every person has the right freely to profess a religious faith, and to manifest and practice it both in public and in private.

Article IV

Every person has the right to freedom of investigation, of opinion, and the expression and dissemination of ideas, by any medium whatsoever.

Article V

Every person has the right to the protection of the law against abusive attacks upon his honor, his reputation, and his private and family life.

* * *

Article X

Every person has the right to the inviolability and transmission of his correspondence.

* * *

Article XII

Every person has the right to an education, which should be based on the principles of liberty, morality and human solidarity.

Likewise every person has the right to an education that will prepare him to attain a decent life, to raise his standard of living, and to be a useful member of society.

The right to an education includes the right to equality of opportunity in every case, in accordance with natural talents, merit and the desire to realize the resources that the state or the community is in a position to provide.

Every person has the right to receive, free, at least a primary education.

Article XIII

Every person has the right to take part in the cultural life of the community, to enjoy the arts, and to participate in the benefits that result from intellectual progress, especially scientific discoveries.

He likewise has the right to the protection of his moral and material interests as regards his inventions or any literary, scientific or artistic work of which he is the author.

*   *   *

Article XXI

Every person has the right to assemble peaceably with others in a formal public meeting or an informal gathering, in connection with matters of common interest of any nature.

Article XXII

Every person has the right to associate with others to promote, exercise and protect his legitimate interests of a political, economic, religious, social, cultural, professional, labor union or other nature.

AMERICAN CONVENTION ON HUMAN RIGHTS, 1969

Preamble

The American states signatory to the present Convention,

Reaffirming their intention to consolidate in this hemisphere, within the framework of democratic institutions, a system of personal liberty and social justice based on respect for the essential rights of man;

Recognizing that the essential rights of man are not derived from one's being a national of a certain state, but are based upon attributes of the human personality, and that they therefore justify international protection in the form of a convention reinforcing or complementing the protection provided by the domestic law of the American states;

Considering that these principles have been set forth in the Charter of the Organization of American States, in the American Declaration of the Rights and Duties of Man, and in the Universal Declaration of Human Rights, and that they have been reaffirmed and refined in other international instruments, worldwide as well as regional in scope;

Reiterating that, in accordance with the Universal Declaration of Human Rights, the ideal of free men enjoying freedom from fear and want can be achieved only if conditions are created whereby everyone may enjoy his economic, social and cultural rights, as well as his civil and political rights; and

Considering that the Third Special Inter-American Conference (Buenos Aires, 1967) approved the incorporation into the Charter of the Organization itself of broader standards with respect to economic, social, and educational rights and resolved that an inter-American convention on human rights should determine the structure, competence, and procedure of the organs responsible for these matters,

Have agreed upon the following:

Part I State Obligations and Rights Protected
Chapter 1. General Obligations
Obligation to Respect Rights

Article 1

1. The States Parties to this Convention undertake to respect the rights and freedoms recognized herein and to ensure to all persons subject to their jurisdiction the free and full exercise of those rights and freedoms, without any discrimination for reasons of race, color, sex, language, religion, political or other opinion, national or social origin, economic status, birth, or any other social condition.

2. For the purposes of this Convention 'person' means every human being.

Article 2

Where the exercise of any of the rights or freedoms referred to in Article I is not already ensured by legislative or other provisions, the States Parties undertake to adopt, in accordance with their constitutional processes and the provisions of this Convention, such legislative or other measures as may be necessary to give effect to those rights or freedoms.

*   *   *

Right to Privacy

Article 11

1. Everyone has the right to have his honor respected and his dignity recognized.

2. No one may be the object of arbitrary or abusive interference with his private life, his family, his home, or his correspondence, or of unlawful attacks on his honor or reputation.

3. Everyone has the right to the protection of the law against such interference or attacks.

Freedom of Conscience and Religion

Article 12

1. Everyone has the right to freedom of conscience and of religion. This includes freedom to maintain or to change one's religion or beliefs, and freedom to profess or disseminate one's religion or beliefs either individually or together with others, in public or in private.

2. No one shall be subject to restrictions that might impair his freedom to maintain or to change his religion or beliefs.

3. Freedom to manifest one's religion and beliefs may be subject only to the limitations prescribed by law that are necessary to protect public safety, order, health, or morals, or the rights or freedoms of others.

4. Parents or guardians, as the case may be, have the right to provide for the religious and moral education of their children or wards that is in accord with their own convictions.

Freedom of Thought and Expression

Article 13

1. Everyone shall have the right to freedom of thought and expression. This right shall include freedom to seek, receive, and impart information and ideas of all kinds, regardless of frontiers, either orally, in writing, in print, in the form of art, or through any other medium of one's choice.

2. The exercise of the right provided for in the foregoing paragraph shall not be subject to prior censorship but shall be subject to subsequent imposition of liability, which shall be expressly established by law to the extent necessary in order to ensure:

(a)   respect for the rights or reputations of others; or
(b)   the protection of national security, public order, or public health or morals.

3. The right of expression may not be restricted by indirect methods or means, such as the abuse of government or private controls over newsprint, radio broadcasting frequencies, or equipment used in the dissemination of information, or by any other means tending to impede the communication and circulation of ideas and opinions.

4. Notwithstanding the provisions of paragraph 2 above, public entertainments may be subject by law to prior censorship for the sole purpose of regulating access to them for the moral protection of childhood and adolescence.

5. Any propaganda for war and any advocacy of national, racial, or religious hatred that constitute incitements to lawless violence or to any other similar illegal action against any person or group of persons on any grounds including those of race, color, religion, language, or national origin shall be considered as offenses punishable by law.

Right of Reply

Article 14

1. Anyone injured by inaccurate or offensive statements or ideas disseminated to the public in general by a legally regulated medium of communication has the right to reply or make a correction using the same communications outlet, under such conditions as the law may establish.

2. The correction or reply shall not in any case remit other legal liabilities that may have been incurred.

3. For the effective protection of honor and reputation, every publisher, and every newspaper, motion picture, radio, and television company, shall have a person responsible, who is not protected by immunities or special privileges.

Right of Assembly

Article 15

The right of peaceful assembly, without arms, is recognized. No restrictions may be placed on the exercise of this right other than those imposed in conformity with the law and necessary in a democratic society in the interest of national security, public safety or public order, or to protect public health or morals or the rights or freedoms of others.

Freedom of Association

Article 16

1. Everyone has the right to associate freely for ideological, religious, political, economic, labor, social, cultural, sports, or other purposes.

2. The exercise of this right shall be subject only to such restrictions established by law as may be necessary in a democratic society, in the interest of national security, public safety or public order, or to protect public health or morals or the rights and freedoms of others.

3. The provisions of this article do not bar the imposition of legal restrictions, including even deprivation of the exercise of the right of association, on members of the armed forces and the police.

* * *

Part II
Means of Protection
Chapter VI. Competent Organs

Article 33

The following organs shall have competence with respect to matters relating to the fulfillment of the commitments made by the States Parties to this Convention:

(a) the Inter-American Commission on Human Rights, referred to as 'The Commission'; and

(b) the.Inter-American Court of Human Rights, referred to as 'The Court.'

* * *

CHARTER OF THE ORGANIZATION OF AFRICAN UNITY, 1963 (OAU)

We, the Heads of African and Malagasy States and Governments assembled in the City of Addis Ababa, Ethiopia;

Convinced that it is the inalienable right of all people to control their own destiny;

Conscious of the fact that freedom, equality, justice, and dignity are essential objectives for the achievement of the legitimate aspirations of the African peoples;

Conscious of our responsibility to harness the natural and human resources of our continent for the total advancement of our peoples in spheres of human endeavour;

Inspired by a common determination to promote understanding among our peoples and co-operation among our States in response to the aspirations of our peoples for brotherhood and solidarity, in a larger unity transcending ethnic and national differences;

Convinced that, in order to translate this determination into a dynamic force in the cause of human progress, conditions for peace and security must be established and maintained;

Determined to safeguard and consolidate the hard-won independence as well as the sovereignty and territorial integrity of our States, and to resist neo-colonialism in all its forms;

Dedicated to the general progress of Africa;

Persuaded that the Charter of the United Nations and the Universal Declaration of Human Rights, to the principles of which we reaffirm our adherence, provide a solid foundation for peaceful and positive cooperation among states;

Desirous that all African States should henceforth unite so that the welfare and well-being of their peoples can be assured;

Resolved to reinforce the links between our States by establishing and strengthening common institutions;

Have agreed to the present Charter.

Establishment

Article 1

1. The High Contracting Parties do by the present Charter establish an Organization to be known as the *Organization of African Unity.*

2. The Organization shall include the Continental African States, Madagascar and other Islands surrounding Africa.

Purposes

Article 2

1. The Organization shall have the following purposes:

(a)   To promote the unity and solidarity of the African States;
(b)   To co-ordinate and intensify their collaboration and efforts to achieve a better life for the peoples of Africa;
(c)   To defend their sovereignty, their territorial integrity and independence;
(d)   To eradicate all forms of colonialism from the continent of Africa; and
(e)   To promote international co-operation, having due regard to the Charter of the United Nations and the Universal Declaration of Human Rights.

2. To these ends, the Member States shall co-ordinate and harmonize their general policies, especially in the following fields:

(a)   Political and diplomatic co-operation;
(b)   Economic co-operation, including transport and communications;
(c)   Educational and cultural co-operation;
(d)   Health, sanitation, and nutritional co-operation;
(e)   Scientific and technical co-operation; and
(f)   Co-operation for defence and security.

Principles

Article 3

The Member States, in pursuit of the purposes stated in Article 2, solemnly affirm and declare their adherence to the following principles:

1. The sovereign equality of all Member States;

2. Non-interference in the internal affairs of States;

3. Respect for the sovereignty and territorial integrity of each State and for its inalienable right to independent existence;

4. Peaceful settlement of disputes by negotiation, mediation, conciliation, or arbitration;

5. Unreserved condemnation, in all its forms, of political assassination as well as of subversive activities on the part of neighbouring States or any other States;

6. Absolute dedication to the total emancipation of the African territories which are still dependent;

7. Affirmation of a policy of non-alignment with regard to all blocs.

THE ASSOCIATION OF SOUTHEAST ASIAN NATIONS DECLARATION, 1967 (ASEAN)

The Presidium Minister for Political Affairs/Minister of Foreign Affairs of Indonesia, the Deputy Prime Minister of Malaysia, the Secretary for Foreign Affairs of Singapore and the Minister of Foreign Affairs of Thailand;

   Mindful of the existence of mutual interests and common problems among the countries of South-East Asia and convinced of the need to strengthen further the existing bonds of regional solidarity and co-operation;

   Aspiring to establish a firm foundation for common action to promote regional co-operation in South-East Asia in the spirit of equality and partnership and thereby contribute towards peace, progress and prosperity in the region;

Conscious that in an increasingly interdependent world, the cherished aims of peace, freedom, social justice and economic well-being are best reached by fostering good understanding, good neighborliness and meaningful co-operation among the countries of the region already bound together by ties of history and culture;

Considering that the countries of South-East Asia share a primary responsibility for strengthening the economic and social stability of the region and ensuring their peaceful and progressive national development, and that they are determined to ensure their stability and security from external interference in any form or manifestation in order to preserve their national identities in accordance with the ideals and aspirations of their peoples;

Affirming that all foreign bases are temporary and remain only with the expressed concurrence of the countries concerned and are not intended to be used directly or indirectly to subvert the national independence and freedom of States in the area or prejudice the orderly processes of their national development;

Hereby declare:

First, the establishment of an Association for Regional Co-operation among the countries of South-East Asia to be known as the Association of South-East Asian Nations (ASEAN).

Second, that the aims and purposes of the Association shall be:

1. To accelerate the economic growth, social progress and cultural development in the region through joint endeavors in the spirit of equality and partnership in order to strengthen the foundation for a prosperous and peaceful community of South-East Asian Nations;

2. To promote regional peace and stability through abiding respect of justice and the rule of law in the relationship among countries of the region and adherence to the principles of the United Nations Charter;

3. To promote active collaboration and mutual assistance on matters of common interest in the economic, social, cultural, technical, scientific and administrative fields;

4. To provide assistance to each other in the form of training and research facilities in the education, professional, technical and administrative spheres;

5. To collaborate more effectively for the greater utilization of their agriculture and industries, the expansion of their trade, including the study of the problems of international commodity trade, the improvement of their transportation and communication facilities and the raising of the living standards of their peoples;

6. To promote South-East Asian studies;

7. To maintain close and beneficial co-operation with existing international and regional organizations with similar aims and purposes, and explore all avenues for even closer co-operation among themselves.

Third, that, to carry out these aims and purposes, the following machinery shall be established:

(a) Annual Meeting of Foreign Ministers, which shall be by rotation and referred to as ASEAN Ministerial Meeting. Special Meetings of Foreign Ministers may be convened as required.

(b) A standing Committee, under the chairmanship of the Foreign Minister of the host country or his representative and having as its members the accredited Ambassadors of the other member countries, to carry on the work of the Association in between Meetings of Foreign Ministers.

(c) *Ad Hoc* Committees and Permanent Committees of specialists and officials on specific subjects.

(d) A National Secretariat in each member country to carry out the work of the Association on behalf of that country and to service the Annual or Special

Meetings of Foreign Ministers, the Standing Committee and such other committees as may hereafter be established.

Fourth, that the Association is open for participation to all States in the South-East Asian Region subscribing to the aforementioned aims, principles and purposes.

Fifth, that the Association represents the collective will of the nations of South-East Asia to bind themselves together in friendship and co-operation and, through joint efforts and sacrifices, secure for their peoples and for posterity the blessings of peace, freedom and prosperity.

Done in Bangkok on the Eighth Day of August in the Year One Thousand Nine Hundred and Sixty-Seven.

PACT OF THE LEAGUE OF ARAB STATES, 1945

His Excellency the President of the Syrian Republic;
His Royal Highness the Amir of Trans-Jordan;
His Majesty the King of Iraq;
His Majesty the King of Saudi Arabia;
His Excellency the President of the Lebanese Republic;
His Majesty the King of Egypt;
His Majesty the King of the Yemen;
Desirous of strengthening the close relations and numerous ties which link the Arab states;

And anxious to support and stabilize these ties upon a basis of respect for the independence and sovereignty of these states, and to direct their efforts towards the common good of all the Arab countries, the improvement of their status, the security of their future, the realization of their aspirations and hopes;

And responding to the wishes of Arab public opinion in all Arab lands;

Have agreed to conclude a Pact to that end and have appointed as their representatives the persons whose names are listed hereinafter; who, after having exchanged their plenary powers which were found to be in good and due form, have agreed upon the following provisions:

Article 1

The League of Arab States is composed of the independent Arab States which have signed this Pact.

Any independent Arab State has the right to become a member of the League. If it desires to do so, it shall submit a request which will be deposited with the Permanent Secretariat-General and submitted to the Council at the first meeting held after submission of the request.

Article 2

The League has as its purpose the strengthening of the relations between the member states; the co-ordination of their policies in order to achieve co-operation between them and to safeguard their independence and sovereignty; and a general concern with the affairs and interests of the Arab countries. It has also as its purpose the close co-operation of the member states, with due regard to the organization and circumstances of each state, on the following matters:

(a) Economic and financial affairs, including commercial relations, customs, currency, and questions of agriculture and industry.
(b) Communications; this includes railroads, roads, aviation, navigation, telegraphs, and posts.
(c) Cultural affairs.
(d) Nationality, passports, visas, execution of judgements, and extradition of criminals.

(e)   Social affairs.
(f)   Health problems.

Article 3

The League shall possess a Council composed of the representatives of the member states of the League; each state shall have a single vote, irrespective of the number of its representatives.

It shall be the task of the Council to achieve the realization of the objectives of the League and to supervise the execution of agreements which the member states have concluded on the questions enumerated in the preceding article, or on any other questions.

It likewise shall be the Council's task to decide upon the means by which the League is to co-operate with the international bodies to be created in the future in order to guarantee security and peace and regulate economic and social relations.

Article 4

For each of the questions listed in Article 2 there shall be set up a special committee in which the member states of the League shall be represented. These committees shall be charged with the task of laying down the principles and extent of co-operation. Such principles shall be formulated as draft agreements, to be presented to the Council for examination preparatory to their submission to the aforesaid states.

Representatives of the other Arab countries may take part in the work of the aforesaid committees. The Council shall determine the conditions under which these representatives may be permitted to participate and the rules governing such representation.

*   *   *

Article 7

Unanimous decisions of the Council shall be binding upon all member states of the League; majority decisions shall be binding only upon those states which have accepted them.

In either case the decisions of the Council shall be enforced in each member state according to its respective basic laws.

*   *   *

Article 12

The League shall have a permanent Secretariat-General, which shall consist of a Secretary-General, Assistant Secretaries, and an appropriate number of officials.

The Council of the League shall appoint the Secretary-General by a majority of two-thirds of the states of the League. The Secretary-General, with the approval of the Council, shall appoint the Assistant Secretaries and the principal officials of the League.

The Council of the League shall establish an administrative regulation for the functions of the Secretariat-General and matters relating to the Staff.

The Secretary-General shall have the rank of Ambassador and the Assistant Secretaries that of Ministers Plenipotentiary.

The first Secretary-General of the League is named in an Annex to this Pact.

*   *   *

Article 19

This Pact may be amended with the consent of two-thirds of the states belonging to the League, especially in order to make firmer and stronger the ties between the member states, to create an Arab Tribunal of Arbitration, and to regulate the relations of the League with any international bodies to be created in the future to guarantee security and peace.

Final action on an amendment cannot be taken prior to the session following the session in which the motion was initiated.

If a state does not accept such an amendment it may withdraw at such time as the amendment goes into effect, without being bound by the provisions of the preceding article.

CONVENTION OF THE ORGANISATION FOR ECONOMIC CO-OPERATION AND DEVELOPMENT, 1960 (OECD)

The Governments of the Republic of Austria, the Kingdom of Belgium, Canada, the Kingdom of Denmark, the French Republic, the Federal Republic of Germany, the Kingdom of Greece, the Republic of Iceland, Ireland, the Italian Republic, the Grand Duchy of Luxembourg, the Kingdom of the Netherlands, the Kingdom of Norway, the Portuguese Republic, Spain, the Kingdom of Sweden, the Swiss Confederation, the Turkish Republic, the United Kingdom of Great Britain and Northern Ireland and the United States of America;

Considering that economic strength and prosperity are essential for the attainment of the purposes of the United Nations, the preservation of individual liberty and the increase of general well-being;

Believing that they can further these aims most effectively by strengthening the tradition of co-operation which has evolved among them;

Recognising that the economic recovery and progress of Europe to which their participation in the Organisation for European Economic Co-operation has made a major contribution, have opened new perspectives for strengthening that tradition and applying it to new tasks and broader objectives;

Convinced that broader co-operation will make a vital contribution to peaceful and harmonious relations among the peoples of the world;

Recognising the increasing inter-dependence of their economies;

Determined by consultation and co-operation to use more effectively their capacities and potentialities so as to promote the highest sustainable growth of their economies and improve the economic and social well-being of their peoples;

Believing that the economically more advanced nations should co-operate in assisting to the best of their ability the countries in process of economic development;

Recognising that the further expansion of world trade is one of the most important factors favouring the economic development of countries and the improvement of international economic relations; and

Determined to pursue these purposes in a manner consistent with their obligations in other international organizations or institutions in which they participate or under agreements to which they are a party;

Have therefore agreed on the following provisions for the reconstitution of the Organisation for European Economic Co-operation as the Organisation for Economic Co-operation and Development:

Article 1

The aims of the Organisation for Economic Co-operation and Development (hereinafter called the "Organisation") shall be to promote policies designed:

(a)   to achieve the highest sustainable economic growth and employment and a rising standard of living in Member countries, while maintaining financial stability, and thus to contribute to the development of the world economy;

(b)   to contribute to sound economic expansion in Member as well as non-member countries in the process of economic development; and

(c) to contribute to the expansion of world trade on a multilateral, non-discriminatory basis in accordance with international obligations.

Article 2

In the pursuit of these aims, the Members agree that they will, both individually and jointly:

(a) promote the efficient use of their economic resources;
(b) in the scientific and technological field, promote the development of their resources, encourage research and promote vocational training;
(c) pursue policies designed to achieve economic growth and internal and external financial stability and to avoid developments which might endanger their economies or those of other countries;
(d) pursue their efforts to reduce or abolish obstacles to the exchange of goods and services and current payments and maintain and extend the liberalisation of capital movements; and
(e) contribute to the economic development of both Member and non-member countries in the process of economic development by appropriate means and, in particular, by the flow of capital to those countries, having regard to the importance to their economies of receiving technical assistance and of securing expanding export markets.

Article 3

With a view to achieving the aims set out in Article 1 and to fulfilling the undertakings contained in Article 2, the Members agree that they will:

(a) keep each other informed and furnish the Organisation with the information necessary for the accomplishment of its tasks:
(b) consult together on a continuing basis, carry out studies and participate in agreed projects; and
(c) co-operate closely and where appropriate take co-ordinated action.

Article 4

The Contracting Parties to this Convention shall be Members of the Organisation.

Article 5

In order to achieve its aims, the Organisation may:

(a) take decisions which, except as otherwise provided, shall be binding on all the Members;
(b) make recommendations to Members; and
(c) enter into agreements with Members, non-member States and international organisations.

Article 6

1. Unless the Organisation otherwise agrees unanimously for special cases, decisions shall be taken and recommendations shall be made by mutual agreement of all the Members.

2. Each Member shall have one vote. If a Member abstains from voting on a decision or recommendation, such abstention shall not invalidate the decision or recommendation, which shall be applicable to the other Members but not to the abstaining Member.

3. No decision shall be binding on any Member until it has complied with the requirements of its own constitutional procedures. The other Members may agree that such a decision shall apply provisionally to them.

Article 7

A Council composed of all the Members shall be the body from which all acts of the Organisation derive. The Council may meet in sessions of Ministers or of Permanent Representatives.

Article 8

The Council shall designate each year a Chairman, who shall preside at its ministerial sessions, and two Vice-Chairmen. The Chairman may be designated to serve one additional consecutive term.

Article 9

The Council may establish an Executive Committee and such subsidiary bodies as may be required for the achievement of the aims of the Organisation.

Article 10

1. A Secretary-General responsible to the Council shall be appointed by the Council for a term of five years. He shall be assisted by one or more Deputy Secretaries-General or Assistant Secretaries-General appointed by the Council on the recommendation of the Secretary-General.

2. The Secretary-General shall serve as Chairman of the Council meeting at sessions of Permanent Representatives. He shall assist the Council in all appropriate ways and may submit proposals to the Council or to any other body of the Organisation.

*   *   *

POLITICAL DECLARATION
SIXTH SUMMIT CONFERENCE OF HEADS OF STATE OR
GOVERNMENT OF NON-ALIGNED COUNTRIES, HAVANA, 1979

The Policy of Non-Alignment and the Strengthening
of its Independent Role

12. Taking into consideration the principles on which non-alignment has been based and the elaboration of those principles through the successive Summit Conferences held in Belgrade, Cairo, Lusaka, Algiers and Colombo, the Sixth Conference reaffirmed that the quintessence of the policy of non-alignment, in accordance with its original principles and essential character, involved the struggle against imperialism, colonialism, neo-colonialism, *apartheid,* racism including Zionism and all forms of foreign aggression, occupation, domination, interference or hegemony, as well as against great-Power and bloc policies. In other words, the rejection of all forms of subjugation, dependency, interference or intervention, direct or indirect, and of all pressures, whether political, economic, military or cultural, in international relations.

13. Recalling these fundamental goals and purposes of the Movement which have guided it since its inception in 1961, the Heads of State or Government reaffirmed their adherence in particular to the following principles:

National independence, sovereignty and territorial integrity, sovereign equality, and the free social development of all countries; independence of non-aligned countries from great-Power or bloc rivalries and influences and opposition to participation in military pacts and alliances arising therefrom; the struggle against imperialism, colonialism, neo-colonialism, racism including Zionism, and all forms of expansionism, foreign occupation and domination and hegemony; active peaceful coexistence among all States; indivisibility of peace and security; non-interference and non-intervention in the internal and external affairs of other countries; freedom of all States to determine their political systems and pursue economic, social and cultural development without intimidation, hindrance and pressure; establishment of a new international economic order and development of international co-operation on the basis of equality; the right to self-determination and independence of all peoples under colonial and alien domination and constant support to the struggle of national liberation movements; respect for human rights and military-political alliances and blocs and rejection of outmoded doctrines such as spheres of influence and balance of terror; permanent sovereignty over natural resources; inviolability of legally established international boundaries; non-use of force or threat of use of force and non-recognition of situations brought about by the threat or use of force; and peaceful settlement of disputes.

Basing themselves on the above-mentioned principles, the Heads of State or Government considered the following to be the essential objectives of the Non-Aligned Movement.

Preservation of the national independence, sovereignty, territorial integrity and security of non-aligned countries; elimination of foreign interference and intervention in the internal and external affairs of States and the use of the threat of force; strengthening of non-alignment as an independent non-bloc factor and the further spread of non-alignment in the world; elimination of imperialism, colonialism, neo-colonialism, *apartheid,* racism including Zionism, and all forms of expansionism, foreign occupation and domination and hegemony; support to national liberation movements struggling against colonial and alien domination and foreign occupation; safeguarding international peace and security and the universalization of the relaxation of international tensions; promotion of unity, solidarity and co-operation among non-aligned countries with a view to the achievement of the objectives of non-alignment, thus preserving its essential character; ending the arms race, particularly the nuclear arms race, and the achievement of general and complete disarmament under effective international control; the early establishment of the New International Economic Order with a view to accelerating the development of developing countries, eliminating the inequality between developed and developing countries and eradicating poverty, hunger, sickness and illiteracy in the developing countries; participation on the basis of equality in solving international issues; establishment of a democratic system of international relations based on the equality of States and respect for and the preservation of human rights and fundamental freedoms; the strengthening of the United Nations as an effective instrument for promoting international peace and security, resolving international problems and struggling against colonialism, neo-colonialism, racism, Zionism, racial discrimination and *apartheid* and as an important factor in the development of international co-operation and the establishment of equitable economic relations between States; dissolution of great-Power pacts and military alliances and interlocking arrangements arising therefrom, withdrawal of foreign military forces and dismantling of foreign military bases; promotion of economic co-operation among the non-aligned and other developing countries with a view to the achievement of collective self-reliance; establishment of a new international order in the field of information and mass media for the purpose of forging new international relations in general; and revival, preservation and enrichment of the cultural heritage of the peoples of non-aligned countries and promotion of cultural co-operation among them.

* * *

17. In the context of the above principles and objectives, the Heads of State or Government of Non-Aligned Countries reaffirmed the following criteria for participation in the Movement as members agreed upon in 1961:

   i. The country should have adopted an independent policy based on the co-existence of States with different political and social systems and on non-alignment or should be showing a trend in favour of such a policy.

   ii. The country concerned should be consistently supporting the movements for national independence.

iii. The country should not be a member of a multilateral military alliance concluded in the context of great-Power conflicts.

iv. If a country has a bilateral military agreement with a great Power or is a member of a regional defence pact, the agreement or pact should not be one deliberately concluded in the context of great-Power conflicts.

v. If it has conceded military bases to a foreign Power, the concession should not have been made in the context of great-Power conflicts.

18. The Policy of non-alignment, by acting as an independent global factor, represents an important step in mankind's search for freely established, peaceful and equitable relations among nations, irrespective of their size, geographic location, power or social systems.

19. The Conference considered that unity and mutual solidarity among the non-aligned countries were indispensable for maintaining the independence and strength of the Movement and for the realization of its objectives. Over a period of nearly two decades the Movement of Non-Aligned Countries has brought together a growing number of States and liberation movements which, despite their ideological, political, economic, social and cultural diversity, have accepted these fundamental principles and have shown their readiness to translate them into reality.

20. The non-aligned countries have demonstrated their ability, through democratic dialogue, to overcome their differences and to find a common denominator for action leading to mutual co-operation.

21. Meeting in Havana, the Conference confirmed that the policy of non-alignment constituted an important and indispensable factor in the struggle for freedom and independence of all peoples and countries, for world peace and security for all States, for the universal application of active peaceful co-existence, for the democratization of international relations, for the establishment for the New International Economic Order and for economic development and social progress. The Conference acknowledged the co-operation received by non-aligned countries from other peace-, freedom- and justice-loving, democratic and progressive States and forces in the achievement of their goals and objectives and expressed its readiness to continue to co-operate with them on the basis of equality.

FIFTH CONFERENCE OF HEADS OF STATE OR GOVERNMENT OF NON-ALIGNED COUNTRIES, COLOMBO, 1976

Decision regarding the Composition and Mandate of the Co-ordinating Bureau and Co-ordination of Action Programme

I

The Conference, at its final session, adopted the recommendations on the Composition and Mandate of the Co-ordinating Bureau, made by the Conference of Foreign Ministers, which met in Colombo.

These recommendations are as follows:

1. In the intervening period between conferences of Heads of State or Government of Non-Aligned Countries, the Co-ordinating Bureau is the organ of Non-Aligned countries entrusted with the co-ordination of their joint activities aimed at implementing decisions and programmes adopted at Summit Conferences, Ministerial Conferences, meetings of the Group of Non-Aligned Countries at the United Nations and at other gatherings of Non-Aligned countries.

2. The Co-ordinating Bureau shall be composed of representatives of Non-Aligned countries (up to 25) chosen by the Conference of Heads of State or Government of Non-Aligned Countries, taking into consideration the principles of balanced geographical distribution, continuity and rotation.

3. The Co-ordinating Bureau shall meet:

   i. at the level of Ministers of Foreign Affairs or Special Government representatives once a year or as necessary;

   ii. on a continuing basis, at the level of permanent representatives of Non-
Aligned countries at the United Nations Headquarters in New York once a
month as a rule.

4. In carrying out the functions entrusted to it by the Conference of Heads of State
or Government of Non-Aligned Countries and Ministerial Conferences of Non-
Aligned Countries, the Co-ordinating bureau shall:

   i. follow the implementation of the decisions and programmes adopted by the
conferences of Non-Aligned countries; ensure the co-ordination of activities of
Non-Aligned countries aimed at carrying out the said decisions and programmes and propose measures for ensuring and promoting their implementation;

   ii. carry out work connected with the preparation of Conferences of Heads of
States or Government, Ministerial Conferences and, if need be other meetings;

   iii. meet to consider international problems special crises situations or a matter of
immediate common concern to the Non-Aligned countries. It may recommend
appropriate action as necessary; it may also set up when necessary working or
contact groups from among all the Non-Aligned countries;

   iv. review and assist in the implementation of the sectors of the Action Programme for Economic Co-operation among Non-Aligned Countries in respect
of which responsibilities have been assigned to various member States individually or jointly;

   v. co-ordinate the joint activities of Non-Aligned countries within the framework
of the United Nations system on the basis of the decisions of conferences of
Non-Aligned countries and carry out tasks assigned to it by the Group of Non-
Aligned Countries in the United Nations, bearing in mind the necessity to co-
ordinate activity with the Group of 77; keep the Group of Non-Aligned Countries in the United Nations continually informed of its activity and maintain
constant working contact with it;

   vi. the Bureau may issue press releases or hold press conferences in order to inform the public about its activities and decisions.

*   *   *

II

The Conference decided that the Bureau will consist of 25 seats and that these seats
will be allocated between the different regions in the following manner:

Africa	12
Asia	8
Latin America	4
Europe	1

III

The Conference also decided that each of the above regions will select on the basis of
consensus, the countries which will occupy the seats allocated to it.

FINAL ACTS

CONFERENCE ON SECURITY AND CO-OPERATION IN EUROPE, HELSINKI
1975

Motivated by the political will, in the interest of peoples, to improve and intensify their relations and to contribute in Europe to peace, security, justice and co-operation as well as to rapprochement among themselves and with the other States of the world,

Determined, in consequence, to give full effect to the results of the Conference and to assure, among their States and throughout Europe, the benefits deriving from those results and thus to broaden, deepen and make continuing and lasting the process of détente,

The High Representatives of the participating States have solemnly adopted the following:

Questions Relating to Security in Europe

The States participating in the Conference on Security and Co-operating in Europe,

Reaffirming their objective of promoting better relations among themselves and ensuring conditions in which their people can live in true and lasting peace free from any threat to or attempt against their security;

Convinced of the need to exert efforts to make détente both a continuing and an increasingly viable and comprehensive process, universal in scope, and that the implementation of the results of the Conference on Security and Co-operation in Europe will be a major contribution to this process;

Considering that solidarity among peoples, as well as the common purpose of the participating States in achieving the aims as set forth by the Conference on Security and Co-operation in Europe, should lead to the development of better and closer relations among them in all fields and thus to overcoming the confrontation stemming from the character of their past relations, and to better mutual understanding;

Mindful of their common history and recognising that the existence of elements common to their traditions and values can assist them in developing their relations, and desiring to search, fully taking into account the individuality and diversity of their positions and views, for possibilities of joining their efforts with a view to overcoming distrust and increasing confidence, solving the problems that separate them and co-operating in the interest of mankind;

Recognising the indivisibility of security in Europe as well as their common interest in the development of co-operation throughout Europe and among themselves and expressing their intention to pursue efforts accordingly;

Recognising the close link between peace and security in Europe and in the world as a whole and conscious of the need for each of them to make its contribution to the strengthening of world peace and security and to the promotion of fundamental rights, economic and social progress and well-being for all peoples;

Have adopted the following:

1
(a) Declaration on Principles Guiding Relations between Participating States

The participating States,

Reaffirming their commitment to peace, security and justice and the continuing development of friendly relations and co-operation;

Recognising that this commitment, which reflects the interest and aspirations of peoples, constitutes for each participating State a present and future responsibility, heightened by experience of the past;

Reaffirming, in conformity with their membership in the United Nations and in accordance with the purposes and principles of the United Nations, their full and active support for the United Nations and for the enhancement of its rôle and effectiveness in strengthening international peace, security and justice, and in promoting the solution of international problems, as well as the development of friendly relations and co-operation among States;

Expressing their common adherence to the principles which are set forth below and are in conformity with the Charter of the United Nations, as well as their common will to act, in the application of these principles, in conformity with the purposes and principles of the Charter of the United Nations;

Declare their determination to respect and put into practice, each of them in its relations with all other participating states, irrespective of their political, economic or social systems as well as of their size, geographical location or level of economic development, the following principles, which all are of primary significance, guiding their mutual relations:

I. Sovereign equality, respect for the rights inherent in sovereignty

The participating States will respect each other's sovereign equality and individuality as well as all the rights inherent in and encompassed by its sovereignty, including in particular the right of every State to juridical equality, to territorial integrity and to freedom and political independence. They will also respect each other's right freely to choose and develop its political, social, economic and cultural systems as well as its right to determine its laws and regulations.

Within the framework of international law, all the participating States have equal rights and duties. They will respect each other's right to define and conduct as it wishes its relations with other States in accordance with international law and in the spirit of the present Declaration. They consider that their frontiers can be changed, in accordance with international law, by peaceful means and by agreement. They also have the right to belong or not to belong to international organizations, to be or not to be a party to bilateral or multilateral treaties including the right to be or not to be a party to treaties of alliance; they also have the right to neutrality.

II. Refraining from the threat or use of force

The participating States will refrain in their mutual relations, as well as in their international relations in general, from the threat or use of force against the territorial integrity or political independence of any State, or in any other manner inconsistent with the purposes of the United Nations and with the present Declaration. No consideration may be invoked to serve to warrant resort to the threat or use of force in contravention of this principle.

Accordingly, the participating States will refrain from any acts constituting a threat of force or direct or indirect use of force against another participating State. Likewise they will refrain from any manifestation of force for the purpose of inducing another participating State to renounce the full exercise of its sovereign rights. Likewise they will also refrain in their mutual relations from any act of reprisal by force.

No such threat or use of force will be employed as a means of settling disputes, or questions likely to give rise to disputes, between them.

III. Inviolability of frontiers

The participating States regard as inviolable all one another's frontiers as well as the frontiers of all States in Europe and therefore they will refrain now and in the future from assaulting these frontiers.

Accordingly, they will also refrain from any demand for, or act of, seizure and usurpation of part or all of the territory of any participating State.

IV. Territorial integrity of States

The participating States will respect the territorial integrity of each of the participating States.

Accordingly, they will refrain from any action inconsistent with the purposes and principles of the Charter of the United Nations against the territorial integrity, political independence or the unity of any participating State, and in particular from any such action constituting a threat or use of force.

The participating States will likewise refrain from making each other's territory the object of military occupation or other direct or indirect measures of force in contravention of international law, or the object of acquisition by means of such measures or the threat of them. No such occupation or acquisition will be recognised as legal.

V. Peaceful settlement of disputes

The participating States will settle disputes among them by peaceful means in such a manner as not to endanger international peace and security, and justice.

They will endeavour in good faith and a spirit of co-operation to reach a rapid and equitable solution on the basis of international law.

For this purpose they will use such means as negotiation, enquiry, mediation, conciliation, arbitration, judicial settlement or other peaceful means of their own choice including any settlement procedure agreed to in advance of disputes to which they are parties.

In the event of failure to reach a solution by any of the above peaceful means, the parties to a dispute will continue to seek a mutually agreed way to settle the dispute peacefully.

Participating States, parties to a dispute among them, as well as other participating States, will refrain from any action which might aggravate the situation to such a degree as to endanger the maintenance of international peace and security and thereby make a peaceful settlement of the dispute more difficult.

VI. Non-intervention in internal affairs

The participating States will refrain from any intervention, direct or indirect, individual or collective, in the internal or external affairs falling within the domestic jurisdiction of another participating State, regardless of their mutual relations.

They will accordingly refrain from any form of armed intervention or threat of such intervention against another participating State.

They will likewise in all circumstances refrain from any other act of military, or of political, economic or other coercion designed to subordinate to their own interest the exercise by another participating State of the rights inherent in its sovereignty and thus to secure advantages of any kind.

Accordingly, they will, *inter alia*, refrain from direct or indirect assistance to terrorist activities, or to subversive or other activities directed towards the violent overthrow of the régime of another participating State.

VII. Respect for human rights and fundamental freedoms, including the freedom of thought, conscience, religion or belief

The participating States will respect human rights and fundamental freedoms, including the freedom of thought, conscience, religion or belief, for all without distinction as to race, sex, language or religion.

They will promote and encourage the effective exercise of civil, political, economic, social, cultural and other rights and freedoms all of which derive from the inherent dignity of the human person and are essential for his free and full development.

Within this framework the participating States will recognise and respect the freedom of the individual to profess and practise, alone or in community with others, religion or belief acting in accordance with the dictates of his own conscience.

The participating States on whose territory national minorities exist will respect the right of persons belonging to such minorities to equality before the law, will afford them the full opportunity for the actual enjoyment of human rights and fundamental freedoms and will, in this manner, protect their legitimate interests in this sphere.

The participating States recognise the universal significance of human rights and fundamental freedoms, respect for which is an essential factor for the peace, justice and well-being necessary to ensure the development of friendly relations and co-operation among themselves as among all States.

They will constantly respect these rights and freedoms in their mutual relations and will endeavor jointly and separately, including in co-operation with the United Nations, to promote universal and effective respect for them.

They confirm the right of the individual to know and act upon his rights and duties in this field.

In the field of human rights and fundamental freedoms, the participating States will act in conformity with the purposes and principles of the Charter of the United Nations and with the Universal Declaration of Human Rights. They will also fulfil their obligations as set forth in the international declarations and agreements in this field, including *inter alia* the International Covenants on Human Rights, by which they may be bound.

VIII. Equal rights and self-determination of peoples

The participating States will respect the equal rights of peoples and their right to self-determination, acting at all times in conformity with the purposes and principles of the Charter of the United Nations and with the relevant norms of international law, including those relating to territorial integrity of States.

By virtue of the principle of equal rights and self-determination of peoples, all peoples always have the right, in full freedom, to determine, when and as they wish, their internal and external political status, without external interference, and to pursue as they wish their political, economic, social and cultural development.

The participating States reaffirm the universal significance of respect for and effective exercise of equal rights and self-determination of peoples for the development of friendly relations among themselves as among all States; they also recall the importance of the elimination of any form of violation of this principle.

IX. Co-operation among States

The participating States will develop their co-operation with one another and with all States in all fields in accordance with the purposes and principles of the Charter of the United Nations. In developing their co-operation the participating States will place special emphasis on the fields as set forth within the framework of the Conference on Security and Co-operation in Europe, with each of them making its contribution in conditions of full equality.

They will endeavour, in developing their co-operation as equals, to promote mutual understanding and confidence, friendly and good-neighbourly relations among themselves, international peace, security and justice. They will equally endeavour, in developing their co-operation, to improve the well-being of peoples and contribute to the fulfilment of their aspirations through, *inter alia*, the benefits resulting from increased mutual knowledge and from progress and achievement in the economic, scientific, technological, social, cultural and humanitarian fields. They will take steps to promote conditions favourable to making these benefits available to all; they will take into account the interest of all in the narrowing of differences in the levels of economic development, and in particular the interest of developing countries throughout the world.

They confirm that governments, institutions, organisations and persons have a relevant and positive rôle to play in contributing toward the achievement of these aims of their co-operation.

They will strive, in increasing their co-operation as set forth above, to develop closer relations among themselves on an improved and more enduring basis for the benefit of peoples.

X. Fulfilment in good faith of obligations under international law

The participating States will fulfil in good faith their obligations under international law, both those obligations arising from the generally recognised principles and rules of international law and those obligations arising from treaties or other agreements, in conformity with international law, to which they are parties.

In exercising their sovereign rights, including the right to determine their laws and regulations, they will conform with their legal obligations under international law; they will furthermore pay due regard to and implement the provisions in the Final Act of the Conference on Security and Co-operation in Europe.

The participating States confirm that in the event of a conflict between the obligations of the members of the United Nations under the Charter of the United Nations and their obligations under any treaty or other international agreement, their obligations under the Charter will prevail, in accordance with Article 103 of the Charter of the United Nations.

All the principles set forth above are of primary significance and, accordingly, they will be equally and unreservedly applied, each of them being interpreted taking into account the others.

The participating States express their determination fully to respect and apply these principles, as set forth in the present Declaration, in all aspects, to their mutual relations and co-operation in order to ensure to each participating State the benefits resulting from the respect and application of these principles by all.

The participating States, paying due regard to the principles above and, in particular, to the first sentence of the tenth principle, "Fulfilment in good faith of obligations under international law", note that the present Declaration does not affect their rights and obligations, nor the corresponding treaties and other agreements and arrangements.

*   *   *

PART TWO
INFORMATION LAW

In international law there is at present no generally recognized or agreed category known as 'information law'. This expression is used to cover diverse subject matters. Often it designates rules concerning freedom of information and media regulation but in other cases the same concept refers to computerized information systems and transborder data flows. Also, some subject matters included under this heading are sometimes referred to as 'the international law of communications', which is taken to include telecommunications law.

In order to reflect the evolution of concepts and the shifting concerns of the international community, the texts in this section have been divided into two sets: the first set concerns traditional concepts such as freedom of information, free flow of information and associated subject matters; the second set reflects new and emerging approaches dealing with communications development and policy, and the new international information order.

Information law in its traditional formulation is mainly associated with human rights and comprises both freedom of information and the free flow of information. The distinction between these two concepts is to some extent arbitrary since they are often seen as not only overlapping but inseparable. However, this distinction has provided the basis for the traditional division of work between the UN and Unesco. The UN under the heading of 'freedom of information' has mainly dealt with the politico-juridical aspects while Unesco's mandate has been related to practical measures to promote the flow of information.

Most of the instruments included in the first set of texts were intended to have general validity and therefore refer to information, public opinion and similar general expressions. The earlier texts often seem formulated with mainly the printed word in mind while in later texts reference is increasingly made to more encompassing concepts which also include the electronic media, such as the media of information or the mass media.

Some of the texts are more specific in that they refer to specified classes of documents or other information materials, or even to specific media. Included are also texts dealing with such related subject matters as the practice of journalism and the protection of individual rights (privacy).

In recent years, the traditional concepts of freedom of information and free flow of information and the distinction between them have been to some extent overtaken by events through the emergence of new concepts which attempt to provide a more comprehensive approach. The second set of documents reflects these emerging approaches which still have not been formulated in binding instruments.

This shift in emphasis is also reflected in a change of vocabulary. In the context both of the UN and of Unesco, the expression information is increasingly associated with the expression communication(s). Thus, relevant instruments concern 'communications' generally, communication policies and the development of communications. It is significant that recent international debate originally concerned the 'new international information order' which now has been changed to the 'new world information and communication order' to indicate the more comprehensive nature of the issues and the inter-relationship between international and national policy and practice.

The material in this section has thus been organised as follows:

A. Traditional legal regimes
  1. Historic documents
  2. Freedom of information
  3. Free flow of information
  4. Media regulation
  5. Protection of journalists and codes of ethics
  6. Protection of individual rights: privacy

B. Recent and emerging concepts
  7. Development of communications
  8. Communications policies
  9. New World Information and Communication Order
  10. Other emerging concepts: the right to communicate

1. Historic documents

The constitutional regulation of human rights found its first full expression in the French Declaration of the Rights of Man 1789 and in the US Bill of Rights 1791. Both include provisions concerning freedom of information which have influenced many constitutions in the nineteenth century and later, and international instruments of this century.

Documents

  i. Declaration of the Rights of Man and of the Citizen, France, 1789,
      – Articles 1–2, 4, 10–11
  ii. Bill of Rights, USA, 1791
      – Articles I, IV, V

DECLARATION OF THE RIGHTS OF
MAN AND OF THE CITIZEN, FRANCE, 1789

Article 1

Men are born and remain free and equal in respect of rights. Social distinctions shall be based solely upon public utility.

Article 2

The purpose of all civil associations is the preservation of the natural and imprescriptible rights of man. These rights are liberty, property and resistance to oppression.

*　　*　　*

Article 4

Liberty consists in the power of doing whatever does not injure another. Accordingly the exercise of the natural rights of every man has no other limits than those which are necessary to secure to every other man the free exercise of the same rights; and these limits are determinable only by the law.

*   *   *

Article 10

No man is to be interfered with because of his opinions, not even because of religious opinions, provided his avowal of them does not disturb public order as established by law.

Article 11

The unrestrained communication of thoughts or opinions being one of the most precious rights of man, every citizen may speak, write and publish freely, provided he be responsible for the abuse of this liberty, in the cases determined by law.

BILL OF RIGHTS, UNITED STATES, 1791

Article I

Congress shall make no law respecting an establishment of religion, or prohibiting the free exercise thereof; or abridging the freedom of speech, or of the press; or the right of the people peaceably to assemble, and to petition the government for a redress of grievances.

*   *   *

Article IV

The rights of the people to be secure in their persons, houses, papers, and effects, against unreasonable searches and seizures, shall not be violated, and no warrants shall issue, but upon probable cause, supported by Oath or affirmation, and particularly describing the place to be searched, and the persons or things to be seized.

Article V

No person shall be held to answer for a capital, or otherwise infamous crime, unless on a presentment or indictment of a Grand Jury, except in cases arising in the land or naval forces, or in the Militia, when in actual service in time of War or public danger; nor shall any person be subject for the same offence to be twice put in jeopardy of life or limb; nor shall be compelled in any Criminal Case to be a witness against himself, nor be deprived of life, liberty, or property, without due process of law; nor shall private property be taken for public use, without just compensation.

2. Freedom of information

The classical formulation of freedom of information in the modern context of human rights is to be found in the Universal Declaration of Human Rights, 1948. These provisions were later incorporated in binding instruments, the two international covenants on human rights of 1966.

Following the adoption of the general standards laid down in the Universal Declaration of Human Rights, work proceeded in the UN context on more specific agreements concerning freedom of information. In 1948, the UN convened a conference on freedom of information in Geneva which drafted proposals for three conventions;

- *on freedom of information*
- *on access to information and its transmission from country to country*

—   *on the international right of correction*

After further discussion in the Economic and Social Council (ECOSOC) and other UN organs, and in the General Assembly, agreement could, however, only be reached on the right of correction: in the form of a separate international instrument a convention was opened for signature in 1952. Adhesion though was slow and the convention did not enter into force until 1962 and has so far been ratified only by a few countries.

In 1960, ECOSOC adopted a draft Declaration on Freedom of Information which, however, has not been approved by the General Assembly. Also, a draft Convention on Freedom of Information has for a long time been the subject of debate within different organs of the UN. However, only the preamble and a few articles have been adopted by the General Assembly at successive sessions. A draft Convention on the Gathering and International Transmission of News has been approved in principle but is not yet in force.

At the regional level, the most important instruments which provide for freedom of information are the European and American conventions on human rights.

The regulation of freedom of information is clearly related to the rules concerning the free flow of information which are included in the next section.

The expression 'freedom of information' is also used in a more specific sense referring to rules for access to official documents as provided for in national legislation (e.g. the Swedish Constitution and the US Freedom of Information Act). This aspect has, however, not been regulated at the international level.

Documents

(a)   Texts adopted by the United Nations
Universal Declaration of Human Rights and subsequent Treaties
   i.   Universal Declaration of Human Rights, 1948
         —   see Articles 18–20, 29 (text included in Part One)
  ii.   International Covenant on Civil and Political Rights, 1966
         —   see Articles 18, 19, 21 (text included in Part One)
 iii.   Convention on the International Right of Correction, 1952
         —   Full text

Resolutions, draft conventions, etc.
  iv.   Calling of an International Conference on Freedom of Information
         General Assembly Resolution 59 (I), 1946
         —   Full text
   v.   False or distorted reports, General Assembly Resolution 127 (II) 1947
         —   Full text
  vi.   Draft Convention on the Gathering and International Transmission of News, ECOSOC 1948
         —   Full text
 vii.   Freedom of Information; interference with radio signals General Assembly Resolution 424 (V), 1950
         —   Full text
viii.   Draft Declaration on Freedom of Information Economic and Social

Council Resolution 756 (XXIX), 1960
 − Full text (i.e. Preamble, Articles 1-5)
ix. Freedom of Information General Assembly Resolution 2448 (XXIII), 1968
 − Full text
x. Draft Convention on Freedom of Information Third Committee of the General Assembly, 1973
 − Text as adopted by Third Committee

(b) Regional Treaties
 xi. European Convention on Human Rights, 1954
 − see Articles 9-11, (full text included in previous section)
 xii. American Convention on Human Rights, 1969
 − Articles 13, 15 (text included in previous section)

CONVENTION ON THE INTERNATIONAL RIGHT OF CORRECTION, 1952

Preamble

The Contracting States,
Desiring to implement the right of their peoples to be fully and reliably informed,
  Desiring to improve understanding between their peoples through the free flow of information and opinion,
  Desiring thereby to protect mankind from the scourge of war, to prevent the recurrence of aggression from any source, and to combat all propaganda which is either designed or likely to provoke or encourage any threat to the peace, breach of the peace, or act of aggression,
  Considering the danger to the maintenance of friendly relations between peoples and to the preservation of peace, arising from the publication of inaccurate reports,
  Considering that at its second regular session the General Assembly of the United Nations recommended the adoption of measures designed to combat the dissemination of false or distorted reports likely to injure friendly relations between States,
  Considering, however, that it is not at present practicable to institute, on the international level, a procedure for verifying the accuracy of a report which might lead to the imposition of penalties for the publication of false or distorted reports,
  Considering, moreover, that to prevent the publication of reports of this nature or to reduce their pernicious effects, it is above all necessary to promote a wide circulation of news and to heighten the sense of responsibility of those regularly engaged in the dissemination of news,
  Considering that an effective means to these ends is to give States directly affected by a report, which they consider false or distorted and which is disseminated by an information agency, the possibility of securing commensurate publicity for their corrections,
  Considering that the legislation of certain States does not provide for a right of correction of which foreign governments may avail themselves, and that it is therefore desirable to institute such a right on the international level, and
  Having resolved to conclude a Convention for these purposes,
  Have agreed as follows:

Article I

For the purposes of the present Convention:
1. "News dispatch" means news material transmitted in writing or by means of

telecommunications, in the form customarily employed by information agencies in transmitting such news material, before publication, to newspapers, news periodicals and broadcasting organizations.

2. "Information agency" means a Press, broadcasting, film, television or facsimile organization, public or private, regularly engaged in the collection and dissemination of news material, created and organized under the laws and regulations of the Contracting State in which the central organization is domiciled and which in each Contracting State where it operates, functions under the laws and regulations of that State.

3. "Correspondent" means a national of a contracting State or an individual employed by an information agency of a Contracting State, who in either case is regularly engaged in the collection and the reporting of news material, and who when outside his State is identified as a correspondent by a valid passport or by a similar document internationally acceptable.

Article II

1. Recognizing that the professional responsibility of correspondents and information agencies requires them to report facts without discrimination and in their proper context and thereby to promote respect for human rights and fundamental freedoms, to further international understanding and co-operation and to contribute to the maintenance of international peace and security,

   Considering also that, as a matter of professional ethics, all correspondents and information agencies should, in the case of news dispatches transmitted and published by them and which have been demonstrated to be false or distorted, follow the customary practices of transmitting through the same channels, or of publishing corrections of such dispatches,

   The Contracting States agree that in cases where the Contracting State contends that a news dispatch capable of injuring its relations with other States or its national prestige or dignity transmitted from one country to another by correspondents or information agencies of a Contracting or non-Contracting State and published or disseminated abroad is false or distorted, it may submit its version of the facts (hereinafter call "communiqué") to the Contracting States within whose territory such dispatch has been published or disseminated. A copy of the communiqué shall be forwarded at the same time to the correspondent or information agency concerned to enable that correspondent or information agency to correct the news dispatch in question.

2. A communiqué may be issued only with respect to news dispatches and must be without comment or expression of opinion. It should not be longer than is necessary to correct the alleged inaccuracy or distortion and must be accompanied by a verbatim text of the dispatch as published or disseminated, and by evidence that the dispatch has been transmitted from abroad by a correspondent or an information agency.

Article III

1. With the least possible delay and in any case not later than five clear days from the date of receiving a communiqué transmitted in accordance with provisions of article II, a Contracting State, whatever be its opinion concerning the facts in question, shall:

   (a) Release the communiqué to the correspondents and information agencies operating in its territory through the channels customarily used for the release of news concerning international affairs for publication; and

   (b) Transmit the communiqué to the headquarters of the information agency whose correspondent was responsible for originating the dispatch in question, if such headquarters are within its territory.

2. In the event that a Contracting State does not discharge its obligation under this article, with respect to the communiqué of another Contracting State, the latter may accord, on the basis of reciprocity, similar treatment to a communiqué thereafter submitted to it by the defaulting State.

Article IV

1. If any of the Contracting States to which a communiqué has been transmitted in accordance with article II fails to fulfil, within the prescribed time-limit, the obligations laid down in article III, the Contracting State exercising the right of correction may submit the said communiqué, together with a verbatim text of the dispatch as published or disseminated, to the Secretary-General of the United Nations and shall at the same time notify the State complained against that it is doing so. The latter State, may, within five clear days after receiving such notice, submit its comments to the Secretary-General, which shall relate only to the allegation that it has not discharged its obligations under article III.

2. The Secretary-General shall in any event, within ten clear days after receiving the communiqué, give appropriate publicity through the information channels at his disposal to the communiqué, together with the dispatch and the comments, if any, submitted to him by the State complained against.

Article V

Any dispute between any two or more Contracting States concerning the interpretation or application of the present Convention which is not settled by negotiations shall be referred to the International Court of Justice for decision unless the Contracting States agree to another mode of settlement.

Article VI

1. The present Convention shall be open for signature to all States Members of the United Nations, to every State invited to the United Nations Conference on Freedom of Information held at Geneva in 1948, and to every other State which the General Assembly may, by resolution, declare to be eligible.

2. The present Convention shall be ratified by the States signatory hereto in conformity with their respective constitutional processes. The instruments of ratification shall be deposited with the Secretary-General of the United Nations.

Article VII

1. The present Convention shall be open for accession to the States referred to in article VI(1).

2. Accession shall be effected by the deposit of an instrument of accession with the Secretary-General of the United Nations.

Article VIII

When any six of the States referred to in article VI(1) have deposited their instruments of ratification or accession, the present Convention shall come into force among them on the thirtieth day after the date of the deposit of the sixth instrument of ratification or accession. It shall come into force for each State which ratifies or accedes after that date on the thirtieth day after the deposit of its instrument of ratification or accession.

Article IX

The provisions of the present Convention shall extend to or be applicable equally to a contracting metropolitan State and to all territories, be they Non-Self-Governing,

Trust or Colonial Territories, which are being administered or governed by such metropolitan State.

Article X

Any contracting State may denounce the present Convention by notification to the Secretary-General of the United Nations. Denunciation shall take effect six months after the date of receipt of the notification by the Secretary-General.

Article XI

The present Convention shall cease to be in force as from the date when the denunciation which reduces the number of parties to less than six becomes effective.

Article XII

1. A request for the revision of the present Convention may be made at any time by any Contracting State by means of a notification to the Secretary-General of the United Nations.

2. The General Assembly shall decide upon the steps, if any, to be taken in respect of such request.

Article XIII

The Secretary-General of the United Nations shall notify the States referred to in article VI(1) of the following:

(a) Signatures, ratifications and accessions received in accordance with articles VI and VII;
(b) The date upon which the present Convention comes into force in accordance with article VIII:
(c) Denunciations received in accordance with article X;
(d) Abrogation in accordance with article XI;
(e) Notifications received in accordance with article XII.

Article XIV

1. The present Convention, of which the Chinese, English, French, Russian and Spanish texts shall be equally authentic, shall be deposited in the archives of the United Nations.

2. The Secretary-General of the United Nations shall transmit a certified copy to each State referred to in article VI(1).

3. The present Convention shall be registered with the Secretariat of the United Nations on the date of its coming into force.

CALLING OF AN INTERNATIONAL
CONFERENCE ON FREEDOM OF INFORMATION

General Assembly Resolution 59(I), 1946

The General Assembly,
Whereas
Freedom of information is a fundamental human right and is the touchstone of all the freedoms to which the United Nations is consecrated;

Freedom of information implies the right to gather, transmit and publish news anywhere and everywhere without fetters. As such it is an essential factor in any serious effort to promote the peace and progress of the world;

Freedom of information requires as an indispensable element the willingness and capacity to employ its privileges without abuse. It requires as a basic discipline the moral obligation to seek the facts without prejudice and to spread knowledge without malicious intent;

Understanding and co-operation among nations are impossible without an alert and sound world opinion which, in turn, is wholly dependent upon freedom of information;

Resolves therefore, in the spirit of paragraphs 3 and 4 of Article 1 of the Charter, to authorize the holding of a conference of all Members of the United Nations on freedom of information;

Instructs the Economic and Social Council to undertake, pursuant to Article 50 and Article 62 paragraph 4, of the Charter, the convocation of such a conference in accordance with the following guiding principles:

(a) The purpose of the Conference shall be to formulate its views concerning the rights, obligations and practices which should be included in the concept of the freedom of information;

(b) Delegations to the Conference shall include in each instance persons actually engaged or experienced in press, radio, motion pictures and other media for the dissemination of information;

(c) The Conference shall be held before the end of 1947, at such place as may be determined by the Economic and Social Council, in order to enable the Council to submit a report on the deliberations and recommendations of the Conference to the following regular session of the General Assembly.

FALSE OR DISTORTED REPORTS

General Assembly Resolution 127 (II), 1947

The General Assembly considering that under Article 1 of the Charter members are bound to develop friendly relations among themselves and to achieve international co-operation in promoting and encouraging respect for human rights and fundamental liberties;

Considering that to attain this end it is essential to facilitate and increase the diffusion in all countries of information calculated to strengthen mutual understanding and ensure friendly relations between the peoples;

Considering that substantial progress in this sphere can be achieved only if measures are taken to combat, within the limits of constitutional procedures, the publication of false or distorted reports likely to injure friendly relations between States,

Invites the Governments of States Members

1. To study such measures as might with advantage be taken on the national plane to combat, within the limits of constitutional procedures, the diffusion of false or distorted reports likely to injure friendly relations between States;

2. To submit reports on this subject to the Conference on Freedom of Information so as to provide the Conference with the data it requires to enable it to start its work immediately on a concrete basis;

DRAFT CONVENTION ON THE GATHERING AND INTERNATIONAL TRANSMISSION OF NEWS

Submitted by the Economic and Social Council to the General Assembly, 1948

The Contracting States,
Desiring to implement the right of their peoples to be fully informed,

Desiring to improve understanding between their peoples through the free flow of information and opinion,

Having resolved to conclude a Convention for this purpose,

Have agreed as follows:

Article 1

For the purposes of the present Convention:

1. "Information agency" means any Press, radio or film organization created or organized under the laws and regulations of a Contracting State, regularly engaged in the collection and dissemination of news material, and includes Press associations, news feature services, newspapers, periodicals and radio, television, facsimile and any other broadcasting organization and newsreel companies;

2. "Correspondent" means an individual employed by an information agency or a national of a Contracting State, who in either case is regularly engaged in the collection and reporting of news material, and who, when outside his State, is the holder of a valid passport identifying him as a correspondent or of a similar document internationally accepted identifying him as such;

3. "News material" means all news material, whether of information or opinion and whether visual or auditory, for dissemination to the public.

Article 2

In order to encourage the freest possible movement of correspondents in the performance of their functions, the Contracting States shall expedite, in a manner consistent with their respective laws and procedures, the administrative measures necessary for the entry into, residence in, travel through, and egress from their respective territories of correspondents of other Contracting States together with their professional equipment, and shall not impose restrictions which discriminate against such correspondents with respect to ingress into, residence in, travel through or egress from such territories.

Article 3

Each Contracting State shall, within the limits compatible with national security, permit and encourage access to news, official and non-official, for all correspondents of other Contracting States so far as possible on the same basis as for its own correspondents, and shall not discriminate among correspondents of other Contracting States as regards such access.

Article 4

The Contracting States shall permit egress from their territories of all news material of correspondents and information agencies of other Contracting States without censorship, editing or delay; provided that each of the Contracting States may make and enforce regulations relating directly to the maintenance of national security. Such of these regulations as relate to the transmission of news material shall be communicated by the State to correspondents and information agencies of other Contracting States in its territory and shall apply equally to all correspondents and information agencies of other Contracting States.

If the requirements of national security should compel a Contracting State to establish censorship in peacetime it shall:

1. Establish in advance which categories of news material are subject to previous inspection; and publish the directives of the censor announcing forbidden matters;

2. Carry out censorship as far as possible in the presence of the correspondent or of a representative of the information agency concerned;

3. Where censorship in the presence of the person concerned is not possible:

(a) Fix the time-limit allowed the censors for the return of the news material to the correspondent or information agency concerned;

(b) Require the return of news material submitted for censorship direct to the correspondent or information agency concerned so that the correspondent or agency may know at once what has been censored in the text and what use may be made of the censored information;

(c) In the case of a telegram, base the charge on the number of words composing the telegram after censorship;

(d) Return the total telegraph charges for telegrams submitted for censorship, if the transmission has been delayed more than six hours by reason of censorship and the sender has cancelled the telegram before its transmission.

Article 5

The Contracting States, while recognizing that correspondents must conform to the laws in force in the countries in which they are operating, agree that correspondents of other Contracting States legally admitted into their territories shall not be expelled on account of any lawful exercise of their right to seek, receive or impart information or opinion.

Article 6

Correspondents and information agencies of one Contracting State in the territory of another Contracting State shall have access to all facilities in that territory generally and publicly used for the international transmission of news material and may transmit news material from one territory to another including transmissions between the metropolitan and non-metropolitan territories of any State on the same basis and at the same rates applicable to all other users of such facilities for similar purposes.

Article 7

Each Contracting State shall permit all news material of correspondents and information agencies of other Contracting States to enter its territory and reach information agencies operating therein on conditions which are not less favourable than those accorded to any correspondents or information agency of any other Contracting or non-Contracting State.

Article 8

The present Convention shall not apply to any correspondent of a Contracting State who, while not otherwise admissible under article 2 into the territory of another Contracting State, is nevertheless admitted conditionally in accordance with an agreement between that other Contracting State and the United Nations, or a specialized agency thereof, in order to cover its proceedings, or pursuant to a special arrangement made by that other Contracting State in order to facilitate the entry of such correspondents.

Article 9

Nothing in this Convention shall be construed as depriving any Contracting State of its right to make and enforce laws and regulations for the protection of national security and public order.

Nothing herein contained shall be construed as depriving any Contracting State of its right to make and enforce laws and regulations prohibiting obscene news material.

Nothing in the present Convention shall limit the discretion of any Contracting

State to refuse entry into its territory to any particular person, or to restrict the period of his residence therein, provided any such restriction does not conflict with the provisions of article 5.

Article 10

(Not agreed.)

Article 11

In time of war or any other public emergency, a Contracting State may take measures derogating from its obligations under the present Convention to the extent strictly limited by the exigencies of the situation.

Any contracting State availing itself of this right of derogation shall promptly inform the Secretary-General of the United Nations of the measures which it has thus adopted and of the reasons therefor.

It shall also inform him as and when the measures cease to operate.

Article 12

The present Convention shall be ratified on behalf of the States signatory hereto in conformity with their respective constitutional procedures. The instruments of ratification shall be deposited with the Secretary-General of the United Nations, who shall notify all signatory and acceding States of each such deposit.

Article 13

The present Convention shall remain open for the accession of all States which are not signatories. Instruments of accession shall be deposited with the Secretary-General of the United Nations, who shall notify all signatory and acceding States of each such deposit.

Article 14

The present Convention shall come into force as soon as . . . States have deposited their respective instruments of ratification or accession. The Convention thereafter shall come into force with respect to each other State on the date of the deposit of its instrument of ratification or accession.

Article 15

1. Each Contracting State undertakes to take as soon as possible the necessary steps with a view to extending the provisions of the present Convention to the territories for whose foreign relations it is responsible.

To this end, having due regard to the position of each territory and particularly to the constitutional practice applicable thereto, each Contracting State may, at the time of its accession or at any time thereafter, by notification addressed to the Secretary-General of the United Nations, declare that the present Convention shall extend to any of the territories for the international relations of which it is responsible. The Convention shall extend to the territories named in the notification as from the thirtieth day after the date of receipt by the Secretary-General of the United Nations of the notification.

2. Each State which has made a declaration under paragraph 1 above extending the present Convention may, subject to the same conditions, at any time thereafter, by notification to the Secretary-General of the United Nations, declare that the Convention shall cease to extend to any territory named in the notification. The Convention shall then cease to extend to such territory as from the thirtieth day after the date of receipt by the Secretary-General of the United Nations of the notification.

Article 16

The present Convention shall remain in force indefinitely, but may be denounced by any Contracting State by means of six months' notice in writing given to the Secretary-General of the United Nations, who shall transmit a copy of the notice to each of the other Contracting States. After the expiration of this period of six months, the Convention shall cease in its effect as regards the State which denounces it, but shall remain in force for the remaining Contracting States.

In witness whereof, the Plenipotentiaries of the respective States, being duly authorized thereto, have signed the present Convention.

FREEDOM OF INFORMATION: INTERFERENCE WITH RADIO SIGNALS

General Assembly Resolution 424 (V), 1950

The General Assembly,

Whereas freedom to listen to radio broadcasts regardless of source is embodied in article 19 of the Universal Declaration of Human Rights, which reads: "everyone has the right to freedom of opinion and expression" and whereas this right "includes freedom to hold opinions without interference and to seek, receive and impart information and ideas through any media and regardless of frontier",

Whereas article 44 of the International Telecommunication Convention, Atlantic City, 1947, provides that "All stations, whatever their purpose, must be established and operated in such a manner as not to result in harmful interference to the radio service or communications of other members or associate members . . . [and that] Each member or associate member undertakes to require the private operating agencies which it recognizes and the other operating agencies duly authorized for this purpose, to observe the provisions of the preceding paragraph",

Considering that the duly authorized radio operating agencies in some countries are deliberately interfering with the reception by the people of those countries of certain radio signals originating beyond their territories, and bearing in mind the discussion which took place in the Economic and Social Council and in the Sub-Commission on Freedom of Information and of the Press on this subject,

Considering that peace among nations rests on the goodwill of all peoples and governments and that tolerance and understanding are prerequisites for establishing goodwill in the international field,

1. *Adopts* the declaration of the Economic and Social Council contained in its resolution 306 B (XI) of 9 August 1950 to the effect that this type of interference constitutes a violation of the accepted principles of freedom of information;

2. *Condemns* measures of this nature as a denial of the right of all persons to be fully informed concerning news, opinions and ideas regardless of frontiers;

3. *Invites* the governments of all Member States to refrain from such interference with the right of their peoples to freedom of information;

4. *Invites* all governments to refrain from radio broadcasts that would mean unfair attacks or slanders against other peoples anywhere and in so doing to conform strictly to an ethical conduct in the interest of world peace by reporting facts truly and objectively;

5. *Invites* also Member States to give every possible facility so that their peoples may know objectively the activities of the United Nations in promoting peace and, in particular, to facilitate the reception and transmission of the United Nations official broadcasts.

DRAFT DECLARATION ON FREEDOM OF INFORMATION

Economic and Social Council Resolution 756 (XXIX), 1960

The Economic and Social Council,
Recalling its resolutions 720 (XXVII) of 24 April 1959 and 732 (XXVIII) of 30 July 1959,
   Having in mind General Assembly Resolution 1459 (XIV) of 10 December 1959,
   Desiring to ensure freedom of information as a fundamental human right,
   Recognizing the great importance of freedom of information in the development of friendly relations among peoples and nations and in the fulfilment of the purposes of the Charter of the United Nations,
   Being aware that the General Assembly is engaged in considering the draft Convention on Freedom of Information with a view to its early adoption,
   Noting that nothing should be allowed to interrupt, hinder or prejudice General Assembly action in achieving this task as soon as possible,
   Having considered and completed a draft Declaration on Freedom of Information in the light of the comments submitted by Member States in accordance with Council resolution 732 (XXVIII), with the hope that it will promote the realization of freedom of information and assist the General Assembly in the completion of its work in this field,
   Decides to transmit to the General Assembly for its consideration the text of the draft Declaration on Freedom of Information annexed to the present resolution.

ANNEX

Draft Declaration on Freedom of Information

Preamble

Whereas the development of friendly relations among nations and the promotion of respect for human rights and fundamental freedoms for all are basic purposes of the United Nations,
   Whereas the Universal Declaration of Human Rights affirms: "Everyone has the right to freedom of opinion and expression; this right includes freedom to hold opinions without interference and to seek, receive and impart information and ideas through any media and regardless of frontiers",
   Whereas freedom of information is essential to the respect for other human rights and fundamental freedoms, since no other liberty is secure if information cannot be freely sought, received and imparted,
   Whereas freedom of information is also fundamental to peaceful and friendly relations between peoples and nations, since the erection of barriers to the free flow of information obstructs international understanding and thus impairs prospects for world peace,
   Whereas newspapers, periodicals, books, radio, television, films and other media of information play an important role in enabling people to acquire the knowledge of public affairs necessary for the discharge of their responsibilities as citizens, and in shaping the attitudes of peoples and nations to each other, and therefore bear a great responsibility for conveying accurate information,
   Now, therefore, the General Assembly,
   Desiring to reaffirm the principles which should be upheld and observed and which domestic law and international conventions and other instruments for the protection of freedom of information should support and endeavour to promote,
   Proclaims this Declaration on Freedom of Information in proof of its determination

that all peoples should fully enjoy free interchange of information and access to all media of expression:

Article 1

The right to know and the right freely to seek the truth are inalienable and fundamental rights of man. Everyone has the right, individually and collectively, to seek, receive and impart information.

Article 2

All governments should pursue policies under which the free flow of information, within countries and across frontiers, will be protected. The right to seek and transmit information should be assured in order to enable the public to ascertain facts and appraise events.

Article 3

Media of information should be employed in the service of the people. No Government or public or private body or interests should exercise such control over media for disseminating information as to prevent the existence of a diversity of sources of information or to deprive the individual of free access to such sources. The development of independent national media of information should be encouraged.

Article 4

The exercise of these rights and freedoms entails special responsibilities and duties. Those who disseminate information must strive in good faith to ensure the accuracy of the facts reported and respect the rights and the dignity of nations, and of groups and individuals without distinction as to race, nationality or creed.

Article 5

The rights and freedoms proclaimed above should be universally recognized and respected, and may in no case be exercised contrary to the purposes and principles of the United Nations. They should be subject only to such limitations as are determined by law solely for the purpose of securing due recognition and respect for the rights and freedoms of others and of meeting the just requirements of national security, public order, morality and the general welfare in a democratic society.

FREEDOM OF INFORMATION

General Assembly Resolution 2448 (XXIII), 1968

The General Assembly,
Having regard to article 19 of the Universal Declaration of Human Rights which ensures to everyone the right to freedom of opinion and expression, including freedom to hold opinions without interference and to seek, receive and impart information and ideas through any media and regardless of frontiers,

Recalling further its resolution 2081 (XX) of 20 December 1965 by which it, *inter alia,* decided to hasten the conclusion, among other instruments, of a convention on freedom of information,

Recognizing that freedom of information is indispensable to the enjoyment, promotion and protection of all the other rights and freedoms set forth in the Universal Declaration of Human Rights,

Recalling its resolutions concerning racism, nazism, racial discrimination and other similar ideologies,

Recalling also its resolutions and the decisions of other United Nations bodies regarding the dissemination of information on the evils of *apartheid,* racial discrimination and colonialism,

Recalling the deep interest which the United Nations has shown since 1947 in problems of freedom of information and the various measures, thus far inadequate, which it has taken to promote and safeguard this freedom,

Mindful that recent technological advances in the field of telecommunications have, by enormously extending the reach and scope of words, images and ideas, greatly magnified the potentialities, for good or evil, of the media of information,

Recognizing that the existence of monopolies in the media of information is an obstacle to economic and social progress and prevents the full achievement of freedom of information,

Believing that the time has come for the international community to take a renewed interest in measures calculated to promote freedom of information and to encourage the responsible exercise of this freedom,

1. *Affirms* the principle that the primary function of media of information anywhere in the world is to gather and impart freely and responsibly objective and accurate information;

2. *Emphasizes* that the objectives of freedom of information could best be attained if everyone had access to diverse sources of news and opinions;

3. *Recommends* to all States and international organizations concerned that freedom of information should be particularly promoted in the case of dissemination of information on the evils of *apartheid,* racism, nazism, colonialism and racial discrimination;

4. *Appeals* to the media of information everywhere to co-operate in the strengthening of democratic institutions, the promotion of economic and social progress and friendly relations among nations, and combating propaganda for war or for national, racial or religious hatred, in accordance with the principles of the United Nations;

5. *Draws* the attention of the United Nations bodies and specialized agencies concerned to the continuing need for assistance in the development and improvement of information media in the developing countries in order to enable the latter to share in the benefits flowing from the modern technological revolution and to redress the inequality in this field between the developed and the developing countries;

6. *Commends* the existing practice of triennial reporting on freedom of information under the system of periodic reports on human rights and recommends the consideration of the possibility of appointing, as may be necessary, a special rapporteur on freedom of information to conduct an independent and objective study of the actual situation and developments in this field;

7. *Decides,* pending completion of the draft Convention on Freedom of Information, to give priority at its twenty-fourth session to the consideration and adoption of the draft Declaration on Freedom of Information so that it may serve as an inspiration and set a standard for information media as well as Governments anywhere in the world.

DRAFT CONVENTION ON FREEDOM OF INFORMATION, AS ADOPTED BY THE THIRD COMMITTEE, 1973

Preamble

The States Parties to this Convention,
Bearing in mind the Charter of the United Nations and the Universal Declaration of Human Rights,

Considering that freedom of expression, information and opinions are fundamental human rights,

Considering that the free interchange of accurate, objective and comprehensive information and of opinions, both in the national and in the international spheres, is essential to the causes of democracy and peace and for the achievement of political, social, cultural and economic progress,

Considering that freedom of information implies respect for the right of everyone to form an opinion through the fullest possible knowledge of the facts,

Desiring to co-operate fully with one another to guarantee these freedoms and to promote democratic institutions, friendly relations between States and peoples and the peace and welfare of mankind, and

Recognizing that in order to achieve these aims the media of information should be free from pressure or dictation, but that these media, by virtue of their power for influencing public opinion, bear to the peoples of the world a great responsibility, and have the duty to respect the truth and to promote understanding among nations,

Have accepted the following provisions:

Article 1

Subject to the provisions of this Convention,

(a) Each Contracting State undertakes to respect and protect the right of every person to have at his disposal diverse sources of information;

(b) Each Contracting State shall secure to its own nationals, and to such of the nationals of every other Contracting State as are lawfully within its territory, freedom to gather, receive and impart without governmental interference, save as provided in article 2, and regardless of frontiers, information and opinions orally, in writing or in print, in the form of art or by duly licensed visual or auditory devices;

(c) No Contracting State shall regulate or control the use or availability of any of the means of communication referred to in the preceding paragraph in any manner discriminating against any of its own nationals or of such of the nationals of any other Contracting State as are lawfully within its territory on political grounds or on the basis of their race, sex, language or religion.

Article 2

1. The exercise of the freedoms referred to in article 1 carries with it duties and responsibilities. It may, however, be subject only to such necessary restrictions as are clearly defined by law and applied in accordance with the dissemination of false reports harmful to friendly relations among nations and of expressions inciting to war or to national, racial or religious hatred; attacks on founders of religions, incitement to violence and crime; public health and morals; the rights, honour and reputation of others, and the fair administration of justice.

2. The restrictions specified in the preceding paragraph shall not be deemed to justify the imposition by any State of prior censorship on news comments and political opinions and may not be used as grounds for restricting the right to criticize the Government.

Article 3

Nothing in the present Convention may be interpreted as limiting or derogating from any of the rights and freedoms to which the present Convention refers which may be guaranteed under the laws of any Contracting State or any convention to which it is a party.

Article 4

The Contracting States recognize that the right of reply is a corollary of freedom of information and may establish appropriate means for safeguarding that right.

Articles 5 to 8 of the draft Convention on Freedom of Information, not yet considered by the Third Committee

Article 5

Each Contracting State shall encourage the establishment and functioning within its territory of one or more non-official organizations of persons employed in the dissemination of information and opinions to the public, so that such persons may thus be encouraged to observe high standards of professional conduct and, in particular, the moral obligation to report facts without prejudice and in their proper context and to make comments without malicious intent, and thereby to:

(a) Facilitate the solution of the economic, social and humanitarian problems of the world as a whole, by the free exchange of information bearing on them;
(b) Help to promote respect for human rights and fundamental freedoms without discrimination;
(c) Help to maintain international peace and security;
(d) Counteract the dissemination of false or distorted reports which offend the national dignity of peoples or promote hatred or prejudice against other States, or against persons or groups of different race, language, religion or philosophical conviction; or
(e) Combat any form of propaganda for war.

Article 6

Nothing in the present Convention shall affect the right of any Contracting State to take measures which it deems necessary in order to safeguard its external financial position and balance of payments.

Article 7

Nothing in the present Convention shall affect the right of any Contracting State to take measures which it deems necessary in order:

(a) To develop and protect its national news enterprises until such time as they are fully developed;
(b) To prevent restrictive or monopolistic practices or agreements in restraint of the free flow of information and opinions;
(c) To control international broadcasting originating within its territory, provided that such measures may not be used as a means of preventing the entry, movement or residence of nationals of other Contracting States engaged in the gathering and transmission of information and opinions for dissemination to the public.

Article 8

Nothing in the present convention shall prevent a Contracting State from reserving under its legislation to its own nationals the right to edit newspapers or news periodicals produced within its territory, or the right to own or operate telecommunication facilities, including radio broadcasting stations, within its territory.

3. Free Flow of Information

The concept of the free flow of information is closely related to freedom of information, but the international texts included in this section are specific in their focus on measures designed to promote and facilitate the flow of information whether in general terms or with reference to specific kinds of materials.

The instruments included in this section should be seen in relation to telecommunications law, and to postal agreements and customs regulation with regard to information fixed on a physical support. The flow of information is also conditioned by rules for the protection of private rights as in the case of privacy rules and international agreements concerning intellectual property rights.

Early international agreements concerning the flow of information mainly seem to be of two kinds:

i. Agreements designed to further specific kinds of exchanges as for example:
    − Convention for the International Exchange of Official Documents and of Scientific and Literary Publications, Brussels, 1886
    − Convention for the Exchange of Official Journals and of Parliamentary Records and Documents, Brussels, 1886
    − Convention relative to the Exchange of Official, Scientific, Literary and Industrial Publications, Mexico, 1901
    − Convention on Interchange of Publications, Buenos Aires, 1936
    − Convention concerning Facilities for Educational and Publicity Films, Buenos Aires, 1936
    − Convention concerning Artistic Exhibitions, Buenos Aires, 1936
ii. Agreements designed to prohibit the circulation of certain materials:
    − Convention for the suppression of the circulation of and traffic in obscene publications, concluded at Geneva on 12 September 1923 as amended by the Protocol signed at Lake Success, New York on 12 November 1947.
    − Agreement for the suppression of the circulation of obscene publications, signed at Paris on 3 May 1910, as amended by the Protocol signed at Lake Success, New York, on 4 May 1949.

The texts of the above instruments are not included.

In modern international law general references to the free flow of information are included in human rights instruments and in other binding instruments such as the Unesco Constitution. The Unesco General Conference has regularly considered issues of free flow of information in connection with the bi-annual programme of the Organization (not included in this context). Following the general provisions laid down in its constitution, Unesco has promoted the free flow of information in more specific terms, through the agreements on the circulation and importation of scientific, educational and cultural materials (Beirut and Florence Agreements). References to the free flow of information have been included in such general instruments as the Mass Media Declaration of 1978 (see Section 4 below).

Other recent international instruments include important provisions concerning the flow of information such as the Final Acts of the Conference on Security and Co-operation in Europe and the Buenos Aires Plan of Action for Promoting and Implementing Technical Co-operation among Developing Countries.

It should also be noted that rules for the collection, circulation and exchange of information are often included in international agreements covering a variety of international activities and reporting duties. Examples are rules adopted within the framework of the International Atomic Energy Agency, the World Meteorological Organization, the World Health Organization and others.

In recent years the traditional concept of free flow of information has been questioned particularly by the developing countries which have proposed new approaches such as the 'free and balanced' or the 'free and equitable' flow of information. Since these concepts are generally linked to the demands for a new international information order the relevant texts are to be found in Section 8.

Documents

(a) Unesco sponsored instruments

Treaties
   i. Constitution of the United Nations Educational, Scientific and Cultural Organization, 1945
      – see Preamble and Article 1 (text included in Part One)
  ii. Agreement for facilitating the international circulation of visual and auditory materials of an educational, scientific and cultural character, 1948 (Beirut Agreement)
      – Full text
 iii. Agreements on the Importation of Educational, Scientific and Cultural Materials, 1950 (Florence Agreement) Additional Protocol, 1976
      – Full text

Declarations and Resolutions
See Declaration of Guiding Principles on the Use of Satellites for Broadcasting, 1974; in Part Four: Space Law

Mass Media Declaration, 1978, in Section 4 below

See also texts included in Sections 7–9 concerning Development of Communications, Communications policy and study, New World Information and Communication Order

(b) Instruments adopted by other organisations
  vi. Final Acts, Conference on Security and Co-operation in Europe, 1975
      – Co-operation in Humanitarian and other Fields:
        2–3 (Information, Co-operation and Exchanges in the Field of Culture)
 vii. Buenos Aires Plan of Action for Promoting and Implementing Technical Co-operation among Developing Countries, 1978
      – Introduction
      – Objectives, points 15–16
      – Action, points 17, 23, 29, 31–32, 40, 47, 49–50, 54

AGREEMENT FOR FACILITATING THE
INTERNATIONAL CIRCULATION OF VISUAL AND AUDITORY MATERIALS
OF AN EDUCATIONAL, SCIENTIFIC AND CULTURAL CHARACTER, 1948

The governments of the States signatory to the present Agreement,
   Being convinced that in facilitating the international circulation of visual and auditory materials of an educational, scientific and cultural character, the free flow of ideas by word and image will be promoted and the mutual understanding of peoples thereby encouraged, in conformity with the aims of the United Nations Educational, Scientific and Cultural Organization,
   Have agreed as follows:

Article I

The present Agreement shall apply to visual and auditory materials of the types specified in article II which are of an educational, scientific or cultural character.

Visual and auditory materials shall be deemed to be of an educational, scientific and cultural character:

(a) when their primary purpose or effect is to instruct or inform through the development of a subject or aspect of a subject, or when their content is such as to maintain, increase or diffuse knowledge, and augment international understanding and goodwill; and

(b) when the materials are representative, authentic, and accurate; and

(c) when the technical quality is such that it does not interfere with the use made of the material.

Article II

The provisions of the preceding article shall apply to visual and auditory materials of the following types and forms:

(a) Films, filmstrips and microfilm in either negative form, exposed and developed, or positive form, printed and developed;

(b) Sound recordings of all types and forms;

(c) Glass slides: models, static and moving; wall charts, maps and posters.

These materials are hereinafter referred to as 'material'.

Article III

1. Each of the contracting States shall accord, within six months from the coming into force of the present Agreement with respect to that State, exemption from all customs duties and quantitative restrictions and from the necessity of applying for an import licence in respect of the importation, either permanent or temporary, of material originating in the territory of any of the other contracting States.

2. Nothing in this Agreement shall exempt material from those taxes, fees, charges or exactions which are imposed on the import of all articles without exception and without regard to their nature and origin, even though such articles are exempt from customs duties; such taxes, fees and exactions shall include, but are not limited to, nominal statistical fees and stamp duties.

3. Material entitled to the privileges provided by paragraph 1 of this article shall be exempt, in the territory of the country of entry, from all internal taxes, fees, charges or exactions other or higher than those imposed on like products of that country, and shall be accorded treatment no less favourable than that accorded like products of that country in respect of all internal laws, regulations or requirements affecting its sale, transportation or distribution or affecting its processing, exhibition or other use.

4. Nothing in this Agreement shall require any contracting State to deny the treatment provided for in this article to like material of an educational, scientific or cultural character originating in any State not a party to this Agreement in any case in which the denial of such treatment would be contrary to an international obligation or to the commercial policy of such contracting State.

Article IV

1. To obtain the exemption, provided under the present Agreement for material for which admission into the territory of a contracting State is sought, a certificate that such material is of an educational, scientific or cultural character within the meaning of Article I, shall be filed in connexion with the entry.

2. The certificate shall be issued by the appropriate governmental agency of the State wherein the material to which the certificate relates originated, or by the

United Nations Educational, Scientific and Cultural Organization as provided for in paragraph 3 of this article, and in the forms annexed hereto. The prescribed forms of certificate may be amended or revised upon mutual agreement of the contracting States, provided such amendment or revision is in conformity with the provisions of this Agreement.

3. Certificates shall be issued by the United Nations Educational, Scientific and Cultural Organization for material of educational, scientific or cultural character produced by international organizations recognized by the United Nations or by any of the Specialized Agencies.

4. On the filing of any such certificate, there will be a decision by the appropriate governmental agency of the contracting State into which entry is sought as to whether the material is entitled to the privilege provided by Article III, paragraph 1, of the present Agreement. This decision shall be made after consideration of the material and through the application of the standards provided in Article I. If, as a result of that consideration, such agency of the contracting State into which entry is sought intends not to grant the privileges provided by Article III, paragraph 1, to that material because it does not concede its educational, scientific and cultural character, the government of the State which certified the material, or Unesco, as the case may be, shall be notified prior to any final decision in order that it may make friendly representations in support of the exemption of that material to the government of the other State into which entry is sought.

5. The governmental agency of the contracting State into which entry is sought shall be entitled to impose regulations upon the importer of the material to ensure that it shall only be exhibited or used for non-profit-making purposes.

6. The decision of the appropriate governmental agency of the contracting State into which entry is sought, provided for in paragraph 4 of this article shall be final, but in making its decision the said agency shall give due consideration to any representations made to it by the government certifying the material or by Unesco as the case may be.

Article V

Nothing in the present Agreement shall affect the right of the contracting States to censor material in accordance with their own laws or to adopt measures to prohibit or limit the importation of material for reasons of public security or order.

Article VII

The contracting States undertake jointly to consider means of reducing to a minimum the restrictions that are not removed by the present Agreement which might interfere with the international circulation of the material referred to in Article I.

AGREEMENT ON THE IMPORTATION OF EDUCATIONAL,
SCIENTIFIC AND CULTURAL MATERIALS, 1950

Preamble

The contracting States,
   Considering that the free exchange of ideas and knowledge and, in general, the widest possible dissemination of the diverse forms of self-expression used by civilizations are vitally important both for intellectual progress and international understanding, and consequently for the maintenance of world peace;
   Considering that this interchange is accomplished primarily by means of books, publications and educational, scientific and cultural materials;

Considering that the Constitution of the United Nations Educational, Scientific and Cultural Organization urges cooperation between nations in all branches of intellectual activity, including 'the exchange of publications, objects of artistic and scientific interest and other materials of information' and provides further that the Organization shall 'collaborate in the work of advancing the mutual knowledge and understanding of peoples, through all means of mass communication and to that end recommend such international agreements as may be necessary to promote the free flow of ideas by word and image';

Recognize that these aims will be effectively furthered by an international agreement facilitating the free flow of books, publications and educational, scientific and cultural materials; and

Have, therefore, agreed to the following provisions:

Article I

1. The contracting States undertake not to apply customs duties or other charges on, or in connexion with, the importation of:

(a) Books, publications and documents, listed in Annex A to this Agreement;
(b) Educational, scientific and cultural materials, listed in Annexes B, C, D and E to this Agreement;

which are the products of another contracting State, subject to the conditions laid down in those annexes.

2. The provisions of paragraph 1 of this article shall not prevent any contracting State from levying on imported materials:

(a) Internal taxes or any other internal charges of any kind, imposed at the time of importation or subsequently, not exceeding those applied directly or indirectly to like domestic products;
(b) Fees and charges, other than customs duties, imposed by governmental authorities on, or in connexion with, importation, limited in amount to the approximate cost of the services rendered, and representing neither an indirect protection to domestic products nor a taxation of imports for revenue purposes.

Article II

1. The contracting States undertake to grant the necessary licences and/or foreign exchange for the importation of the following articles:

(a) Books and publications consigned to public libraries and collections and to the libraries and collections of public, educational, research or cultural institutions;
(b) Official government publications, that is, official, parliamentary and administrative documents published in their country of origin;
(c) Books and publications of the United Nations or any of its Specialized Agencies;
(d) Books and publications received by the United Nations Educational, Scientific and Cultural Organization and distributed free of charge by it or under its supervision;
(e) Publications intended to promote tourist travel outside the country of importation, sent and distributed free of charge;
(f) Articles for the blind:
  i. Books, publications and documents of all kinds with raised characters for the blind;
  ii. Other articles specially designed for the educational, scientific or cultural advancement of the blind which are imported directly by institutions or organizations concerned with the welfare of the blind approved by the competent authorities of the importing country for the purpose of duty-free entry of these types of articles.

2. The contracting States which at any time apply quantitative restrictions and ex-

change control measures undertake to grant, as far as possible, foreign exchange and licence necessary for the importation of other educational, scientific or cultural materials, and particularly the materials referred to in the annexes to this Agreement.

Article III

1. The contracting States undertake to give every possible facility to the importation of educational, scientific or cultural materials, which are imported exclusively for showing at a public exhibition approved by the competent authorities of the importing country and for subsequent re-exportation. These facilities shall include the granting of the necessary licences and exemption from customs duties and income taxes and charges of all kinds payable on importation other than fees and charges corresponding to the approximation of services rendered.

2. Nothing in this article shall prevent the authorities of the importing country from taking such steps as may be necessary to ensure that the materials in question shall be re-exported at the close of their exhibition.

Article IV

The contracting States undertake that they will as much as possible:
(a) Continue their common efforts to promote by all means the free circulation of educational, scientific and cultural materials, and abolish or reduce any restrictions to that free circulation which are not referred to in this Agreement;
(b) Simplify the administration procedure governing the importation of educational, scientific or cultural materials;
(c) Facilitate the expeditious and safe customs clearance of educational, scientific or cultural materials.

Article V

Nothing in this Agreement shall affect the right of contracting States to take measures, in conformity with their legislation to prohibit or limit the importation, or the circulation on importation, of articles on grounds relating directly to internal security, public order or public morals.

Article VI

This Agreement shall not modify or affect the laws and regulations of any contracting State or any of its international treaties, conventions, agreements or proclamations, with respect to copyright, trade marks or patents.

ANNEXES

Annex A

Books, publications and documents
  i.   Printed books.
 ii.   Newspapers and periodicals.
iii.   Books and documents produced by duplicating processes other than printing.
 iv.   Official government publications, that is, official, parliamentary and administrative documents published in their country of origin.
  v.   Travel posters and travel literature (pamphlets, guides, time-tables, leaflets and similar publications), whether illustrated or not, including those published by private commercial enterprises, whose purpose is to stimulate travel outside the country of importation.
 vi.   Publications whose purpose is to stimulate study outside the country of importation.

vii. Manuscripts, including typescripts.
viii. Catalogues of books and publications, being books and publications offered for sale by publishers or booksellers established outside the country of importation.
ix. Catalogues of films, recordings or other visual and auditory material of an educational, scientific or cultural character, being catalogues issued by or on behalf of the United Nations or any of its Specialized Agencies.
x. Music in manuscript or printed form, or reproduced by duplicating processes other than printing.
xi. Geographical, hydrographical or astronomical maps and charts.
xii. Architectural, industrial or engineering plans and designs, and reproductions thereof, intended for study in scientific establishments or educational institutions approved by the competent authorities of the importing country for the purpose of duty-free admission of these types of articles.

The exemptions provided by Annex A shall not apply to:
(a) Stationery;
(b) Books, publications and documents (except catalogues, travel posters and travel literature referred to above) published by or for a private commercial enterprise, essentially for advertising purposes;
(c) Newspapers and periodicals in which the advertising matter is in excess of 70 per cent by space;
(d) All other items (except catalogues referred to above) in which the advertising matter is in excess of 25 per cent by space. In the case of travel posters and literature, this percentage shall apply only to private commercial advertising matter.

Annex B

Works of art and collectors' pieces of an educational, scientific or cultural character
i. Paintings and drawings, including copies, executed entirely by hand, but excluding manufactured decorated wares.
ii. Handprinted impressions, produced from hand-engraved or hand-etched blocks, plates or other material, and signed and numbered by the artist.
iii. Original works of art of statuary or sculpture, whether in the round, in relief, or in intaglio, excluding mass-produced reproductions and works of conventional craftsmanship of a commercial character.
iv. Collectors' pieces and objects of art consigned to public galleries, museums and other public institutions, approved by the competent authorities of the importing country for the purpose of duty-free entry of these types of articles, not intended for resale.
v. Collections and collectors' pieces in such scientific fields as anatomy, zoology, botany, mineralogy, palaeontology, archaeology and ethnography, not intended for resale.
vi. Antiques, being articles in excess of 100 years of age.

Annex C

Visual and auditory materials of an educational, scientific or cultural character
i. Films, filmstrips, microfilms and slides, of an educational, scientific or cultural character, when imported by organizations (including, at the discretion of the importing country, broadcasting organizations), approved by the competent authorities of the importing country for the purpose of duty-free admission of these types of articles, exclusively for exhibition by these organizations or by other public or private educational, scientific or cultural institutions or societies approved by the aforesaid authorities.
ii. Newsreels (with or without sound track), depicting events of current news value at the time of importation, and imported in either negative form, ex-

posed and developed, or positive form, printed and developed, when imported by organizations (including, at the discretion of the importing country, broadcasting organizations) approved by the competent authorities of the importing country for the purpose of duty-free admission of such films provided that free entry may be limited to two copies of each subject for copying purposes.

iii. Sound recordings of an educational, scientific or cultural character for use exclusively in public or private educational, scientific or cultural institutions or societies (including, at the discretion of the importing country, broadcasting organizations) approved by the competent authorities of the importing country for the purpose of duty-free admission of these types of articles.

iv. Films, filmstrips, microfilms and sound recordings of an educational, scientific or cultural character produced by the United Nations or any of its Specialized Agencies.

v. Patterns, models and wall charts for use exclusively for demonstrating and teaching purposes in public or private educational, scientific or cultural institutions approved by the competent authorities of the importing country for the purpose of duty-free admission of these types of articles.

Annex D

Scientific instruments or apparatus
Scientific instruments or apparatus, intended exclusively for educational purposes or pure scientific research, provided:

(a) That such scientific instruments or apparatus are consigned to public or private scientific or educational institutions approved by the competent authorities of the importing country for the purpose of duty free entry of these types of articles, and used under the control and responsibility of these institutions;

(b) That instruments or apparatus of equivalent scientific value are not being manufactured in the country of importation.

Annex E

Articles for the blind
i. Books, publications and documents of all kinds in raised characters for the blind.

ii. Other articles specially designed for the educational, scientific, or cultural advancement of the blind, which are imported directly by institutions or organizations concerned with the welfare of the blind approved by the competent authorities of the importing country for the purpose of duty-free entry of these types of articles.

PROTOCOL TO THE AGREEMENT ON THE IMPORTATION OF EDUCATIONAL, SCIENTIFIC AND CULTURAL MATERIALS, 1976

The contracting States parties to the Agreement on the Importation of Educational, Scientific and Cultural Materials, adopted by the General Conferences of the United Nations Educational, Scientific and Cultural Organization at its fifth session held in Florence in 1950,

Reaffirming the principles on which the Agreement, hereinafter called "the Agreement", is based,

Considering that this Agreement has proved to be an effective instrument in lowering customs barriers and reducing other economic restrictions that impede the exchange of ideas and knowledge,

Considering, nevertheless, that in the quarter of a century following the adoption of the Agreement, technical progress has changed the ways and means of transmitting information and knowledge, which is the fundamental objective of that Agreement,

Considering, further, that the developments that have taken place in the field of international trade during this period have, in general, been reflected in greater freedom of exchanges,

Considering that since the adoption of the Agreement, the international situation has changed radically owing to the development of the international community, in particular through the accession of many States to independence,

Considering that the needs and concerns of the developing countries should be taken into consideration, with a view to giving them easier and less costly access to education, science, technology and culture,

Recalling the provision of the Convention on the means of prohibiting and preventing the illicit import, export and transfer of ownership of cultural property, adopted by the General Conference of Unesco in 1970, and those of the Convention concerning the protection of the world cultural and natural heritage, adopted by the General Conference in 1972,

Recalling, moreover, the customs conventions concluded under the auspices of the Customs Co-operation Council, in consultation with the United Nations Educational, Scientific and Cultural Organization, concerning the temporary importation of educational, scientific and cultural materials,

Convinced that new arrangements should be made and that such arrangements will contribute even more effectively to the development of education, science and culture which constitute the essential bases of economic and social progress,

Recalling resolution 4.112 adopted by the General Conference of Unesco at its eighteenth session,

Have agreed as follows:

I

1. The contracting States undertake to extend to the materials listed in Annexes A, B, D and E and also, where the annexes in question have not been the subject of a declaration under paragraph 16 (a) below, Annexes C.1, F, G and H, to the present protocol exemption from customs duties and other charges on, or in connexion with, their importation, as set out in Article I, paragraph 1, of the Agreement, provided such materials fulfil the conditions laid down in these annexes and are the products of another contracting State.

2. The provisions of paragraph 1 of this protocol shall not prevent any contracting State from levying on imported materials:

(a) internal taxes or any other internal charges of any kind, imposed at the time of importation or subsequently, not exceeding those applied directly or indirectly to like domestic products;

(b) fees and charges, other than customs duties, imposed by governmental or administrative authorities on, or in connexion with, importation, limited in amount to the approximate cost of the services rendered, and representing neither an indirect protection to domestic products nor a taxation of imports for revenue purposes.

II

3. Notwithstanding paragraph 2 (a) of this protocol, the contracting States undertake not to levy on the materials listed below any internal taxes or other internal charges of any kind, imposed at the time of importation or subsequently:

(a) books and publications consigned to the libraries referred to in paragraph 5 of this protocol;

(b) official, parliamentary and administrative documents published in their country of origin;

(c)   books and publications of the United Nations or any of its Specialized Agencies;

(d)   books and publications received by the United Nations Educational, Scientific and Cultural Organization and distributed free of charge by it or under its supervision;

(e)   publications intended to promote tourist travel outside the country of importation, sent and distributed free of charge;

(f)   articles for the blind and other physically and mentally handicapped persons:
    i.   books, publications and documents of all kinds in raised characters for the blind;
    ii. other articles specially designed for the educational, scientific or cultural advancement of the blind and other physically or mentally handicapped persons which are imported directly by institutions or organizations concerned with the education of, or assistance to the blind and other physically or mentally handicapped persons approved by the competent authorities of the importing country for the purpose of duty-free entry of these types of articles.

III

4. The contracting States undertake not to levy on the articles and materials referred to in the annexes to this protocol any customs duties, export duties or duties levied on goods leaving the country, or other internal taxes of any kind, levied on such articles and materials when they are intended for export to other contracting States.

IV

5. The contracting States undertake to extend the granting of the necessary licences and/or foreign exchange provided for in Article II, paragraph 1, of the Agreement, to the importation of the following materials:

(a)   books and publications consigned to libraries serving the public interest, including the following:
    i.   national libraries and other major research libraries:
    ii.   general and specialized academic libraries, including university libraries, college libraries, institute libraries and university extra-mural libraries;
    iii. public libraries;
    iv.   school libraries;
    v.   special libraries serving a group of readers who form an entity, having particular and identifiable subjects of interest, such as government libraries, public authority libraries, industrial libraries and libraries of professional bodies;
    vi.   libraries for the handicapped and for readers who are unable to move around, such as libraries for the blind, hospital libraries and prison libraries;
    vii. music libraries, including record libraries;

(b)   books adopted or recommended as textbooks in higher educational establishments and imported by such establishments;

(c)   books in foreign languages, with the exception of books in the principal native language or languages of the importing country;

(d)   films, slides, video-tapes, and sound recordings of an educational, scientific or cultural nature, imported by organizations approved by the competent authorities of the importing country for the purpose of duty-free entry of these types of articles.

V

6. The contracting States undertake to extend the granting of the facilities provided

for in Article III of the Agreement to materials and furniture imported exclusively for showing at a public exhibition of objects of an educational, scientific or cultural nature approved by the competent authorities of the importing country and for subsequent re-exportation.

7. Nothing in the foregoing paragraph shall prevent the authorities of an importing country from taking such steps as may be necessary to ensure that the materials and furniture in question will in fact be re-exported at the close of the exhibition.

VI

8. The contracting States undertake:

(a) to extend to the importation of the articles covered by the present protocol the provisions of Article IV of the Agreement;
(b) to encourage through appropriate measures the free flow and distribution of educational, scientific and cultural objects and materials produced in the developing countries.

VII

9. Nothing in this protocol shall affect the right of contracting States to take measures, in conformity with their legislation, to prohibit or limit the importation of articles, or their circulation after importation, on grounds relating directly to national security, public order or public morals.

10. Notwithstanding other provisions of this protocol, a developing country, which is defined as such by the practice established by the General Assembly of the United Nations and which is a party to the protocol, may suspend or limit the obligations under this protocol relating to importation of any object or material if such importation causes or threatens to cause serious injury to the nascent indigenous industry in that developing country. The country concerned shall implement such action in a non-discriminatory manner. It shall notify the Director-General of the United Nations Educational, Scientific and Cultural Organization of any such action, as far as practicable in advance of implementation, and the Director-General of the United Nations Educational, Scientific and Cultural Organization shall notify all Parties to the protocol.

11. This protocol shall not modify or affect the laws and regulations of any contracting State or any of its international treaties, conventions, agreements or proclamations, with respect to copyright, trade marks or patents.

12. Subject to the provisions of any previous conventions to which they may have subscribed for the settlement of disputes, the contracting States undertake to have recourse to negotiation or conciliation with a view to settlement of any disputes regarding the interpretation or the application of this protocol.

13. In case of a dispute between contracting States relating to the education, scientific or cultural character of imported materials, the interested parties may, by common agreement refer it to the Director-General of the United Nations Educational, Scientific and Cultural Organization for an advisory opinion.

VIII

14. (a) This protocol, of which the English and French texts are equally authentic, shall bear today's date and shall be open to signature by all States Parties to the Agreement, as well as by customs or economic unions, provided that all the Member States constituting them are also Parties to the protocol.

The term "State" or "Country" as used in this protocol, or in the protocol referred to in paragraph 18, shall be taken to refer also, as the context may require, to the customs or economic unions and, in all matters which fall within their competence with regard to the scope of this protocol, to the whole of the territories of the Member States which constitute them, and not to the territory of each of these States.

It is understood that, in a Contracting Party to this protocol, such customs or economic unions will also apply the provisions of the Agreement on the same basis as is provided in the preceding paragraph with respect to the protocol.

(b) This protocol shall be subject to ratification or acceptance by the signatory States in accordance with their respective constitutional procedures.

(c) The instruments of ratification or acceptance shall be deposited with the Secretary-General of the United Nations.

15. (a) The States referred to in paragraph 14 (a) which are not signatories of this protocol may accede to this protocol.

(b) Accession shall be effected by the deposit of a formal instrument with the Secretary-General of the United Nations.

16. (a) The States referred to in paragraph 14 (a) of this protocol may, at the time of signature, ratification, acceptance or accession, declare that they will not be bound by Part II, Part IV, Annex C.1, Annex F, Annex G and Annex H, or by any of these Parts or Annexes. They may also declare that they will be bound by Annex C.1 only in respect of contracting States which have themselves accepted that Annex.

(b) Any contracting State which has made such a declaration may withdraw it, in whole or in part, at any time by notification to the Secretary-General of the United Nations, specifying the date on which such withdrawal takes effect.

(c) States which have declared, in accordance with sub-paragraph (a) of this paragraph, that they will not be bound by Annex C.1 shall necessarily be bound by Annex C.2. Those which have declared that they will be bound by Annex C.1 only in respect of contracting States which have themselves accepted that Annex shall necessarily be bound by Annex C.2 in respect of contracting States which have not accepted Annex C.1.

17. (a) This protocol shall come into force six months after the date of the fifth instrument of ratification, acceptance or accession with the Secretary-General of the United Nations.

(b) It shall come into force for every other State six months after the date of the deposit of its instrument of ratification, acceptance or accession.

(c) Within one month following the expiration of the periods mentioned in sub-paragraphs (a) and (b) of this paragraph, the contracting States to this protocol shall submit a report to the United Nations Educational, Scientific and Cultural Organization on the measures which they have taken to give full effect to the protocol.

(d) The United Nations Educational, Scientific and Cultural Organization shall transmit these reports to all States parties to this protocol.

18. The protocol annexed to the Agreement, and made an integral part thereof, as provided for in Article XVII of the Agreement, is hereby made an integral part of this protocol and shall apply to obligations incurred under this protocol and to products covered by this protocol.

19. (a) Two years after the date of the coming into force of this protocol any contracting State may denounce this protocol by an instrument in writing deposited with the Secretary-General of the United Nations.

(b) The denunciation shall take effect one year after the receipt of the instrument of denunciation.

(c) Denunciation of the Agreement pursuant to Article XIV thereof shall automatically imply denunication of this protocol.

20. The Secretary-General of the United Nations shall inform the States referred to in paragraph 14 (a), as well as the United Nations Educational, Scientific and Cultural Organization, of the deposit of all the instruments of ratification, acceptance or accession referred to in paragraphs 14 and 15; of declarations made and

withdrawn under paragraph 16 of the dates of entry into force of this protocol in accordance with paragraph 17 (a) and (b); and of the denunciations provided for in paragraph 19.

21. (a) This protocol may be revised by the General Conference of the United Nations Educational, Scientific and Cultural Organization. Any such revision, however, shall be binding only upon States that become parties to the revising protocol.

(b) Should the General Conference adopt a new protocol revising this protocol either totally or in part, and unless the new protocol provides otherwise, the present protocol shall cease to be open to signature, ratification, acceptance or accession as from the date of the coming into force of the new revising protocol.

22. This protocol shall not change or modify the Agreement.

23. Annexes A, B, C.1, C.2, D, E, F, G and H are hereby made an integral part of this protocol.[1]

24. In accordance with Article 102 of the Charter of the United Nations, this protocol shall be registered by the Secretary-General of the United Nations on the date of its coming into force.

In faith whereof the undersigned, duly authorized, have signed this protocol on behalf of their respective governments.

FINAL ACTS
CONFERENCE ON SECURITY AND CO-OPERATION IN EUROPE, 1975
CO-OPERATION IN HUMANITARIAN AND OTHER FIELDS

The participating States,

Desiring to contribute to the strengthening of peace and understanding among peoples and to the spiritual enrichment of the human personality without distinction as to race, sex, language or religion,

Conscious that increased cultural and educational exchanges, broader dissemination of information, contacts between people, and the solution of humanitarian problems will contribute to the attainment of these aims,

Determined therefore to co-operate among themselves, irrespective of their political, economic and social systems, in order to create better conditions in the above fields, to develop and strengthen existing forms of co-operation and to work out new ways and means appropriate to these aims,

Convinced that this co-operation should take place in full respect for the principles guiding relations among participating States as set forth in the relevant document,

Have adopted the following:

* * *

2. Information

The participating States,

Conscious of the need for an ever wider knowledge and understanding of the various aspects of life in other participating States,

Acknowledging the contribution of this process to the growth of confidence between peoples,

Desiring, with the development of mutual understanding between the par-

---

[1] These annexes which give further details of the various categories of material covered by the Agreement are not included.

ticipating States and with the further improvements of their relations, to continue
further efforts towards progress in this field,

Recognising the importance of the dissemination of information from the other participating States and of a better acquaintance with such information,

Emphasising therefore the essential and influential rôle of the press, radio, television, cinema and news agencies and of the journalists working in these fields,

Make it their aim to facilitate the freer and wider dissemination of information of
all kinds, to encourage co-operation in the field of information and the exchange of
information with other countries, and to improve the conditions under which journalists from one participating State exercise their profession in another participating
State, and

Express their intention in particular:

(a) Improvement of the Circulation of, Access to, and Exchange of Information

i.   *Oral Information*

To facilitate the dissemination of oral information through the encouragement of lectures and lecture tours by personalities and specialists from the other participating
States, as well as exchanges of opinions at round table meetings, seminars, symposia, summer schools, congresses and other bilateral and multilateral meetings.

ii.   *Printed information*

To facilitate the improvement of the dissemination, on their territory, of newspapers
and printed publications, periodical and non-periodical, from the other participating
States. For this purpose:

they will encourage their competent firms and organisations to conclude agreements
and contracts designed gradually to increase the quantities and the number of titles
of newspapers and publications imported from the other participating States. These
agreements and contracts should in particular mention the speediest conditions of
delivery and the use of the normal channels existing in each country for the distribution of its own publications and newspapers, as well as forms and means of payment
agreed between the parties making it possible to achieve the objectives aimed at by
these agreements and contracts;

where necessary, they will take appropriate measures to achieve the above objectives and to implement the provisions contained in the agreements and contracts.

To contribute to the improvement of access by the public to periodical and non-
periodical printed publications imported on the bases indicated above. In particular:

they will encourage an increase in the number of places where these publications
are on sale;

they will facilitate the availability of these periodical publications during congresses,
conferences, official visits and other international events and to tourists during the
season;

they will develop the possibilities for taking out subscriptions according to the
modalities particular to each country;

they will improve the opportunities for reading and borrowing these publications in
large public libraries and their reading rooms as well as in the university libraries.

They intend to improve the possibilities for acquaintance with bulletins of official
information issued by diplomatic missions and distributed by those missions on the
basis of arrangements acceptable to the interested parties.

iii.   *Filmed and Broadcast Information*

To promote the improvement of the dissemination of filmed and broadcast information. To this end:

they will encourage the wider showing and broadcasting of a greater variety of
recorded and filmed information from the other participating States, illustrating the

various aspects of life in their countries and received on the basis of such agreements or arrangements as may be necessary between the organizations and firms directly concerned;

they will facilitate the import by competent organizations and firms of recorded audio-visual material from the other participating States.

The participating States note the expansion in the dissemination of information broadcast by radio and express the hope for the continuation of this process, so as to meet the interest of mutual understanding among peoples and the aims set forth by this Conference.

(b) Co-operation in the Field of Information

To encourage co-operation in the field of information on the basis of short or long term agreements or arrangements. In particular:

they will favour increased co-operation among mass media organisations, including press agencies, as well as among publishing houses and organisations;

they will favour co-operation among public or private, national or international radio and television organisations, in particular through the exchange of both live and recorded radio and television programmes, and through the joint production and the broadcasting and distribution of such programmes;

they will encourage meetings and contacts both between journalists' organizations and between journalists from the participating States;

they will view favourably the possibilities of arrangements between periodical publications as well as between newspapers from the participating States, for the purposes of exchanging and publishing articles;

they will encourage the exchange of technical information as well as the organization of joint research and meetings devoted to the exchange of experience and views between experts in the field of the press, radio and television.

(c) Improvement of Working Conditions for Journalists

The participating States, desiring to improve the conditions under which journalists from one participating State exercise their profession in another participating State, intend in particular to:

examine in a favourable spirit and within a suitable and reasonable time scale requests from journalists for visas;

grant to permanently accredited journalists of the participating States, on the basis of arrangements, multiple entry and exit visas for specified periods;

facilitate the issue to accredited journalists of the participating States of permits for stay in their country of temporary residence and, if and when these are necessary, of other official papers which it is appropriate for them to have;

ease on a basis of reciprocity, procedures for arranging travel by journalists of the participating States in the country where they are exercising their profession, and to provide progressively greater opportunities for such travel, subject to the observance of regulations relating to the existence of areas closed for security reasons;

ensure that requests by such journalists for such travel receive, in so far as possible, an expeditious response, taking into account the time scale of the request;

increase the opportunities for journalists of the participating States to communicate personally with their sources, including organizations and official institutions;

grant to journalists of the participating States the right to import, subject only to its being taken out again, the technical equipment (photographic, cinematographic, tape recorder, radio and television) necessary for the exercise of their profession;

enable journalists of the other participating States, whether permanently or temporarily accredited, to transmit completely, normally and rapidly by means recognised by the participating States to the information organs which they represent, the results of their professional activity, including tape recordings and undeveloped film, for the purpose of publication or of broadcasting on the radio or television.

The participating States reaffirm that the legitimate pursuit of their professional activity will neither render journalists liable to expulsion nor otherwise penalise them. If an accredited journalist is expelled, he will be informed of the reasons for this act and may submit an application for re-examination of his case.

3. Co-operation and Exchanges in the Field of Culture

The participating States,

Considering that cultural exchanges and co-operation contribute to a better comprehension among people and among peoples, and thus promote a lasting understanding among States,

Confirming the conclusions already formulated in this field at the multilateral level, particularly at the Intergovernmental Conference on Cultural Policies in Europe, organised by Unesco in Helsinki in June 1972, where interest was manifested in the active participation of the broadest possible social groups in an increasingly diversified cultural life,

Desiring, with the development of mutual confidence and the further improvement of relations between the participating States, to continue further efforts toward progress in this field,

Disposed in this spirit to increase substantially their cultural exchanges, with regard both to persons and to cultural works, and to develop among them an active co-operation, both at the bilateral and the multilateral level, in all the fields of culture,

Convinced that such a development of their mutual relations will contribute to the enrichment of the respective cultures, while respecting the originality of each, as well as to the reinforcement among them of a consciousness of common values, while continuing to develop cultural co-operation with other countries of the world,

Declare that they jointly set themselves the following objectives:

(a) to develop the mutual exchange of information with a view to a better knowledge of respective cultural achievements,
(b) to improve the facilities for the exchange and for the dissemination of cultural property,
(c) to promote access by all to respective cultural achievements,
(d) to develop contacts and co-operation among persons active in the field of culture,
(e) to seek new fields and forms of cultural co-operation,

Thus *give expression* to their common will to take progressive, coherent and long-term action in order to achieve the objectives of the present declaration; and

Express their intention now to proceed to the implementation of the following:

Extension of Relations

To expand and improve at the various levels co-operation and links in the field of culture, in particular by:

concluding, where appropriate, agreements on a bilateral or multilateral basis, providing for the extension of relations among competent state institutions and non-governmental organizations in the field of culture, as well as among people engaged in cultural activities, taking into account the need both for flexibility and the fullest possible use of existing agreements, and bearing in mind that agreements and also other arrangements constitute important means of developing cultural co-operation and exchanges;

contributing to the development of direct communication and co-operation among relevant state institutions and non-governmental organizations, including, where necessary, such communication and co-operation carried out on the basis of special agreements and arrangements;

encouraging direct contacts and communications among persons engaged in cultural activities, including, where necessary, such contacts and communications carried out on the basis of special agreements and arrangements.

Mutual Knowledge

Within their competence to adopt, on a bilateral and multilateral level, appropriate measures which would give their peoples a more comprehensive and complete mutual knowledge of their achievements in the various fields of culture, and among them:

to examine jointly if necessary with the assistance of appropriate international organizations, the possible creation in Europe and the structure of a bank of cultural data, which would collect information from the participating countries and make it available to its correspondents on their request, and to convene for this purpose a meeting of experts from interested States;

to consider, if necessary in conjunction with appropriate international organizations, ways of compiling in Europe an inventory of documentary films of a cultural or scientific nature from the participating States;

to encourage more frequent book exhibitions and to examine the possibility of organizing periodically in Europe a large-scale exhibition of books from the participating States;

to promote the systematic exchange, between the institutions concerned and publishing houses, of catalogues of available books as well as of pre-publication material which will include, as far as possible, all forthcoming publications; and also to promote the exchange of material between firms publishing encyclopaedias, with a view to improving the presentation of each country;

to examine jointly questions of expanding and improving exchanges of information in the various fields of culture, such as theatre, music, library work as well as the conservation and restoration of cultural property.

Exchanges and Dissemination

To contribute to the improvement of facilities for exchanges and the dissemination of cultural property, by appropriate means, in particular by:

studying the possibilities for harmonising and reducing the charges relating to international commercial exchanges of books and other cultural materials, and also for new means of insuring works of art in foreign exhibitions and for reducing the risks of damage or loss to which these works are exposed by their movement;

facilitating the formalities of customs clearance, in good time for programmes of artistic events, of the works of art, materials and accessories appearing on lists agreed upon by the organisers of these events;

encouraging meetings among representatives of competent organisations and relevant firms to examine measures within their field of activity – such as the simplification of orders, time limits for sending supplies and modalities of payment – which might facilitate international commercial exchanges of books;

promoting the loan and exchange of films among their film institutes and film libraries;

encouraging the exchange of information among interested parties concerning events of a cultural character foreseen in the participating States, in fields where this is most appropriate, such as music, theatre and the plastic and graphic arts, with a view to contributing to the compilation and publication of a calendar of such events, with the assistance, where necessary, of the appropriate international organizations;

encouraging a study of the impact which the foreseeable development, and a possible harmonization among interested parties, of the technical means used for the dissemination of culture might have on the development of cultural co-operation and exchanges, while keeping in view the preservation of the diversity and originality of their respective cultures;

encouraging, in the way they deem appropriate, within their cultural policies, the further development of interest in the cultural heritage of the other participating States, conscious of the merits and the value of each culture;

endeavouring to ensure the full and effective application of the international agreements and conventions on copyrights and on circulation of cultural property to which they are party or to which they may decide in the future to become party.

Access

To promote fuller mutual access by all to the achievements – works, experiences and performing arts – in the various fields of culture of their countries, and to that end to make the best possible efforts, in accordance with their competence, more particularly:

to promote wider dissemination of books and artistic works, in particular by such means as:

facilitating, while taking full account of the international copyright conventions to which they are party, international contacts and communications between authors and publishing houses as well as other cultural institutions, with a view to a more complete mutual access to cultural achievements;

recommending that, in determining the size of editions, publishing houses take into account also the demand from the other participating States, and that rights of sale in other participating States be granted, where possible, to several sales organizations of the importing countries, by agreement between interested partners;

encouraging competent organizations and relevant firms to conclude agreements and contracts and contributing, by this means, to a gradual increase in the number and diversity of works by authors from the other participating States available in the original and in translation in their libraries and bookshops;

promoting, where deemed appropriate, an increase in the number of sales outlets where books by authors from the other participating States, imported in the original on the basis of agreements and contracts, and in translation, are for sale;

promoting, on a wider scale, the translation of works in the sphere of literature and other fields of cultural activity, produced in the languages of the other participating States, especially from the less widely-spoken languages, and the publication and dissemination of the translated works by such measures as:

encouraging more regular contacts between interested publishing houses;

developing their efforts in the basic and advanced training of translators;

encouraging, by appropriate means, the publishing houses of their countries to publish translations;

facilitating the exchange between publishers and interested institutions of lists of books which might be translated;

promoting between their countries the professional activity and co-operation of translators;

carrying out joint studies on ways of further promoting translations and their dissemination;

improving and expanding exchanges of books, bibliographies and catalogue cards between libraries;

to envisage other appropriate measures which would permit, where necessary by mutual agreement among interested parties, the facilitation of access to their respective cultural achievements, in particular in the field of books;

to contribute by appropriate means to the wider use of the mass media in order to improve mutual acquaintance with the cultural life of each;

to seek to develop the necessary conditions for migrant workers and their families to preserve their links with their national culture, and also to adapt themselves to their new cultural environment;

to encourage the competent bodies and enterprises to make a wider choice and effect wider distribution of full-length and documentary films from the other participating States, and to promote more frequent non-commercial showings, such as premières, film weeks and festivals, giving due consideration to films from countries whose cinematographic works are less well known;

to promote, by appropriate means, the extension of opportunities for specialists from the other participating States to work with materials of a cultural character from film and audio-visual archives, within the framework of the existing rules for work on such archival materials;

to encourage a joint study by interested bodies, where appropriate with the assistance of the competent international organizations, of the expedience and the conditions for the establishment of a repertory of their recorded television programmes of a cultural nature, as well as of the means of viewing them rapidly in order to facilitate their selection and possible acquisition.

Contacts and Co-operation

To contribute, by appropriate means, to the development of contacts and co-operation in the various fields of culture, especially among creative artists and peoples engaged in cultural activities, in particular by making efforts to:

promote for persons active in the field of culture, travel and meetings including, where necessary, those carried out on the basis of agreements, contracts or other special arrangements and which are relevant to their cultural co-operation;

encourage in this way performing artists and artistic groups with a view to their working together, making known their works in other participating States or exchanging views on topics relevant to their common activity;

encourage, where necessary through appropriate arrangements, exchanges of trainees and specialists and the granting of scholarships for basic and advanced training in various fields of culture such as the arts and architecture, museums and libraries, literary studies and translation, and contribute to the creation of favourable conditions of reception in their respective institutions;

encourage the exchange of experience in the training of organisers of cultural activities as well as of teachers and specialists in fields such as theatre, opera, ballet, music and fine arts;

continue to encourage the organization of international meetings among creative artists, especially young creative artists, on current questions of artistic and literary creation which are of interest for joint study;

study other possibilities for developing exchanges and co-operation among persons active in the field of culture, with a view to a better mutual knowledge of the cultural life of the participating States.

Fields and Forms of Co-operation

To encourage the search for new fields and forms of cultural co-operation, to these ends contributing to the conclusion among interested parties, where necessary, of appropriate agreements and arrangements, and in this context to promote:

joint studies regarding cultural policies, in particular in their social aspects, and as they relate to planning, town-planning, educational and environmental policies, and the cultural aspects of tourism;

the exchange of knowledge in the realm of cultural diversity, with a view to contributing thus to a better understanding by interested parties of such diversity where it occurs;

the exchange of information, and as may be appropriate, meetings of experts, the elaboration and the execution of research programmes and projects, as well as their joint evaluation, and the dissemination of the results, on the subjects indicated above;

such forms of cultural co-operation and the development of such joint projects as:

international events in the fields of the plastic and graphic arts, cinema, theatre, ballet, music, folklore, etc.; book fairs and exhibitions, joint performances of operatic and dramatic works, as well as performances given by soloists, instrumental ensembles, orchestras, choirs and other artistic groups, including those composed of amateurs, paying due attention to the organization of international cultural youth events and the exchange of young artists;

the inclusion of works by writers and composers from the other participating States in the repertoires of soloists and artistic ensembles;

the preparation, translation and publication of articles, studies and monographs, as well as of low-cost books and of artistic and literary collections, suited to making better known respective cultural achievements, envisaging for this purpose meetings among experts and representatives of publishing houses;

the co-production and the exchange of films and of radio and television programmes, by promoting, in particular, meetings among producers, technicians and representatives of the public authorities with a view to working out favourable conditions for the execution of specific joint projects and by encouraging, in the field of co-production, the establishment of international filming teams;

the organization of competitions for architects and town-planners, bearing in mind the possible implementation of the best projects and the formation, where possible, of international teams;

the implementation of joint projects for conserving, restoring and showing to advantage works of art, historical and archaeological monuments and sites of cultural interest, with the help, in appropriate cases, of international organizations of a governmental or non-governmental character as well as of private institutions – competent and active in these fields – envisaging for this purpose:

periodic meetings of experts of the interested parties to elaborate the necessary proposals, while bearing in mind the need to consider these questions in a wider social and economic context; the publication in appropriate periodicals of articles designed to make known and to compare, among the participating States, the most significant achievements and innovations;

a joint study with a view to the improvement and possible harmonization of the different systems used to inventory and catalogue the historical monuments and places of cultural interest in their countries;

the study of the possibilities for organizing international courses for the training of specialists in different disciplines relating to restoration.

*   *   *

National minorities or regional cultures. The participating States, recognizing the contribution that national minorities or regional cultures can make to co-operation among them in various fields of culture, intend, when such minorities or cultures exist within their territory, to facilitate this contribution, taking into account the legitimate interests of their members.

BUENOS AIRES PLAN OF ACTION FOR
PROMOTING AND IMPLEMENTING TECHNICAL CO-OPERATION
AMONG DEVELOPING COUNTRIES, 1978

The United Nations Conference on Technical Co-operation among Developing Countries
Having convened in Buenos Aires, from 30 August to 12 September 1978 pursuant to
General Assembly resolutions 31/179 of 21 December 1976 and 32/183 of 19
December 1977 on technical co-operation among developing countries,

1. *Adopts* the following Plan of Action for Promoting and Implementing Technical
Co-operation among Developing Countries;

2. *Decides* that it be known as the "Buenos Aires Plan of Action";

3. *Urges* all Governments, the entire United Nations development system and the
international community as a whole, to take effective action for its implementation.

I. Introduction

1. The United Nations Conference on Technical Co-operation among Developing
Countries comes at a critical point in the evolution of relations among developing
countries themselves and between them and developed countries.

2. Profound changes are taking place in international political and economic relationships. When the principal institutions of the present international system were
first established, a group of industrialized countries were dominant in world affairs.
However, the historic process of decolonization now makes it possible for a large
number of States, representing an overwhelming proportion of the world's population, to participate in international affairs. Moreover, substantial changes are taking
place at the world level in the control and distribution of resources and in the
capabilities and needs of nations. As a result of these changes and other international
developments, the expansion of international relations and co-operation and the interdependence of nations are progressively increasing. Interdependence, however,
demands sovereign and equal participation in the conduct of international relations
and the equitable distribution of benefits.

3. The international system is in a state of ferment. Concepts, political and
economic positions, institutions and relationships must be adjusted to the new
realities and changing perceptions. It is in this perspective that the countries of the
developing world have made their call for the new international economic order as
an expression of their political will and their determination, based on the principles
of national and collective self-reliance, to work toward a new pattern of international relations more appropriate to the real circumstances and reflecting fully the
interests of the world community as a whole.

4. There is a growing recognition of the urgency and magnitude of the problems that
are being faced and will increasingly be faced by the world community in the future.
The problems of development, social and economic, national and international demand greatly increased, concerted efforts by the developing and developed countries if the new international economic order is to be a reality. While the progress of
the developing countries depends primarily on their own efforts, that progress is
also affected by the policies and performance of the developed countries. At the
same time, it is evident that, as a consequence of widening international relations,
co-operation and interdependence in many fields, the progress of the developed
countries is now and will increasingly be, affected by the policies and performance
of the developing countries.

5. In this historic new stage of progress towards the attainment of the new international economic order, technical co-operation among developing countries (TCDC)
is becoming a critically important dimension. It is a means of building communication and of promoting wider and more effective co-operation among developing

countries. It is a vital force for initiating, designing, organizing and promoting co-operation among developing countries so that they can create, acquire, adapt, transfer and pool knowledge and experience for their mutual benefit and for achieving national and collective self-reliance, which are essential for their social and economic development.

6. This form of co-operation is not new. A large number of co-operative activities have been carried out among developing countries over the years and many are now in progress. What is new, however, is that co-operation among developing countries is now perceived by those countries to be increasingly important in promoting sound development in the present world context. Furthermore, the difficulties currently encountered by the world economy make it even more necessary for the developing countries to evolve strategies based on greater national and collective self-reliance, for which TCDC is an important instrument. This in no way reduces the responsibility of developed countries to undertake the necessary policy measures, in particular, the increase of development assistance for accelerated development of developing countries.

7. TCDC is a multidimensional process. It can be bilateral or multilateral in scope, and subregional, regional or interregional in character. It should be organized by and between Governments which can promote, for this purpose, the participation of public organizations and, within the framework of the policies laid down by Governments, that of private organizations and individuals. It may rely on innovative approaches, methods and techniques particularly adapted to local needs and, at the same time, use existing modalities of technical co-operation to the extent that these are useful. While the main flows of technical co-operation visualized would be between two or more developing countries, the support of developed countries and of regional and interregional institutions may be necessary.

8. TCDC is neither an end in itself nor a substitute for technical co-operation with developed countries. Increased technical co-operation of the developed countries is required for the transfer of appropriate technologies and also for the transfer of advanced technologies and other expertise in which they have manifest advantages. Further contributions from the developed countries are required for the enhancement of technological capabilities of developing countries through support to relevant institutions in those countries. TCDC can serve the purpose of increasing the capacity of developing countries to adapt and absorb appropriate inputs from developed countries.

*   *   *

II. Objectives

15. The basic objectives of TCDC, which are interdependent and mutually supportive, contribute to the wider objectives of the development of the developing countries and international development co-operation. They reinforce those of closely related forms of co-operation, including economic co-operation among developing countries, for which TCDC is a key instrument. The objectives are:

(a) To foster the self-reliance of developing countries through the enhancement of their creative capacity to find solutions to their development problems in keeping with their own aspirations, values and special needs;

(b) To promote and strengthen collective self-reliance among developing countries through exchanges of experience, the pooling, sharing and utilization of their technical resources, and the development of their complementary capacities;

(c) To strengthen the capacity of developing countries to identify and analyse together the main issues of their development and to formulate the requisite strategies in the conduct of their international economic relations, through pooling of knowledge available in those countries through joint studies by their existing institutions, with a view to establishing the new international economic order;

(d) To increase the quantum and enhance the quality of international co-operation as well as to improve the effectiveness of the resources devoted to over-all technical co-operation through the pooling of capacities;

(e) To strengthen existing technological capacities in the developing countries, including the traditional sector, to improve the effectiveness with which such capacities are used and to create new capacities and capabilities and in this context to promote the transfer of technology and skills appropriate to their resource endowments and the development potential of the developing countries so as to strengthen their individual and collective self-reliance;

(f) To increase and improve communications among developing countries, leading to a greater awareness of common problems and wider access to available knowledge and experience as well as the creation of new knowledge in tackling problems of development;

(g) To improve the capacity of developing countries for the absorption and adaptation of technology and skill to meet their specific developmental needs;

(h) To recognize and respond to the problems and requirements of the least developed, land-locked, island developing and most seriously affected countries;

(i) To enable developing countries to attain a greater degree of participation in international economic activities and to expand international co-operation.

16. TCDC clearly serves many other purposes, such as overcoming attitudinal barriers, increasing developing countries' confidence in each other's technical capabilities and enhancing the process of harmonization of their interests so as to take fully into account, within the context of the fundamental concept of solidarity, their specific subregional, regional and interregional characteristics, particularly by identifying priorities in such fields as transport and communications, employment, development and exchange of human resources, as well as agriculture and industry.

III. Action to be taken

17. The recommendations formulated below should strengthen and support co-operation among developing countries, for example, and without implying an indication of priority, through the implementation of current activities and programmes of action decided upon by the developing countries, in such fields as employment and development of human resources, fisheries, food and agriculture, health, industrialization, information, integration of women in development, monetary and financial co-operation, raw materials, science and technology, technical co-operation and consultancy service, telecommunications, tourism, trade, and transport and communications. These recommendations should also facilitate the formulation of programmes of co-operation in other sectors.

* * *

Recommendation 4. The strengthening of national information systems for technical co-operation among developing countries

23. Each developing country should take adequate steps to strengthen the gathering, processing and dissemination of information covering the availability of national capacities, knowledge and experience for application and use in TCDC, if necessary with the support of the information systems of the United Nations development system, and particularly of the Information Referral System (INRES) of the United Nations Development Programme (UNDP), as well as official, professional and other sources. Governments of developing countries should further intensify their co-operation with the appropriate bodies at the regional, interregional and

global levels for the pooling of such information so as to facilitate the communication to other developing countries of the availability of such resources and opportunities for TCDC. These bodies should secure the information for TCDC from Governments and entities officially designated by them and disseminate it through the channels established for this purpose by Governments.

* * *

Recommendation 10. Technical co-operation among developing countries in the cultural spheres

29. The Governments of developing countries should, in order to affirm the cultural identity of their peoples and to enrich and strengthen their collective capacity with a greater awareness of the culture and heritage of other developing countries, increasingly employ TCDC mechanisms to foster cultural and educational links and to strengthen mutual knowledge by promoting exchanges and co-operation in the social sciences, education and culture.

* * *

Recommendation 12. The expansion of TCDC through national public and private enterprises and institutions

31. Having regard to the important and growing contribution that enterprises and institutions in the public sector are making to national development in the developing countries and the rich fund of experience acquired by them over the years, the Governments of developing countries should endeavour to establish or strengthen suitable arrangements to encourage and maintain co-operation and communication between public enterprises and institutions in their own countries and those in other developing countries, especially with a view to promoting closer technical collaboration. Similarly, Governments of developing countries should aim at encouraging comparable arrangements with regard to national private enterprises and institutions, where applicable.

* * *

Recommendation 13. Information and education programmes in support of technical co-operation among developing countries

32. Governments and non-governmental organizations of developing countries should undertake long-term information and education programmes to strengthen their own cultural identities, to encourage greater awareness of their common development problems and opportunities, to mobilize public support for self-reliance, and to break down attitudinal barriers to the expansion of TCDC. The United Nations system should lend intensive support to such programmes, seeking special additional resources for that purpose.

* * *

Recommendation 20. The improvement of regional information for technical co-operation among developing countries

40. The appropriate subregional and regional intergovernmental organizations, including, or with the support of the United Nations regional commissions, at the request of and in close collaboration with the countries concerned and with the support of other United Nations organizations should:

(a)   Contribute towards improving both the qualitative and quantitative aspects of the Information Referral System (INRES) and similar systems being developed by other components of the United Nations development system in specialized technical fields in widening their coverage and utilization of information on technical co-operation among developing countries;

(b) Ensure the effective, speedy and economical pooling and dissemination of information on the technical co-operation requirements and capacities of the developing countries within each region drawing on, *inter alia,* various potential mechanisms such as institutional networks and professional journals, which should also aim at overcoming language barriers;

(c) Prepare or harmonize, where necessary, subregional and regional standards in TCDC information flow.

* * *

Recommendation 24. The exchange of development experience

47. Since a great deal of benefit is to be derived by developing countries from sharing each other's experiences, the organizations of the United Nations development system should, at the request of interested developing countries, provide assistance in their respective sectors in preparing programmes and projects through which the rich experience accumulated in these countries in dealing with the problems connected with improving the living conditions of their populations could be shared and extensively applied.

* * *

Recommendation 26. The improvement of information flows

49. To encourage and intensify the collection, processing, analysis and dissemination at the global level of information on the capacities and needs of developing countries, the Information Referral System (INRES) and other related information systems should be further improved, developed and expanded. They should comprehensively cover the needs that might be met through TCDC in dealing with specific, detailed development problems. The Inquiry Service of INRES should be expanded at an early date in order to be able to match speedily the specific needs of developing countries with available capacities in order to improve channels for the wider use of experts, consultants, training facilities, equipment and other capacities of developing countries through bilateral or multilateral TCDC arrangements. For improved efficiency and better service to developing countries, appropriate linkages should be established between INRES and the information systems of other organizations of the United Nations development system and of the subregional and regional intergovernmental organizations.

50. In order to improve further the efficiency of INRES and to develop it appropriately, the Administrator of the United Nations Development Programme should initiate an evaluation and assessment of the functioning of the System.

* * *

Recommendation 30. The strengthening of transport and communications among developing countries

54. Bearing in mind the fact that the strengthening of transport and communications among developing countries is a necessary condition if TCDC is to become a major element in the development process, the Governments of developing countries should, on the basis of studies carried out by themselves, and by the organizations of the United Nations system when so requested, make specific and sustained efforts to strengthen, improve and maintain all means of transport and communications between their countries. In this context, all countries, the United Nations system and other international organizations should effectively support the implementation of programmes of the Transport and Communications Decade in Africa.

4. Media Regulation

The texts included in the previous sections often deal with information and communications in general terms: the reference is to 'information' without any qualification, to public opinion, public information or similar expressions. Another approach is the one used in the Unesco context through texts concerning certain classes of materials as in the Beirut and Florence Agreements, or information materials of a specific nature as in the case of certain other instruments mentioned in Section 3 above.

The instruments which concern specified media or means of communications can be classified in three main groups:

(a) In recent years there has been an increasing tendency of referring–mostly in non-binding instruments–to the media of information, the mass media, the mass communication media. Relevant rules may directly concern the mass media or refer to the role of the media in the context of other agreed objectives.

(b) A few international instruments concern specific media explicitly stated in the text. To this group belong such texts as the International Convention concerning the Use of Broadcasting for Peace (1936) and the special rules concerning cinema and broadcasting included in the European Convention on Human Rights.

(c) Specific means or services of communication figure prominently in the technical regulation of telecommunications and intellectual property rights. The relevant instruments will be found under the respective headings.

In the mass media field, international instruments adopted at the intergovernmental level are supplemented by agreements concluded by and among professional organizations established by newspaper owners, film producers, broadcasting organizations, journalists, performing artists, etc. Such agreements may cover policy co-ordination, exchanges and co-operation in the most varied areas.

Documents

Treaties

  i. International Convention concerning the Use of Broadcasting for Peace, 1936
     – Full text
 ii. European Convention on Human Rights, *see* Article 10 (Part One, III)

Declarations and Resolutions

iii. Declaration on Mass Communications Media and Human Rights
     Council of Europe, Resolution 428, 1970
     – Full text
 iv. (a) Declaration on the Fundamental Principles Concerning the Contribution of the Mass Media to Strengthening Peace and International Understanding, to the Promotion of Human Rights and to Countering Racialism, Apartheid and Incitement to War
         Unesco, General Conference, Resolution 4/9.3/2, 1978
         – Full text

(b) Application of the Declaration on the Fundamental Principles
etc.
Unesco, General Conference, Resolution 4/20, 1980
– Full text

INTERNATIONAL CONVENTION CONCERNING THE USE OF BROADCASTING IN THE CAUSE OF PEACE, GENEVA, 1936

Albania, the Argentine Republic, Austria, Belgium, the United States of Brazil, the United Kingdom of Great Britain and Northern Ireland, Chile, Colombia, Denmark, the Dominican Republic, Egypt, Spain, Estonia, France, Greece, India, Lithuania, Luxemburg, the United States of Mexico, Norway, New Zealand, the Netherlands, Roumania, Switzerland, Czechoslovakia, Turkey, the Union of Soviet Socialist Republics and Uruguay,
Having recognised the need for preventing, by means of rules established by common agreement, broadcasting from being used in a manner prejudicial to good international understanding;
Prompted, moreover, by the desire to utilise, by the application of these rules, the possibilities offered by this medium of intercommunication for promoting better mutual understanding between peoples;
Have decided to conclude a Convention for this purpose

Article I

The High Contracting Parties mutually undertake to prohibit and, if occasion arises, to stop without delay the broadcasting within their respective territories of any transmission which to the detriment of good international understanding is of such a character as to incite the population of any territory to acts incompatible with the internal order or the security of a territory of a High Contracting Party.

Article 2

The High Contracting Parties mutually undertake to ensure that transmissions from stations within their respective territories shall not constitute an incitement either to war against another High Contracting Party or to acts likely to lead thereto.

Article 3

The High Contracting Parties mutually undertake to prohibit and, if occasion arises, to stop without delay within their respective territories any transmission likely to harm good international understanding by statements the incorrectness of which is or ought to be known to the persons responsible for the broadcast.
They further mutually undertake to ensure that any transmission likely to harm good international understanding by incorrect statements shall be rectified at the earliest possible moment by the most effective means, even if the incorrectness has become apparent only after the broadcast has taken place.

Article 4

The High Contracting Parties mutually undertake to ensure, especially in time of crisis, that stations within their respective territories shall broadcast information concerning international relations the accuracy of which shall have been verified – and that by all means within their power – by the persons responsible for broadcasting the information.

Article 5

Each of the High Contracting Parties undertakes to place at the disposal of the other

High Contracting Parties, should they so request, any information that, in his opinion, is of such a character as to facilitate the broadcasting, by the various broadcasting services, of items calculated to promote a better knowledge of the civilization and the conditions of life of his own country as well as of the esssential features of the development of his relations with other peoples and of his contribution to the organization of peace.

Article 6

In order to give full effect to the obligations assumed under the preceding Articles, the High Contracting Parties mutually undertake to issue, for the guidance of governmental broadcasting services, appropriate instructions and regulations, and to secure their application by these services.

With the same end in view, the High Contracting Parties mutually undertake to include appropriate clauses for the guidance of any autonomous broadcasting organizations, either in the constitutive charter of a national institution, or in the conditions imposed upon a concessionary company, or in the rules applicable to other private concerns, and to take the necessary measures to ensure the application of these clauses.

Article 7

Should a dispute arise between the High Contracting Parties regarding the interpretation or application of the present convention for which it has been found impossible to arrive at a satisfactory settlement through the diplomatic channel, it shall be settled in conformity with the provisions in force between the Parties concerning the settlement of international disputes.

In the absence of any such provisions between the Parties to the dispute, the said Parties shall submit it to arbitration or to judicial settlement. Failing agreement concerning the choice of another tribunal, they shall submit the dispute, at the request of one of them, to the Permanent Court of International Justice, provided they are all Parties to the Protocol of December 16th, 1920, regarding the Statute of the Court; or, if they are not all Parties to the above Protocol, they shall submit the dispute to an arbitral tribunal, constituted in conformity with the Hague Convention of October 18th, 1907, for the Pacific Settlement of International Disputes.

Before having recourse to the procedures specified in paragraphs 1 and 2 above, the High Contracting Parties may, by common consent, appeal to the good offices of the International Committee on Intellectual Co-operation, which would be in a position to constitute a special committee for this purpose.

Article 8

The present Convention, of which the French and English texts are both authentic, shall bear this day's date, and shall be open for signature until May 1st, 1937, on behalf of any Member of the League of Nations, or any non-member State represented at the Conference which drew up the present Convention, or any non-member State to which the Council of the League of Nations shall have communicated a copy of the said Convention for that purpose.

Article 9

The present Convention shall be ratified. The instruments of ratification shall be sent to the Secretary-General of the League of Nations, who shall notify the deposit thereof to all the Members of the League and to the non-member States referred to in the preceding Article.

Article 10

After May 1st, 1937, any Member of the League of Nations and any non-member State referred to in Article 8 may accede to the present Convention.

DECLARATION ON MASS COMMUNICATION MEDIA AND HUMAN RIGHTS
CONSULTATIVE ASSEMBLY OF THE COUNCIL OF EUROPE, RESOLUTION 428, 1970

A. *Status and independence of the press and the other mass media*

1. The press and the other mass media, though generally not public institutions, perform an essential function for the general public. In order to enable them to discharge that function in the public interest, the following principles should be observed:

2. The right to freedom of expression shall apply to mass communication media.

3. This right shall include freedom to seek, receive, impart, publish and distribute information and ideas. There shall be a corresponding duty for the public authorities to make available information on matters of public interest within reasonable limits and a duty for mass communication media to give complete and general information on public affairs.

4. The independence of the press and other mass media from control by the state should be established by law. Any infringement of this independence should be justifiable by courts and not by executive authorities.

5. There shall be no direct or indirect censorship of the press, or of the contents of radio and television programmes, or of news or information conveyed by other media such as news reels shown in cinemas. Restrictions may be imposed within the limits authorised by Article 10 of the European Convention on Human Rights. There shall be no control by the state of the contents of radio and television programmes, except on the grounds set out in paragraph 2 of that Article.

6. The internal organisation of mass media should guarantee the freedom of expression of the responsible editors. Their editorial independence should be preserved.

7. The independence of mass media should be protected against the dangers of monopolies. The effects of concentration in the press, and possible measures of economic assistance require further consideration.

8. Neither individual enterprises, nor financial groups should have the right to institute a monopoly in the fields of press, radio or television, nor should government-controlled monopoly be permitted. Individuals, social groups, regional or local authorities should have – as far as they comply with the established licensing provisions – the right to engage in these activities.

9. Special measures are necessary to ensure the freedom of foreign correspondents, including the staff of international press agencies, in order to permit the public to receive accurate information from abroad. These measures should cover the status, duties and privileges of foreign correspondents and should include protection from arbitrary expulsion. They impose a corresponding duty of accurate reporting.

B. *Measures to secure responsibility of the press and other mass media*

It is the duty of the press and other mass media to discharge their functions with a sense of responsibility towards the community and towards the individual citizens. For this purpose, it is desirable to institute (where not already done):

(a) professional training for journalists under the responsibility of editors and journalists;

(b) a professional code of ethics for journalists; this should cover *inter alia* such matters as accurate and well balanced reporting, rectification of inaccurate information, clear distinction between reported information and comments, avoidance of calumny, respect for privacy, respect for the right to a fair trial as guaranteed by Article 6 of the European Convention on Human Rights;

(c) press councils empowered to investigate and even to censure instances of unprofessional conduct with a view to the exercising of self-control by the press itself.

C. Measures to protect the individual against interference with his right to privacy

1. There is an area in which the exercise of the right of freedom of information and freedom of expression may conflict with the right to privacy protected by Article 8 of the Convention on Human Rights. The exercise of the former right must not be allowed to destroy the existence of the latter.

2. The right to privacy consists essentially in the right to live one's own life with a minimum of interference. It concerns private, family and home life, physical and moral integrity, honour and reputation, avoidance of being placed in a false light, non-revelation of irrelevant and embarrassing facts, unauthorised publication of private photographs, protection against misuse of private communications, protection from disclosure of information given or received by the individual confidentially. Those who, by their own actions, have encouraged indiscreet revelations about which they complain later on, cannot avail themselves of the right to privacy.

3. A particular problem arises as regards the privacy of persons in public life. The phrase "where public life begins, private life ends" is inadequate to cover this situation. The private lives of public figures are entitled to protection, save where they may have an impact upon public events. The fact that an individual figures in the news does not deprive him of a right to a private life.

4. Another particular problem arises from attempts to obtain information by modern technical devices (wire-tapping, hidden microphones, the use of computers etc.), which infringe the right to privacy. Further consideration of this problem is required.

5. Where regional, national or international computer-data banks are instituted the individual must not become completely exposed and transparent by the accumulation of information referring even to his private life. Data banks should be restricted to the necessary minimum of information required for the purposes of taxation, pension schemes, social security schemes and similar matters.

6. In order to counter these dangers, national law should provide a right of action enforceable at law against persons responsible for such infringements of the right to privacy.

7. The right to privacy afforded by Article 8 of the Convention on Human Rights should not only protect an individual against interference by public authorities, but also against interference by private persons or institutions, including the mass media. National legislations should comprise provisions guaranteeing this protection.

DECLARATION ON FUNDAMENTAL PRINCIPLES CONCERNING THE CONTRIBUTION OF THE MASS MEDIA TO STRENGTHENING PEACE AND INTERNATIONAL UNDERSTANDING, TO THE PROMOTION OF HUMAN RIGHTS AND TO COUNTERING RACIALISM, APARTHEID AND INCITEMENT TO WAR

Unesco General Conference, Resolution 4/9.3/2, 1978

Preamble

The General Conference,
Recalling that by virtue of its Constitution the purpose of Unesco is to 'contribute peace and security by promoting collaboration among the nations through education, science and culture in order to further universal respect for justice, for the rule of law and for the human rights and fundamental freedoms' (Art. I, 1), and that to realize this purpose the Organization will strive 'to promote the free flow of ideas by word and image' (Art. I, 2),

Further recalling that under the Constitution the Member States of Unesco, 'believing in full and equal opportunities for education for all, in the unrestricted pursuit of objective truth, and in the free exchange of ideas and knowledge, are agreed and determined to develop and to increase the means of communication between their peoples and to employ these means for the purposes of mutual understanding and a truer and more perfect knowledge of each other's lives' (sixth preambular paragraph),

Recalling the purposes and principles of the United Nations, as specified in its Charter,

Recalling the Universal Declaration of Human Rights, adopted by the General Assembly of the United Nations in 1948 and particularly Article 19 thereof, which provides that 'everyone has the right to freedom of opinion and expression; this right includes freedom to hold opinions without interference and to seek, receive and impart information and ideas through any media and regardless of frontiers'; and the International Covenant on Civil and Political Rights, adopted by the General Assembly of the United Nations in 1966, Article 19 of which proclaims the same principles and Article 20 of which condemns incitement to war, the advocacy of national, racial or religious hatred and any form of discrimination, hostility or violence,

Recalling Article 4 of the International Convention on the Elimination of all forms of Racial Discrimination, adopted by the General Assembly of the United Nations in 1965, and the International Convention on the Suppression and Punishment of the Crime of Apartheid, adopted by the General Assembly of the United Nations in 1973, whereby the States acceding to these Conventions undertook to adopt immediate and positive measures designed to eradicate all incitement to, or acts of, racial discrimination, and agreed to prevent any encouragement of the crime of apartheid and similar segregationist policies or their manifestations,

Recalling the Declaration on the Promotion among Youth of the Ideals of Peace, Mutual Respect and Understanding between Peoples, adopted by the General Assembly of the United Nations in 1965,

Recalling the declarations and resolutions adopted by the various organs of the United Nations concerning the establishment of a new international economic order and the role Unesco is called upon to play in this respect,

Recalling the Declaration of the Principles of International Cultural Co-operation, adopted by the General Conference of Unesco in 1966,

Recalling Resolution 59(I) of the General Assembly of the United Nations, adopted in 1946 and declaring:

> 'Freedom of information is a fundamental human right and is the touchstone of all the freedoms to which the United Nations is consecrated; . . . Freedom of information requires as an indispensable element the willingness and capacity to employ its privileges without abuse. It requires as a basic discipline the moral obligation to seek the facts without prejudice and to spread knowledge without malicious intent; . . . '

Recalling Resolution 110(II) of the General Assembly of the United Nations, adopted in 1947, condemning all forms of propaganda which are designed or likely to provoke or encourage any threat to the peace, breach of the peace, or act of aggression,

Recalling resolution 127(II), also adopted by the General Assembly in 1947, which invites Member States to take measures, within the limits of constitutional procedures, to combat the diffusion of false or distorted reports likely to injure friendly relations between States, as well as the other resolutions of the General Assembly concerning the mass media and their contribution to strengthening peace, trust and friendly relations among States,

Recalling resolution 9.12 adopted by the General Conference of Unesco in 1968, reiterating Unesco's objective to help to eradicate colonialism and racialism, and resolution 12.1 adopted by the General Conference in 1976, which proclaims that colonialism, neo-colonialism and racialism in all its forms and manifestations are incompatible with the fundamental aims of Unesco,

Recalling resolution 4.301 adopted in 1970 by the General Conference of Unesco on the contribution of the information media to furthering international understanding and co-operation in the interests of peace and human welfare, and to countering propaganda on behalf of war, racialism, apartheid and hatred among nations, and *aware* of the fundamental contribution that mass media can make to the realization of these objectives,

Recalling the Declaration on Race and Racial Prejudice adopted by the General Conference of Unesco at its twentieth session,

Conscious of the complexity of the problems of information in modern society, of the diversity of solutions which have been offered to them, as evidenced in particular by the consideration given to them within Unesco, and of the legitimate desire of all parties concerned that their aspirations, points of view and cultural identity be taken into due consideration,

Conscious of the aspirations of the developing countries for the establishment of a new, more just and more effective world information and communication order,

Proclaims on this twenty-eighth day of November 1978 this Declaration on Fundamental Principles concerning the Contribution of the Mass Media to strengthening Peace and International Understanding, to the Promotion of Human Rights and to Countering Racialism, Apartheid and Incitement to War.

Article I

The strengthening of peace and international understanding, the promotion of human rights and the countering of racialism, apartheid and incitement to war demand a free flow and a wider and better balanced dissemination of information. To this end, the mass media have a leading contribution to make. This contribution will be the more effective to the extent that the information reflects the different aspects of the subject dealt with.

Article II

1. The exercise of freedom of opinion, expression and information, recognized as an integral part of human rights and fundamental freedoms, is a vital factor in the strengthening of peace and international understanding.

2. Access by the public to information should be guaranteed by the diversity of the sources and means of information available to it, thus enabling each individual to check the accuracy of facts and to appraise events objectively. To this end, journalists must have freedom to report and the fullest possible facilities of access to information. Similarly, it is important that the mass media be responsive to concerns of peoples and individuals, thus promoting the participation of the public in the elaboration of information.

3. With a view to the strengthening of peace and international understanding, to promoting human rights and to countering racialism, apartheid and incitement to war, the mass media throughout the world, by reasons of their role, contribute to promoting human rights, in particular by giving expression to oppressed peoples who struggle against colonialism, neo-colonialism, foreign occupation and all forms of racial discrimination and oppression and who are unable to make their voices heard within their own territories.

4. If the mass media are to be in a position to promote the principles of this Declaration in their activities, it is essential that journalists and other agents of the mass media, in their own country or abroad, be assured of protection guaranteeing them the best conditions for the exercise of their profession.

Article III

1. The mass media have an important contribution to make to the strengthening of peace and international understanding and in countering racialism, apartheid and incitement to war.

2. In countering aggressive war, racialism, apartheid and other violations of human

rights which are *inter alia* spawned by prejudice and ignorance, the mass media, by disseminating information on the aims, aspirations, cultures and needs of all peoples, contribute to eliminate ignorance and misunderstanding between peoples, to make nations of a country sensitive to the needs and desires of others, to ensure the respect of the rights and dignity of all nations, all peoples and all individuals without distinction of race, sex, language, religion or nationality and and to draw attention to the great evils which afflict humanity, such as poverty, malnutrition and diseases, thereby promoting the formulation by States of the policies best able to promote the reduction of international tension and the peaceful and equitable settlement of international disputes.

Article IV

The mass media have an essential part to play in the education of young people in a spirit of peace, justice, freedom, mutual respect and understanding, in order to promote human rights, equality of rights as between all human beings and all nations, and economic and social progress. Equally, they have an important role to play in making known the views and aspirations of the younger generation.

Article V

In order to respect freedom of opinion, expression and information and in order that information may reflect all points of view, it is important that the points of view presented by those who consider that the information published or disseminated about them has seriously prejudiced their effort to strengthen peace and international understanding, to promote human rights or to counter racialism, apartheid and incitement to war be disseminated.

Article VI

For the establishment of a new equilibrium and greater reciprocity in the flow of information, which will be conducive to the institution of a just and lasting peace and to the economic and political independence of the developing countries, it is necessary to correct the inequalities in the flow of information to and from developing countries, and between those countries. To this end, it is essential that their mass media should have conditions and resources enabling them to gain strength and expand, and to co-operate both among themselves and with the mass media in developed countries.

Article VII

By disseminating more widely all of the information concerning the universally accepted objectives and principles which are the bases of the resolutions adopted by the different organs of the United Nations, the mass media contribute effectively to the strengthening of peace and international understanding, to the promotion of human rights, and to the establishment of a more just and equitable international economic order.

Article VIII

Professional organizations, and people who participate in the professional training of journalists and other agents of the mass media and who assist them in performing their functions in a responsible manner should attach special importance to the principles of this Declaration when drawing up and ensuring application of their codes of ethics.

Article IX

In the spirit of this Declaration, it is for the international community to contribute to the creation of the conditions for a free flow and wider and more balanced dissemination of information, and of the conditions for the protection, in the exercise of their functions, of journalists and other agents of the mass media. Unesco is well placed to make a valuable contribution in this respect.

Article X

1. With due respect for constitutional provisions designed to guarantee freedom of information and for the applicable international instruments and agreements, it is indispensable to create and maintain throughout the world the conditions which make it possible for the organizations and persons professionally involved in the dissemination of information to achieve the objectives of the Declaration.

2. It is important that a free flow and wider and better balanced dissemination of information be encouraged.

3. To this end, it is necessary that States facilitate the procurement of the mass media in the developing countries of adequate conditions and resources enabling them to gain strength and expand, and that they support co-operation by the latter both among themselves and with the mass media in developed countries.

4. Similarly, on a basis of equality of rights, mutual advantage and respect for the diversity of the cultures which go to make up the common heritage of mankind, it is essential that bilateral and multilateral exchanges of information among all States, and in particular between those which have different economic and social systems, be encouraged and developed.

Article XI

For this Declaration to be fully effective it is necessary, with due respect for the legislative and administrative provisions and the other obligations of Member States, to guarantee the existence of favourable conditions for the operation of the mass media, in conformity with the provisions of the Universal Declaration of Human Rights and with the corresponding principle proclaimed in the International Covenant on Civil and Political Rights adopted by the General Assembly of the United Nations in 1966.

APPLICATION OF THE DECLARATION ON FUNDAMENTAL PRINCIPLES CONCERNING THE CONTRIBUTION OF THE MASS MEDIA TO STRENGTHENING PEACE AND INTERNATIONAL UNDERSTANDING, TO THE PROMOTION OF HUMAN RIGHTS AND TO COUNTERING RACISM, APARTHEID AND INCITEMENT TO WAR

Unesco General Conference Resolution 4/20, 1980

The General Conference,
Realizing the enormous and growing part played by the modern mass media in the lives of individuals and nations in the fields of communication, education and information, as well as in the achievement of the noble aims assigned to Unesco by its Constitution,

Taking account of the Unesco Declaration on Fundamental Principles concerning the Contribution of the Mass Media to Strengthening Peace and International Understanding, to the Promotion of Human Rights and to Countering Racialism, Apartheid and Incitement to War, which was adopted at its twentieth session,

Considering that, if communication between nations and individuals is to become a reciprocal process beneficial to all, Unesco must not only contribute to the maintenance of peace and security but must also promote the free flow of ideas by word and image and access by all nations to whatever is published in each of them,

1. *Calls upon* Member States to take all necessary steps to ensure that public opinion, journalists and others working in the mass media in their countries become

even more conversant with the aforesaid Declaration, and to publish it in as many languages as possible, if they have not already done so;

2. *Calls upon* Member States, intergovernmental and non-governmental organizations, journalists and other professionals working in the mass media, as well as their professional associations to contribute actively to the implementation of the aforesaid Declaration of Unesco;

3. *Calls upon* Member States, in accordance with their constitutional provisions, and governmental and non-governmental organizations having co-operative relations with Unesco to provide the Director-General with any information at their disposal concerning the way in which the principles set forth in the aforesaid Declaration have been put into effect;

4. *Invites* the Director-General:

(a) to have the 1978 Declaration concerning the mass media circulated as widely as possible and in as many languages as possible;

(b) to ensure that Unesco's programmes in the field of communication are based upon the fundamental principles stated therein;

(c) to convene in 1983, on the occasion of the fifth anniversary of the adoption of the Declaration, an international congress (Category IV), to be financed from extra-budgetary funds, to further the application of the Declaration;

5. *Invites* the Director-General to prepare on the basis of data collected and any other information in his possession, a comprehensive study on the implementation of the principles set forth in the Declaration and to include that study in the report on the activities of the Organization which he will submit to the General Conference for consideration at its twenty-second session.

5. Practice of journalism

The international rules concerning the mass media are closely related to the legal provisions dealing with the practice of journalism. The relevant texts, none of which are of a binding nature, comprise two main areas: the protection of journalists and codes of ethics. These matters have in the last few years attracted renewed attention in the perspective of the protection of human rights and of the debates on the new international information order.

Documents

Protection of journalists
  i. Protection of journalists engaged in dangerous missions in areas of armed conflict
     United Nations General Assembly Resolution 2673 (XXV) 1970
     – Full Text
 ii. Preliminary draft international convention on the protection of journalists engaged in dangerous missions
     United Nations Economic and Social Council, Resolution 1597 (L), 1971
     – Full text

Code of ethics
 iv. Draft International Code of Ethics
     United Nations Economic and Social Council, Resolution 442B (XIV) 1952
     – Full text

PROTECTION OF JOURNALISTS ENGAGED IN
DANGEROUS MISSIONS IN AREAS OF ARMED CONFLICT

United Nations General Assembly Resolution 2673 (XXV), 1970

The General Assembly,
Recalling its resolution 2444 (XXIII) of 19 December 1968, in which it invited the Secretary-General, in consultation with the International Committee of the Red Cross and other appropriate international organizations, to study:

(a) Steps which could be taken to secure the better application of existing humanitarian international conventions and rules in all armed conflicts,

(b) The need for additional humanitarian international conventions or for other appropriate legal instruments to ensure the better protection of civilians, prisoners and combatants in all armed conflicts,

Recalling also the fundamental principle that a distinction must be made at all times between combatants and persons not taking part in the hostilities,

Considering that it is essential for the United Nations to obtain complete information concerning armed conflicts and that journalists, whatever their nationality, have an important role to play in that regard,

Noting with regret that journalists engaged in missions in areas where an armed conflict is taking place sometimes suffer as a result of their professional duty, which is to inform world public opinion objectively,

Bearing in mind the appeal made by the Secretary-General on 30 September 1970 on behalf of missing journalists,

Recognizing that certain types of protection can be granted to journalists under:

(a) Article 4 of the Geneva Convention relative to the Treatment of Prisoners of War, of 12 August 1949,

(b) Article 13 of the Geneva Convention for the Amelioration of the Condition of the Wounded and Sick in Armed Forces in the Field, of 12 August 1949,

(c) Article 13 of the Geneva Convention for the Amelioration of the Condition of Wounded, Sick and Shipwrecked Members of Armed Forces at Sea, of 12 August 1949,

(d) Article 4 of the Geneva Convention relative to the Protection of Civilian Persons in time of War, of 12 August 1949,

Being aware, however, that these provisions do not cover some categories of journalists engaged in dangerous missions and do not correspond to their present needs,

Convinced of the need for an additional humanitarian international instrument to ensure the better protection of journalists engaged in dangerous missions, particularly in areas where an armed conflict is taking place,

1. *Expresses its grave concern* about the fate of press correspondents carrying out dangerous missions;

2. *Expresses its deepest regret* that some of those correspondents have paid with their lives for their conscientious approach to their missions;

3. *Invites* all States and all authorities parties to an armed conflict to respect and apply in all circumstances the provisions of the Geneva Conventions of 12 August 1949 in so far as they are applicable, in particular, to war correspondents who accompany armed forces but are not actually a part of them;

4. *Invites* the Economic and Social Council to request the Commission on Human Rights to consider at its twenty-seventh session the possibility of preparing a draft international agreement ensuring the protection of journalists engaged in dangerous missions and providing, *inter alia,* for the creation of a universally recognized and guaranteed identification document;

5. *Invites* the Commission on Human Rights to consider this question as a matter of priority at its twenty-seventh session in order that a draft international agreement

may be adopted as soon as possible by the General Assembly or by some other appropriate international body;

6. *Requests* the Secretary-General, in consultation with the International Committee of the Red Cross and other appropriate international organizations, to submit a report on this question to the General Assembly at its twenty-sixth session;

7. *Decides* to give the highest priority to the consideration of this question at its twenty-sixth session.

PRELIMINARY DRAFT INTERNATIONAL CONVENTION ON THE PROTECTION OF JOURNALISTS ENGAGED IN DANGEROUS MISSIONS

(Transmitted to the General Assembly by the Economic and Social Council in its resolution 1597 (L), 1971)

The High Contracting Parties,
Considering that the Universal Declaration of Human Rights has proclaimed in this Article 19 the right of everyone to freedom of opinion and expression, including freedom to seek, receive and impart information through any media and regardless of frontiers,

Considering that it is important to promote the right to complete, objective and truthful information,

Considering that the press plays a vital role in that connexion,

Considering that the quest for information may expose journalists to dangerous situations when their mission leads them to carry on their activity in areas where there is armed conflict,

Considering that those whose recognized function is to gather information for dissemination through an information organ should be afforded adequate protection in time of armed conflict,

Considering that without prejudice to the application of the Geneva Conventions of 12 August 1949 it is desirable to guarantee for all categories of journalists, in view of the present-day requirements of their profession, effective protection when they carry out dangerous missions,

Have agreed on the following provisions:

Article 1

This Convention shall apply to journalists who engage in dangerous missions and who hold the safe-conduct card provided for in article 3 below.

It shall not apply to war correspondents covered by the provisions of the Geneva Conventions of 12 August 1949.

Article 2

For the purposes of the application of this Convention, the word "journalist" shall mean any correspondent, reporter, photographer, film cameraman or press technician who has that status by virtue of his country's law or practice, in the case of a State Member of the United Nations or member of a specialized agency of the International Atomic Energy Agency or any other State party to the Statute of the International Court of Justice or Party to this Convention.

The words "dangerous mission" shall mean any mission carried out in an area where there is an armed conflict, whether or not of an international character for the purpose of gathering information for dissemination through a medium of public information.

Article 3

A journalist who is to carry out a dangerous mission may hold a safe-conduct card.

The said card shall be issued by the International Professional Committee for the Protection of Journalists Engaged in Dangerous Missions, whose composition and functions are defined in a Protocol annexed to this Convention.

Article 4

The validity of the safe-conduct shall be limited to a specified geographical area and to the expected duration of the mission.

It shall certify the status of the journalist and the references which entitle him to that status within the meaning of article 2 above; it shall, in particular, bear his photograph and state his name, date and place of birth, habitual residence and nationality.

Article 5

Every party to an armed conflict shall recognize the validity of the safe-conduct cards issued by the International Committee.

The Committee shall give wide circulation to the model of the card and distinguishing mark provided for in the following article.

Article 6

When engaged in a dangerous mission, a journalist who holds a safe-conduct card must be able to produce it on any occasion and, in particular, at the request of any competent authority.

A journalist who holds a safe-conduct card may also, at his discretion, wear a readily recognizable distinguishing mark, an exact description of which shall be drawn up by the International Committee.

Article 7

The States Parties to this Convention and all parties to the conflict shall:

1. Recognize persons holding a safe-conduct card as journalists within the meaning of the provisions of articles 2, 3 and 4 above;

2. Enable such persons to identify themselves;

3. Extend to them the same protection of their persons as to their own journalists;

4. Recognize, in case of internment, that the regulations for the treatment of internees laid down in the Geneva Convention relative to the Protection of Civilian Persons in Time of War, of 12 August 1949 shall apply;

5. Make public the internment order;

6. Also make public any information on journalists who have been wounded or who have died.

Such facts may be made public through all appropriate media, in the quickest and most effective manner and, preferably, through the International Committee on the Red Cross or any organ of the United Nations family in order that the International Professional Committee for the Protection of Journalists Engaged in Dangerous Missions may be informed without delay.

Article 8

The application of this Convention shall have no legal effect on the situation of the parties to a conflict.

Article 9

This Convention shall not affect national regulations concerning the crossing of frontiers or the movement or residence of aliens.

Article 10

None of the provisions of this Convention may be interpreted as affecting the provisions of the Geneva Conventions of 12 August 1949.

DRAFT INTERNATIONAL CODE OF ETHICS

United Nations Economic and Social Council, Resolution 442B (XIV), 1952

Preamble

Freedom of information and of the Press is a fundamental human right and is the touchstone of all the freedoms consecrated in the Charter of the United Nations and proclaimed in the Universal Declaration of Human Rights; and it is essential to the promotion and to the preservation of peace.

That freedom will be the better safeguarded when the personnel of the Press and of all other media of information constantly and voluntarily strive to maintain the highest sense of responsibility, being deeply imbued with the moral obligation to be truthful and to search for the truth in reporting, in explaining and in interpreting facts.

This International Code of Ethics is therefore proclaimed as a standard of professional conduct for all engaged in gathering, transmitting, disseminating and commenting on news and information and in describing contemporary events by the written word, by word of mouth or by any other means of expression.

Article I

The personnel of the Press and of all other media of information should do all in their power to ensure that the information the public receives is factually accurate. They should check all items of information to the best of their ability. No fact should be wilfully distorted and no essential fact should be deliberately suppressed.

Article II

A high standard of professional conduct requires devotion to the public interest. The seeking of personal advantage and the promotion of any private interest contrary to the general welfare, for whatever reason, is not compatible with such professional conduct.

Wilful calumny, slander, libel and unfounded accusations are serious professional offences; so also is plagiarism.

Good faith with the public is the foundation of good journalism. Any published information which is found to be harmfully inaccurate should be spontaneously and immediately rectified. Rumour and unconfirmed news should be identified and treated as such.

Article III

Only such tasks as are compatible with the integrity and dignity of the profession should be assigned or accepted by personnel of the Press and other media of information, as also by those participating in the economic and commercial activities of information enterprises.

Those who make public any information or comment should assume full responsibility for what is published unless such responsibility is explicitly disclaimed at the time.

The reputation of individuals should be respected and information and comment on their private lives likely to harm their reputation should not be published unless it serves the public interest, as distinguished from public curiosity. If charges against reputation or moral character are made, opportunity should be given for reply.

Discretion should be observed concerning sources of information. Professional secrecy should be observed in matters revealed in confidence; and this privilege may always be invoked to the furthest limits of law.

Article IV

It is the duty of those who describe and comment upon events relating to a foreign country to acquire the necessary knowledge of such country which will enable them to report and comment accurately and fairly thereon.

Article V

This Code is based on the principle that the responsibility for ensuring the faithful observance of professional ethics rests upon those who are engaged in the profession, and not upon any government. Nothing herein may therefore be interpreted as implying any justification for intervention by a government in any manner whatsoever to enforce observance of the moral obligations set forth in this Code.

6. Protection of the individual: privacy and related matters

General provisions for the protection of the right of the individual to privacy have been included in all the major human rights instruments. They have though not been followed by specific agreements at the international level.

In the UN context work has proceeded on the implications of scientific and technical developments for the exercise of human rights and fundamental freedoms with particular focus on the effects of new recording and other devices on the rights of the person.

Protection of privacy in relation to automated data systems has at the regional level already been formulated in a European convention; this and related texts will be noted in Part Seven: Informatics Law.

Related to the rules concerning privacy is the protection of secrecy of correspondence included in the International Telecommunication Convention. A more specific rule referring to the protection of diplomatic correspondence is included in the Vienna Convention on Diplomatic Relations.

At the national level, protection of the individual is also expressed in rules against libel and slander. The approaches adopted in the various legal systems vary considerably with regard both to substantive rules and to legal procedure; no international agreements have been concluded on this subject matter.

Documents

(a) Human Rights Instruments
   i.   Universal Declaration of Human Rights (see text in Part One).
        −   Article 12
   ii. International Covenant on Civil and Political Rights (see text in Part One).
        −   Article 17
   iii. European Convention on Human Rights (see text in Part One)
        −   Article 8
   iv. American Convention on Human Rights (see text in Part One)
        −   Article 11

(b) Implications of technological development
  v. Human Rights and scientific and technological development
     United Nations General Assembly Resolution 2450 (XXIII), 1968
     − Preamble
     − Point 1
  vi. Declaration on the Use of Scientific and Technological Progress in the
     Interests of Peace and for the Benefit of Mankind,
     United Nations General Assembly, Resolution 3348 (XXX), 1975
     − Full text
  vii. Points for possible inclusion in draft international standards concern-
     ing respect for the privacy of the individual in the light of modern
     recording and other devices. Report by the Secretary General, UN
     document E/CN.4/1116, 1976
     − Paragraph 177

(c) Secrecy of correspondence
  viii. International Telecommunication Convention (see text in Part Three)
     − Article 22

(d) Other agreements
See Part Seven: Informatics Law

HUMAN RIGHTS AND SCIENTIFIC AND
TECHNOLOGICAL DEVELOPMENT

United Nations General Assembly Resolution 2450 (XXIII), 1968

The General Assembly,
Having taken note of paragraph 18 of the Proclamation of Teheran adopted by the International Conference on Human Rights and of resolution XI concerning human
rights and scientific and technological developments adopted by the Conference on
12 May 1968,
  Sharing the concern expressed by the Conference that recent scientific discoveries
and technological advances, although they open up vast prospects for economic,
social and cultural progress, may nevertheless endanger the rights and freedoms of
individuals and peoples and consequently call for constant attention,
  Endorsing the idea that these problems require thorough and continuous interdisciplinary studies, both national and international, which may serve as a basis for
drawing up appropriate standards to protect human rights and fundamental
freedoms,

1. *Invites* the Secretary-General to undertake, with the assistance, *inter alia,* of the
Advisory Committee on the Application of Science and Technology to Development
and in co-operation with the executive heads of the competent specialized agencies,
a study of the problems in connexion with human rights arising from developments
in science and technology, in particular from the following standpoints:
  (a) Respect for the privacy of individuals and the integrity and sovereignty of na-
      tions in the light of advances in recording and other techniques;
  (b) Protection of the human personality and its physical and intellectual integrity,
      in the light of advances in biology, medicine and biochemistry;
  (c) Uses of electronics which may affect the rights of the person and the limits
      which should be placed on such uses in a democratic society;
  (d) More generally, the balance which should be established between scientific

and technological progress and the intellectual, spiritual, cultural and moral advancement of humanity.

* * *

DECLARATION ON THE USE OF SCIENTIFIC AND TECHNOLOGICAL PROGRESS IN THE INTERESTS OF PEACE AND FOR THE BENEFIT OF MANKIND

United Nations General Assembly Resolution 3348 (XXX), 1975

The General Assembly,
Noting that scientific and technological progress has become one of the most important factors in the development of human society,

Taking into consideration that, while scientific and technological developments provide ever increasing opportunities to better the conditions of life of people and nations, in a number of instances they can give rise to social problems, as well as threaten the human rights and fundamental freedoms of the individual,

Noting with concern that scientific and technological achievements can be used to intensify the arms race, suppress national liberation movements and deprive individuals and peoples of their human rights and fundamental freedoms,

Also noting with concern that scientific and technological achievements can entail dangers for the civil and political rights of the individual or of the group and for human dignity,

Noting the urgent need to make full use of scientific and technological developments for the welfare of man and to neutralize the present and possible future harmful consequences of certain scientific and technological achievements,

Recognizing that scientific and technological progress is of great importance in accelerating the social and economic development of developing countries,

Aware that the transfer of science and technology is one of the principal ways of accelerating the economic development of developing countries,

Reaffirming the right of peoples to self-determination and the need to respect human rights and freedoms and the dignity of the human person in the conditions of scientific and technological progress,

Desiring to promote the realization of the principles which form the basis of the Charter of the United Nations, the Universal Declaration of Human Rights, the International Covenants on Human Rights, the Declaration on the Granting of Independence to Colonial Countries and Peoples, the Declaration on Principles of International Law concerning Friendly Relations and Co-operation among States in accordance with the Charter of the United Nations, the Declaration on Social Progress and Development, and the Charter of Economic Rights and Duties of States,

Solemnly proclaims that:

1. All States shall promote international co-operation to ensure that the results of scientific and technological developments are used in the interests of strengthening international peace and security, freedom and independence, and also for the purpose of the economic and social development of peoples and the realization of human rights and freedoms in accordance with the Charter of the United Nations.

2. All States shall take appropriate measures to prevent the use of scientific and technological developments, particularly by the State organs, to limit or interfere with the enjoyment of the human rights and fundamental freedoms of the individual as enshrined in the Universal Declaration of Human Rights, the International Covenants on Human Rights and other relevant international instruments.

3. All States shall take measures to ensure that scientific and technological achievements satisfy the material and spiritual needs of all sectors of the population.

4. All States shall refrain from any acts involving the use of scientific and technological achievements for the purposes of violating the sovereignty and ter-

ritorial integrity of other States, interfering in their internal affairs, waging aggressive wars, suppressing national liberation movements, or pursuing a policy of
racial discrimination. Such acts are not only a flagrant violation of the Charter of the
United Nations and principles of international law, but constitute an inadmissible
distortion of the purposes that should guide scientific and technological
developments for the benefit of mankind.

5. All States shall co-operate in the establishment, strengthening and development
of the scientific and technological capacity of developing countries with a view to accelerating the realization of the social and economic rights of the peoples of those
countries.

6. All States shall take measures to extend the benefits of science and technology to
all strata of the population and to protect them, both socially and materially, from
possible harmful effects of the misuse of scientific and technological developments,
including their misuse to infringe upon the rights of the individual or of the group,
particularly with regard to respect for privacy and the protection of the human personality and its physical and intellectual integrity.

7. All States shall take the necessary measures, including legislative measures, to
ensure that the utilization of scientific and technological achievements promotes the
fullest realization of human rights and fundamental freedoms without any
discrimination whatsoever on grounds of race, sex, language or religious beliefs.

8. All States shall take effective measures, including legislative measures, to prevent
and preclude the utilization of scientific and technological achievements to the detriment of human rights and fundamental freedoms and the dignity of the human person.

9. All States shall, whenever necessary, take action to ensure compliance with
legislation guaranteeing human rights and freedoms in the conditions of scientific
and technological developments.

POINTS FOR POSSIBLE INCLUSION IN DRAFT INTERNATIONAL
STANDARDS CONCERNING RESPECT FOR THE PRIVACY OF THE
INDIVIDUAL IN THE LIGHT OF MODERN RECORDING AND OTHER DEVICES

Report by the Secretary General, United Nations, doc. E/CN.4/1116, 1976

177. In view of the considerable differences of opinion as to the practical effects
which the creation on the national level of a statutory right to privacy would have on
the protection of other rights, as well as of the different legal contexts in which such
legislation would operate, it seems inadvisable to recommend a uniform adoption of
legislation establishing a general right to privacy. International standards might,
however, be adopted, indicating other types of action which should be taken to protect the privacy of the individual against invasions by modern recording and other
techniques, along the following lines:
1. States shall adopt legislation, or bring up to date existing legislation, so as to provide protection for the privacy of the individual against invasions by modern
technological devices;
2. Legislation might be drafted in such a manner as to make it easily adaptable to
future technological developments;
3. States shall, in particular, take the following minimum steps:
(a) Penal Codes should designate as offences and provide for penalties of fine, imprisonment or both, for:
    i. the clandestine monitoring or recording of conversations except, possibly,
        by participants to the conversations, and except by judicial or ministerial

order, and in accordance with that order, in countries which permit monitoring or recording-in-criminal investigation or for reasons of national security;

ii.   the disclosure by any person of information so obtained;

iii.   the clandestine viewing, photographing, filming or televising of members of households and their guests in their dwellings, except by judicial or ministerial order, and in accordance with that order, in countries which permit such actions in criminal investigations or for reasons of national security;

(b)   States which permit the utilization by their own agencies of modern recording and other techniques in the investigation of crimes or for reasons of national security shall make provision to restrict the use of these techniques to cases of the most serious crimes or the most serious threats to national security. They shall lay down by law the conditions for their use, which conditions shall include:

i.   prior authorization in each case by a judicial authority (or by an official of Ministerial rank), upon a showing of "probable cause" or its equivalent and a showing that alternative methods of surveillance are not available or not effective in the particular case;

ii.   specification, in the authorization, of the person to be monitored, the suspected offence, the person who is to do the monitoring, and the length of the period of surveillance. States shall make provision to ensure that such authorizations are not issued in a routine manner or by delegation of authority;

iii.   specification of the extent to which use may be made in criminal proceedings of information gained;

(c)   States permitting the operations of private detectives shall license such detectives individually;

(d)   States shall favour the establishment of journalists' codes of ethics including provisions concerning respect for the privacy of the individual;

(e)   In addition to any possible criminal liability, civil liability should attach to either the use of an auditory or visual device in relation to a person, under circumstances which would entitle him to assume that he could not be seen or heard by unauthorized persons, or the unauthorized disclosure of information so gained;

(f)   Civil remedies shall allow a person to apply for the cessation of acts thus violating his privacy and, where the act has been completed, to recover damages, including damages for non-pecuniary injury;

(g)   Legislative or administrative steps shall be taken to control effectively the importation, manufacture, advertisement, sale, transfer and possession of devices suitable primarily for clandestine auditory or visual surveillance. These steps shall include the following:

i.   the manufacturers of such devices shall be required to hold a valid government licence, renewable periodically and revocable for good cause, and to submit appropriate records periodically for State inspection;

ii.   the manufacturers of such devices shall be forbidden to sell them to anyone not having a valid government licence authorizing possession thereof;

iii.   the unlicensed manufacture or possession of such devices shall be punishable;

iv.   the responsible governmental authority shall compile and keep current a catalogue of the devices and components subject to its control;

(h)   Legal provision shall be made for the confiscation and destruction without compensation of recording and other devices utilized in an offence involving clandestine auditory or visual surveillance, whether or not the device was intended primarily for such use.

4. States shall establish expert bodies to follow scientific and technological developments affecting the right to privacy and to draw the attention of the legislature, the executive and the public to the effects of such developments, existing or new, upon the right to privacy and to possible safeguards required.

7. Development of communications

The following four sections include texts which reflect current and recent concerns of the international community in the field of communications.

The documents in this first section deal with measures to promote the development of communications, particularly in developing countries. These concerns were reflected in resolutions of the UN General Assembly as early as 1952. In the last few years increasing attention has been paid to this matter particularly in the context of the UN and Unesco, as well as in more specific terms by such organizations as the International Telecommunication Union and the Intergovernmental Bureau of Informatics.

The question of the development of communications is closely interrelated with the formation of communications policy and with the issues that have come to be subsumed under the expression of the 'new international information order'. In view of the increasing number of relevant documents and the differences in approach it seemed useful to distinguish between the sets of documents which refer to these three issues.

The documents included in this section comprise a selection of UN General Assembly resolutions; the resolutions adopted by the Unesco General Conference generally refer to the specific objectives and activities of the organization with regard to the promotion of infrastructures, training; included here is the recent decision to establish an International Programme for the Development of Communications. Relevant decisions by the International Telecommunication Union are mentioned in Section Three.

Documents

United Nations
   i. Information facilities in underdeveloped regions of the world, General Assembly Resolution 633 (VII), 1952
      – Full text
  ii. Freedom of Information, General Assembly Resolution 1313 (XIII), 1958
      – Preamble, Parts A, B
 iii. International cooperation to assist in the development of information media in less developed countries, General Assembly Resolution 1778 (XVII), 1962
      – Full text
  iv. Cooperation and assistance in the application and improvement of national information and mass communication systems for social progress and development, General Assembly Resolution 31/139, 1976
      – Full text
   v. Questions Relating to Information, General Assembly Resolution 33/115, 1978
      – Part A

vi.   Questions Relating to Information, General Assembly Resolution
      35/201, 1981
      −   Part I

Unesco
vii. International Programme for the Development of Communications,
      General Conference Resolution 4/21, 1980
      −   Full text (including Annexes)
See also Texts adopted by the Intergovernmental Conferences on Communication Policies, (1976, 1978, 1980) in next section.

INFORMATION FACILITIES IN UNDERDEVELOPED
REGIONS OF THE WORLD

United Nations General Assembly Resolution 633 (VII), 1952

The General Assembly,
Considering that it is essential for the proper development of public opinion in under-
developed countries that independent domestic information enterprises should be
given facilities and assistance in order that they may be enabled to contribute to the
spread of information, to the development of national culture and to international
understanding,
      Convinced that the development of information media contributes greatly to the
economic and social progress of peoples,
      Convinced that the time has arrived for the elaboration of a concrete programme
and plan of action in this respect,
      Taking note with approval of the decision taken by the Economic and Social Coun-
cil in resolution 442 E (XIV) of 13 June 1952 with regard to the study of ways and
means of encouraging and developing independent domestic information enterprises,
      Noting, however, that the above decision only refers to the encouragement and
development of independent domestic information enterprises, including Press,
radio, newsreels and television, therefore,
1. *Invites* the Economic and Social Council to consider, in the light of the discussions
at the seventh session of the General Assembly, the desirability of expanding the
area of its study of this question; and, to that end,

2. *Requests* the Secretary-General, in preparing the report called for under the
above-mentioned resolution of the Council, also to elaborate a programme of concrete action which would include, *inter alia:*

(a)   Measures to reduce economic and financial obstacles in the field of information;
(b)   Measures to organize and promote among countries the exchange of informa-
      tion personnel;
(c)   Measures to assist the training of information personnel, the raising of profes-
      sional and technical standards, the provision of fellowships and the holding of
      regional seminars;
(d)   All necessary measures in connexion with the supply of newsprint;

3. *Calls upon* the Economic and Social Council to submit the above-mentioned programme, together with recommendations thereon, to the General Assembly at its
eighth session;

4. *Further invites* the Council to recommend to the organizations participating in the
technical assistance and other programmes providing aid or assistance at the request
of Member States that they give sympathetic consideration to requests which

governments may submit for such aid or assistance within the framework of those programmes with a view to improving information facilities and increasing the quantity and improving the quality of information available to the peoples of the world, as one means of implementing the right of freedom of information as enunciated in the provisions of Article 1, paragraph 3, and Article 55 of the Charter of the United Nations and in article 19 of the Universal Declaration of Human Rights.

FREEDOM OF INFORMATION

United Nations General Assembly Resolution 1313 (XIII), 1958

A

The General Assembly,
Noting that the Commission on Human Rights at its fourteenth session requested the Economic and Social Council and, through it, the United Nations Educational, Scientific and Cultural Organization and other specialized agencies concerned to initiate action to consider and implement the suggestions of the Committee on Freedom of Information concerning under-developed countries wherever possible and as expeditiously as possible, with the object of assisting them to build up adequate media of information which could facilitate the free flow of accurate and undistorted news and information within these countries and throughout the membership of the United Nations,

Noting that the Commission on Human Rights will give further consideration at its fifteenth session to the suggestions of the Committee on Freedom of Information and that the Economic and Social Council has requested the Commission on Human Rights to complete its recommendations on freedom of information,
1. *Expresses the hope* that the Economic and Social Council, on the basis of the analysis to be prepared by the Secretary-General in response to Council resolutions 574 D (XIX) of 26 May 1955 and 643 (XXIII) of 25 April 1957, and taking into account recommendations of the Commission on Human Rights to be submitted in response to Council resolution 683 C (XXVI) of 21 July 1958, will formulate at its twenty-eighth session a programme of concrete action and measures on the international plane which could be undertaken for the development of information enterprises in under-developed countries, with an evaluation of the material, financial and professional requirements and resources for the implementation of this programme;
2. *Invites* the Economic and Social Council to request the Commission on Human Rights to give particular attention to procedures by which constant review of the problems of providing technical assistance to under-developed countries in the field of information may be assured, and to report regularly to the Council on progress in this field;
3. *Invites* the United Nations Educational, Scientific and Cultural Organization and other specialized agencies as appropriate to formulate concrete proposals to assist in meeting the needs of less developed countries in building up adequate media of information, and to include an account of their efforts on this and other aspects of freedom of information in their annual reports to the Economic and Social Council.

B

The General Assembly,
Reiterating its belief in the free flow of undistorted news and information within countries and across national frontiers as the essential basis for an accurate and undistorted understanding of events and situations,

Recognizing however that the development of media of information constitutes only a partial measure in ensuring freedom of information.

Recognizing further that greater freedom of communications would lessen international tension and promote mutual understanding and confidence, thereby allowing countries and peoples more easily to understand and compose their differences,

Recommends that all Member States, as a contribution to building peace and confidence, should encourage better mutual understanding by taking practical measures, in co-operation with the programmes of the United Nations and its specialized agencies, to open their countries to greater freedom of communications by:

(a)   Facilitating access to United Nations information programmes;
(b)   Supporting the activities of United Nations information centres;
(c)   Facilitating the free flow of accurate information through all media.

*   *   *

INTERNATIONAL CO-OPERATION TO ASSIST IN THE DEVELOPMENT OF INFORMATION MEDIA IN LESS DEVELOPED COUNTRIES

United Nations General Assembly Resolution 1778 (XVII), 1962

The General Assembly,

Recalling its resolution 1313 A (XIII) of 12 December 1958, by which it requested the Economic and Social Council to formulate a programme of concrete action and measures on the international plane which could be undertaken for the development of information enterprises in under-developed countries, with an evaluation of the material, financial and professional requirements and resources for the implementation of this programme,

Recalling that the Economic and Social Council, in resolution 718 (XXVII) of 24 April 1959, requested the United Nations Educational, Scientific and Cultural Organization to undertake a survey designed to provide the elements for the programme of concrete action desired by the General Assembly,

Noting with satisfaction Economic and Social Council resolution 888 E (XXXIV) of 24 July 1962, transmitting to the General Assembly the reports on the survey which has been carried out by the United Nations Educational, Scientific and Cultural Organization by means of a series of regional meetings in Asia, Africa and Latin America, held in co-operation with the respective United Nations regional economic commissions,

Expressing its concern that, according to the survey, 70 per cent of the population of the world lack adequate information facilities and are thus denied effective enjoyment of the right to information,

Considering that the information media have an important part to play in education and in economic and social progress generally and that new techniques of communication offer special opportunities for acceleration of the education process,

1. *Invites* the Governments concerned to include adequate provision in their economic plans for the development of national information media;

2. *Invites* the Technical Assistance Board, the Special Fund, the specialized agencies concerned, the regional economic commissions and other public and private agencies and institutions to assist, as appropriate, the less developed countries in developing and strengthening their national information media;

3. *Requests* the United Nations Educational, Scientific and Cultural Organization to continue to further the programme for the development of information media including the application of new techniques of communication for achievement of rapid progress in education, to keep up to date as far as possible its survey on this subject and to report as appropriate to the Commission on Human Rights and to the Economic and Social Council;

4. *Recommends* that the Governments of Member States should take this programme into account in connexion with the United Nations Development Decade;

5. *Invites* the governments of the more developed countries to co-operate with less developed countries with a view to meeting the urgent needs of the less developed countries in connexion with this programme for the development of independent national information media, with due regard for the culture of each country.

CO-OPERATION AND ASSISTANCE IN THE APPLICATION AND IMPROVEMENT OF NATIONAL INFORMATION AND MASS COMMUNICATION SYSTEMS FOR SOCIAL PROGRESS AND DEVELOPMENT

United Nations General Assembly Resolution 31/139, 1976

The General Assembly,
Recalling its resolution 1778 (XVII) of 7 December 1962 and convinced that the establishment and/or development of national information and mass communication systems will play an important role in the promotion of opportunities for the peoples of the developing nations to participate fully in national development and in the promotion of international co-operation, including the efforts to achieve the goals of the International Development Strategy for the Second United Nations Development Decade and the establishment of the new international economic order,

Further recalling its resolution 3148 (XXVIII) of 14 December 1973 and convinced that the establishment and/or improvement of national information and mass communication systems will greatly help preserve and enhance the cultural values of a country and will be one of the most efficient methods for transmitting scientific and technological knowledge and the cultural values of a country,

Desirous that the benefits of co-operation and assistance in the application and the establishment and/or improvement of national information and mass communication systems for social progress and development be considered with a view to disseminating those benefits to all countries regardless of their stages of economic and social development,

Acknowledging the important contributions made and the significant roles being played by the specialized agencies, intergovernmental organizations, regional economic and social commissions, non-governmental organizations and regional communication media training and research institutions in assisting developing countries in the field of mass communications,

Noting with appreciation the relevant decisions taken by the General Conference of the United Nations Educational, Scientific and Cultural Organization at its nineteenth session in the field of mass communications,

Convinced that consideration of ways and means of achieving the application and improvement of national information and mass communication systems for social progress and development will pave the way for improved international co-operation in the field of mass communications,

1. *Invites* the Governments of the developing countries to give due regard to the establishment and/or strengthening of their national mass communication systems within the framework of their over-all development plans;

2. *Requests* the Director-General of the United Nations Educational, Scientific and Cultural Organization to continue and intensify its programme for the development of mass communication systems, especially for the benefit of developing countries;

3. *Requests* the Director-General of the United Nations Educational, Scientific and Cultural Organization, in co-operation with the United Nations, the specialized agencies concerned and other interested organizations, to report to the General Assembly at its thirty-third session on progress achieved in the development of mass

communication systems, which report will be used as a basis for discussion at that session of the Assembly;

4. *Decides* to include in the provisional agenda of its thirty-third session an item entitled "Co-operation and assistance in the application and improvement of national information and mass communication systems for social progress and development" and to consider it at that session as a matter of priority.

QUESTIONS RELATING TO INFORMATION

United Nations General Assembly Resolution 33/115, 1978

A

Co-operation and assistance in the application and improvement of national information and mass communication systems for social progress and development

The General Assembly,

Recalling its resolution 1778 (XVII) of 7 December 1962 and convinced that the establishment and/or development of national information and mass communication systems will play an important role in the promotion of opportunities for the peoples of the developing nations to participate fully in national development and in the promotion of international co-operation, including the efforts to achieve the goals of the International Development Strategy for the Second United Nations Development Decade and the establishment of the new international economic order,

Recalling its resolution 3148 (XXVIII) of 14 December 1973 and convinced that the establishment and/or the improvement of national information and mass communication systems will greatly help preserve and enhance the cultural values of a country and will be one of the most efficient methods for transmitting scientific and technological knowledge and the cultural values of a country,

Recalling its resolution 31/139 of 16 December 1976, in which, *inter alia*, it established the need to discuss this item and requested the United Nations Educational, Scientific and Cultural Organization to continue and intensify its programme for the development of mass communication systems, especially for the benefit of developing countries,

Desirous that the benefits of co-operation and assistance in the application and the establishment and/or improvement of national information and mass communication systems for social progress and development be considered with a view to disseminating those benefits to all countries regardless of their stages of economic and social development,

Recognizing that the potential of the field of communications should be applicable to all developing countries so that it could be used appropriately to enhance further the economic and social progress of developing countries and to allow all developing countries to have equal access to communication technology and principles in order to develop and operate their own communication systems and policies and to have equal access to the channels of information,

Noting with appreciation the relevant decisions in the field of mass communications adopted by the General Conference of the United Nations Educational, Scientific and Cultural Organization at its twentieth session,

Taking into consideration the need for finding ways to improve existing channels of communication within the United Nations and between developing countries,

Convinced that consideration of ways and means of achieving the application and improvement of national information and mass communication systems for social progress and development will pave the way for improved international co-operation in the field of mass communications,

1. *Takes note with appreciation* of the report of the Director-General of the United Nations Educational, Scientific and Cultural Organization, prepared in co-operation with the International Telecommunication Union;

2. *Invites* the Secretary-General, in co-operation with the United Nations Educational, Scientific and Cultural Organization and other specialized agencies as well as interested organizations, to carry out consultations on ways and means by which assistance for developing countries can be increased in the field of communication technology and systems for their social progress and economic development;

3. *Requests* the Director-General of the United Nations Educational, Scientific and Cultural Organizations, on the basis of the result of the consultation referred to in paragraph 2 above, to draw up a model plan for co-operation and assistance in the application and improvement of national information and mass communication systems for social progress and development, including the elaboration of a proposal for institutional arrangements to systematize collaborative consultation on communication development activities, needs and plans;

4. *Requests* the Director-General of the United Nations Educational, Scientific and Cultural Organization to submit a progress report, in pursuance of paragraph 3 above, to the General Assembly at its thirty-fourth session;

5. *Decides* to include in the provisional agenda of its thirty-fourth session the item entitled "Co-operation and assistance in the application and improvement of national information and mass communication systems for social progress and development" and to consider it at that session as a matter of priority.

* * *

QUESTIONS RELATING TO INFORMATION

United Nations General Assembly Resolution 35/201, 1981

The General Assembly,

I

1. *Expresses its satisfaction* with the relevant resolutions as adopted by the General Conference of the United Nations Educational, Scientific and Cultural Organization at its twenty-first session, held at Belgrade from 23 September to 28 October 1980, in particular the resolution on the report of the Director-General on the findings of the International Commission for the Study of Communication;

2. *Takes note* of the invitation of the Director-General of the United Nations Educational, Scientific and Cultural Organization to take immediate steps to initiate studies with a view to drawing up the fundamental principles underlying a new world information and communication order and exploring the possibility and desirability of such studies serving as a basis for a Declaration on the Establishment of a New World Information and Communication Order;

3. *Expresses its satisfaction* at the establishment within the United Nations Educational, Scientific and Cultural Organization of the International Programme for the Development of Communication, which constitutes an important step in the establishment of a new world information and communication order and which aims at the development of infrastructures of communications of the developing countries in order to contribute to narrowing the gap in the fields of information and communication between developed and developing countries as well as among developing countries themselves;

4. *Invites* Governments, non-governmental organizations and other entities in Member States to extend financial as well as technical support for the development of communication structures in developing countries and, in particular, to the International Programme for the Development of Communication;

5. *Calls upon* the Secretary-General to render full co-operation and support to the International Programme for the Development of Communication and to seek and encourage interagency co-operation and the participation of the agencies in the activities of the Programme and its Intergovernmental Council;

6. *Invites* Member States to facilitate the widespread circulation and study of the final report of the International Commission for the Study of Communication Problems, to take into account its recommendations in the preparation and strengthening of their national communication capabilities and to include the questions relating to information and communication in their development strategy;

7. *Takes note* of the significant activities which the United Nations Educational, Scientific and Cultural Organization is undertaking with regard to the effects of the activities of transnational corporations in developing countries within the fields of its competence;

8. *Reaffirms* the vital need, at the operational level, for co-operation and coordination between the United Nations Educational, Scientific and Cultural Organization and other organizations of the United Nations system that are concerned with the question of information and communication;

9. *Requests* the Director-General of the United Nations Educational, Scientific and Cultural Organization to submit a progress report on the implementation of the International Programme for the Development of Communication to the General Assembly at its thirty-sixth session.

* * *

INTERNATIONAL PROGRAMME
FOR THE DEVELOPMENT OF COMMUNICATION

Unesco General Conference Resolution 4/21, 1980

The General Conference,
Recalling resolution 4/9.1/3 adopted at its twentieth session, calling for the establishment of 'a new, more just and more effective world information and communication order',
    Conscious of the Declaration on Fundamental Principles concerning the Contribution of the Mass Media to the Strengthening of Peace and International Understanding, to the Promotion of Human Rights and to Countering Racialism, Apartheid and Incitement to War,
    Taking note of the declarations and recommendations of the Intergovernmental Conferences on Communication Policies held at San José in July 1976, Kuala Lumpur in February 1979 and Yaoundé in July 1980,
    Recalling also resolution 4/9.4/2 adopted at its twentieth session, requesting the Director-General to encourage and intensify communication development and to convene for this purpose a planning meeting of the representatives of governments to develop a proposal for institutional arrangements to systematize collaborative consultation on communications development activities, needs and plans,
    Appreciating the Director-General's prompt action in convening the Intergovernmental Conference for Co-operation on Activities, Needs and Programmes for Communication Development (DEVCOM), held in Paris in April 1980,
    Taking note of the recommendation of the Intergovernmental Conference inviting the Director-General to submit to the General Conference a project for the establishment, within the framework of Unesco, of an International Programme for the Development of Communication (IPDC),
    Taking fully into account the line of action suggested in the document submitted to this session and entitled 'Intergovernmental Conference for Co-operation on Activities, Needs and Programmes for Communication Development – Director-

General's Report and Proposals' (21C/86),

Stressing that this international programme, aiming to increase co-operation and assistance for the development of communication infrastructures and to reduce the gap between various countries in the communication field, must form part of the efforts for the establishment of a new, more just and more effective world information and communication order,

I

1. *Approves* the recommendation on the International Programme for the Development of Communication, adopted by consensus at the Intergovernmental Conference, the text of which is reproduced in Annex I;

II

2. *Resolves:*

(a) to establish, within the framework of Unesco, an International Programme for the Development of Communication (IPDC) in accordance with the provisions of Part III to VI of the aforementioned recommendation, which define the objectives, competence and measures necessary for the effective functioning of the programme;

(b) to set up without delay the appropriate system of financing and resources, referred to in Part V and VI of the recommendation;

(c) to adopt the Statutes of the Intergovernmental Council of the International Programme for the Development of Communication, the text of which is contained in Annex II;

(d) to elect the Intergovernmental Council composed of thirty-five Member States, on the basis of equitable geographical distribution and applying the principles of rotation, as a co-ordinating body responsible to the General Conference of Unesco, with the task of implementing the objectives of the IPDC;

III

3. *Invites* Member States to take appropriate self-reliant measures for the more intensive development of communication facilities and activities, and further invites them, as well as various international organizations and relevant non-governmental and professional associations, to collaborate extensively between themselves and with Unesco in the fields of communication development and to lend their support to the activities of the IPDC, bearing in mind that implementation of the objectives of the International Programme for the Development of Communication needs the co-operation of all those interested and concerned;

IV

4. *Invites* the Director-General:

(a) to take appropriate measures and make necessary arrangements, in the context of existing programme activities and staffing (more particularly in the framework of Objective 9.4), which will facilitate the establishment, development and efficient implementation of the IPDC;

(b) to set up the necessary secretariat to assist the Intergovernmental Council as soon as possible, in accordance with the Statutes of the Council;

(c) to make available within the framework of the approved regular budget for 1981–1983 the sum of $1,750,000 for launching and implementing the initial phase of the IPDC;

(d) to take necessary action leading to the establishment of an inter-agency working group of the appropriate organizations in the United Nations system, bearing in mind that wider co-operation between Unesco, the United Nations and the various Specialized Agencies and other bodies having competence in this field is vital for the satisfactory implementation of the IPDC;

(e) to make the appropriate arrangements, in consultation with the Intergovernmental Council, to mobilize resources needed for the International Programme and to seek contributions from Member States and other parties concerned;

(f) to explore, in consultation with the Intergovernmental Council, among other alternatives, the possibilities of elevating the appropriate system of financing and resources to the status of an international fund within the framework of Unesco;

V

5. *Expresses* its hope that all developed and developing countries, organizations and agencies of the United Nations system as well as other intergovernmental and non-governmental organizations, professional groups and other available sources will lend their support to the expansion of IPDC resources, in the form of finances, manpower, materials, technology and training, for a speedy and satisfactory implementation of the International Programme of the Development of Communication;

6. *Invites* the Intergovernmental Council to submit to the General Conference of Unesco at its twenty-second session the first report on its activities, in conformity with Article 11 of the Statutes;

7. *Expresses* the conviction that the progressive implementation of these recommendations constitutes an essential stage towards the establishment of a new, more just and more effective world information and communication order;

VI

8. *Elects* in accordance with paragraph 1 of Article 2 of the Statutes of the Intergovernmental Council of the International Programme for the Development of Communication, the following Member States to be members of the Council:

Argentina	India	Sri Lanka
Austria	Indonesia	Tunisia
Bangladesh	Iraq	Union of Soviet
Benin	Japan	Socialist Republics
Canada	Mexico	United Republic
China	Mozambique	of Cameroon
Cuba	Netherlands	United Republic
Democratic Yemen	Nicaragua	of Tanzania
Egypt	Nigeria	United States of America
France	Norway	Venezuela
Gabon	Peru	Yugoslavia
German Democratic Republic	Saudi Arabia	Zaire
Federal Republic of Germany	Senegal	

9. *Decides*, in accordance with paragraph 3 of Article 2 of the Statutes of the Intergovernmental Council of the International Programme for the Development of Communication, that the term of office of the following members of the Council shall cease at the end of the twenty-second session of the General Conference:

Argentina	Mozambique	Tunisia
Benin	Netherlands	United Republic
Canada	Nigeria	of Cameroon

Cuba	Norway	United Republic
Egypt	Saudi Arabia	of Tanzania
France	Senegal	Yugoslavia
Federal Republic of Germany		

Annex I. Recommendation on the International Programme for the Development of Communication adopted by the Intergovernmental Conference for Co-operation on Activities, Needs and Programmes for Communication Development (Paris, 14–21 April 1980)

The Conference,

1. *Conscious* of the increasing role of communication among peoples and nations in promoting political, economic, social, scientific, educational and cultural progress, as well as in improving mutual understanding, strengthening international peace and safeguarding national sovereignty and cultural identity,

2. *Conscious* of the close relationship linking the concepts, objectives and results of the overall development of each country and of all countries with the systems, practices, means and infrastructures of social communication,

3. *Noting* the deplorable situations of dependence and the significant inequalities of a technological, professional, material and financial nature which exist between developed countries and developing countries in most fields of communication, and further noting calls for larger participation in, and democratization of, international relations in the field of information and for the overcoming of vestiges of colonialism,

4. *Observing* also that the circulation of information among countries still shows numerous deficiencies,

5. *Reaffirming* that it is indispensable to change the state of dependency of developing countries in the field of information and communication by assuring wider and better balanced circulation and dissemination of information among all partners and by guaranteeing the diversity of sources and free access to information,

6. *Underlining* that pursuit of the objectives and elimination of the obstacles cited above depends on strengthening the potential of developing countries in the different fields of communication,

7. *Underlining* the need to establish a new international information and communication order, as indicated in the relevant resolutions adopted by the General Conference of Unesco at its twentieth session,

8. *Considering* that international co-operation in the field of communication development should take place on the basis of equality, justice, mutual advantage and the principles of international law, and mindful of the fundamental contribution that the information media and mass communications can make to the establishment of a new international economic order, the strengthening of peace and international understanding, the realization of the goal of general and complete disarmament under effective international control, the promotion of universal respect for human rights and the struggle against racism, apartheid and colonialism,

9. *Considering* that assistance to developing countries should not be politically tied and that favourable conditions should be enhanced to facilitate better access to modern communication technology for developing countries,

10. *Recalling* the 'Declaration on Fundamental Principles concerning the Contribution of the Mass Media to Strengthening Peace and International Understanding, to the Promotion of Human Rights and to Countering Racialism, Apartheid and Incitement to War', adopted by the General Conference of Unesco at its twentieth session, in particular Article VI, which states that in order to achieve a new equilibrium and assure greater reciprocity in the flow of information it is essential that the mass

media in developing countries 'should have conditions and resources enabling them to gain strength and expand, and to co-operate both among themselves and with the mass media in developed countries',

11. *Recalling* resolution 4/9.4/2 adopted at the twentieth session of the General Conference of Unesco, requesting the Director-General to intensify and encourage communications development and to hold consultations designed to lead to the provision to developing countries of technological and other means for promoting a free flow and a wider and better balanced exchange of information of all kinds, and inviting him, for this purpose, to convene as early as possible after the conclusion of its twentieth session a planning meeting of representatives of governments, to develop a proposal for institutional arrangements to systematize collaborative consultation on communications development activities, needs and plans,

12. *Recalling* propositions made by the delegates of certain developed countries during the twentieth session of Unesco's General Conference to engage in technical co-operation and practical assistance,

13. *Recalling* also the resolutions adopted by the General Assembly of the United Nations at its 33rd and 34th sessions, supporting the action undertaken by Unesco and the orientations it has adopted in the field of communication,

14. *Recalling* resolution 34/181 adopted by the 34th session of the General Assembly of the United Nations which asks the Director-General of Unesco to study, among other alternatives, the possibility of creating, under the auspices of Unesco, an international fund for the development of communication,

15. *Recalling* also resolution 34/182 adopted by the General Assembly of the United Nations at its 34th session recognizing in particular the central and important role of Unesco in the field of information and mass communications and in the implementation of decisions relating thereto,

16. *Reaffirming* the need to strengthen the co-operation and co-ordination between the institutions of the United Nations system which deal with different aspects of communication and contribute to operational action for the development of communication systems,

17. *Recalling* in this context the notable role already played in communications development by several agencies of the United Nations system and particularly the International Telecommunication Union (ITU), which has been given the responsibility for establishing an integrated worldwide telecommunications network,

18. *Reaffirming* that in order to reduce the existing gaps in communication within, as well as among, nations it is indispensable to develop appropriate infrastructures, equipment, training programmes, resources and means in developing countries in order to increase their indigenous capacity for the production and distribution of messages,

19. *Recognizing* the necessity for all countries to utilize fully all possible forms of mutual consultation, co-operation and assistance, both multilateral and bilateral, to accelerate the development and improvement of communication and information systems,

20. *Observing* that signs of solidarity are appearing within the international community to correct in different fields, including communication, the present disequilibrium between developed and developing countries, and anxious to transform these signs of constructive solidarity into concrete actions,

21. *Recalling* that the existing disparity in communication among different countries will not be eliminated by the mere material development of infrastructures and professional resources and by the transfer of know-how and technologies but that the solution depends also on the elimination of all political, ideological, psychological, economic and technical obstacles which run counter to the development of indepen-

dent national communication systems and to a freer, wider and more balanced circulation of information,

I

Recommends Member States, taking into account the objectives of their national communication development policies and priorities:

i.   to promote the formulation, at national and regional levels, of general communication development policies in order to facilitate the mobilization of available human and material resources, while ensuring the coherent coordination and planning of their use;

ii.   to identify the priority areas in national investment plans and communication development programmes which justify support and financing by competent national or international bodies;

iii.   to make provision in economic, social and cultural development projects for the necessary facilities for the acquisition, installation and operation of different means of information and communication to meet professional needs, as well as for the production of telecommunication and information material and equipment;

iv.   to contribute to the creation and consolidation of appropriate systems of communication at the material and logistic level, taking into account the requirements of endogenous development;

v.   to take appropriate measures to overcome, more effectively than in the past, the different political, economic, commercial, financial and technical obstacles which hamper the introduction of conditions conducive to the freer and better balanced exchange of information;

vi.   to undertake measures such as will stimulate the efforts of the developing countries, by increasing resources from various countries and ensuring the harmonious utilization of available national and international means;

vii.   to give highest priority, in their co-operation agreements, to the creation or development of the national and regional infrastructures which are necessary for communication, to the improvement of professional and technical training as well as to the setting up of production structures to ensure a more balanced exchange of information and cultural products;

viii.   to intensify substantially their efforts in the various fields of technical assistance in the form of training, expertise, equipment, etc.;

II

Recommends international and regional organizations, and especially those belonging to the United Nations system:

i.   to intensify their reciprocal co-operation with a view to the more effective utilization of their existing or potential human and material resources, in the communication development field, in support of the common aims which these organizations pursue;

ii.   to provide additional resources to information and communication development programmes, and to support efforts made by developing countries to set up infrastructures and facilities for social communication, telecommunication or informatics which will enable them to transmit or receive information of all kinds at an acceptable cost;

iii.   to contribute to the development of the training of specialized professionals and skilled personnel so as to master different communication technologies;

III

Invites the Director-General of Unesco, in conformity with the resolution 4/9.4/2 adopted at the twentieth session of the General Conference, to submit to the General Conference, at its next session, a project for the establishment, within the framework of Unesco, of an International Programme for the Development of Communication;

Recommends that the main objectives of this programme should be:

i.   to assist developing countries, at their request, in the elaboration and implementation of their information and communication development plans, as well as in the identification of needs and priority areas;

ii.   to promote in developing countries, in accordance with their communication policies and development plans, the creation or extension of infrastructures for the different communication sectors, in order, in particular, to increase the contribution of the means of communication to endogenous economic, social and cultural development, as well as to promote improved international exchange of information;

iii. to proceed with the analysis of technical and financial needs and resources in the fields of information and communication at national and international levels;

iv.   to ensure reciprocal consultation and better co-ordination among the parties interested in the development of communication and in various related programmes of co-operation;

v.   to pursue all available avenues, both public and private, for the securing of funds and other resources to support projects or classes of projects of communications development;

vi.   to bring together proposed projects with sources of financial and other help that it may have obtained or identified;

vii. to encourage contributions to these projects from all possible financing sources, in accordance with such plans and common interests as may emerge;

viii. to strengthen co-operation and co-ordination of Unesco's activities with other Specialized Agencies concerned, especially with the International Telecommunication Union (ITU);

ix.   to give particular attention, at an early stage of its activities, to the promotion of viable regional institutional arrangements which should assist the programme in pursuing the above-mentioned objectives, through integrated regional co-operation in the field of communication development; in this connection, regional communication institutions established with Unesco's assistance should be encouraged to play an extensive role in the planning and execution of regional projects within the programme;

x.   to provide consultative and advisory services to the developing countries in the field of communications development, with a view to making optimum use of available resources;

xi.   to take measures to promote the awareness of all parties concerned (be they developing or developed countries, international organizations and agencies of the United Nations system, non-governmental organizations or other public and private bodies active in this field) of the important role that communication plays in the development process, thus contributing to mobilize technical and financial resources necessary to the pursuance of the objectives of the programme;

xii. to encourage maximum co-operation, co-ordination and concentration of efforts among all who are interested in national or international communications development;

xiii. to support, particularly among developing countries, the conclusion of arrangements on the exchange of information, programmes and experience and on co-operation and co-production between radio and television organizations, news agencies and journalists' associations;

xiv. to prepare studies based on experience gained in international co-operation in

the field of information and communication development, particularly between developing and developed countries;

IV

Recommends that:

i. the International Programme for the Development of Communication should
    be co-ordinated by an Intergovernmental Council composed of thirty-five
    Member States elected by and responsible to the General Conference of
    Unesco on the basis of equitable geographical distribution and applying the
    principle of rotation. It will be the task of the Intergovernmental Council to
    implement the objectives set out in this recommendation. In its deliberations,
    priority should be given to seeking a consensus. The Intergovernmental
    Council will administer funds which may be contributed to the programme to
    promote communication development in the developing countries and
    allocate them to projects and programmes in accordance with criteria and
    priorities it will define;

ii. the organizations and agencies of the United Nations system, as well as other
    intergovernmental and non-governmental organizations and professional
    groups which are active in the field of communication development, should
    be closely associated with the activities of the Intergovernmental Council so
    as to play a significant role in the accomplishment of its objectives;

Invites the Director-General of Unesco:

(a) to take the necessary steps to facilitate the establishment and functioning of the
    International Programme for the Development of Communication;

(b) to consult with appropriate organizations of the United Nations system with a
    view to establishing a consultative framework in which to co-ordinate and har-
    monize the communication development efforts of each;

(c) to put at the disposal of the Intergovernmental Council the necessary
    secretariat. The director of the secretariat will be appointed by the Director-
    General on the recommendation of the Intergovernmental Council, following
    those provisions of the Constitution of Unesco and of prevailing procedures that
    lead towards this end;

V

Recommends that, to secure satisfactory implementation of the International Programme for the Development of Communication, additional resources should be
sought from all possible sources – developing and developed countries, international
organizations and agencies of the United Nations system as well as other intergovernmental and non-governmental organizations, professional groups and
other available sources – in the form of financial means, manpower, materials,
technology and training for the development of communication. To this effect an appropriate system of financing and resources should be established;

VI

Requests the Director-General to make the appropriate arrangements, in consultation with the Intergovernmental Council, to mobilize the resources needed for the
International Programme, and to seek contributions from Member States and other
parties concerned;

VII

Expresses the conviction that the gradual implementation of these recommendations constitutes an essential stage on the way to the establishment of a new, more just and more effective world information and communication order.

Annex II. Statutes of the Intergovernmental Council of the International Programme for the Development of Communication

Article 1

An Intergovernmental Council of the International Programme for the Development of Communication is hereby established within the United Nations Educational, Scientific and Cultural Organization.

Article 2

1. The Council shall be composed of thirty-five Member States of the United Nations Educational, Scientific and Cultural Organization, elected by the General Conference, taking into account the need to ensure equitable geographical distribution and appropriate rotation.

2. The term of office of Members of the Council shall extend from the end of the ordinary session of the General Conference during which they are elected until the end of its second subsequent ordinary session.

3. Notwithstanding the provisions of paragraph 2 above, the term of office of seventeen members designated at the time of the first election shall cease at the end of the first ordinary session of the General Conference following that at which they were elected. The names of these members shall be chosen by lot by the President of the General Conference after the first election. The retiring members shall be replaced by members belonging to the same regional group.

4. Members of the Council shall be immediately eligible for re-election.

5. The Council may make recommendations concerning its own membership to the General Conference.

6. The persons appointed by Member States as their representatives on the Council shall preferably be specialists in the fields covered by the International Programme for the Development of Communication. They shall be selected particularly from persons employed in various fields of communication, especially those connected with planning, research or the application of national policies or with activities conducted under international co-operation in those same fields.

Article 3

1. The Council shall normally meet in regular plenary session once a year. Extraordinary sessions may be convened as specified in the Council's Rules of Procedure.

2. When votes are taken, each member of the Council shall have one vote, but the representative of any State member of the Council may be assisted by one or more advisers, a list of whom shall be communicated to the Secretariat, preferably before the opening of the Council's proceedings.

Article 4

1. The Council shall adopt its own Rules of Procedure.

2. Under its Rules of Procedure, the Council may establish whatever subsidiary bodies it considers appropriate, provided that the necessary financial resources are available.

Article 5

Within the framework of the decisions of the General Conference concerning the International Programme for the Development of Communication, the Council shall be responsible for:

(a) guiding the planning and implementation of the International Programme;
(b) considering proposals concerning the development and adaptation of the Programme;
(c) recommending priorities among the various activities or groups of activities constituting that Programme;
(d) reviewing and assessing achievements and defining the basic areas requiring increased international co-operation;
(e) reviewing ways and means whereby Member States might participate more effectively in the International Programme for the Development of Communication;
(f) devising an appropriate system of financing for the Programme;
(g) seeking the necessary resources for the implementation of the Programme and for the development of communication for the benefit of countries requesting assistance from the Programme.

Article 6

1. At the beginning of its first session, and subsequently whenever the membership of the Council is changed by the General Conference in accordance with Article 2 above, the Council shall elect a Chairman, three Vice-Chairmen, a Rapporteur and three other members; these shall form the Council's Bureau.

2. The Bureau shall discharge such duties as the Council may lay upon it.

3. Meetings of the Bureau may be convened between meetings of the Council at the request of an absolute majority of the Council's members, at the request of the Director-General of Unesco or at the request of half the members of the Bureau.

Article 7

1. Member States and Associate Members of Unesco which are not members of the Council may send observers to all meetings of the Council or its subsidiary bodies.

2. Representatives of the United Nations and other organizations of the United Nations system supporting the Programme may take part, without the right to vote, in all meetings of the Council and its subsidiary bodies.

3. The Council shall lay down the conditions under which other international governmental or non-governmental organizations may be invited to participate in its proceedings without the right to vote. The Council shall also lay down the conditions under which certain particularly well qualified persons might be consulted on matters within their competence.

Article 8

1. The International Programme for the Development of Communication shall be administered by the Director-General, who shall make the necessary secretariat and facilities available to the Council. The director of the Programme shall be appointed by the Director-General on the recommendation of the Council, pursuant to the provisions of the Constitution of Unesco and in accordance with the procedures in force governing the appointment of the Organization's staff which are applicable to this end.

2. The secretariat, under the authority of the Director-General, shall carry out the administrative work necessary for the implementation of the International Programme for the Development of Communication and for the sessions of the Council or the meetings of its Bureau.

Article 9

1. The running expenses of the Council and its subsidiary bodies shall be covered by appropriations voted for this purpose by the General Conference of the United Nations Educational, Scientific and Cultural Organization.

2. The expenses incurred by the participation of representatives of Member States in sessions of the Council and its subsidiary bodies shall be covered by appropriations voted for this purpose by the General Conference of the United Nations Educational, Scientific and Cultural Organization.

3. Voluntary contributions shall be accepted in accordance with the Financial Regulations of the United Nations Educational, Scientific and Cultural Organization.

Article 10

The Director-General shall submit to the Council, at each of its sessions, a report on the implementation of the International Programme for the Development of Communication. He shall report to the General Conference on the implementation of the Programme, particularly as it relates to the Regular Programme of the Organization and the activities of other agencies of the United Nations system.

Article 11

The Council shall submit reports on its activities to the General Conference of the United Nations Educational, Scientific and Cultural Organization at each of its ordinary sessions.

8. Communications policies

It is only in the last few years that communications and information policy has appeared as an issue area *per se* at the international level. While specific and mostly technically oriented policy issues have for a long time been dealt with by such organizations as the International Telecommunication Union, the Universal Postal Union and other specialized agencies, general communications policy issues represent a new area of debate and decision-making in international fora.

The documents included in this section reflect the concerns and issues related to general communications policy as they have been expressed in the context of Unesco. These issues are closely related to those mentioned in the preceding and in the following sections. In a more global perspective, most other international legal instruments mentioned in this collection include provisions which give a formalized expression to communications and information policy.

Documents

i.   Culture and communication, Unesco General Conference Resolution 4/0.1, 1978
     − Part III
ii. International Commission for the Study of Communication Problems, Unesco General Conference Resolution 4/19, 1980
     − Preamble
     − Parts I-V
iii. Declaration of San José, Intergovernmental Conference on Communication Policies in Latin America and the Caribbean, San José, 1976
     − Full text

iv. Kuala Lumpur Declaration, Intergovernmental Conference of Communication Policies in Asia and Oceania, Kuala Lumpur, 1979
   - Full text
v. Yaoundé Declaration, Intergovernmental Conference on Communication Policies in Africa, Yaoundé, 1980
   - Full text

CULTURE AND COMMUNICATION

Unesco General Conference Resolution 4/0.1, 1978

The General Conference,

III

Mindful of the fundamental importance of communication, as the link between minds and the instrument of relations between societies, and of the role it must play in improving knowledge and bringing about true mutual understanding between peoples in all their diversity,
   Recalling the concern caused throughout the world by the imbalances and inequalities to be found today in the production, dissemination and exchange of information, both within countries and between countries and regions, whereas the progress achieved by the communication media should enable all peoples to give expression to the way they see their own position and that of the international community of which they form a part,
   Recognizing the role that can and should be assigned to communication in awakening the conscience of, and sensitizing public opinion to the major problems confronting the world and to their indivisible and global character, and in helping towards their solution,
   Recalling the irreplaceable contribution that communication media of all kinds can make in furthering the advance and the renewal of education, facilitating the dissemination and use of scientific and technological innovations, making possible the diffusion of cultural works and, in general, promoting economic and social development,
   Recalling the need to clarify and solve problems involving the professional status and responsibility of those whose business it is to produce and disseminate information, and, similarly, those concerning the establishment of rules, standards and practices such as will provide them with more effective protection and security in the exercise of their duties,
   Considering that utilization of the increasingly numerous and varied opportunities afforded by communication in the world today depends on the availability of human resources, material means and technical infrastructures, all of which are at present very unevenly distributed,
   Mindful of the complexity of communications problems and of their international range, *convinced* of the urgent need for their searching examination and clarification, and *noting* that this task has been entrusted to the International Commission for the Study of Communication Problems set up by the Director-General in 1977,
3. *Invites* the Director-General:
   (a) to continue the work of studying the significance, scope and role of communication;
   (b) to assign high priority to measures likely to reduce inequalities and imbalances in communication, both within countries and between different groups of countries and in particular between developed and developing countries, especially by helping the latter to organize exchanges of information,

under satisfactory conditions, between themselves and the developed countries, and thereby promote a free flow and a wider and better balanced exchange of information between the different regions of the world;

(c)   to take into account all the ways in which communication, by making it possible to involve the different populations in the discovery of innovative solutions, should help to overcome the major problems facing mankind, particularly concerning the preservation of peace, respect for human rights and the drive against poverty, hunger and malnutrition in the context of the establishment of a new international economic order;

(d)   to co-operate with Member States, especially the developing countries, with a view to helping them to build up their infrastructures and train their personnel in the field of communication so as to be able to make full use of the opportunities afforded by the communication media for promoting wider participation in cultural life, educational progress, the establishment of science and technology, and overall development;

(e)   to co-operate with Member States in analysing the problems raised by the rapid expansion of the means of information and of the dissemination of news and in seeking appropriate solutions to those problems;

(f)   to encourage an adoption of a global approach to problems connected with communication, regarded as an essential factor of economic, social and cultural development.

INTERNATIONAL COMMISSION FOR THE STUDY OF COMMUNICATION PROBLEMS

Unesco General Conference Resolution 4/19, 1980

The General Conference,

Reaffirming its attachment to the principles proclaimed in the Charter of the United Nations, the Universal Declaration of Human Rights, the International Covenant on Civil and Political Rights, the Constitution of Unesco and the Declaration on Fundamental Principles concerning the Contribution of the Mass Media to Strengthening Peace and International Understanding, to the Promotion of Human Rights and to Countering Racialism, Apartheid and Incitement to War,

Recalling more particularly Article 19 of the Universal Declaration of Human Rights which provides that 'Everyone has the right to freedom of opinion and expression; this right includes freedom to hold opinions without interference and to seek, receive and impart information and ideas through any media and regardless of frontiers' and Article 29, which stipulates that, like all others, 'These rights and freedoms may in no case be exercised contrary to the purposes and principles of the United Nations',

Recalling also Articles 19 and 20 of the International Covenant on Civil and Political Rights,

Recalling also the declaration in the Constitution of Unesco that 'the States Parties to this Constitution, believing in . . . the unrestricted pursuit of objective truth, and in the free exchange of ideas and knowledge, are agreed and determined to develop and to increase the means of communication between their peoples and to employ these means for the purpose of mutual understanding and a truer and more perfect knowledge of each other's lives',

Recalling moreover that the purpose of Unesco is 'to contribute to peace and security by promoting collaboration among the nations through education, science and culture in order to further universal respect for justice, for the rule of law and for the human rights and fundamental freedoms which are affirmed for the peoples of the world, without distinction of race, sex, language or religion, by the Charter of the United Nations' (Article 1 of the Constitution),

Reaffirming the responsibilities of Unesco and its role in the field of communication and recalling previous General Conference debates on this subject, including resolutions 4/9.1/2 and 4/9.1/3 adopted at its twentieth session (1978),

Noting the increasing attention devoted to communication problems and needs by other intergovernmental organizations, both regional and international, notably the Movement of Non-Aligned Countries which, in the Declaration of the Colombo Summit (1976), stated that 'a new international order in the fields of information and mass communications is as vital as a new international economic order' and, in the Declaration of the Havana Summit (1979), noting progress in the development of national information media, stressed that 'co-operation in the field of information is an integral part of the struggle for the creation of new international relations in general and a new international information order in particular',

Recalling that the Director-General, in pursuance of resolution 100 adopted by the General Conference at its nineteenth session (Nairobi, 1976), set up the International Commission for the Study of Communication Problems, composed of sixteen eminent persons acting in an individual capacity, that the Commission was able to carry out its work in total independence and that it prepared a final report published under the title *Many Voices, One World,*

Considering that the publication by Unesco of the Report of the International Commission for the Study of Communication Problems is not only stimulating a discussion of considerable breadth and intensity, but is, at the same time, encouraging professional circles and the general public to join in the debate,

Noting with satisfaction that the report of the Director-General on the findings of the International Commission for the Study of Communication Problems (21C/85) has greatly facilitated the discussion devoted to communication problems and to the different aspects of the Organization's programme related to them,

Conscious that communication among individuals, nations and peoples, as well as among national minorities and different social, ethnic and cultural groups can and must, provided that its means are increased and practices improved, make a greater contribution to individual and collective development, the strengthening of national and cultural identity, the consolidation of democracy and the advancement of education, science and culture, as well as to the positive transformation of international relations and the expansion of international co-operation,

I

1. *Expresses* its thanks to the Director-General for having put at the disposal of the International Commission for the Study of Communication Problems the means necessary for its work;

2. *Addresses* its appreciation and thanks to the Chairman, Mr Sean MacBride, and to the members of the International Commission for the Study of Communication Problems, and congratulates them on the quality of the work carried out, the breadth of vision they have shown and the praiseworthy efforts they have made to fulfil their mandate in the allotted time;

II

3. *Considers* the publication of the Report of the International Commission for the Study of Communication Problems as a valuable contribution to the study of information and communication problems;

4. *Recognizes* that that Report has succeeded in identifying a large number of the most significant information and communication problems, examining certain questions posed in this field at different levels and pointing to a number of directions in which action with a view to settling those questions in the short, medium and long term might be taken;

5. *Emphasizes* that the debate to which the Report has given rise up to now shows that the international community is becoming aware of the universality of the prob-

lems of information and communication, of the growing interdependence of countries and of the community of interests in this field;

6. *Hopes* that this debate will continue and become more searching, drawing in all those to whom the Report's recommendations were addressed, including 'governments and international organizations, policy-makers and planners, the media and professional organizations, researchers, communication practitioners, organized social groups and the public at large', bearing in mind that communication takes diverse forms and involves large sectors of all societies;

7. *Welcomes* the steps taken by the Director-General to ensure the widest possible distribution of the Final Report of the International Commission for the Study of Communication Problems;

8. *Approves* the comments of the Director-General concerning the Final Report of the Commission, notably those in which he affirms that 'it should be possible to give effect to some' of its recommendations 'in the immediate future, whereas others call for resources or studies which would take varying lengths of time to provide';

9. *Considers* that the Report and its recommendations also constitute valuable encouragement for the continuing examination, analysis and study of information and communication problems within the Secretariat, and in Member States and professional associations;

III

10. *Invites* Member States:

(a) to circulate the Report widely and to study the conclusions and recommendations approved by the Commission, which merit the attention of all Member States;

(b) to study the Final Report in detail, particularly the recommendations it contains, and to communicate their comments and observations on those recommendations to the Director-General of Unesco in time for him to be able to make use of them in the preparation of the second Medium-Term Plan (1984–1989);

(c) to take the Commission's recommendations into consideration in the preparation and strengthening of their national communication capabilities, without losing sight of the fact that differing social, cultural and economic circumstances call for a variety of approaches to the definition and implementation of national policies and systems and to the identification and overcoming of the obstacles to development in the field of information and communication;

(d) to bear in mind also the fundamental need to safeguard freedom of opinion, expression and information; to ensure that the peoples are given the widest and most democratic access possible to the functioning of the mass media; and to make communication an integral part of all development strategy;

(e) to further the development of communication infrastructures, paying special attention to the establishment of fairer telecommunication, postal and other tariffs, and to define in liaison with the International Telecommunication Union and other competent organizations of the United Nations system the conditions necessary for a more equitable utilization of limited natural resources such as the electromagnetic spectrum and geostationary orbits;

IV

11. *Invites* interested international and regional intergovernmental, nongovernmental and professional organizations:

(a) to take note of the recommendations approved by the International Commission for the Study of Communication Problems and to convey their comments and observations to the Director-General;

(b) particularly if they belong to the United Nations system, to expand their co-operation so as to contribute to the solution of the most pressing information and communication problems;

V

12. *Reaffirms* that Unesco, which has been particularly active in the field of information and communication within the United Nations system, plays a major role in the examination and solution of problems in this domain;

13. *Invites* the Director-General to take the necessary measures to follow up the suggestions presented in his report on the findings of the International Commission for the Study of Communication Problems, and in particular:

(a) to continue to promote dissemination of the Commission's Report, within the limits of the regular programme and budget, by providing assistance for this purpose to countries which request it;

(b) to communicate the Commission's Final Report and recommendations to the international and regional intergovernmental and non-governmental organizations concerned in order that they may examine measures that they might be able to carry out;

(c) to take into consideration to the greatest possible extent, in implementing the Programme for 1981–1983, those recommendations of the Commission that lend themselves to rapid application;

(d) to provide in forthcoming programmes for the continuation of studies on those problems of communication about which data are still incomplete, which did not receive sufficient attention from the Commission, or which deserve attention as a possible basis for procedures for implementing national, regional and international action;

(e) to examine how Unesco could help professional journalists to acquire a better knowledge of the cultures and the economic, political and social realities of different Member States, for instance by holding seminars for journalists on the cultures, societies and history of these countries;

(f) to examine the possibility of giving the programme sector concerned a place and a position in keeping with the growing importance which Member States appear to be attaching to it;

(g) to take into account as far as possible in the preparation of the next Medium-Term Plan the comments and observations made by Member States and international intergovernmental and non-governmental organizations on the conclusions and recommendations of the International Commission for the Study of Communication Problems and any other suggestions received from other organizations professionally concerned with communication problems;

(h) to undertake or sponsor, in particular, the studies and analyses necessary for the formulation of specific and practical proposals for the establishment of a new world information and communication order, and to convene an international meeting of experts for that purpose;

* * *

DECLARATION OF SAN JOSÉ

Intergovernmental Conference on Communication Policies
in Latin America and the Caribbean, San José, 1976

The representatives of the governments of the States of Latin America and the Caribbean, members of the United Nations Educational, Scientific and Cultural Organization (Unesco),

Meeting at the Intergovernmental Conference on Communication Policies in Latin America and the Caribbean, convened in San José (Costa Rica) from 12 to 21 July 1976,

Hereby declare:
That man has a vital need to express himself and that therefore his free and spontaneous right to establish relations within his own community should be guaranteed.

That this human attitude is encountered at all times, everywhere and in every type of society.

That man, in his urge to communicate, has created a wide diversity of forms and media that constitute the whole range of cultural expression.

That access to the entire range of cultural resources and the free and democratic participation of all men in the diverse manifestations of the spirit is a human right.

That the growth of the population and the consequent increase in its spiritual and material needs have led men to apply their scientific talent to the creation of more and more efficient media and instruments that facilitate closer relations and communication between human beings.

That those media form part of the resources of society and the scientific heritage of all mankind, and therefore constitute fundamental components of universal culture.

That there are sectors of the population which have yet to emerge from the isolation in which they live and be helped to communicate with one another and to be informed about national and world-wide affairs.

That all the members of a society are responsible for ensuring the peaceful and beneficial use of communication media.

The States have social, economic and ethical obligations and responsibilities in all matters relating to stimulation, support, promotion and dissemination of the resources of the community in the interest of its overall individual and collective development.

That they should therefore encourage individuals and peoples to become aware of their present and future responsibilities and their capacity for autonomy, by multiplying opportunities for dialogue and community mobilization.

That it should be the joint responsibility of the State and the citizen to establish plans and programmes for the extensive and positive use of communication media wthin the framework of development policies.

That national communication policies should be conceived in the context of national realities, free expression of thought and respect for individual and social rights.

That communication policies should contribute to knowledge, understanding, friendship, co-operation and integration of peoples through a process of identification of common goals and needs, respecting national sovereignties and the international legal principle of non-intervention in the affairs of States as well as the cultural and political plurality of societies and individuals, with a view to achieving world solidarity and peace.

That the United Nations and the agencies of its system, especially Unesco, should contribute, to the fullest extent that their possibilities allow, to this universal process.

KUALA LUMPUR DECLARATION

Intergovernmental Conference of Communication Policies
in Asia and Oceania, Kuala Lumpur, 1979

We, the representatives of the governments of the States of Asia and Oceania, members of the United Nations Educational, Scientific and Cultural Organization (Unesco),

Meeting at the first Intergovernmental Conference on Communication Policies in Asia and Oceania, convened in Kuala Lumpur, Malaysia, from 5 to 14 February 1979,

Hereby declare that:

1

People and individuals have the right to acquire an objective picture of reality by means of accurate and comprehensive information through a diversity of sources and means of information available to them, as well as to express themselves through various means of culture and communication.

No human community worth the name can be created and maintained without effective communication among its members, for the social essence of every human being is determined by his ability to communicate with his fellow human beings.

Communication between persons, groups of persons and nations has been, is and will continue to be vital for man's survival, liberation and growth.

In the years ahead the socio-economic and cultural development of mankind, the improvement of the living and cultural standards of nations, as well as their international relations will be increasingly influenced by the proper use of communication potential.

Consequently, since each nation has the right to determine its own communication policies, we call for the elaboration, by States and citizens together, of comprehensive national policies and programmes based on a global vision of communication and on the goals of economic and social development. Countries planning the implementation of these policies and programmes should do it as an integral part of overall national planning.

2

The region of Asia and Oceania, as the cradle of ancient civilizations, religions and systems of thought and as one of the richest treasure houses of culture in the world, is an inexhaustible source that has much to offer the world as a whole.

We, and all mankind, have inherited from our ancestors not only masterpieces of art and thought but also an age-old tradition of living together as well as highly developed forms of interpersonal communication. We now have to strengthen our heritage with its wealth of traditional interpersonal forms of communication and harmonize these with the new but more impersonal forms of modern communication. We must do everything possible to ensure that the best features of our traditional interpersonal communications and of our forms of living together are not harmed or destroyed by the new techniques which we need.

We must find, individually and collectively, some means of combining modern science and technology with a cultural continuity that will avoid any break with the wealth of our traditions. Culture disseminated through the intermediary of mass communications attuned to the needs and values of a society can bring about not only a new dimension in interrelations between States in the region, but also generate greater understanding and tolerance about our different ways of life.

Given the richness of the cultural heritage in this part of the world and the enlightenment which comes from it, together with the vastness of the region of Asia and Oceania and the size of the population in many of our countries, it is indispensable that all forms of communications—from the most traditional to the highly sophisticated, from interpersonal to mass communication—should be adopted, maintained, harmonized and expanded.

The mass media of the developing countries bear a responsibility for contributing to the common task of nation-building and to the further development of the cultural identity of peoples and ethnic minorities, so ensuring national cohesion and creating abilities to derive the utmost benefit from enriching influences coming from outside.

3

National communication systems and practices are of necessity different from each other in view of the varying traditions, cultural values and political options which governments and peoples exercise.

The basic criteria for judging the value of the communication media should be whether they serve the interests of the people and whether they disseminate true and accurate messages without outside interference and with respect for the dignity of all. Such an aim can be attained only if ideas and information, standards and values, are disseminated as widely as possible and in all directions, vertically and horizontally, from the periphery to the centre, within communities and peoples, so that individuals, groups and peoples are involved more actively and meaningfully in shaping their common destiny.

We therefore call for greater participation of people and individuals in the communication process and for more freedom and autonomy for and the assumption of greater social responsibility by mass information media and at the same time for greater individual responsibility by and protection of those who run the media and prepare messages for circulation.

4

In the world of today the maintenance of world peace and security, the strengthening of international co-operation, the assurance of social progress, the raising of living and educational standards, the promotion of human rights and freedom of thought, and the establishment of a new economic order are among the prerequisites for effective communication.

At the same time, within the national communication systems freedom of expression and freedom of information are also prerequisites for effective communication between peoples and individuals.

Various obstacles still prevent the full realization of these prerequisites.

So long as some are powerful in and others lack the means or potential of communication, and so long as conditions have not been created for just and equitable international relations, with all nations living in peaceful coexistence, respecting each other's sovereign equality and abiding by the principle of non-interference in each other's internal affairs, there can be no equity in communication flows and exchanges.

We urge therefore that every effort be made to eliminate the many obstacles impeding the exchange and circulation of information; we urge also that every effort be made to ensure that the mass media contribute to the strengthening of peace and international understanding, and the promotion of progress and development; we also call for a reduction of existing imbalances as well as current disparities in the facilities available for communication both within countries and between countries.

5

Communication messages and programmes in many countries are too often disproportionately at the service of the educated strata and élite in the more affluent parts of more advanced environments and urban and industrialized centres.

At the present time a considerable imbalance of technological development and inadequate provision of the broad masses with the messages transmitted by communication media are typical features in many countries.

Consequently greater attention should be focused on communication activities which cater to the broad masses of people, including those belonging to ethnic and linguistic communities and people living in distant areas, and all others who are isolated from the outside world and unaware of the achievements and events taking place in it. The poor and underprivileged groups should be given the opportunity to give expression to their aspirations and hopes.

We call for the exploration of ways and means to get news, information and ideas across to those people who are still on the fringes of communication circuits.

6

In the regions of Asia and Oceania all material and human resources should be pooled in order to achieve such urgent objectives as higher food output, lower child mortality, increased production rates, a planned population growth, the spread of literacy, faster modernization, an end to violence and the preservation of cultural identity.

We call for greater awareness on the part of the communication media of their potential as catalysts of socio-economic progress and reform.

7

In developing countries of Asia and Oceania, as in other developing parts of the world, there is both a qualitative and a quantitative imbalance in the flow of information: generally, the inflow of information is strong and powerful while the outflow is feeble; mutual exchanges between our countries are still irregular and inadequate.

This shows that the developing countries of our region are still suffering from a dependence upon colonial legacies which have resulted in imbalances in communication structures and information flows.

Our efforts and achievements need to be better known. Our life patterns and aspirations need to be better appreciated. Our difficulties and failures need to be better understood with empathy and accuracy.

This has to be accompanied by a firm determination to increase our own capacities to produce and disseminate messages around the world in order to communicate better our own perceptions of reality, national and international.

We therefore state that the elimination of such imbalances and the equalization of access to news sources are our next priority tasks, to which States, non-governmental bodies, public and private media, information agencies and enterprises, professionals and private citizens could all make an effective contribution.

8

We call for a higher degree of solidarity and co-operation, on both a bilateral and multilateral basis, in the field of communication and information, at the regional and international level, as a testimony of and a contribution to the interdependence of nations.

We call for broader, more efficient and diversified co-operation among all the countries of Asia and Oceania.

We call for a constant exchange of experiences in the establishment of communication policies and in the implementation of such policies.

We call for greater mutual assistance to overcome the disparities in technical and economic levels among the countries of the region.

We call for a wider network of regional bodies for the research in all aspects of communication, training of information specialists, the dissemination of news, the collection and exchange of media programmes, book and film production.

9

We call for more contacts and exchanges of experience between countries in Asia and Oceania and those in other regions of the world.

A new, more just and more effective world information and communication order, the basis of good neighbourliness, demands in turn an opening to the world. Professional, cultural and scientific collaboration between groups, nations and regions must be a vital element of the order we seek to establish.

We believe that international solidarity should be put into practice through co-operation for broader research and training at national level, transfer of technology, creation of national infrastructures, joint use of communication satellites and greater technical and financial assistance, through mutual friendship and respect for each

people's sovereignty and dignity, and, finally, through the establishment and observance of mutually acceptable norms and the elimination of disparities affecting the
circulation of messages especially in regard to disproportions in telecommunication
tariffs, the scarcity of transmitting facilities and the problems of radio frequency
channels.

*We urge the United Nations system as a whole, and more specifically Unesco, to support
these objectives, promote various forms of regional and international co-operation and thus
pave the way for a new, more just and more effective world communication and information order which is an integral part of the efforts to achieve a new international economic
order.*

*We believe that such a new communication and information order would be one of the
most vivid contemporary manifestations of the ideals of justice, independence and equality
between men and nations.*

YAOUNDÉ DECLARATION

Intergovernmental Conference on Communication Policies
in Africa, Yaoundé, 1980

We, the representatives of the African Member States of the United Nations Educational, Scientific and Cultural Organization (Unesco),

Meeting at Yaoundé (Cameroon) from 22 to 31 July 1980 for the Intergovernmental Conference on Communication Policies in Africa,

Mindful of the great significance of the Universal Declaration of Human Rights and
of the necessity of the fullest application of all its principles,

Recalling that one of the cardinal principles of human rights is the right to
knowledge and education, and that communication, always an important vehicle for
information and a tool for the acquisition of knowledge and know-how, has assumed
a more important dimension in the life of societies because of the progress communication has recently made as well as the possibilities it offers for greater
communicability among men and among peoples,

Mindful of the irreplaceable role that the mass media can play in building young
nations, ensuring mutual respect among peoples, international understanding,
educational and scientific progress, and strengthening cultural identity, as well as in
eliminating racialism and apartheid,

Recalling the Declaration on fundamental principles concerning the contribution
of the mass media to strengthening peace and international understanding, to the
promotion of human rights and to countering racialism, apartheid and incitement to
war, which the General Conference of Unesco adopted unanimously at its twentieth
session,

Mindful that Africa has not so far been able to benefit fully from the possibilities afforded by the extraordinary advances in communication, science and technology,
and that even though Africa has made significant strides towards the achievement of
political freedom, the African man's search for the knowledge and information to
which he has a right is seriously hampered by the great difficulties and numerous
obstacles that he encounters in the field of communication, chiefly as a result of the
damage caused by the colonial oppression and exploitation of which he has been the
victim,

Noting that, to remedy the imbalances that are becoming steadily more pronounced between the different nations of the world, particularly between the highly industrialized countries and the Third World countries, there is an urgent need to improve the structure of communication in Africa and the present arrangement for
news exchanges between it and the other continents,

Declare as follows:

I

In Africa, in the communication field more perhaps than in any other, the prevailing situation is the direct result of the heritage of colonization. Political independence has not always been followed by a decolonization of cultural life or by the elimination of many alienating factors imposed by the colonial system. Communication structures often still conform to the old colonial patterns and not to the needs and aspirations of the African peoples. We are resolved to decolonize them in their turn. We are also determined to extend the opportunities for social communication to the various social, cultural, political and economic groups that currently make up African societies.

There is an urgent need to give higher priority to the formulation of global integrated policies in the field of culture and communication, to the establishment and expansion of infrastructures for the exchange of information and cultural life, and to the endogenous production of all kinds of messages and cultural products.

II

Since their accession to independence all African countries have set themselves fundamental economic, social and cultural objectives in order to overcome the serious handicaps stemming from the after-effects of the long period of the slave trade and colonization. For many of them national cohesiveness and social integration within the overall development, the promotion of human rights, freedom of expression and equality between the sexes; similarly, it is resolutely fighting illiteracy, disease, hunger and all forms of social inequality.

We consider that, if information organs are systematically used to strengthen national unity, mobilize energies for development and greater participation by popular masses in communication and reinforce African solidarity and combat all that divides the African continent and prevents it from asserting itself in all its dignity, this will be a means of liberation and an expression of our peoples' freedom.

The Declaration on fundamental principles concerning the contribution of the mass media to strengthening peace and international understanding, to the promotion of human rights and to countering racialism, apartheid and incitement to war, which the General Conference of Unesco adopted at its twentieth session, highlights the responsibility of the mass media in combating the great scourges of mankind and in achieving its most noble ideals. Large-scale action by the mass media and the news agencies, both public and private, can facilitate positive mobilization of the creativity and of the rural and urban masses and make it possible for them to give full expression to their aspirations and to the vision they have of their nation's future evolution. In this national effort, which presupposes a qualitatively new role for communication, free access to information is a factor that stimulates development. We need a new conception of freedom of information such as will truly enfranchise men and society instead of subjecting them to the conditioning of those who control powerful communication media; such as will contribute to the democratization of communication and recognize the rights of individuals and peoples to be informed, to inform and freely to express themselves.

III

We Africans, like all other peoples, have inherited from the past great works of art, brilliant cultural traditions, undeniable original ways of thinking and modes of social life – an entire heritage of knowledge and wisdom of inestimable value. The forms of traditional and interpersonal communication have always been a powerful instrument for transmitting knowledge and the legacy of values accumulated within our societies. They have played an essential part in the fight to throw off the colonial yoke and unify the historical components of our identity. The multiplicity of our languages and our many-faceted cultures, instead of being a cause of divisiveness and conflict, should – once they have been taken into consideration as part of a rational communication policy – be seen as a historical fact, a source of mutual enrichment and a further sign of the strength of the Africa of tomorrow.

Africa represents a special human context, in which the living forms of traditional communication can be harmoniously linked up with the boldest conquests of modern communications. The systematic and apt use of local and national languages by the various media can help to prevent the gulf between the ordinary peoples and the élites from widening. Modern means of communication, by disseminating culture to a vast national and regional public, will enable each African people to gain deeper insight into their own personality and likewise to discover that of other countries.

IV

In Africa may be found a broad spectrum of communication technologies in use today, from the most ancient to the most recent. Messages and knowledge are exchanged by a variety of means ranging from ritual to the computer and from the tom-tom to the satellite.

The use of traditional media and circuits is not incompatible with advanced technologies. In the overall development effort simple and low-cost technologies can be associated with the use of the most sophisticated media.

The expansion of radio broadcasting does not replace the need for printed information, just as the spoken word does not replace the written word and television does not replace the traditional palaver. Consideration must be given to the use of computers, the establishment of earth stations for satellites and the setting up of data banks, while simultaneously developing telecommunication networks. Computer technology must be mastered today. Communication methods and media vary enormously; each country must clear-headedly and judiciously make its own choice.

V

Many obstacles still hamper the satisfactory implementation of national communication policies. Shortage of resources, both human and financial, is the major obstacle; but the rural areas' access to information must be increased, freedom of information guaranteed, the flow of news facilitated and journalists' conditions of work improved.

In addition to the internal obstacles there are also in particular the gross disproportion in communication capacity as between the industrialized and the developing countries, and the grip of the multinationals on world communication. The dearth of bilateral and multilateral help for the development of communications in African countries is also to be deplored.

But the solution of communication problems cannot be reduced simply to the transfer of technology or the mere redistribution of resources, although both for Africa and for the world these measures are an essential part of a new information and communication order. The solution of our problem remains intimately bound up with the defence of the fundamental freedoms of individuals and peoples – all peoples, and especially those who still remain the most underprivileged.

We also consider that we must deploy special efforts to increase the endogenous supply of messages of all kinds in order to fill the gaps of which external producers of messages – especially non-African radio broadcasts – take advantage.

It is also necessary to mobilize more national resources for the needs of communication, by wise overall planning such as to allow recourse to funds from different sources, both public and private.

We are thoroughly convinced of the need to implement communication policies effectively and to democratize the means of communication through active participation by users. We think that this democratization presupposes avoiding control by selfish pressure groups over the means of communication or their surrender to private interests alone to the exclusive benefit of the communication transnationals or monopoly by information professionals.

VI

The success of development in African countries will increasingly depend on the practice of collective self-reliance. This policy, based on increased confidence in inner resources and their capacity for innovation, is the only one calculated to reduce excessive dependence on the outside world. This is true in politics as in culture, in economics as in communication.

Communication and access to communication represent an individual and collective right, instead of being the prerogative of those who possess information facilities. We are therefore resolved to work to help change the present situation, in which man is all too often subjected to news framed by others for their own ends instead of receiving messages that take account of his aspirations and meet his needs. What goes for man goes for African nations: each should become more the subject and originator of its own communication activities.

We must do everything we can, and the international community must help us in this, to achieve independence in the field of communication as we have in the political field, by building communication systems which meet our needs, bear the stamp of our genius, and take account of our situation, needs and aspirations and make it possible to establish relationships of equality, equity and dignity with the rest of the world.

If we need to learn from others, we want their teaching to respect our dignity and be suited to our own needs and priorities. We are fully aware of the fact that Africa also is capable of contributing to the enrichment of the world heritage in the field of culture and communication.

We affirm our collective will, following this meeting in Yaoundé, to work with all our strength for the changes called for by the present world situation, so that every people may freely inform and be informed, full respect being accorded to their dignity. We are determined to work for the strengthening of our communication capacity.

We are prepared to co-operate with all those who, recognizing the need for solidarity among all peoples, are willing to co-operate with us to end the imbalances and historical dependence under which Africa is labouring in the sphere of information and communication.

We consider that all the competent regional and international organizations have a duty to co-operate with us with a view to eliminating all the obstacles that prevent us from affirming our identity and from enjoying freely and fully the freedom for which we have fought so hard.

We undertake to co-operate more closely with each other in the pursuit of our objectives, aware of our common destiny, the congruence of our aspirations and the complementarity of all our countries and also of the need to make more rational use of our limited resources through the widest and most fruitful regional co-operation.

We appeal to Unesco and the other bodies and agencies of the United Nations system to collaborate with us to establish a new world information and communication order that will open the way to progress and complete self-fulfilment for all peoples in peace, justice and freedom.

9. New World International Information and Communication Order

International relations and practices in the communications field based on the traditional concepts of freedom of information and the free flow of information have in recent years been under attack and have to some extent been superseded by new approaches as reflected in the demands for a new international information order. This concept has been linked to measures for the development of communications in Third World countries. For these and other reasons a more extensive formulation is increasingly being used within the framework of the UN and Unesco; a new world information and communication order.

The concept of a new international information order has not yet been laid down in a binding international document. The texts in this section will thus comprise

— relevant resolutions adopted by the UN General Assembly
— relevant texts adopted within the framework of Unesco
— examples of texts adopted by other organizations such as the Conference of non-aligned countries.

Recent agreements reached in other more specific areas such as telecommunications and copyright are related to the demands for a new international information order, either by direct reference or by implication in that they are designed to favour the development of communication and information in Third World countries. Since such provisions have been agreed within the context of technical regulation in specialized fields, they are included under respective headings in the following parts of the collection.

Documents

United Nations
  i. Questions Relating to Information, General Assembly Resolution 33/115, 1978
     — Part B
 ii. Questions Relating to Information, General Assembly Resolution 34/182, 1979
     — Preamble
     — Part I

Unesco
iii. International Commission for the Study of Communication Problems, General Conference Resolution 4/19, 1980
     — Part VI

Other organizations
 iv. Co-operation in the Field of Information and Mass Communication Media, Political Declaration' Sixth Conference of Heads of State or Government of Non-Aligned Countries, Havana, 1979
     — Points 280–282, 286–289, 291–298

QUESTIONS RELATING TO INFORMATION

United Nations General Assembly Resolution 33/115, 1978

B
International Relations in the Sphere of
Information and Mass Communications

The General Assembly,
Recalling its resolutions 3535 (XXX) of 17 December 1975 and 31/139 of 16 December 1976 and other relevant resolutions of the General Assembly relating to the question of information,

Recalling its resolutions 3201 (S-VI) and 3202 (S-VI) of 1 May 1974 containing the Declaration and the Programme of Action on the Establishment of a New International Economic Order, 3281 (XXIX) of 12 December 1974 containing the Charter of Economic Rights and Duties of States and 3362 (S-VII) of 16 September 1975 on development and international economic co-operation,

Taking note of the decisions and recommendations on the question of information made by the Fifth Conference of Heads of State or Government of Non-Aligned Countries, held at Colombo from 16 to 19 August 1976, and the Conference of Ministers for Foreign Affairs of Non-Aligned Countries, held at Belgrade from 25 to 30 July 1978, and by the regional conferences on the same subject organized by the United Nations Educational, Scientific and Cultural Organization,

Aware of the fundamental contribution that the information media can make to the establishment of the new international economic order and to the strengthening of peace and international understanding,

Taking note with satisfaction of the report of the Director-General of the United Nations Educational, Scientific and Cultural Organization and of that organization's contribution to international co-operation in the field of information and communication,

Recalling the relevant decisions on information and mass communications adopted by the General Conference on the United Nations Educational, Scientific and Cultural Organization at its nineteenth and twentieth sessions,

Recalling the Declaration on Fundamental Principles concerning the Contribution of the Mass Media to Strengthening Peace and International Understanding, to the Promotion of Human Rights and to Countering Racialism, *Apartheid* and Incitement to War adopted by the General Conference of the United Nations Educational, Scientific and Cultural Organization at its twentieth session,

Reaffirming the manifest need to change the dependent status of the developing countries in the sphere of information and communication,

Aware of the need to mobilize assistance and make maximum use of all avenues of co-operation for the development of the information and communication systems of the developing countries,

Taking into account the widespread hopes that the United Nations and the specialized agencies, notably the United Nations Educational, Scientific and Cultural Organization, will help to establish a new, more just and better balanced world information and communication order,

1. *Affirms* the need to establish a new, more just and more effective world information and communication order, intended to strengthen peace and international understanding and based on the free circulation and wider and better-balanced dissemination of information;

2. *Approves* the efforts being made to establish this new world order, which should reflect in particular the concerns and legitimate aspirations of the developing countries and the views expressed at the twentieth session of the General Conference of the United Nations Educational, Scientific and Cultural Organization;

3. *Stresses* the essential role of the United Nations system in the attainment of this objective;

4. *Requests* the Secretary-General to take the necessary measures to encourage, through the specialized agencies, especially the United Nations Educational, Scientific and Cultural Organization, co-operation and assistance conducive to strengthening the information and communication systems of the developing countries;

5. *Requests* the specialized agencies to provide co-operation and assistance to the developing countries in order to help them to identify and eliminate obstacles to the establishment of greater reciprocity in the circulation of information and to define needs and objectives in the communication sector by drawing up action programmes and mobilizing the necessary resources to increase their ability to produce and

disseminate information;

6. *Expresses its satisfaction* to the Director-General of the United Nations Educational, Scientific and Cultural Organization for his efforts in the sphere of information and communication and requests him to submit to the General Assembly at its thirty-fourth session a report on the activities of that organization in the field of information and mass communications;

7. *Decides* to include in the provisional agenda of its thirty-fourth session an item entitled "International relations in the sphere of information and mass communications".

QUESTIONS RELATING TO INFORMATION

United Nations General Assembly Resolution 34/182, 1979

The General Assembly,
Recalling its resolutions 3535 (XXX) of 17 December 1975 and 31/139 of 16 December 1976 and other relevant resolutions of the General Assembly on the question of information, in particular resolutions 33/115 A to C of 18 December 1978,
   Recalling article 19 of the Universal Declaration of Human Rights and articles 19 and 20 of the International Covenant on Civil and Political Rights,
   Recalling its resolutions 3201 (S-VI) and 3202 (S-VI) of 1 May 1974, containing the Declaration and the Programme of Action on the Establishment of a New International Economic Order, 3281 (XXIX) of 12 December 1974, containing the Charter of Economic Rights and Duties of States, and 3362 (S-VII) of 16 September 1975 on development and international economic co-operation,
   Recalling the Declaration on Fundamental Principles concerning the Contribution of the Mass Media to Strengthening Peace and International Understanding, to the Promotion of Human Rights and to Countering Racialism, *Apartheid* and Incitement to War, adopted on 28 November 1978 by the General Conference of the United Nations Educational, Scientific and Cultural Organization, as well as the relevant resolutions on information and mass communications adopted by the General Conference at its nineteenth and twentieth sessions,
   Recalling the Final Document of the Tenth Special Session of the General Assembly,
   Taking note of the Final Act of the Conference on Security and Co-operation in Europe, signed at Helsinki on 1 August 1975,
   Recalling also the Declaration on the Preparation of Societies for Life in Peace,
   Recalling further its resolution 32/197 of 20 December 1977 on the restructuring of the economic and social sectors of the United Nations system, in which the General Assembly is recognized as the principal forum for policy-making and the harmonization of international action in respect of international economic, social and related problems,
   Taking note of the recommendations on the question of information of the Sixth Conference of Heads of State or Government of Non-Aligned Countries, held at Havana from 3 to 9 September 1979,
   Mindful of the need for the organizations of the United Nations system, in particular the United Nations Educational, Scientific and Cultural Organization, to continue their co-operation with developing countries by assisting them in identifying and eliminating the obstacles to the establishment of greater reciprocity in the circulation of information and in defining the needs and objectives in the communications sector by the elaboration of action programmes and the mobilization of the necessary resources with a view to increasing their ability to produce and disseminate information,
   Taking into account with satisfaction the report of the Secretary-General on United

Nations public information policies and activities,

Taking note with satisfaction of the reports of the Director-General of the United Nations Educational, Scientific and Cultural Organization,

Also taking note with satisfaction of the report of the Committee to Review United Nations Public Information Policies and Activities and of the report of the *Ad Hoc* Working Group of the Committee,

Mindful of the fundamental contribution that the information media and mass communications can make to the establishment of the new international economic order, the strengthening of peace and international understanding, the realization of the goal of general and complete disarmament under effective international control, the promotion of universal respect for human rights and the struggle against racism, *apartheid* and colonialism,

Reaffirming the manifest need to change the dependent status of the developing countries in the field of information and communications and to guarantee the diversity of the sources of information and the free access to information,

Reaffirming the need to maintain a linguistic balance in the dissemination of information by the United Nations and an equitable geographical distribution of personnel, particularly with regard to the senior and decision-making posts of the Department of Public Information of the Secretariat, in accordance with Article 101, paragraph 3, of the Charter of the United Nations,

I

1. *Decides* to maintain the Committee to Review United Nations Public Information Policies and Activities, which will henceforth be known as the United Nations "Committee on Information" and whose membership will be increased from forty-one to sixty-six, the additional twenty-five members to be appointed on the basis of equitable geographical distribution by the President of the General Assembly, after consultation with the regional groups;

2. *Requests* the Committee on Information:

(a) To continue to examine United Nations public information policies and activities, in the light of the evolution of international relations, particularly during the past two decades, and of the imperatives of the establishment of the new international economic order and of a new world information and communication order;

(b) To evaluate and follow up the efforts made and the progress achieved by the United Nations system in the field of information and communications;

(c) To promote the establishment of a new, more just and more effective world information and communication order intended to strengthen peace and international understanding and based on the free circulation and wider and better balanced dissemination of information and to make recommendations thereon to the General Assembly;

3. *Requests* all organizations of the United Nations system, particularly the United Nations Educational, Scientific and Cultural Organization, to continue to participate actively in the work of the Committee on Information and to facilitate its task in fulfilling its mandate;

4. Affirming the primary role which the General Assembly is to play in elaborating, co-ordinating and harmonizing United Nations policies and activities in the field of information towards the establishment of a new more just and more effective world information and communication order, *recognizes* the central and important role of the United Nations Educational, Scientific and Cultural Organization in the field of information and mass communications and in the implementation of the relevant decisions on information and mass communications adopted by the General Conference of that organization at its twentieth session and of the relevant parts of Assembly resolutions 33/115 A to C;

5. *Requests* the Director-General of the United Nations Educational, Scientific and

Cultural Organization, in the light of the conclusions of the General Conference of that organization at its twenty-first session, to submit to the General Assembly at its thirty-fifth session a progress report on the establishment of a new world information and communication order;

6. *Reaffirms* the need, at the operational level, for co-operation and co-ordination between the United Nations Educational, Scientific and Cultural Organization and the other organizations of the United Nations system that are concerned with the question of information and mass communications;

7. *Expresses its satisfaction* to the Director-General of the United Nations Educational, Scientific and Cultural Organization at the development of the preparations for the Intergovernmental Planning Conference on Communication Development, to be held in Paris from 14 to 21 April 1980, and recommends the undertaking of the necessary consultations concerning the participation of the Committee on Information in the work of that Conference;

8. *Requests* the Director-General of the United Nations Educational, Scientific and Cultural Organization in the light of the foregoing, to make provision for appropriate consultations with the Secretary-General in connexion with the implementation of the pertinent recommendations emanating from the Intergovernmental Planning Conference on Communication Development;

9. *Requests* the organizations concerned within the United Nations system to make an active contribution to the work of that Conference;

10. *Requests* the Secretary-General to continue to take the necessary measures to ensure the close collaboration of organizations within the United Nations system in promoting United Nations policies and programmes in the field of information and mass communication towards the establishment of a new world information and communication order;

INTERNATIONAL COMMISSION FOR THE STUDY OF COMMUNICATION PROBLEMS

Unesco General Conference Resolution 4/19, 1980

The General Conference

VI

14. *Considers* that:

(a) this new world information and communication order could be based, among other considerations, on:
    i. elimination of the imbalances and inequalities which characterize the present situation;
    ii. elimination of the negative effects of certain monopolies, public or private, and excessive concentrations;
    iii. removal of the internal and external obstacles to a free flow and wider and better balanced dissemination of information and ideas;
    iv. plurality of sources and channels of information;
    v. freedom of the press and information;
    vi. the freedom of journalists and all professionals in the communication media, a freedom inseparable from responsibility;
    vii. the capacity of developing countries to achieve improvement of their own situations, notably by providing their own equipment, by training their personnel, by improving their infrastructures and by making their information and communication media suitable to their needs and aspirations;

viii. the sincere will of developed countries to help them attain these objectives;

ix. respect for each people's cultural identity and for the right of each nation to inform the world public about its interests, its aspirations and its social and cultural values;

x. respect for the right of all peoples to participate in international exchanges of information on the basis of equality, justice and mutual benefit;

xi. respect for the right of the public, of ethnic and social groups and of individuals to have access to information sources and to participate actively in the communication process;

(b) this new world information and communication order should be based on the fundamental principles of international law, as laid down in the Charter of the United Nations;

(c) diverse solutions to information and communication problems are required because social, political, cultural and economic problems differ from one country to another and, within a given country, from one group to another;

15. *Expresses the wish* that Unesco demonstrate its willingness in its short-term and medium-term activities to contribute to the clarification, elaboration and application of the concept of a new world information and communication order.

SIXTH CONFERENCE OF THE HEADS OF STATE
OR GOVERNMENT OF NON-ALIGNED COUNTRIES, HAVANA, 1979

1. Political Declaration

Co-operation in the Field of Information and Mass Communication Media

280. The Conference noted with satisfaction the significant results achieved in the development of co-operation in the field of information and mass communication media among non-aligned countries and the successful implementation of the recommendations and decisions adopted at the Fourth and Fifth Summit Conferences.

281. The Conference noted with gratification the fact that non-aligned and other developing countries have made notable progress along the path of emancipation and development of national information media and stressed that the co-operation in this field of information is an integral part of the struggle of non-aligned and other developing countries for the creation of new international relations in general and a new international information order in particular. Relying upon their own forces, and on the basis of solidarity and mutual assistance, non-aligned countries have been undertaking significant steps towards the development of national information media and mass communication systems with the aim of greater emancipation and affirmation of national information sources, as well as the realization of active participation in mutual communication and co-operation on a broader international plane.

282. The Conference considered that the building up of national information media and mass communication systems; affirmation of national information sources concerning issues of relevance for social, economic and cultural development of each country and each people and their joint action on the international levels; training of domestic personnel, independently and with the help of other non-aligned countries and the international community through the United Nations and its specialized agencies; and the development of technical and technological bases were essential preconditions for the establishment of a new international order in the field of information and for setting up a multi-dimensional flow of information.

*   *   *

286. The Conference noted with satisfaction that important results have been achieved in the development and activities of the Pool of News Agencies of Non-Aligned Countries, which, as the broadest form of free exchange of information through news agencies, has contributed to improving the flow of information among non-aligned and other developing countries and to a more rapid development of national information media.

287. The Conference stressed in particular the decisions of the Co-ordinating Committee of the Pool of News Agencies and the Committee on Co-operation of Radio Broadcasting Organizations of Non-Aligned Countries concerning the following: creating favourable conditions for the provision of technical facilities and the transfer of technology in accordance with national development policies and the granting of facilities when determining national and international rates, broadcasts and loans, and co-operation with international organizations; reducing the high rates for telecommunications at the national and international levels as part of the struggle against the unfair privileges enjoyed by the news institutions of most industrialized countries; and stimulating news flows among non-aligned and developing countries. The Conference recommended that the member countries of the Non-Aligned Movement endorse those decisions the implementation of which is significant from the development point of view and constitutes a basic condition for the elimination of the imbalance in the exchange of information.

288. The Conference noted with satisfaction the results achieved in the development of co-operation in the field of radio broadcasting and the efforts which have been invested in the implementation of the Action Programme of Co-operation adopted at the First Conference of Radio Broadcasting Organizations of Non-Aligned Countries in Sarajevo in 1977. The Conference took note of the recommendations of the Committee on Co-operation of Radio Broadcasting Organizations of Non-Aligned Countries adopted at the meetings in Baghdad (1978), Arusha (1979) and Algiers (1979), which are particularly related to the need for the development and strengthening of infrastructure in the field of radio broadcasting at the national level and the rendering of assistance to less developed countries' personnel training, as well as a more comprehensive exchange of radio and television programmes. The results obtained in this area of co-operation are contributing in a most comprehensive manner to the spreading and assertion of the national cultural heritage, the development of systems of education, scientific research, the preservation of national identity and further emancipation and constitute a part of the overall activities of non-aligned countries aimed at the establishment of a new and more just and equitable international information order.

289. The Conference called upon the broadcasting organizations of non-aligned countries to take the necessary joint and co-ordinated action in international forums concerning issues of common concern, so as to improve the situation in this sphere in favour of non-aligned and other developing countries.

*   *   *

291. The Conference endorsed the recommendations adopted at the Conference of Foreign Ministers of Non-Aligned Countries held in Belgrade in 1978, concerning Sri Lanka's proposal to set up a documentation centre of non-aligned countries in Colombo. The Conference welcomed this project, considering that it constitutes an important contribution to the development of the Non-Aligned Movement and an appropriate means for facilitating the research into and study of non-alignment in international politics. The Conference called upon all member countries of the Movement to co-operate with Sri Lanka in establishing the documentation centre of non-aligned countries and to render the centre all possible assistance by making available the documents adopted at the conferences and meetings of non-aligned countries held in their territory.

292. The Conference acknowledged with satisfaction the positive results achieved in the field of information at the thirty-third session of the General Assembly of the United Nations and underlined the contribution of non-aligned and other developing countries in the adoption of the resolution on the establishment of a new international information order.

293. The Conference noted the positive outcome of the twentieth session of the UNESCO General Conference, at which the Declaration on the Fundamental Principles and Contribution of Mass Media to the Strengthening of Peace, International Understanding, the Promotion of Human Rights and the Struggle against Racism, *Apartheid* and the Incitement to War was adopted.

294. The Conference of Heads of State or Government of Non-Aligned Countries recognized the positive role played by UNESCO in studying the problem of communication and in working towards a more balanced flow of information between the developing and the developed countries.

295. The Conference requested UNESCO to continue assisting non-aligned and developing countries in setting up appropriate national and regional structures in the field of communication and in training technical personnel in accordance with General Assembly resolution 33/135 A, B and C.

296. The Conference considered that the results achieved by non-aligned countries in the field of information within the United Nations and UNESCO constitute a remarkable success and called upon the member countries to redouble their efforts in order to achieve their common objectives in the United Nations committee concerned with the study of the policies and activities of the United Nations in the field of information, as well as to facilitate the endorsement of their common objectives at the forthcoming UNESCO Inter-Governmental Conference.

297. The Conference, fully supporting the recommendations of the Inter-Governmental Co-ordinating Council in the field of information of non-aligned countries, requested the member countries of the Movement to support, through their information media, the liberation movements, particularly those in Southern Africa, with a view to putting an end to the negative and biased information about them, and to support the initiative to organize the year of information about their struggle.

298. The Conference noted with satisfaction the creation of a pan-African news agency which will contribute to the promotion of information in Africa and the development of the exchange of news between African and other non-aligned countries and ensure a better knowledge of the just cause of the African liberation struggle, thus contributing to the establishment of a new international information order.

* * *

10. Other emerging concepts: the right to communicate

The current changes in the attitudes towards the organization and conduct of communication and information activities, and the introduction of new communication technologies and services have also resulted in the addition of new dimensions to freedom of information and the right to information as traditionally formulated. Since the early 1970s, work has been undertaken in various fora to formulate a more modern and comprehensive concept under the name of 'the right to communicate'.

In 1974, the Unesco General Conference adopted a resolution on the right to communicate which has provided the basis for further work by the organization. In addition, studies on this concept have been undertaken by various non-governmental organizations. The right to communicate is a still emerging concept which has not yet been given an agreed legal formulation.

Documents

i. Right to communicate Unesco General Conference Resolution 4.121, 1974

RIGHT TO COMMUNICATE

Unesco General Conference Resolution 4.121, 1974

Recalling that the recognition of fundamental human rights is at the origin of the Charter of the United Nations and is proclaimed by the Universal Declaration of Human Rights,

Believing that communication is the foundation of all social organization,

Bearing in mind the relationship between communication and culture,

Taking account of the diverse developments in the technology of communication and the potential availability of an abundance of communications resources, although at the same time noting that there are unresolved problems in the control of and access to these resources,

Bearing in mind the plurality and equality of cultures and the potential now existing for all groups and individuals in society to give full expression to their cultural values,

Noting the growing human need for a wider variety of communication services in an interdependent world,

Recognizing the emergence of a science of communication and the increased need for planning communication resources for the future,

Convinced that all individuals should have equal opportunities to participate actively in the means of communication and to benefit from such means while preserving the right to protection against their abuses,

Authorizes the Director-General to study and *define the Right to Communicate* in consultation with competent organs of the United Nations and with professional organizations and other interested institutions, and to report to the nineteenth General Conference on further steps which should be taken.

PART THREE
TELECOMMUNICATIONS LAW

Telecommunications law is one of the oldest branches of modern functional international law. Following a series of bilateral arrangements among European governments, the first multilateral agreements were concluded in 1865 regulating international telegraph transmissions and setting up an administrative structure. As new communications technologies developed, additions were made to the international regulations and to the administrative structure. Today the International Telecommunication Convention covers all forms of telecommunications and the International Telecommunication Union (ITU) is within the UN system the responsible body for virtually all international regulation in this field.

This historical development explains certain peculiarities both of the Convention and of the Union. Most modern international organizations are based on a charter, constitution or similar document which is adopted in a permanent form, subject to special procedures for amendments. The International Telecommunication Convention represents an older form of international instrument which has to be re-adopted *in toto* by each ITU Plenipotentiary Conference, the supreme organ of the Union. The Convention is a dual-purpose document which contains provisions relating to the structure and general purpose of the ITU as well as to provisions of technical law.

The rule-making function of the ITU is carried out not only by the Plenipotentiary Conference but also by Administrative Conferences which are convened, when the need arises, to develop and revise the international administrative regulations: the Radio Regulations which govern the use of the radio frequency spectrum and the Telegraph and Telephone Regulations which specify standards and procedures concerning the operation of international telephone and telegraph networks. These administrative regulations once adopted are binding upon member states as annexes to the Convention.

The establishment of technical standards is the responsibility of two permanent organs of the Union, the two Consultative Committees, one for Radio Communication (CCIR) and another for Telegraph and Telephone (CCITT). The decisions of the Committees are not binding upon member states; however since the Committees operate on the basis of consensus the standards recommended generally gain wide international acceptance.

A regulatory function is performed by the International Frequency Registration Board (IFRB) which was set up in 1947 in order to ensure the orderly use of the radio frequency spectrum. The IFRB is responsible for the implementation of the Radio Regulations and maintains a Master Register for all frequency assignments made by the national authorities. The registration of frequency assignments often involving interpretation of the complex Radio Regulations confers upon the IFRB an important quasi-juridical function.

The international legal texts adopted within the framework of the ITU are voluminous and complex since they contain both general principles and regulation, in painstaking detail, of technical characteristics and criteria, operational procedures, and administrative procedures with reference to the different telecommunication services. The selection of relevant provisions has been made so as to include

- general principles of international telecommunications law, the organization of the ITU and the mandates of its major organs as laid down in the International Telecommunication Convention in its current version of 1973
- general principles from the Telegraph and Telephone Regulations, 1973
- in the case of the Radio Regulations as revised by the World Administrative Radio Conference, Geneva, 1979, the selection is more substantial in view of their importance and applicability in related legal areas (i.e. space law): furthermore, a number of general principles and measures related to the situation of developing countries were formulated in the resolutions and recommendations adopted by the 1979 Conference.

Agreements related to telecommunications law have been concluded in other contexts than the ITU. At the European level, the Council of Europe has sponsored an agreement prohibiting 'pirate broadcasting' and similar provisions have been proposed for inclusion in the Law of the Sea conventions which also provide for freedom to lay submarine cables and for the maintenance of communications to ensure safety of life at sea.

Documents

1. Instruments adopted within the framework of the International Telecommunications Union

   i.   International Telecommunication Convention, Malaga-Torremolinos, 1973
- Preamble
- Articles 1–12 (only 9.1) 15, 18–28, 31–39, 42–44, 50

  ii.   Telegraph and Telephone Regulations, Geneva, 1973
   (a) Telegraph Regulations
- Articles 1–4, 8

   (b) Telephone Regulations
- Articles 1–6

iii.   Radio Regulations
In the version adopted by the World Administration Radio Conference, Geneva, 1979

CHAPTER NI Terminology
  Article N1/1   Terms and definitions
      Section I. General Terms
- Nos. 1.1–1.7

         II. Specific Terms Related to Frequency Management
- Nos. 2.1–2.3

       III. Radio Services
- Nos. 3.1–3.3, 3.8, 3.17, 3.18, 3.29, 3.30, 3.33–3.38

       IV. Radio Stations and Systems (not included)
        V. Operational Terms

Resolution AU
Relating to the Establishment of Agreements and Associated Plans for the Broadcasting-Satellite Service

Resolution AY
Relating to the Equitable Use, by All Countries, with Equal Rights, of the Geostationary Orbit and of Frequency Bands for Space Radio-Communication Services

Resolution BJ
Relating to Improvements in the Design and Use of Radio Equipment

Resolution BP
Relating to the Use of the Geostationary Orbit and to the Planning of Space Services Utilizing it

Resolution BZ
Relating to Improvements in Assistance to Developing Countries in Securing Access to the HF Bands for their Fixed Services and in Ensuring Protection of their Assignments from Harmful Interference

Resolution CE
Relating to Technical Cooperation with the Developing Countries in Maritime Telecommunications

Resolution CX
Relating to the Role of Telecommunications in Integrated Rural Development

Resolution CZ
Relating to International Cooperation and Technical Assistance in the Field of Space Radiocommunications

Resolution DG
Relating to the Transfer of Technology

Recommendation ZG
Relating to the Measures to be taken to prevent the Operation of Broadcasting Stations on Board Ships or Aircraft outside National Territories

Recommendation ZI
Relating to the Examination by World Administrative Radio Conferences of the Situation with Regard to Occupation of the Frequency Spectrum in Space Radiocommunications

Recommendation ZN
Relating to the Standardization of the Technical and Operational Characteristics of Radio Equipment

Recommendation ZP
Relating to Specifications of Low-Cost Television Receivers

Recommendation XC
Relating to the Utilization of Frequency Bands Allocated to Space Radiocommunications

Recommendation XE
Relating to the Use of Space Radiocommunication Systems in the Event of Natural Disasters, Epidemics, Famines and Similar Emergencies

Recommendation XH
Relating to the Practical Needs of Countries in Need of Special Assistance

Recommendation XM
Relating to the Convening of Future Administrative Radio Conferences to Deal with Specific Services

2. Other instruments

i. Conventions adopted by the United Nations Conference on the Law of the Sea, 29 April 1958
    (a) The High Seas
        - Preamble
        - Articles 1, 2, 10
    (b) The Continental Shelf
        - Articles 1, 4

ii. European Agreement for the Prevention of Broadcasts Transmitted From Stations Outside National Territories, Council of Europe, 1969
    - Full text

INTERNATIONAL TELECOMMUNICATION CONVENTION,
MALAGA-TORREMOLINOS 1973

First Part

Basic Provisions

Preamble

1   While fully recognizing the sovereign right of each country to regulate its telecommunication, the plenipotentiaries of the Contracting Governments, with the object of facilitating relations and cooperation between the peoples by means of efficient telecommunication services, have agreed to establish this Convention which is the basic instrument of the International Telecommunication Union.

Chapter 1 Composition, Purposes and Structure of the Union

Article 1 Composition of the Union

2   1. The International Telecommunication Union shall comprise Members which, having regard to the principle of universality and the desirability of universal participation in the Union, shall be:

3   (a) any country listed in Annex 1 which signs and ratifies, or accedes to, the Convention;

4   (b) any country, not listed in Annex 1, which becomes a Member of the United Nations and which accedes to the Convention in accordance with Article 46;

5   (c) any sovereign country, not listed in Annex 1 and not a Member of the United Nations, which applies for Membership of the Union and which, after having secured approval of such application by two-thirds of the Members of the Union, accedes to the Convention in accordance with Article 46.

6   2. For the purpose of 5, if an application for membership is made, by diplomatic channel and through the intermediary of the country of the seat of the

Union, during the interval between two Plenipotentiary Conferences, the Secretary-General shall consult the Members of the Union; a Member shall be deemed to have abstained if it has not replied within four months after its opinion has been requested.

Article 2 Rights and Obligations of Members

7 1. Members of the Union shall have the rights and shall be subject to the obligations provided for in the Convention.

8 2. Rights of Members in respect of their participation in the conferences, meetings and consultations of the Union are:

(a) all Members shall be entitled to participate in conferences of the Union, shall be eligible for election to the Administrative Council and shall have the right to nominate candidates for election to any of the permanent organs of the Union;

9 (b) each Member shall have one vote at all conferences of the Union, at all meetings of the International Consultative Committees and, if it is a Member of the Administrative Council, at all sessions of that Council;

10 (c) each Member shall also have one vote in all consultations carried out by correspondence.

Article 3 Seat of the Union

11 The seat of the Union shall be at Geneva.

Article 4 Purposes of the Union

12 1. The purposes of the Union are:

(a) to maintain and extend international cooperation for the improvement and rational use of telecommunications of all kinds;

13 (b) to promote the development of technical facilities and their most efficient operation with a view to improving the efficiency of telecommunications services, increasing their usefulness and making them, so far as possible, generally available to the public;

14 (c) to harmonize the actions of nations in the attainment of those ends.

15 2. To this end, the Union shall in particular:

(a) effect allocation of the radio frequency spectrum and registration of radio frequency assignments in order to avoid harmful interference between radio stations of different countries;

16 (b) coordinate efforts to eliminate harmful interference between radio stations of different countries and to improve the use made of the radio frequency spectrum;

17 (c) coordinate efforts with a view to harmonizing the development of telecommunications facilities, notably those using space techniques, with a view to full advantage being taken of their possibilities;

18 (d) foster collaboration among its Members with a view to the establishment of rates at levels as low as possible consistent with an efficient service and taking into account the necessity for maintaining independent financial administration of telecommunication on a sound basis;

19 (e) foster the creation, development and improvement of telecommunication equipment and networks in developing countries by every means at its disposal, especially its participation in the appropriate programmes of the United Nations;

20 (f) promote the adoption of measures for ensuring the safety of life through the cooperation of telecommunication services;

21 (g) undertake studies, make regulations, adopt resolutions, formulate recòm-
mendations and opinions, and collect and publish information concerning
telecommunication matters.

Article 5 Structure of the Union

22 The Union shall comprise the following organs:
1. The Plenipotentiary Conference, which is the supreme organ of the Union;
23 2. administrative conferences;
24 3. the Administrative Council;
25 4. the permanent organs of the Union, which are:

(a) the General Secretariat;
26 (b) the International Frequency Registration Board (I.F.R.B.);
27 (c) the International Radio Consultative Committee (C.C.I.R.);
28 (d) the International Telegraph and Telephone Consultative Committee
(C.C.I.T.T.).

Article 6 Plenipotentiary Conference

29 1. The Plenipotentiary Conference shall be composed of delegations representing Members. It shall be convened at regular intervals and normally every five
years.

30 2. The Plenipotentiary Conference shall:

(a) determine the general policies for fulfilling the purposes of the Union
prescribed in Article 4 of this Convention;
31 (b) consider the report by the Administrative Council on the activities of all the
organs of the Union since the previous Plenipotentiary Conference;
32 (c) establish the basis for the budget of the Union and determine a fiscal limit
for the expenditure of the union until the next Plenipotentiary Conference
after considering a programme of the administrative conferences and
meetings of the Union foreseen in that period;
33 (d) fix the basic salaries, the salary scales and the system of allowances and pension for all the officials of the Union; and, if necessary, provide any general
directives dealing with the staffing of the Union;
34 (e) examine the accounts of the Union and finally approve them, if appropriate;
35 (f) elect the Members of the Union which are to serve on the Administrative
Council;
36 (g) elect the Secretary-General and the Deputy Secretary-General and fix the
dates of their taking office;
37 (h) elect the members of the I.F.R.B. and fix the dates of their taking office;
38 (i) revise the Convention if it considers this necessary;
39 (j) conclude or revise, if necessary, agreements between the Union and other
international organizations, examine any provisional agreements with such
organizations concluded, on behalf of the Union, by the Administrative
Council, and take such measures in connection therewith as it deems appropriate;
40 (k) deal with such other telecommunication questions as may be necessary.

Article 7 Administrative Conferences

41 1. Administrative conferences of the Union shall comprise:

(a) world administrative conferences;
42 (b) regional administrative conferences.
43 2. Administrative conferences shall normally be convened to consider specific
telecommunication matters. Only items included in their agenda may be discussed

by such conferences. The decisions of such conferences must in all circumstances be in conformity with the provisions of the Convention.

44   3. (1)The agenda of a world administrative conference may include:

(a) the partial revision of the Administrative Regulations mentioned in 571;

45   (b) exceptionally, the complete revision of one or more of those Regulations;

46   (c) any other question of a worldwide character within the competence of the conference.

47   (2) The agenda of a regional administrative conference may provide only for specific telecommunication questions of a regional nature, including instructions to the International Frequency Registration Board regarding its activities in respect of the region concerned, provided such instructions do not conflict with the interests of other regions. Furthermore, the decisions of such a conference must in all circumstances be in conformity with the provisions of the Administrative Regulations.

Article 8 Administrative Council

48   1. (1) The Administrative Council shall be composed of thirty-six Members of the Union elected by the Plenipotentiary Conference with due regard to the need for equitable distribution of the seats on the Council among all regions of the world. Except in the case of vacancies arising as provided for in the General Regulations, the Members of the Union elected to the Administrative Council shall hold office until the date on which a new Administrative Council is elected by the Plenipotentiary Conference. They shall be eligible for re-election.

49   (2) Each Member of the Council shall appoint a person to serve on the Council who may be assisted by one or more advisers.

50   2. The Administrative Council shall adopt its own rules of procedure.

51   3. In the interval between Plenipotentiary Conferences the Administrative Council shall act on behalf of the Plenipotentiary Conference within the limits of the powers delegated to it by the latter.

52   4. (1) The Administrative Council shall take all steps to facilitate the implementation by the Members of the provisions of the Convention, of the Administrative Regulations, of the decisions of the Plenipotentiary Conference, and, where appropriate, of the decisions of other conferences and meetings of the Union, and perform any duties assigned to it by the Plenipotentiary Conference.

53   (2) It shall ensure the efficient coordination of the work of the Union and exercise effective financial control over its permanent organs.

54   (3) It shall promote international cooperation for the provision of technical cooperation to the developing countries by every means at its disposal, especially through the participation of the Union in the appropriate programmes of the United Nations, in accordance with the purposes of the Union, one of which is to promote by all possible means the development of telecommunications.

Article 9 General Secretariat

55   1. (1) The General Secretariat shall be directed by a Secretary-General, assisted by one Deputy Secretary-General.

56   (2) The Secretary-General and the Deputy Secretary-General shall take up their duties on the dates determined at the time of their election. They shall normally remain in office until dates determined by the following Plenipotentiary Conference, and they shall be eligible for re-election.

57   (3) The Secretary-General shall take all the action required to ensure economic use of the Union's resources and he shall be responsible to the Administrative Council for all the administrative and financial aspects of the Union's activities. The Deputy Secretary-General shall be responsible to the Secretary-General.

*   *   *

Article 10 International Frequency Registration Board

63 1. The International Frequency Registration Board (I.F.R.B.) shall consist of five independent members, elected by the Plenipotentiary Conference. These members shall be elected from the candidates sponsored by countries, Members of the Union, in such a way as to ensure equitable distribution amongst the regions of the world. Each member of the Union may propose only one candidate who shall be a national of its country.

64 2. The members of the International Frequency Registration Board shall serve, not as representing their respective countries, or of a region, but as custodians of an international public trust.

65 3. The essential duties of the International Frequency Registration Board shall be:

(a) to effect an orderly recording of frequency assignments made by the different countries so as to establish, in accordance with the procedure provided for in the Radio Regulations and in accordance with any decisions which may be taken by competent conferences of the Union, the date, purpose and technical characteristics of each of these assignments, with a view to ensuring formal international recognition thereof;

66 (b) to effect, in the same conditions and for the same purpose, an orderly recording of the positions assigned by countries to geostationary satellites;

67 (c) to furnish advice to Members with a view to the operation of the maximum practicable number of radio channels in those portions of the spectrum where harmful interference may occur, and with a view to the equitable, effective and economical use of the geostationary satellite orbit;

68 (d) to perform any additional duties, concerned with the assignment and utilization of frequencies and with the utilization of the geostationary satellite orbit, in accordance with the procedures provided for in the Radio Regulations, and as prescribed by a competent conference of the Union, or by the Administrative Council with the consent of a majority of the Members of the Union, in preparation for or in pursuance of the decisions of such a conference;

69 (e) to maintain such essential records as may be related to the performance of its duties.

Article 11 International Consultative Committees

70 1. (1) The duties of the International Radio Consultative Committee (C.C.I.R.) shall be to study technical and operating questions relating specifically to radiocommunication and to issue recommendations on them.

71 (2) The duties of the International Telegraph and Telephone Consultative Committee (C.C.I.T.T.) shall be to study technical, operating and tariff questions relating to telegraphy and telephony and to issue recommendations on them.

72 (3) In the performance of its studies, each Consultative Committee shall pay due attention to the study of questions and to the formulation of recommendations directly connected with the establishment, development and improvement of telecommunication in developing countries in both the regional and international fields.

73 2. The International Consultative Committees shall have as members:

(a) of right, the administrations of all Members of the Union;

74 (b) any recognized private operating agency which, with the approval of the Member which has recognized it, expresses a desire to participate in the work of these Committees.

75 3. Each International Consulative Committee shall work through the medium of:

(a) its Plenary Assembly;

76 (b) study groups set up by it;

77 (c) a Director, elected by a Plenary Assembly and appointed in accordance with the General Regulations.

78 4. There shall be a World Plan Committee, and such Regional Plan Committees as may be jointly approved by the Plenary Assemblies of the International Consultative Committees. These Plan Committees shall develop a General Plan for the international telecommunication network to facilitate coordinated development of international telecommunication services. They shall refer to the International Consultative Committees questions the study of which is of particular interest to developing countries and which are within the terms of reference of those Consultative Committees.

79 5. The working arrangements of the International Consultative Committees are defined in the General Regulations.

Article 12 Coordination Committee

80 1. (1) The Coordination Committee shall assist and advise the Secretary-General on all administrative, financial and technical cooperation matters affecting more than one permanent organ, and on external relations and public information, keeping fully in view the decisions of the Administrative Council and the interest of the Union as a whole.

81 (2) The Committee shall also consider any important matters referred to it by the Administrative Council. After examining them, the Committee shall report, through the Secretary-General, to the Council.

82 2. The Coordination Committee shall be composed of the Deputy Secretary-General, the Directors of the International Consultative Committees and the Chairman of the International Frequency Registration Board and shall be presided over by the Secretary-General.

*   *   *

Article 15 Finances of the Union

90 1. The expenses of the Union shall comprise the costs of;

(a) the Administrative Council and the permanent organs of the Union;

91 (b) Plenipotentiary Conferences and world administrative conferences.

92 2. The expenses of the Union shall be met from the contributions of its Members, each Member paying a sum proportional to the number of units in the class of contribution it has chosen from the following scale:

30	Unit	class		5	Unit	class
25	"	"		4	"	"
20	"	"		3	"	"
18	"	"		2	"	"
15	"	"		1½	"	"
13	"	"		1	"	"
10	"	"		½	"	"
8	"	"				

93 3. Members shall be free to choose their class of contribution for defraying Union expenses.

94 4. No reduction in a unit classification established in accordance with the Convention can take effect during the life of this Convention.

95 5. Expenses incurred by the regional administrative conferences referred to in 42 shall be borne in accordance with their unit classification by all the Members of the region concerned and, where appropriate, on the same basis by any Members of other regions which have participated in such conferences.

96 6. Members shall pay in advance their annual contributory shares, calculated on the basis of the budget approved by the Administrative Council.

97 7. A Member which is in arrear in its payments to the Union shall lose its right to vote as defined in 9 and 10 for so long as the amount of its arrears equals or exceeds the amount of the contribution due from it for the preceding two years.

98 8. The provisions which apply to the financial contributions by recognized private operating agencies, scientific or industrial organizations and international organizations are in the General Regulations.

* * *

Article 18 The Right of the Public to use the International Telecommunication Service

108 Members recognize the right of the public to correspond by means of the international service of public correspondence. The services, the charges and the safeguards shall be the same for all users in each category of correspondence without any priority or preference.

Article 19 Stoppage of Telecommunications

109 1. Members reserve the right to stop the transmission of any private telegram which may appear dangerous to the security of the State or contrary to their laws, to public order or to decency, provided that they immediately notify the office of origin of the stoppage of any such telegram or any part thereof, except when such notification may appear dangerous to the security of the State.

110 2. Members also reserve the right to cut off any other private telecommunications which may appear dangerous to the security of the State or contrary to their laws, to public order or to decency.

Article 20 Suspension of Services

111 Each Member reserves the right to suspend the international telecommunication service for an indefinite time, either generally or only for certain relations and/or for certain kinds of correspondence, outgoing, incoming or in transit, provided that it immediately notifies such action to each of the other Members through the medium of the Secretary-General.

Article 21 Responsibility

112 Members accept no responsibility towards users of the international telecommunication services, particularly as regards claims for damages.

Article 22 Secrecy of Telecommunications

113 1. Members agree to take all possible measures, compatible with the system of telecommunication used, with a view to ensuring the secrecy of international correspondence.

114 2. Nevertheless, they reserve the right to communicate such correspondence to the competent authorities in order to ensure the application of their internal laws or the execution of international conventions to which they are parties.

Article 23 Establishment, Operation, and Protection of Telecommunication Channels and Installations

115 1. Members shall take such steps as may be necessary to ensure the establishment, under the best technical conditions, of the channels and installations necessary to carry on the rapid and uninterrupted exchange of international telecommunications.

116 2. So far as possible, these channels and installations must be operated by the methods and procedures which practical operating experience has shown to be the best. They must be maintained in proper operating condition and kept abreast of scientific and technical progress.

117 3. Members shall safeguard these channels and installations within their jurisdiction.

118 4. Unless other conditions are laid down by special arrangements, each Member shall take such steps as may be necessary to ensure maintenance of those sections of international telecommunication circuits within its control.

Article 24 Notification of Infringements

119 In order to facilitate the application of the provisions of Article 44 Members undertake to inform one another of infringements of the provisions of this Convention and of the Regulations annexed thereto.

Article 25 Priority of Telecommunications concerning Safety of Life

120 The international telecommunication services must give absolute priority to all telecommunications concerning safety of life at sea, on land, in the air or in outer space, as well as to epidemiological telecommunications of exceptional urgency of the World Health Organization.

Article 26 Priority of Government Telegrams and Telephone Calls

121 Subject to the provisions of Articles 25 and 36 government telegrams shall enjoy priority over other telegrams when priority is requested for them by the sender. Government telephone calls may also be given priority, upon specific request and to the extent practicable, over other telephone calls.

Article 27 Secret Language

122 1. Government telegrams and service telegrams may be expressed in secret language in all relations.

123 2. Private telegrams in secret language may be admitted between all countries with the exception of those which have previously notified, through the medium of the Secretary-General, that they do not admit this language for that category of correspondence.

124 3. Members which do not admit private telegrams in secret language originating in, or destined for their own territory must let them pass in transit, except in the case of suspension of service provided for in Article 20.

Article 28 Charges and Free Services

125 The provisions regarding charges for telecommunications and the various cases in which free services are accorded are set forth in the Administrative Regulations annexed to this Convention.

* * *

Article 31 Special Arrangements

128 Members reserve for themselves, for the private operating agencies recognized by them and for other agencies duly authorized to do so, the right to make special arrangements on telecommunications matters which do not concern

Members in general. Such arrangements, however, shall not be in conflict with the terms of this Convention or of the Administrative Regulations annexed thereto, so far as concerns the harmful interference which their operation might be likely to cause to the radio services of other countries.

Article 32 Regional Conferences, Arrangements and Organizations

129   Members reserve the right to convene regional conferences, to make regional arrangements and to form regional organizations, for the purpose of settling telecommunication questions which are susceptible of being treated on a regional basis. Such arrangements shall not be in conflict with this Convention.

Chapter III Special Provisions for Radio

Article 33 Rational Use of the Radio Frequency Spectrum and of the Geostationary Satellite Orbit

130   1. Members shall endeavour to limit the number of frequencies and the spectrum space used to the minimum essential to provide in a satisfactory manner the necessary services. To that end they shall endeavour to apply the latest technical advances as soon as possible.

131   2. In using frequency bands for space radio services Members shall bear in mind that radio frequencies and the geostationary satellite orbit are limited natural resources, that they must be used efficiently and economically so that countries or groups of countries may have equitable access to both in conformity with the provisions of the Radio Regulations according to their needs and the technical facilities at their disposal.

Article 34 Intercommunication

132   1. Stations performing radiocommunication in the mobile service shall be bound, within the limits of their normal employment, to exchange radiocommunications reciprocally without distinction as to the radio system adopted by them.

133   2. Nevertheless, in order not to impede scientific progress, the provisions of 132 shall not prevent the use of a radio system incapable of communicating with other systems, provided that such incapacity is due to the specific nature of such system and is not the result of devices adopted solely with the object of preventing intercommunication.

134   3. Notwithstanding the provisions of 132, a station may be assigned to a restricted international service of telecommunication, determined by the purpose of such service, or by other circumstances independent of the system used.

Article 35 Harmful Interference

135   1. All stations, whatever their purpose, must be established and operated in such a manner as not to cause harmful interference to the radio services or communications of other Members or of recognized private operating agencies, or of other duly authorized operating agencies which carry on radio service, and which operate in accordance with the provisions of the Radio Regulations.

136   2. Each Member undertakes to require the private operating agencies which it recognizes and the other operating agencies duly authorized for this purpose, to observe the provisions of 135.

137   3. Further, the Members recognize the desirability of taking all practicable steps to prevent the operation of electrical apparatus and installations of all kinds from causing harmful interference to the radio services or communications mentioned in 135.

Article 36 Distress Calls and Messages

138 Radio stations shall be obliged to accept, with absolute priority, distress calls and messages regardless of their origin, to reply in the same manner to such messages, and immediately to take such action in regard thereto as may be required.

Article 37 False or deceptive Distress, Urgency, Safety or Identification Signals

139 Members agree to take the steps required to prevent the transmission or circulation of false or deceptive distress, urgency, safety or identification signals, and to collaborate in locating and identifying stations transmitting such signals from their own country.

Article 38 Installations for National Defense Services

140 1. Members retain their entire freedom with regard to military radio installations of their army, naval and air forces.

141 2. Nevertheless, these installations must, so far as possible, observe statutory provisions relative to giving assistance in case of distress and to the measures to be taken to prevent harmful interference, and the provisions of the Administrative Regulations concerning the types of emission and the frequencies to be used, according to the nature of the services performed by such installations.

142 3. Moreover, when these installations take part in the service of public correspondence or other services governed by the Administrative Regulations annexed to this Convention, they must, in general, comply with the regulatory provisions for the conduct of such services.

Chapter IV Relations with the United Nations and with International Organizations

Article 39 Relations with the United Nations

143 1. The relationship between the United Nations and the International Telecommunication Union is defined in the Agreement concluded between these two organizations, the text of which appears in Annex 3 to this Convention.

144 2. In accordance with the provision of Article XVI of the above-mentioned Agreement, the telecommunication operating services of the United Nations shall be entitled to the rights and bound by the obligations of this Convention and of the Administrative Regulations annexed thereto. Accordingly, they shall be entitled to attend all conferences of the Union, including meetings of the International Consultative Committees, in a consultative capacity.

*   *   *

Article 42 Administrative Regulations

147 1. The provisions of the Convention are completed by the Administrative Regulations which regulate the use of telecommunication and shall be binding on all Members.

148 2. Ratification of this Convention in accordance with Article 45 or accession in accordance with Article 46 involves acceptance of the Administrative Regulations in force at the time of ratification or accession.

149 3. Members shall inform the Secretary-General of their approval of any revision of these Regulations by competent administrative conferences. The Secretary-General shall inform Members promptly regarding receipt of such notifications of approval.

150 4. In case of inconsistency between a provision of the Convention and a provision of the Administrative Regulations, the Convention shall prevail.

Article 43 Validity of Administrative Regulations in Force

151 The Administrative Regulations referred to in 147 are those in force at the time of signature of this Convention. They shall be regarded as annexed to this Convention and shall remain valid, subject to such partial revisions as may be adopted in consequence of the provisions of 44 until the time of entry into force of new Regulations drawn up by the competent world administrative conferences to replace them as annexes to this Convention.

Article 44 Execution of the Convention and Regulations

152 1. The Members are bound to abide by the provisions of this Convention and the Administrative Regulations in all telecommunication offices and stations established or operated by them which engage in international services or which are capable of causing harmful interference to radio services of other countries, except in regard to services exempted from these obligations in accordance with the provisions of Article 38.

153 2. They are also bound to take the necessary steps to impose the observance of the provisions of this Convention and of the Administrative Regulations upon private operating agencies authorized by them to establish and operate telecommunications and which engage in international services or which operate stations capable of causing harmful interference to the radio services of other countries.

* * *

Article 50 Settlement of Disputes

165 1. Members may settle their disputes on questions relating to the interpretation or application of this Convention or of the Regulations contemplated in Article 42, through diplomatic channels, or according to procedures established by bilateral or multilateral treaties concluded between them for the settlement of international disputes, or by any other method mutually agreed upon.

166 2. If none of these methods of settlement is adopted, any Member party to a dispute may submit the dispute to arbitration in accordance with the procedure defined in the General Regulations or in the Optional Additional Protocol, as the case may be.

* * *

TELEGRAPH REGULATIONS

Final Acts of the World Administrative
Telegraph and Telephone Conference, Geneva 1973

Article 1 Purpose of the Telegraph Regulations

1 1.(1) The Telegraph Regulations lay down the general principles to be observed in the international telegraph service.

(2) In implementing the principles of the Regulations, Administrations*) should comply with the C.C.I.T.T. Recommendations, including any Instructions forming part of those Recommendations, on any matters not covered by the Regulations.

*) or recognized private operating agency(ies)

2   2. These Regulations shall apply regardless of the means of transmission used, so far as the Radio Regulations and the Additional Radio Regulations do not provide otherwise.

Article 2 Definitions

International Route
An international route comprises the circuits to be used for telecommunication traffic between two international terminal exchanges or offices.

International Public Telegram Service
The Service which provides for the exchange of various classes of international telegrams.

International Telegraph Service
Denotes the generality of the various kinds of international telegraph-type services therein comprised, including the telegram and radiotelegram services, the phototelegraph service, the telex service, the data transmission service, the scheduled radiocommunication service and the leased telegraph circuit service.

Ordinary Private Telegrams
Ordinary private telegrams are obligatory private telegrams other than safety of life telegrams, meteorological telegrams and telegrams concerning persons protected in time of war by the Geneva Conventions of 12 August 1949.

Accounting Rate
The accounting rate is the rate agreed between Administrations in a given relation which is used for the establishment of international accounts.

Collection Charge
The collection charge is the charge established and collected by Administrations from its customers for the use of the international telecommunication service.

Instructions
Instructions consist of a Recommendation (or a group of Recommendations) prepared by the C.C.I.T.T. and dealing with practical procedure for operation and rate-fixing, which may be published in the form of a separate manual and made available to Administrations and recognized private operating agencies for use by their operational services.

Article 3 International system

3   1. The circuits and installation provided for the international telegraph service shall be sufficient to meet all requirements of the service.

4   2. Administrations shall cooperate in the establishment, operation and maintenance of the circuits and installations used for the international telegraph service to ensure the best possible quality of service.

Article 4 Services offered to users

5   1.(1) The following classes of telegrams shall be obligatory in the international public telegram service:
   1. Telegrams relating to the safety of life.
   2. Government telegrams and telegrams relative to the application of the United Nations Charter.

*   *   *

Article 8 Accounting rates for telegrams

26   1. The Administrations shall fix their terminal and transit rates for telegrams taking into account the Recommendations of the C.C.I.T.T. and the cost. The terminal rates fixed by an Administration for a relation with another country shall be the same regardless of the route used.

TELEPHONE REGULATIONS

Final Acts of the World Administrative
Telegraph and Telephone Conference, Geneva 1973

Article 1 Purpose of the Telephone Regulations

1   1.(1) The Telephone Regulations lay down the general principles to be observed in the international telephone service.

(2) In implementing the principles of the Regulations, Administrations should comply with the C.C.I.T.T. Recommendations, including any Instructions forming part of those Recommendations, on any matters not covered by the Regulations.

2   2. These Regulations shall apply regardless of the means of transmission used, so far as the Radio Regulations and the Additional Radio Regulations do not provide otherwise.

Article 2 Definitions

International route
   An international route comprises the circuits to be used for telecommunication traffic between two international terminal exchanges or offices.

Accounting rate
   The accounting rate is the rate agreed between Administrations in a given relation which is used for the establishment of international accounts.

Collection charge
   The collection charge is the charge established and collected by Administrations from its customers for the use of the international telecommunication service.

Instructions
   Instructions consist of a Recommendation (or a group of Recommendations) prepared by the C.C.I.T.T. and dealing with practical procedure for operation and rate fixing, whch may be published in the form of a separate manual and made available to Administrations and recognized private operating agencies for use by their operational services.

Article 3 International system

3   1. All Administrations shall promote the provision of telephone service on a world-wide scale and shall endeavour to extend the international service to their national network.

4   2. Adminstrations shall designate the exchanges in the territory they serve which are to be regarded as international exchanges.

5   3. The circuits and installations provided for the international telephone service shall be sufficient to meet all requirements of the service.

6   4. Administrations shall cooperate in the establishment, operation and maintenance of the circuits and installations used for the international telephone service to ensure the best possible quality of service.

7 5. The Administrations shall determine by mutual agreement which routes are to be used.

Article 4 Services offered to users

8 1. Administrations shall determine by mutual agreement the classes of calls, special facilities and special transmissions using telephone circuits to be admitted in their reciprocal international telephone relations observing the provisions of Articles 39 and 40 of the Convention (Montreux, 1965). To this end, the Administrations may conclude bilateral or regional agreements with a view to improving services available to users.

9 2. Administrations shall determine by mutual agreement the conditions under which they place international telephone type circuits at the exclusive disposal of users for an appropriate charge in those relations where telephone type circuits remain available after the needs of the public telecommunication services have been satisfied.

Article 5 Operating methods

10 Administrations shall agree among themselves upon the operating methods best suited to the needs of the international relations which concern them, taking account of the conditions and the possibilities of operation.

Article 6 Accounting rates

11 1. Accounting rates shall be made up of terminal rates and any transit rates.

12 2. Administrations shall fix their terminal and transit rates.

13 3. However, Administrations may by agreement fix the overall accounting rate applicable in a given relation and may divide that rate into terminal shares payable to the Administrations of terminal countries, and where appropriate, into transit shares payable to the Administrations of transit countries.

14 4. If no agreement as mentioned in **13** is reached, the overall accounting rate shall be determined in accordance with **11** and **12** above.

*   *   *

THE RADIO REGULATIONS

Final Acts of the World Administrative
Radio Conference, Geneva, 1979

Chapter NI Terminology

Article N1/1

Section I. General Terms

3001A 1.1 *Administration:* Any governmental department or service responsible for discharging the obligations undertaken in the Convention of the International Telecommunication Union and the Regulations.

3002 1.2 *Telecommunication:* Any transmission, *emission* or reception of signs, signals, writing, images and sounds or intelligence of any nature by wire, radio, optical or other electromagnetic systems.

3006 1.3 *Radio:* A general term applied to the use of *radio waves.*

3005 1.4 *Radio Waves* or *Hertzian Waves:* Electromagnetic waves of frequencies arbitrarily lower than 3 000 GHz, propagated in space without artificial guide.

3004 1.5 *Radiocommunication: Telecommunication* by means of *radio waves.*

3025 1.6 *Terrestrial Radiocommunication:* Any radiocommunication other than *space radiocommunication* or *radio astronomy.*

3024 1.7 *Space Radiocommunication:* Any *radiocommunication* involving the use of one or more *space stations* or the use of one or more *reflecting satellites* or other objects in space.

* * *

Section II. Specific Terms Related to Frequency Management

3023B 2.1 *Allocation* (of a frequency band): Entry in the Table of Frequency Allocations of a given frequency band for the purpose of its use by one or more [terrestrial or space] *radiocommunication services* or the *radio astronomy service* under specified conditions. This term shall also be applied to the frequency band concerned.

3023C 2.2 *Allotment* (of a radio frequency or radio frequency channel): Entry of a designated frequency channel in an agreed plan, adopted by a competent Conference, for use by one or more administrations for a [terrestrial or space] *radiocommunication service* in one or more identified countries or geographical areas and under specified conditions.

3023D 2.3 *Assignment* (of a radio frequency or radio frequency channel): Authorization given by an administration for a radio *station* to use a radio frequency or radio frequency channel under specified conditions.

* * *

Section III. Radio Services

3023E 3.1 *Radiocommunication Service:* A service as defined in this Section involving the transmission, *emission* and/or reception of *radio waves* for specific *telecommunication* purposes.

In these Regulations, unless otherwise stated, any *radiocommunication service* relates to *terrestrial radiocommunication.*

3036 3.2 *Fixed Service:* A *radiocommunication service* between specified fixed points.

3102 3.3 *Fixed-Satellite Service:* A *radiocommunication service* between *earth stations* at specified fixed points when one or more *satellites* are used; in some cases this service includes satellite-to-satellite links, which may also be effected in the *inter-satellite service;* the fixed-satellite service may also include *feeder links* for other *space radiocommunication* services.

* * *

3115 3.8 *Mobile-Satellite Service:* A *radiocommunication service:*
- between *mobile earth stations* and one or more *space stations,* or between *space stations* used by this service; *or*
- between *mobile earth stations* by means of one or more *space stations.*

This service may also include *feeder links* necessary for its operation.

* * *

3040 3.17 *Broadcasting Service:* A *radiocommunication service* in which the transmissions are intended for direct reception by the general public. This service may include sound transmissions, *television* transmissions or other types of transmission.

3103 3.18 *Broadcasting-Satellite Service:* A *radiocommunication service* in which signals transmitted or retransmitted by *space stations* are intended for direct reception by the general public.

In the broadcasting-satellite service, the term "direct reception" shall encompass both *individual reception* and *community reception.*

* * *

3106 3.29 *Earth Exploration-Satellite Service:* A *radiocommunication service* between *earth stations* and one or more *space stations,* which may include links between *space stations,* in which:
- information relating to the characteristics of the Earth and its natural phenomena is obtained from *active sensors* or *passive sensors* on earth *satellites;*

- similar information is collected from air-borne, or earth-based platforms;
- such information may be distributed to *earth stations* within the system concerned;
- platform interrogation may be included.

This service may also include *feeder links* necessary for its operation.

3107 3.30 *Meteorological-Satellite Service:* An *earth exploration-satellite service* for meteorological purposes.   *   *   *

3099 3.33 *Space Research Service:* A *radiocommunication* service in which *spacecraft* or other objects in space are used for scientific or technological research purposes.

3044 3.34 *Amateur Service:* A *radiocommunication service* for the purpose of self-training, intercommunication and technical investigations carried out by amateurs, that is, by duly authorized persons interested in radio technique solely with a personal aim and without pecuniary interest.

3108 3.35 *Amateur-Satellite Service:* A *radiocommunication service* using *space stations* on earth *satellites* for the same purposes as those of the *amateur service.*

3121 3.36 *Radio Astronomy Service:* A service involving the reception of radio waves of cosmic origin.

3029 3.37 *Safety Service:* Any *radiocommunication service* used permanently or temporarily for the safeguarding of human life and property.

3030 3.38 *Special Service:* A *radiocommunication service,* not otherwise defined in this Section, carried on exclusively for specific needs of general utility, and not open to *public correspondence.*   *   *   *

Section V. Operational Terms

3094B 5.1 *Public Correspondence:* Any *telecommunication* which the offices and *stations* must, by reason of their being at the disposal of the public, accept for transmission.

3007 5.2 *Telegraphy:* A form of *telecommunication* which is concerned in any process providing transmission and reproduction at a distance of documentary matter, such as written or printed matter or fixed images, or the reproduction at a distance of any kind of information in such a form. For the purposes of the Radio Regulations, unless otherwise specified therein, telegraphy shall mean a form of *telecommunication* for the transmission of written matter by the use of a signal code.

3010 5.3 *Telegram:* Written matter intended to be transmitted by *telegraphy* for delivery to the addressee. This term also includes *radiotelegrams* unless otherwise specified.

In this definition the term *telegraphy* has the same general meaning as defined in the Convention.   *   *   *

3016 5.7 *Facsimile:* A form of *telegraphy* for the transmission of fixed images, with or without half-tones, with a view to their reproduction in a permanent form.

In this definition the term *telegraphy* has the same general meaning as defined in the Convention.

3013 5.8 *Telephony:* A form of *telecommunication* set up for the transmission of speech or, in some cases, other sounds.

3014 5.9 *Radiotelephone Call:* A telephone call, originating in or intended for a *mobile station* or a *mobile earth station,* transmitted on all or part of its route over the *radiocommunication* channels of the *mobile service* or of the *mobile-satellite service.*

3015 5.13 *Television:* A form of *telecommunication* for the transmission of transient images of fixed or moving objects.

3104 5.14 *Individual Reception* (in the broadcasting-satellite service): The reception of *emissions* from a *space station* in the *broadcasting-satellite service* by simple domestic installations and in particular those possessing small antennae.

3105 5.15 *Community Reception* (in the broadcasting-satellite service): The reception of *emissions* from a *space station* in the *broadcasting-satellite service* by receiving equipment, which in some cases may be complex and have antennae larger than those used for *individual reception,* and intended for use:
- by a group of the general public at one location; *or*
- through a distribution system covering a limited area.

3017 5.16 *Telemetry:* The use of *telecommunication* for automatically indicating or recording measurement at a distance from the measuring instrument.

* * *

Section VII. Frequency Sharing

3140A 7.1 *Interference:* The effect of unwanted energy due to one or a combination of *emissions, radiations,* or inductions upon reception in a *radiocommunication* system, manifested by any performance degradation, misinterpretation, or loss of information which could be extracted in the absence of such unwanted energy.

3142A 7.2 *Permissible Interference:* Observed or predicted *interference* which complies with quantitative *interference* and sharing criteria contained in these Regulations or in CCIR Recommendations or in special agreements as provided for in these Regulations.

3142A.1 The terms "permissible interference" and "accepted interference" are used in the coordination of frequency assignments between administrations.

3140B 7.3 *Accepted Interference:* Interference at a higher level than that defined as *permissible interference* and which has been agreed upon between two or more administrations without prejudice to other administrations.

3142 7.4 *Harmful Interference:* Interference which endangers the functioning of a *radionavigation service* or of other *safety services* or seriously degrades, obstructs, or repeatedly interrupts a *radiocommunication service* operating in accordance with the Radio Regulations.

* * *

Article N2 Nomenclature of the Frequency and Wavelength Bands Used in Radiocommunication

3183 §1. The radio spectrum shall be subdivided into nine frequency bands, which shall be designated by progressive whole numbers in accordance with the following table. As the unit of frequency is the hertz (Hz), frequencies shall be expressed:
- in kilohertz (kHz), up to and including 3 000 kHz,
- in megahertz (MHz), above 3 MHz, up to and including 3 000 MHz,
- in gigahertz (GHz), above 3 GHz, up to and including 3 000 GHz.

For bands above 3 000 GHz, i.e. centimillimetric waves, micrometric waves, decimicrometric waves, it would be appropriate to use "terahertz (THz)".

However, where adherence to these provisions would introduce serious difficulties, for example in connection with the notification and registration of frequencies, the lists of frequencies and related matters, reasonable departures may be made.

Band number	Symbols	Frequency range (lower limit exclusive, upper limit inclusive)	Corresponding metric subdivision
4	VLF	3–30kHz	Myriametric waves
5	LF	30–300kHz	Kilometric waves
6	MF	300–3000kHz	Hectometric waves
7	HF	3–30MHz	Decametric waves
8	VHF	30–300MHz	Metric waves
9	UHF	300–3000 MHz	Decimetric waves

10	SHF	3–30 GHz	Centimetric waves
11	EHF	30–300 GHz	Millimetric waves
12		300–3000 GHz	Decimillimetric waves

Note 1: "Band Number N" (N = band number) extends from 0.3×10^N Hz to 3×10^N Hz.

Note 2: Prefix: k = kilo (10^3), M = mega (10^6), G = giga (10^9), T = tera (10^{12}).

*   *   *

Chapter NII

Article N4/12 Technical Characteristics of Stations

3242 § 1. (1) The choice and performance of equipment to be used in a station and any emissions therefrom shall satisfy the provisions of these Regulations.

3243 (2) Also, as far as is compatible with practical considerations, the choice of transmitting, receiving and measuring equipment shall be based on the most recent advances in the technique as indicated, inter alia, in CCIR Recommendations.

3244 § 2. Transmitting and receiving equipment intended to be used in a given part of the frequency spectrum should be designed to take into account the technical characteristics of transmitting and receiving equipment likely to be employed in neighbouring and other parts of the spectrum, provided that all technically and economically justifiable measures have been taken to reduce the level of unwanted emissions from the latter transmitting equipment and to reduce the susceptibility to interference of the latter receiving equipment.

*   *   *

3250 § 6. To ensure compliance with these Regulations, administrations shall arrange for frequent checks to be made of the emissions of stations under their jurisdiction. For this purpose, they shall use the means indicated in Article N18/13, if required. The technique of measurements and the intervals of measurements to be employed shall be, as far as is practicable, in accordance with the most recent CCIR Recommendations.

*   *   *

Chapter NIII Frequencies

Article N5/3 General Rules for the Assignment and Use of Frequencies

3276A § 0. Members shall endeavour to limit the number of frequencies and the spectrum space used to the minimum essential to provide in a satisfactory manner the necessary services. To that end they shall endeavour to apply the latest technical advances as soon as possible.

3277 § 1. Members undertake that in assigning frequencies to stations which are capable of causing harmful interference to the services rendered by the stations of another country, such assignments are to be made in accordance with the Table of Frequency Allocations and other provisions of these Regulations.

3278 § 2. Any new assignment or any change of frequency or other basic characteristic of an existing assignment (see Appendix 1 or Appendix 1A) shall be made in such a way as to avoid causing harmful interference to services rendered by stations using frequencies assigned in accordance with the Table of Frequency Allocations in this Chapter and other provisions of these Regulations, the characteristics of which assignments are recorded in the Master International Frequency Register.

3279 § 3. Administrations of the Members shall not assign to a station any frequency in derogation of either the Table of Frequency Allocations given in this Chapter or the other provisions of these Regulations, except on the express condition that harmful interference shall not be caused to services carried on by stations operating in accordance with the provisions of the Convention and of these Regulations.

3280 § 4. The frequency assigned to a station of a given service shall be separated from the limits of the band allocated to this service in such a way that, taking account of the frequency band assigned to a station, no harmful interference is caused to services to which frequency bands immediately adjoining are allocated.

3281 § 5. For the purpose of resolving cases of harmful interference, the radio astronomy service shall be treated as a radiocommunication service. However, protection from services in other bands shall be afforded the radio astronomy service only to the extent that such services are afforded protection from each other.

3281A § 5A. For the purpose of resolving cases of harmful interference the space research (passive) service and the earth exploration-satellite (passive) service shall be afforded protection from different services in other bands only to the extent that these different services are protected from each other.

3282 § 6. Where, in adjacent Regions or sub-Regions, a band of frequencies is allocated to different services of the same category (see Sections I and II of Article N7/5), the basic principle is the equality of right to operate. Accordingly, the stations of each service in one Region or sub-Region must operate so as not to cause harmful interference to services in the other Regions or sub-Regions.

3283 § 6A. No provision of these Regulations prevents the use by a station in distress of any means of radiocommunication at its disposal to attract attention, make known its condition and location, and obtain assistance.

3284 § 6B. No provision of these Regulations prevents the use by a station, in the exceptional circumstances described in No. 3283, of any means of radiocommunication at its disposal to assist a station in distress.

*   *   *

Section I. Regions and Areas

For the allocation of frequencies, the world has been divided into three Regions. In general terms the Regions have been defined so that
- Region 1 comprises Europe and Africa, including the USSR and Mongolia
- Region 2 comprises the Americas
- Region 3 comprises Asia and the Pacific.

For the allocation of frequencies to the broadcasting service, the "European Broadcasting Zone" is defined so as to comprise Europe, including the Western part of the USSR and the countries bordering the Mediterranean, including the northern part of Saudi Arabia, Iraq and Jordan.

In addition, the "Tropical Zone" is defined as the whole of the area between the Tropics of Cancer and Capricorn in Region 2, and in Regions 1 and 3, in principle the area between the parallels 30° North and 35° South (with certain special additions).

The World Administrative Radio Conference, Geneva, 1979 resolved that the present division in Regions should be reviewed in the light of developments in radio communication technology and increase in the membership of the union with countries of different stages of development. The Conference requested the CCIR to undertake a study of the technical and operational bases for the possible revision based on all relevant factors such as radio propagation, climatic conditions, geographical configurations, state of economic and technical development which would permit improvement in the utilization of the radio frequency spectrum by all member states of the Union.

Section II. Categories of Services and Allocations

3427 Primary, Permitted and Secondary Services

3428 Where [in a box of the Table in Section IV of this Article,] a band is indicated as allocated to more than one service, either on a worldwide or Regional basis, such services are listed in the following order:

(a) services, the names of which are printed in "capitals" (example: FIXED); these are called "primary" services;

(b) services, the names of which are printed in capitals between oblique strokes (example: /RADIOLOCATION/); these are called "permitted" services (see No. 3429/138);

(c) services, the names of which are printed in "normal characters" (example: Mobile); these are called "secondary" services (see No. 3430/139).

Additional remarks shall be printed in normal characters (example: MOBILE except aeronautical mobile).

3429 Permitted and primary services have equal rights, except that, in the preparation of frequency plans, the primary service, as compared with the permitted service, shall have prior choice of frequencies.

3430 Stations of a secondary service;

(a) shall not cause harmful interference to stations of primary or permitted services to which frequencies are already assigned or to which frequencies may be assigned at a later date;

(b) cannot claim protection from harmful interference from stations of a primary or permitted service to which frequencies are already assigned or may be assigned at a later date;

(c) can claim protection, however, from harmful interference from stations of the same or other secondary service(s) to which frequencies may be assigned at a later date.

3431 Where a band is indicated in a footnote of the Table as allocated to a service "on a secondary basis" in an area smaller than a Region, or in a particular country, this is a secondary service (see No. 3430/139).

3432 Where a band is indicated in a footnote of the Table as allocated to a service "on a primary basis", or "on a permitted basis" in an area smaller than a Region, or in a particular country, this is a primary service or a permitted service only in that area or country (see No. 3429/138).

3433 Additional Allocations

3434 Where a band is indicated in a footnote of the Table as "also allocated" to a service in an area smaller than a Region, or in a particular country, this is an "additional" allocation, i.e. an allocation which is added in this area or in this country to the service or services which are indicated in the Table (see No. 3435/143).

3435 If the footnote does not include any restriction on the service or services concerned apart from the restriction to operate only in a particular area or country, stations of this service or these services shall have equality of right to operate with stations of the other primary service or services indicated in the Table.

3436 If restrictions are imposed on an additional allocation in addition to the restriction to operate only in a particular area or country, this is indicated in the footnote of the Table.

3437 Alternative Allocations

3438 Where a band is indicated in a footnote of the Table as "allocated" to one or more services in an area smaller than a Region, or in a particular country, this is an "alternative" allocation, i.e. an allocation which replaces, in this area or in this country, the allocation indicated in the Table (see No. 3439/146).

3439 If the footnote does not include any restriction on stations of the service or services concerned, apart from the restriction to operate only in a particular area or country, these stations of such a service or services shall have an equality of right to operate with stations of the primary service or services, indicated in the Table, to which the band is allocated in other areas or countries.

3440 If restrictions are imposed on stations of a service to which an alternative allocation is made, in addition to the restriction to operate only in a particular country or area, this is indicated in the footnote.

3441 *Miscellaneous Provisions*

3442 Where it is indicated in these Regulations that a service may operate in a specific frequency band subject to not causing harmful interference, this means also that this service cannot claim protection from harmful interference caused by other services to which the band is allocated under Chapter NIII/II of these Regulations.

* * *

Article N8/6 Special Rules for the Assignment and Use of Frequencies

3916A § 0. Members recognize that the safety aspects of radionavigation and other safety services require special measures to ensure their freedom from harmful interference; it is necessary therefore to take this factor into account in the assignment and use of frequencies.

3917 § 1. (1) Members recognize that among frequencies which have long-distance propagation characteristics, those in the bands between 5 and 30 MHz are particularly useful for long-distance communications; they agree to make every possible effort to reserve these bands for such communications. Whenever frequencies in these bands are used for short or medium-distance communications, the minimum power necessary shall be employed.

3918 (2) To reduce requirements for frequencies in the bands between 5 and 30 MHz and thus to prevent harmful interference to long-distance radiocommunications, administrations are encouraged to use, whenever practicable, any other possible means of communication.

* * *

3925 § 7. Any emission capable of causing harmful interference to distress, alarm, urgency or safety communications on the international distress and emergency frequencies established for these purposes by these Regulations is prohibited. Supplementary distress frequencies available on less than a worldwide basis should be afforded adequate protection.

* * *

Chapter NIV/III Co-ordination, Notification and Registration of Frequencies. International Frequency Registration Board

Article N9/8 International Frequency Registration Board

Section I. Functions of the Board

3951 § 1. The constitution and the essential duties of the International Frequency Registration Board are defined in the Convention.

3952 § 2. The functions of the Board shall include:

3953 (*a*) the processing of frequency assignment notices, including information about any associated orbital locations of geostationary satellites,

received from administrations for recording in the Master International Frequency Register;

3953A (aa) the processing of information received in application of the advance publication, coordination and other procedures of the Radio Regulations and the Final Acts of Administrative Radio Conferences; and the provision of assistance to administrations in these matters, at their request;

3954 (b) the processing and coordination of seasonal schedules of high frequency broadcasting with a view to accommodating requirements of all administrations for that service;

3955 (c) the compilation, for publication in suitable form and at appropriate intervals by the Secretary-General, of frequency lists reflecting the data recorded in the Master International Frequency Register, as well as other material relating to the assignment and use of frequencies;

3956 (d) the review of entries in the Master International Frequency Register with a view to amending or eliminating, as appropriate, those which do not reflect actual frequency usage, in agreement with the administrations which notified the assignments concerned;

3957 (e) the study, on a long-term basis, of the usage of the radio frequency spectrum, with a view to making recommendations for its more effective use;

3958 (f) the investigation, at the request of one or more of the interested administrations, of harmful interference and the formulation of recommendations with respect thereto;

3959 (g) the provision of assistance to administrations in the field of radio spectrum utilization, in particular to those administrations in need of special assistance, and the recommendation to administrations, where appropriate, of adjustments in their frequency assignments in order to obtain a better use of the radio spectrum;

3960 (h) the collection of such results of monitoring observations as administrations and organizations may be able to supply and the making of arrangements, through the Secretary-General, for their publication in suitable form;

3960A (ha) the development of Technical Standards in accordance with 4471/636 and 4648/639DV and of Rules of Procedure for internal use by the Board in the exercise of its functions.

3961 (i) the formulation and reference to the CCIR of all general technical questions arising from the Board's examination of frequency assignments;

3962 (j) the technical assistance in the preparation for and organization of radio conferences in consultation, as appropriate, with the other permanent organs of the Union, and with due regard for the pertinent directives of the Administrative Council in accordance with the Convention;

3963 (k) the participation in an advisory capacity, upon invitation by the organizations or countries concerned, in conferences and meetings where questions relating to the assignment and utilization of frequencies are discussed;

3963A (ka) the provision of assistance to administrations, at their request, in the training of senior staff in the fields of spectrum management and utilization, particularly for those countries in special need;

3963B (kb) the discharge of such other functions as are specified in the Radio Regulations and in the Final Acts of Administrative Radio Conferences.

3965 § 4. The Specialized Secretariat of the IFRB shall work under the immediate direction of the Board to enable it to discharge its prescribed duties and functions.

3966 to 3990 NOT Allocated.

Article N10/11

Section II. Methods of Work of the Board

3991 § 1. The Board shall meet as frequently as necessary to deal expeditiously with its work and, normally, at least once a week.

3992 § 2. (1) In accordance with the Convention, the members of the Board shall elect from among their number a Chairman and a Vice-Chairman, each to hold office for a term of one year. Thereafter, the Vice-Chairman shall succeed annually to the Chairmanship and a new Vice-Chairman shall be elected.

* * *

3997 (4) The Board shall endeavour to reach its decisions by unanimous agreement. If the Board fails in that endeavour, it shall thereafter decide the problem on the basis of a two-thirds majority vote of the members present and voting for or against.

* * *

3998 § 4. The documents of the Board, which shall comprise a complete record of its official actions and minutes of its meetings, shall be maintained by the Board in the working languages of the Union as defined in the Convention; for this purpose, as well as for the meetings of the Board, the necessary linguistic personnel, and such other facilities as may be required, shall be provided by the Secretary-General. A copy of all documents of the Board shall be available for public inspection at the offices of the Board.

3999 to 4098 NOT allocated.

* * *

Chapter NV Measures against Interference. Tests

Article N16 Interference

4996 § 1. Administrations shall cooperate in the detection and elimination of harmful interference, employing where appropriate the facilities described in Article N18/13 and the procedures detailed in Article N20/15.

Section I. General Interference

4997 § 2. All stations are forbidden to carry out:
- unnecessary transmissions;
- the transmission of superfluous signals and correspondence;
- the transmission of false or misleading signals;
- the transmission of signals without identification (except as provided for in Article N23/19).

4998 § 3. All stations shall radiate only as much power as is necessary to ensure a satisfactory service.

4999 § 4. In order to avoid interference:
- locations of transmitting stations and, where the nature of the service permits, locations of receiving stations shall be selected with particular care;
- radiation in and reception from unnecessary directions shall be minimized by taking the maximum practical advantage of the properties of directional antennae whenever the nature of the service permits;

- the choice and use of transmitters and receivers shall be in accordance with the provisions of Article **N4**/12;
- the conditions specified under No. **6105** shall be fulfilled.

4999A § 4A. Special consideration shall be given to avoiding interference on distress and safety frequencies and those related to distress and safety identified in Article **N35**.

5000 § 5. The class of emission to be employed by a station should be such as to achieve minimum interference and to assure efficient spectrum utilization. In general this requires that in selecting the class of emission to meet these objectives every effort shall be made to minimize the bandwidth occupied, taking into account the operational and technical considerations of the service to be performed.

* * *

Article N18 International Monitoring

5058 § 1. To assist to the extent practicable in the implementation of these Regulations, in particular to help ensure efficient and economical use of the radio frequency spectrum and to help in the prompt elimination of harmful interference, administrations agree to continue the development of monitoring facilities and, to the extent practicable, to co-operate in the continued development of the international monitoring system.

* * *

Article N20/15 Procedure in a Case of Harmful Interference

5126 § 1. It is essential that Members exercise the utmost goodwill and mutual assistance in the application of the provisions of Article 35 of the Convention and of this Article to the settlement of problems of harmful interference.

5127 § 2. In the settlement of these problems, due consideration shall be given to all factors involved, including the relevant technical and operating factors, such as: adjustment of frequencies, characteristics of transmitting and receiving antennae, time sharing, change of channels within multichannel transmissions.

* * *

5132 § 7. Having determined the source and characteristics of the harmful interference, the administration having jurisdiction over the transmitting station whose service is being interfered with shall inform the administration having jurisdiction over the interfering station, giving all useful information in order that this administration may take such steps as may be necessary to eliminate the interference.

5133A § 8A. An administration receiving a communication to the effect that one of its stations is causing harmful interference to a safety service shall promptly investigate the matter and take any necessary remedial action.

* * *

5136A § 11A. Recognizing that transmissions on the distress and safety frequencies (see Article **N35**) require absolute international protection and that the elimination of harmful interference to such transmissions is imperative, administrations undertake to act immediately when their attention is drawn to any such harmful interference.

* * *

Chapter NVI Administrative Provisions for Stations

Article N21/17 Secrecy

5193 In the application of the appropriate provisions of the Convention, administrations bind themselves to take the necessary measures to prohibit and prevent:

5193   (a)   the unauthorized interception of radiocommunications not intended for the general use of the public;

5194   (b)   the divulgence of the contents, simple disclosure of the existence, publication or any use whatever, without authorization of information of any nature whatever obtained by the interception of the radiocommunications mentioned in No. **5194**.

5196 to 5220 NOT allocated.

Article N22/18 Licences

5221 § 1. (1) No transmitting station may be established or operated by a private person or by any enterprise without a licence issued in an appropriate form and in conformity with the provisions of these Regulations by the government of the country to which the station in question is subject. (However, see Nos. **5222, 5228** and **5230A**).   * * *

5224 § 2. The holder of a licence is required to preserve the secrecy of telecommunications, as provided in the relevant provisions of the Convention. Moreover, the licence shall mention, specifically or by reference, that if the station includes a receiver, the interception of radiocommunication correspondence, other than that which the station is authorized to receive, is forbidden, and that in the case where such correspondence is involuntarily received, it shall not be reproduced, nor communicated to third parties, nor used for any purpose, and even its existence shall not be disclosed.

* * *

Chapter NVIII Provisions Relating to Groups of Services and to Specific Services and Stations

Article N28/7 Broadcasting Service and Broadcasting-Satellite Service

Section I. Broadcasting Service

6213 *A. General*

6214 § 1. (1) The establishment and use of broadcasting stations (sound broadcasting and television broadcasting stations) on board ships, aircraft or any other floating or airborne objects outside national territories is prohibited.

6215 (2) In principle, except in the frequency band 3 900–4 000 kHz broadcasting stations using frequencies below 5 060 kHz or above 41 MHz shall not employ power exceeding that necessary to maintain economically an effective national service of good quality within the frontiers of the country concerned.

* * *

Section II. Broadcasting-Satellite Service

6222 § 3. In devising the characteristics of a space station in the broadcasting-satellite service, all technical means available shall be used to reduce, to the maximum extent practicable, the radiation over the territory of other countries unless an agreement has been previously reached with such countries.

* * *

CONVENTIONS ADOPTED BY THE UNITED NATIONS CONFERENCE ON THE LAW OF THE SEA, 29 APRIL 1958

The High Seas

The States Parties to this Convention,
Desiring to codify the rules of international law relating to the high seas,
   Recognizing that the United Nations Conference on the Law of the Sea, held at Geneva from 24 February to 27 April 1958, adopted the following provisions as generally declaratory of established principles of international law,
   Have agreed as follows:

Article 1

The term 'high seas' means all parts of the sea that are not included in the territorial sea or in the internal waters of a State.

Article 2

The high seas being open to all nations, no State may validly purport to subject any part of them to its sovereignty. Freedom of the high seas is exercised under the conditions laid down by these articles and by the other rules of international law. It comprises, *inter alia,* both for coastal and non-coastal States:

(1) Freedom of navigation;
(2) Freedom of fishing;
(3) Freedom to lay submarine cables and pipelines;
(4) Freedom to fly over the high seas.

These freedoms, and others which are recognized by the general principles of international law, shall be exercised by all States with reasonable regard to the interests of other States in their exercise of the freedom of the high seas.

* * *

Article 10

1. Every State shall take such measures for ships under its flag as are necessary to ensure safety at sea with regard *inter alia* to:

(a) The use of signals, the maintenance of communications and the prevention of collisions;
(b) The manning of ships and labour conditions for crews taking into account the applicable international labour instruments;
(c) The construction, equipment, and seaworthiness of ships.

2. In taking such measures each State is required to conform to generally accepted international standards and to take any steps which may be necessary to ensure their observance.

The Continental Shelf

The States Parties to this Convention
Have agreed as follows:

Article 1

For the purpose of these Articles, the term 'continental shelf' is used as referring (a) to the seabed and subsoil of the submarine areas adjacent to the coast but outside the area of the territorial sea, to a depth of 200 metres or, beyond that limit, to where the depth of the superjacent waters admits of the exploitation of the natural resources of the said areas; (b) to the seabed and subsoil of similar submarine areas adjacent to the coasts of islands.

* * *

Article 4

Subject to its right to take reasonable measures for the exploitation of the continental shelf and the exploitation of its natural resources, the coastal State may not impede the laying or maintenance of submarine cables or pipelines on the continental shelf.

EUROPEAN AGREEMENT FOR THE PREVENTION OF
BROADCASTS TRANSMITTED FROM STATIONS
OUTSIDE NATIONAL TERRITORIES

Council of Europe, 1969

The member States of the Council of Europe signatory hereto,

Considering that the aim of the Council of Europe is to achieve a greater unity between its Members;

Considering that the Radio Regulations annexed to the International Telecommunication Convention prohibit the establishment and use of broadcasting stations on board ships, aircraft or any other floating or airborne objects outside national territories;

Considering also the desirability of providing for the possibility of preventing the establishment and use of broadcasting stations on objects affixed to or supported by the bed of the sea outside national territories;

Considering the desirability of European collaboration in this matter,

Have agreed as follows:

Article 1

This Agreement is concerned with broadcasting stations which are installed or maintained on board ships, aircraft, or any other floating or airborne objects and which, outside national territories, transmit broadcasts intended for reception or capable of being received, wholly or in part, within the territory of any Contracting Party, or which cause harmful interference to any radio-communication service operating under the authority of a Contracting Party in accordance with the Radio Regulations.

Article 2

1. Each Contracting Party undertakes to take appropriate steps to make punishable as offences, in accordance with its domestic law, the establishment or operation of broadcasting stations referred to in Article 1, as well as acts of collaboration knowingly performed.

2. The following shall, in relation to broadcasting stations referred to in Article 1, be acts of collaboration:

(a)   the provision, maintenance or repairing of equipment;
(b)   the provision of supplies;
(c)   the provision of transport for, or the transporting of, persons, equipment or supplies;
(d)   the ordering or production of material of any kind, including advertisements, to be broadcast;
(e)   the provision of services concerning advertising for the benefit of the stations.

Article 3

Each Contracting Party shall, in accordance with its domestic law, apply the provisions of this Agreement in regard to:

(a)   its nationals who have committed any act referred to in Article 2 on its territory, ships, or aircraft, or outside national territories on any ships, aircraft or any other floating or airborne object;
(b)   non-nationals who, on its territory, ships or aircraft, or on board any floating or airborne object under its jurisdiction have committed any act referred to in Article 2.

Article 4

Nothing in this Agreement shall be deemed to prevent a Contracting Party:

(a)   from also treating as punishable offences acts other than those referred to in Article 2 and also applying the provisions concerned to persons other than those referred to in Article 3;
(b)   from also applying the provisions of this Agreement to broadcasting stations installed or maintained on objects affixed to or supported by the bed of the sea.

Article 5

The Contracting Parties may elect not to apply the provisions of this Agreement in respect of the services of performers which have been provided elsewhere than on the stations referred to in Article 1.

Article 6

The provisions of Article 2 shall not apply to any acts performed for the purpose of giving assistance to a ship or aircraft or any other floating or airborne object in distress or of protecting human life.

Article 7

No reservation may be made to the provisions of this Agreement.

Article 8

1. This Agreement shall be open to signature by the member States of the Council of Europe, which may become Parties to it either by:
(a) signature without reservation in respect of ratification or acceptance, or
(b) signature with reservation in respect of ratification or acceptance followed by ratification or acceptance.

2. Instruments of ratification or acceptance shall be deposited with the Secretary-General of the Council of Europe.

Article 9

1. This Agreement shall enter into force one month after the date on which three member States of the Council shall, in accordance with the provisions of Article 8, have signed the Agreement without reservation in respect of ratification or acceptance, or shall have deposited their instrument of ratification or acceptance.

2. As regards any member State which shall subsequently sign the Agreement without reservation in respect of ratification or acceptance or which shall ratify or accept it, the Agreement shall enter into force one month after the date of such signature or the date of deposit of the instrument of ratification or acceptance.

Article 10

1. After this Agreement has entered into force, any Member or Associate Member of the International Telecommunication Union which is not a Member of the Council of Europe may accede to it subject to the prior agreement of the Committee of Ministers.

2. Such accession shall be effected by depositing with the Secretary-General of the Council of Europe an instrument of accession which shall take effect one month after the date of its deposit.

Article 11

1. Any Contracting Party may, at the time of signature or when depositing its instrument of ratification, acceptance or accession, specify the territory or territories to which this Agreement shall apply.

2. Any Contracting Party may, when depositing its instrument of ratification, acceptance or accession or at any later date, by declaration addressed to the Secretary-General of the Council of Europe, extend this Agreement to any other territory or territories specified in the declaration and for whose international relations it is responsible or on whose behalf it is authorised to give undertakings.

3. Any declaration made in pursuance of the preceding paragraph may, in respect of

any territory mentioned in such declaration, be withdrawn according to the procedure laid down in Article 12 of this Agreement.

Article 12

1. This Agreement shall remain in force indefinitely.

2. Any Contracting Party may, in so far as it is concerned, denounce this Agreement by means of a notification addressed to the Secretary-General of the Council of Europe.

3. Such denunciation shall take effect six months after the date of receipt by the Secretary-General of such notification.

Article 13

The Secretary-General of the Council of Europe shall notify the member States of the Council and the Government of any State which has acceded to this Agreement, of:

(a) any signature without reservation in respect of ratification or acceptance;
(b) any signature with reservation in respect of ratification or acceptance;
(c) any deposit of an instrument of ratification, acceptance or accession;
(d) any date of entry into force of this Agreement in accordance with Articles 9 and 10 thereof;
(e) any declaration received in pursuance of paragraph 2 and 3 of Article 11;
(f) any notification received in pursuance of the provisions of Article 12 and the date on which denunciation takes effect.

PART FOUR
POSTAL LAW

The Universal Postal Union (UPU) was founded in 1874, as the Postal Bureau, to provide for international co-operation among its members and to promote standardization of postal operation. The current constitution of the UPU was drawn up in Vienna 1964 and its states that the 'Universal Postal Convention and its Detailed Regulations embody the rules applicable throughout the international postal service and the provisions concerning the letter post services'. Thus, the current international regulation of the flow of material on mainly written or printed support is the Universal Postal Convention Lausanne, 1974.

The UPU enjoys the virtually universal membership of some 156 member nations and its aims include the development of communication between peoples through efficient operation of postal services. To this end, its members form a single postal territory for the reciprocal exchange of letter post items and guarantee freedom of transit for correspondence. The Union participates in the United Nations Development Programme and its technical co-operation activities include an extensive postal assistance programme.

The international postal agreements are supplemented by regional agreements which, however, have not been included in the collection.

The provisions in this field should be seen in conjunction with, (a) such instruments on free flow of information as the Florence and Beirut agreements, and (b) relevant customs regulations.

Documents
  i. Constitution of the Universal Postal Union, Vienna, 1964
      – Preamble
      – Articles 1–3, 8–10, 22, 24, 32
  ii. Universal Postal Convention, Lausanne, 1974
      – Preamble
      – Articles 1–9, 33, 34, 77
Examples of regional postal agreements
  – Asian-Oceanic Postal Convention, Manila, 1961
  – Convention on the Postal Union of the Americas and Spain, Santiago, 1971
    (not included)

CONSTITUTION OF THE UNIVERSAL POSTAL UNION, VIENNA, 1964

Preamble
With a view to developing communications between peoples by the efficient operation of the postal services, and to contributing to the attainment of the noble aims of international collaboration in the cultural, social and economic fields,

The Plenipotentiaries of the Governments of the Contracting Countries have, subject to ratification, adopted this Constitution.

Section I Organic Provisions
Chapter I General

Article 1 Scope and objectives of the Union

1. The Countries adopting this Constitution comprise, under the title of the Universal Postal Union, a single postal territory for the reciprocal exchange of letter post items. Freedom of transit is guaranteed throughout the entire territory of the Union.

2. The aim of the Union is to secure the organization and improvement of the postal services and to promote in this sphere the development of international collaboration.

3. The Union takes part, as far as possible, in postal technical assistance sought by its Member Countries.

Article 2 Members of the Union

Member Countries of the Union are:

(a) Countries which have membership status at the date on which this Constitution comes into force.

(b) Countries admitted to membership in accordance with Article 11.

Article 3 Jurisdiction of the Union

The Union has within its jurisdiction:

(a) the territories of Member Countries;

(b) post offices set up by Member Countries in territories not included in the Union;

(c) territories which, without being members of the Union, are included in it because from the postal point of view they are dependent on Member Countries.

*   *   *

Article 8 Restricted Unions. Special Agreements

1. Member Countries, or their Postal Administrations if the legislation of those Countries so permits, may establish Restricted Unions and make Special Agreements concerning the international postal service, provided always that they do not introduce provisions less favourable to the public than those provided for by the Acts to which the Member Countries concerned are parties.

2. Restricted Unions may send observers to Congresses, Conferences and meetings of the Union, to the Executive Council and to the Consultative Committee for Postal Studies.

3. The Union may send observers to Congresses, Conferences and meetings of Restricted Unions.

Article 9 Relations with the United Nations

The relations between the Union and the United Nations are governed by the Agreements whose texts are annexed to this Constitution.

Article 10 Relations with international organizations

In order to secure close co-operation in the international postal sphere, the Union may collaborate with international organizations having related interests and activities.

*   *   *

Article 22 Acts of the Union

1. The Constitution is the basic Act of the Union. It contains the organic rules of the Union.

2. The General Regulations embody those provisions which ensure the application of the Constitution and the working of the Union. They shall be binding on all Member Countries.

3. The Universal Postal Convention and its Detailed Regulations embody the rules applicable throughout the international postal service and the provisions concerning the letter post services. These Acts shall be binding on all Member Countries.

4. The Agreements of the Union, and their Detailed Regulations, regulate the services other than those of the letter post between those Member Countries which are parties to them. They shall be binding on those Countries only.

5. The Detailed Regulations, which contain the rules of application necessary for the implementation of the Convention and of the Agreements, shall be drawn up by the Postal Administrations of the Member Countries concerned.

6. The Final Protocols annexed to the Acts of the Union referred to in paragraphs 3, 4 and 5 contain the reservations to those Acts.

* * *

Article 24 National legislation

The provisions of the Acts of the Union do not derogate from the legislation of any Member Country in respect of anything which is not expressly provided for by those Acts.

* * *

Article 32 Arbitration

In the event of a dispute between two or more Postal Administrations of Member Countries concerning the interpretation of the Acts of the Union or the responsibility imposed on a Postal Administration by the application of those Acts, the question at issue shall be settled by arbitration.

* * *

UNIVERSAL POSTAL CONVENTION, LAUSANNE, 1974

The undersigned, Plenipotentiaries of the Governments of the member countries of the Union, having regard to Article 22, § 3, of the Constitution of the Universal Postal Union concluded at Vienna on 10 July 1964, have by common consent and subject to Article 25, § 3, of the Constitution drawn up in this Convention the rules applicable in common throughout the international postal service concerning the letter-post services.

Part 1 Rules Applicable in Common throughout the International Postal Service
Chapter 1 General Provisions

Article 1 Freedom of transit

1. Freedom of transit, the principle of which is set forth in Article 1 of the Constitution, shall carry with it the obligation for each postal administration to forward always by the quickest routes which it uses for its own items, closed mails and à découvert letter-post items which are passed to it by another administration. This obligation shall also apply to airmail correspondence, whether or not the intermediate postal administration take part in reforwarding it.

2. Member countries which do not participate in the exchange of letters containing perishable biological substances or radioactive substances shall have the option of not admitting these items in transit *à découvert* through their territory. The same shall apply to the items referred to in Article 33, § 6.

3. Member countries not providing the insured letters service or not accepting liability for insured *letters* carried by their sea or air services may not, however, refuse transit of such items in closed mails through their territory or conveyance of them by their sea or air services; but those countries' liability shall be limited to that laid down for registered items.

4. Freedom of transit for postal parcels to be forwarded by land and sea routes shall be limited to the territory of the countries taking part in this service.

5. Freedom of transit for air parcels shall be guaranteed throughout the territory of the Union. Nevertheless, member countries which are not parties to the Postal Parcels Agreement shall not be required to forward air parcels by surface.

6. Member countries which are parties to the Postal Parcels Agreement but which do not provide an insured parcels service or which do not accept liability for insured items carried by their sea or air services, may not, however, refuse transit of such parcels in closed mails through their territory or conveyance of them by their sea or air services; but those countries' liability shall be limited to that laid down for uninsured parcels of the same weight.

Article 2 Failure to give freedom of transit

When a member country fails to observe the provisions of Article 1 of the Constitution and of Article 1 of the Convention regarding freedom of transit, postal administrations of other member countries may discontinue their postal service with that country. They shall give prior notice of this step to the administrations concerned by telegram, and inform the International Bureau of the fact.

Article 3 Land transit without the participation of the services of the country crossed

The conveyance of mail in transit through a country without the participation of the services of that country shall be subject to the prior authorization of the country crossed. This form of transit shall not involve the liability of the latter country.

Article 4 Temporary suspension and resumption of services

When, owing to exceptional circumstances, a postal administration is obliged to suspend temporarily its services wholly or in part, it shall announce the fact immediately, if need be by telegram, to the administration or administrations concerned. It shall do likewise when the suspended services are resumed. In addition, the International Bureau must be notified of the suspension or resumption of services if a general announcement is considered necessary.

Article 5 Ownership of postal items

A postal item shall remain the property of the sender until it is delivered to the rightful owner, except when the item has been seized in pursuance of the legislation of the country of destination.

Article 6 Creation of new service

Administrations may by mutual consent create a new service not expressly provided for in this Convention. Charges for a new service shall be laid down by the administration concerned, having regard to expenses of operating the service.

Article 7 Charges

1. The charges for the various international postal services shall be laid down in the Convention and the Agreements.

2. No postal charge of any kind may be collected other than those provided for in the Convention and Agreements.

Article 8 Equivalents

In each member country, the charges shall be fixed on the basis of the closest possible equivalent of the value of the gold franc in the currency of that country.

Article 9 Postage stamps

Postage stamps for denoting payment of postage shall be issued by postal administrations only.

*   *   *

Article 33 Prohibitions

1. Letter-post items which, by their packing, may expose officials to danger or soil or damage other items or postal equipment shall not be admitted.

Article 34 Customs control

The postal administrations of the countries of origin and destination shall be authorized to submit to customs control, according to the legislation of those countries, letter-post items and, if necessary, to open them officially.

*   *   *

Article 77 Conditions of approval of proposals concerning the Convention and its Detailed Regulations

1. To become effective, proposals submitted to Congress relating to this Convention and its Detailed Regulations must be approved by a majority of the member countries present and voting. At least half of the member countries represented at Congress shall be present at the time of voting.

2. To become effective, proposals introduced between Congresses relating to this Convention and its Detailed Regulations must obtain:

(a) unanimity of votes if they involve amendments to Articles 1 to 17 (part I), 18, 19, 20, 21 (f), (n), (o) and (p), 24, 27, 40, 41, 42, 44 to 57 (part II), 77 and 78 (part IV) of the Convention, to any of the Articles of its Final Protocol or to Articles 102 to 104, 105, § 1, 125, 145, 146, §§ 1 and 3, 163, 174, 175 and 207 of its Detailed Regulations;

(b) two-thirds of the votes if they involve amendments of substance to provisions other than those mentioned under (a);

(c) a majority of the votes if they involve:

    (i) drafting amendments to the provisions of the Convention and its Detailed Regulations other than those mentioned under (a);

    (ii) interpretation of the provisions of the Convention, its Final Protocol and its Detailed Regulations, except in case of a dispute to be submitted to arbitration as provided for in Article 32 of the Constitution.

*   *   *

PART FIVE
SPACE LAW

Space law is that body of international legal norms governing outer space activities which has been developed since the beginning of the 1960s, primarily under the auspices of the UN (Committee on the Peaceful Uses of Outer Space).

The origin of this work was linked to questions of disarmament and the common desire to prevent the extension of cold-war rivalry into outer space. Provisions to this effect were introduced into the Treaty banning nuclear weapon tests in the atmosphere, in outer space, and under water (1963). Simultaneously, the scope and substance of the UN work in this area was widened. Following a number of basic resolutions concerning international co-operation in the peaceful uses of outer space, in particular 1721 (XVI), 1961 and 1802 (XVII), 1962, the General Assembly in 1963 adopted a 'Declaration of Legal Principles Governing the Activities of States in the Exploration and Use of Outer Space'. Most of these principles were incorporated in the Outer Space Treaty of 1967 which provides the cornerstone of the developing space law.

Following the 1967 Treaty, the Outer Space Committee has continued work on the development of space law through a series of agreements on specific issues such as liability for outer space activities, the rescue of astronauts and the exploration and use of the moon and other celestial bodies. As part of this task, the Committee has for a number of years worked on agreements covering two communication issues: legal principles for satellite broadcasting and legal principles for remote sensing of the earth via satellites. So far, the required consensus has not been achieved.

New communications technologies and services are in the most cases incorporated in the mandates of already existing organizations. This is the case with agreements on the technical aspects of space communications which have been adopted within the context of the International Telecommunication Union. Similarly, the Brussels Convention prohibiting piracy of satellite signals which was discussed within the context of intellectual property rights was sponsored by Unesco and WIPO. The advent of satellite communication, though, has led to the establishment of new international organizations for the planning and operation of space communication systems. The constituent documents of the relevant organizations have also been included (i.e. Intelsat, Intersputnik and Inmarsat).

Documents

    i. Treaty on Principles Governing the Activities of States in the Exploration and Use of Outer Space, including the Moon and other Celestial Bodies (Outer Space Treaty), 1967
- Full text

Texts adopted by the United Nations

    ii. Declaration of Legal Principles Governing the Activities of States in the Exploration and the Use of Outer Space, General Assembly Resolution 1962 (XVIII), 1963
- Full text

iii. International co-operation in the peaceful uses of outer space, General Assembly Resolution 1721 (XVI), 1961
   - Full text

iv. International co-operation in the peaceful uses of outer space, General Assembly Resolution 1802 (XVII), 1962
   - Preamble and Section IV

v. International co-operation in the peaceful uses of outer space, General Assembly Resolution 2733 (XXV), 1970
   - Section A

vi. Preparation of an international convention on principles governing the use by States of artificial earth satellites for direct television broadcasting, General Assembly Resolution 2916 (XXVIII), 1972
   - Full text

vii. Draft principles on direct broadcast satellites contained in the report of the Legal Sub-Committee on the work of its twentieth session, (document A/AC 105/288), 1981
   - Full text

viii. Draft principles (on remote sensing) as contained in the report of the Legal Sub-Committee on the work of its nineteenth session, (document A/AC 105/271), 1981
   - Full text

Texts adopted by specialized agencies

ix. Radio Regulations, 1979.
   - See Part Three (in particular Art. N1, N28)

x. Declaration of Guiding Principles on the Use of Satellite Broadcasting for the Free Flow of Information, the Spread of Education and Greater Cultural Exchanges, Unesco, General Conference Resolution, 1972
   - Full text

xi. Brussels Satellite Convention
   - See Part Six

Operational Agreements

i. Agreement Relating to the International Telecommunications Satellite Organization 'Intelsat', 1971
   - Preamble
   - Articles I–III, V–VII (a–c i–iv), VIII (a–b), IX (a), X (a, i–viii)

The annexes to the Agreement concern (not included)

Annex A   Functions of the Secretary General
Annex B   Functions of the Management Services Contractor and Guidelines of the Management Services Contract
Annex C   Provisions on Procedures Relating to Settlement of Disputes
Annex D   Transition Provisions

The Agreement is supplemented by Operating Agreement Relating to the International Telecommunications Satellite Organization 'Intelsat'.

ii. Agreement on the Establishment of the 'Intersputnik' International System and Organization of Space Communications, 1971
   - Preamble
   - Articles 1–7, 11, 12, 16.

iii. Convention on the International Maritime Satellite Organization (Inmarsat), 1978

– Preamble
– Articles 1–7

TREATY ON PRINCIPLES GOVERNING THE ACTIVITIES OF STATES IN THE EXPLORATION AND USE OF OUTER SPACE, INCLUDING THE MOON AND OTHER CELESTIAL BODIES (OUTER SPACE TREATY), 1967

The States Parties to this Treaty,
Inspired by the great prospects opening up before mankind as a result of man's entry into outer space,
Recognizing the common interest of all mankind in the progress of the exploration and use of outer space for peaceful purposes,
Believing that the exploration and use of outer space should be carried on for the benefit of all peoples irrespective of the degree of their economic or scientific development,
Desiring to contribute to broad international co-operation in the scientific as well as the legal aspects of the exploration and use of outer space for peaceful purposes,
Believing that such co-operation will contribute to the development of mutual understanding and to the strengthening of friendly relations between States and peoples,
Recalling resolution 1962 (XVIII), entitled "Declaration of Legal Principles Governing the Activities of States in the Exploration and Use of Outer Space," which was adopted unanimously by the United Nations General Assembly on 13 December 1963,
Recalling resolution 1884 (XVIII), calling upon States to refrain from placing in orbit around the Earth any objects carrying nuclear weapons or any other kinds of weapons of mass destruction or from installing such weapons on celestial bodies, which was adopted unanimously by the United Nations General Assembly on 17 October 1963,
Taking account of United Nations General Assembly resolution 110 (11) of 3 November 1947, which condemned propaganda designed or likely to provoke or encourage any threat to the peace, breach of the peace or act of aggression, and considering that the aforementioned resolution is applicable to outer space,
Convinced that a Treaty on Principles Governing the Activities of States in the Exploration and Use of Outer Space, including the Moon and Other Celestial Bodies, will further the purposes and principles of the Charter of the United Nations,
Have agreed on the following:

Article I

The exploration and use of outer space, including the Moon and other celestial bodies, shall be carried out for the benefit and in the interests of all countries, irrespective of their degree of economic or scientific development, and shall be the province of all mankind.

Outer space, including the Moon and other celestial bodies, shall be free, for exploration and use by all States without discrimination of any kind, on a basis of equality and in accordance with international law, and there shall be free access to all areas of celestial bodies.

There shall be freedom of scientific investigation in outer space, including the Moon and other celestial bodies, and States shall facilitate and encourage international co-operation in such investigation.

Article II

Outer space, including the Moon and other celestial bodies, is not subject to national appropriation by claim of sovereignty, by means of use or occupation, or by any other means.

Article III

States Parties to the Treaty shall carry on activities in the exploration and use of outer space, including the Moon and other celestial bodies, in accordance with international law, including the Charter of the United Nations, in the interest of maintaining peace and security and promoting international co-operation and understanding.

Article IV

States Parties to the Treaty undertake not to place in orbit around the Earth any objects carrying nuclear weapons or any other kinds of weapons of mass destruction, install such weapons on celestial bodies, or station weapons in outer space in any other manner.

The Moon and other celestial bodies shall be used by all States Parties to the Treaty exclusively for peaceful purposes. The establishment of military bases, installations and fortifications, the testing of any type of weapons and the conduct of military manoeuvres on celestial bodies shall be forbidden. The use of military personnel for scientific research or for any other peaceful purposes shall not be prohibited. The use of any equipment or facility necessary for peaceful exploration of the Moon and other celestial bodies shall also not be prohibited

Article V

States Parties to the Treaty shall regard astronauts as envoys of mankind in outer space and shall render to them all possible assistance in the event of accident, distress, or emergency landing on the territory of another State Party or on the high seas. When astronauts make such a landing, they shall be safely and promptly returned to the State of registry of their space vehicle.

In carrying on activities in outer space and on celestial bodies, the astronauts of one State Party shall render all possible assistance to the astronauts of other States Parties.

States Parties to the Treaty shall immediately inform the other States Parties to the Treaty or the Secretary-General of the United Nations of any phenomena they discover in outer space, including the Moon and other celestial bodies, which could constitute a danger to the life or health of astronauts.

Article VI

States Parties to the Treaty shall bear international responsibility for national activities in outer space, including the Moon and other celestial bodies, whether such activities are carried on by governmental agencies or by non-governmental entities, and for assuring that national activities are carried out in conformity with the provisions set forth in the present Treaty. The activities of non-governmental entities in outer space, including the Moon and other celestial bodies, shall require authorization and continuing supervision by the appropriate State Party to the Treaty. When activities are carried on in outer space, including the Moon and other celestial bodies, by an international organization, responsibility for compliance with this Treaty shall be borne both by the international organization and by the States Parties to the Treaty participating in such organization.

Article VII

Each State Party to the Treaty that launches or procures the launching of an object into outer space, including the Moon and other celestial bodies, and each State Party from whose territory or facility an object is launched, is internationally liable for damage to another State Party to the Treaty or to its natural or juridical persons by such object or its component parts on the Earth, in air space or in outer space, including the Moon and other celestial bodies.

Article VIII

A State Party to the Treaty on whose registry an object launched into outer space is carried shall retain jurisdiction and control over such object, and over any personnel thereof, while in outer space or on a celestial body. Ownership of objects launched into outer space, including objects landed or constructed on a celestial body, and of their component parts, is not affected by their presence in outer space or on a celestial body or by their return to the Earth. Such objects or component parts found beyond the limits of the State Party to the Treaty on whose registry they are carried shall be returned to that State Party, which shall, upon request, furnish identifying data prior to their return.

Article IX

In the exploration and use of outer space, including the Moon and other celestial bodies, States Parties to the Treaty shall be guided by the principle of co-operation and mutual assistance and shall conduct all their activities in outer space, including the Moon and other celestial bodies, with due regard to the corresponding interests of all other States Parties to the Treaty. States Parties to the Treaty shall pursue studies of outer space, including the Moon and other celestial bodies, and conduct exploration of them so as to avoid their harmful contamination and also adverse changes in the environment of the Earth resulting from the introduction of extraterrestrial matter and, where necessary, shall adopt appropriate measures for this purpose. If a State Party to the Treaty has reason to believe that an activity or experiment planned by it or its nationals in outer space, including the Moon and other celestial bodies, would cause potentially harmful interference with activities of other States Parties in the peaceful exploration and use of outer space, including the Moon and other celestial bodies, it shall undertake appropriate international consultations before proceeding with any such activity or experiment. A State Party to the Treaty which has reason to believe that an activity or experiment planned by another State Party in outer space, including the Moon and other celestial bodies, would cause potentially harmful interference with activities in the peaceful exploration and use of outer space, including the Moon and other celestial bodies, may request consultation concerning the activity or experiment.

Article X

In order to promote international co-operation in the exploration and use of outer space, including the Moon and other celestial bodies, in conformity with the purposes of this Treaty, the States Parties to the Treaty shall consider on a basis of equality any requests by other States Parties to the Treaty to be afforded an opportunity to observe the flight of space objects launched by those States.

The nature of such an opportunity for observation and the conditions under which it could be afforded shall be determined by agreement between the States concerned.

Article XI

In order to promote international co-operation in the peaceful exploration and use of outer space, States Parties to the Treaty conducting activities in outer space, including the Moon and other celestial bodies, agree to inform the Secretary-General of the United Nations as well as the public and the international scientific community, to the greatest extent feasible and practicable, of the nature, conduct, locations and results of such activities. On receiving the said information, the Secretary-General of the United Nations should be prepared to disseminate it immediately and effectively.

Article XII

All stations, installations, equipment and space vehicles on the Moon and other celestial bodies shall be open to representatives of other States Parties to the Treaty on a basis of reciprocity. Such representatives shall give reasonable advance notice of a projected visit, in order that appropriate consultations may be held and that maximum precautions may be taken to assure safety and to avoid interference with normal operations in the facility to be visited.

Article XIII

The provisions of this Treaty shall apply to the activities of States Parties to the Treaty in the exploration and use of outer space, including the Moon and other celestial bodies, whether such activities are carried on by a single State Party to the Treaty or jointly with other States, including cases where they are carried on within the framework of international intergovernmental organizations.

Any practical questions arising in connexion with activities carried on by international intergovernmental organizations in the exploration and use of outer space, including the Moon and other celestial bodies, shall be resolved by the States Parties to the Treaty either with the appropriate international organization or with one or more States members of that international organization, which are Parties to this Treaty.

Article XIV

1. This Treaty shall be open to all States for signature. Any State which does not sign this Treaty before its entry into force in accordance with paragraph 3 of this article may accede to it at any time.

2. This Treaty shall be subject to ratification by signatory States. Instruments of ratification and instruments of accession shall be deposited with the governments of the Union of Soviet Socialist Republics, the United Kingdom of Great Britain and Northern Ireland and the United States of America, which are hereby designated the Depository Governments.

3. This Treaty shall enter into force upon the deposit of instruments of ratification by five Governments including the Governments designated as Depository Governments under this Treaty.

4. For States whose instruments of ratification or accession are deposited subsequent to the entry into force of this Treaty, it shall enter into force on the date of the deposit of their instruments of ratification or accession.

5. The Depository Governments shall promptly inform all signatory and acceding States of the date of each signature, the date of deposit of each instrument of ratification of and accession to this Treaty, the date of its entry into force and other notices.

6. This Treaty shall be registered by the Depository Governments pursuant to Article 102 of the Charter of the United Nations.

Article XV

Any State Party to the Treaty may propose amendments to this Treaty. Amendments shall enter into force for each State Party to the Treaty accepting the amendments upon their acceptance by a majority of the States Parties to the Treaty and thereafter for each remaining State Party to the Treaty on the date of acceptance by it.

Article XVI

Any State Party to the Treaty may give notice of its withdrawal from the Treaty one year after its entry into force by written notification to the Depository Governments. Such withdrawal shall take effect one year from the date of receipt of this notification.

Article XVII

This Treaty, of which the Chinese, English, French, Russian and Spanish texts are equally authentic, shall be deposited in the archives of the Depository Governments. Duly certified copies of this Treaty shall be transmitted by the Depository Governments to the Governments of the signatory and acceding States.

   In witness whereof the undersigned, duly authorized, have signed this Treaty.

   Done in triplicate at the cities of London, Moscow and Washington, this twenty-seventh day of January, one thousand nine hundred sixty-seven.

DECLARATION OF LEGAL PRINCIPLES GOVERNING THE ACTIVITIES OF STATES IN THE EXPLORATION AND USE OF OUTER SPACE

United Nations General Assembly Resolution 1962 (XVIII), 1963

The General Assembly,
Inspired by the great prospects opening up before mankind as a result of man's entry into outer space,

   Recognizing the common interest of all mankind in the progress of the exploration and use of outer space and peaceful purposes,

   Believing that the exploration and use of outer space should be for the betterment of mankind and for the benefit of States irrespective of their degree of economic or scientific development,

   Desiring to contribute to broad international cooperation in the scientific as well as in the legal aspects of exploration and use of outer space for peaceful purposes,

   Believing that such co-operation will contribute to the development of mutual understanding and to the strengthening of friendly relations between nations and peoples,

   Recalling General Assembly resolution 110 (II) of 3 November 1947, which condemned propaganda designed or likely to provoke or encourage any threat to the peace, breach of the peace, or act of aggression, and considering that the aforementioned resolution is applicable to outer space,

   Taking into consideration General Assembly resolutions 1721 (XVI) of 20 December 1961 and 1802 (XVII) of 14 December 1962, approved unanimously by the States Members of the United Nations,

   Solemnly declares that in the exploration and use of outer space States should be guided by the following principles:

1. The exploration and use of outer space shall be carried on for the benefit and in the interests of all mankind.

2. Outer space and celestial bodies are free for exploration and use by all States on a basis of equality and in accordance with international law.

3. Outer space and celestial bodies are not subject to national appropriation by claim of sovereignty, by means of use or occupation, or by any other means.

4. The activities of States in the exploration and use of outer space shall be carried on in accordance with international law including the Charter of the United Nations, in the interest of maintaining international peace and security and promoting international co-operation and understanding.

5. States bear international responsibility for national activities in outer space, whether carried on by governmental agencies or by non-governmental entities, and for assuring that national activities are carried on in conformity with the principles set forth in this Declaration. The activities of non-governmental entities in outer space shall require authorization and continuing supervision by the State concerned.

When activities are carried on in outer space by an international organization, responsibility for compliance with the principles set forth in this Declaration shall be borne by the international organization and by the States participating in it.

6. In the exploration and use of outer space, States shall be guided by the principles of co-operation and mutual assistance and shall conduct all their activities in outer space with due regard for the corresponding interests of other States. If a State has reason to believe that an outer space activity or experiment planned by it or its nationals would cause potentially harmful interference with activities of other States in the peaceful exploration and use of outer space, it shall undertake appropriate international consultations before proceeding with any such activity or experiment. A State which has reason to believe that an outer space activity or experiment planned by another State would cause potentially harmful interference with activities in the peaceful exploration and use of outer space may request consultation concerning the activity or experiment.

7. The State on whose registry an object launched into outer space is carried shall retain jurisdiction and control over such object, and any personnel thereon, while in outer space. Ownership of objects launched into outer space, and of their component parts, is not affected by their passage through outer space or by their return to the earth. Such objects or component parts found beyond the limits of the State of registry shall be returned to that State, which shall furnish identifying data upon request prior to return.

8. Each State which launches or procures the launching of an object into outer space, and each State from whose territory or facility an object is launched, is internationally liable for damage to a foreign State or to its natural or juridical persons by such object or its component parts on the earth, in air space, or in outer space.

9. States shall regard astronauts as envoys of mankind in outer space, and shall render to them all possible assistance in the event of accident, distress, or emergency landing on the territory of a foreign State or on the high seas. Astronauts who make such a landing shall be safely and promptly returned to the State of registry of their space vehicle.

INTERNATIONAL CO-OPERATION IN THE PEACEFUL USES OF OUTER SPACE

United Nations General Assembly Resolution 1721 (XVI), 1961

A

The General Assembly,
Recognizing the common interest of mankind in furthering the peaceful uses of outer space and the urgent need to strengthen international co-operation in this important field,

Believing that the exploration and use of outer space should be only for the betterment of mankind and to the benefit of States irrespective of the stage of their economic or scientific development,

1. *Commends* to States for their guidance in the exploration and use of outer space the following principles:

(a) International law, including the Charter of the United Nations, applies to outer space and celestial bodies;

(b) Outer space and celestial bodies are free for exploration and use by all States in conformity with international law and are not subject to national appropriation;

2. *Invites* the Committee on the Peaceful Uses of Outer Space to study and report on the legal problems which may arise from the exploration and use of outer space.

B

The General Assembly,
Believing that the United Nations should provide a focal point for international co-operation in the peaceful exploration and use of outer space,

1. *Calls upon* States launching objects into orbit or beyond to furnish information promptly to the Committee on the Peaceful Uses of Outer Space, through the Secretary-General, for the registration of launchings;

2. *Requests* the Secretary-General to maintain a public registry of the information furnished in accordance with paragraph 1 above;

3. *Requests* the Committee on the Peaceful Uses of Outer Space, in co-operation with the Secretary-General and making full use of the functions and resources of the Secretariat:

(a)   To maintain close contact with governmental and non-governmental organizations concerned with outer space matters:

(b)   To provide for the exchange of such information relating to outer space activities as Governments may supply on a voluntary basis, supplementing but not duplicating existing technical and scientific exchanges.

(c)   To assist in the study of measures for the promotion of international co-operation in outer space activities;

4. *Further requests* the Committee on the Peaceful Uses of Outer Space to report to the General Assembly on the arrangements undertaken for the performance of those functions and on such developments relating to the peaceful uses of outer space as it considers significant.

C

The General Assembly,
Noting with gratification the marked progress for meteorological science and technology opened up by the advances in outer space,

Convinced of the world-wide benefits to be derived from international co-operation in weather research and analysis,

1. *Recommends* to all Member States and to the World Meteorological Organization and other appropriate specialized agencies the early and comprehensive study, in the light of developments in outer space, of measures:

(a)   To advance the state of atmospheric science and technology so as to provide greater knowledge of basic physical forces affecting climate and the possibility of large-scale weather modification;

(b)   To develop existing weather forecasting capabilities and to help Member States make effective use of such capabilities through regional meteorological centres;

2. *Requests* the World Meteorological Organization, consulting as appropriate with the United Nations Educational, Scientific and Cultural Organization and other specialized agencies and governmental and non-governmental organizations, such as the International Council of Scientific Unions, to submit a report to the Governments of its Member States and to the Economic and Social Council at its thirty-fourth session regarding appropriate organizational and financial arrangements to achieve those ends, with a view to their further consideration by the General Assembly at its seventeenth session;

3. *Requests* the Committee on the Peaceful Uses of Outer Space, as it deems appropriate, to review that report and submit its comments and recommendations.

D

The General Assembly,
Believing that communication by means of satellites should be available to the nations of the world as soon as practicable on a global and non-discriminatory basis,
   Convinced of the need to prepare the way for the establishment of effective operational satellite communication,

1. *Notes with satisfaction* that the International Telecommunication Union plans to call a special conference in 1963 to make allocations of radio frequency bands for outer space activities;

2. *Recommends* that the International Telecommunication Union consider at that conference those aspects of space communication in which international co-operation will be required;

3. *Notes* the potential importance of communication satellites for use by the United Nations and its principal organs and specialized agencies for both operational and informational requirements;

4. *Invites* the Special Fund and the Expanded Programme of Technical Assistance, in consultation with the International Telecommunication Union, to give sympathetic consideration to requests from Member States for technical and other assistance for the survey of their communication needs and for the development of their domestic communication facilities, so that they may make effective use of space communication;

5. *Requests* the International Telecommunication Union, consulting as appropriate with Member States, the United Nations Educational, Scientific and Cultural Organization and other specialized agencies and governmental and non-governmental organizations, such as the Committee on Space Research of the International Council of Scientific Unions, to submit a report on the implementation of these proposals to the Economic and Social Council at its thirty-fourth session and to the General Assembly at its seventeenth session;

6. *Requests* the Committee on the Peaceful Uses of Outer Space, as it deems appropriate, to review that report and submit its comments and recommendations to the Economic and Social Council and to the General Assembly.

INTERNATIONAL CO-OPERATION IN THE
PEACEFUL USES OF OUTER SPACE

United Nations General Assembly Resolution 1802 (XVII), 1962

The General Assembly,
Recalling its resolution 1721 (XVI) of 20 December 1961 on international co-operation in the peaceful uses of outer space,
   Believing that the activities of States in the exploration and use of outer space should be carried out in conformity with international law including the Charter of the United Nations, in the interest of friendly relations among nations,
   Stressing the necessity of the progressive development of international law pertaining to the further elaboration of basic legal principles governing the activities of States in the exploration and use of outer space and to liability for space vehicle accidents and to assistance to and return of astronauts and space vehicles and to other legal problems,
   Bearing in mind that the application of scientific and technological advances in outer space, particularly in the fields of meteorology and communications, can bring great advantages to mankind and contribute to the economic and social progress of the developing countries as envisaged in the United Nations Development Decade programme,

Having considered the report submitted by the Committee on the Peaceful Uses of Outer Space in response to resolution 1721 (XVI).

* * *

IV

1. *Notes with appreciation* the prompt initial response of the International Telecommunication Union to the request of the General Assembly, as embodied in resolution 1721 D (XVI), that it report on those aspects of space communications in which international co-operation will be required;

2. *Believes* that communication by satellite offers great benefits to mankind, as it will permit the expansion of radio, telephone and television transmissions, including the broadcast of United Nations activities, thus facilitating contact among the peoples of the world;

3. *Emphasizes* the importance of international co-operation to achieve effective satellite communications which will be available on a world-wide basis;

4. *Observes* that the Secretary-General of the International Telecommunication Union has invited member States to submit information on:
   (a) Technical progress and developments in space telecommunications;
   (b) Subjects which they regard as appropriate for international co-operation in order to achieve the objectives set forth in resolution 1721 D (XVI);
   (c) Which of those subjects, if any, should be included in the agenda of the Extraordinary Administrative Radio Conference to be held in October 1963;

5. *Notes* that the Secretary-General of the International Telecommunication Union, in the light of the replies, will report on these questions to the next meeting of its Administrative Council in March 1963 in order that the Council may complete the agenda for this Conference;

6. *Considers* it of the utmost importance that this Conference make allocations of radio frequency bands sufficient to meet expected outer space needs;

* * *

INTERNATIONAL CO-OPERATION IN THE
PEACEFUL USES OF OUTER SPACE

United Nations General Assembly Resolution 2733 (XXV), 1970

A

The General Assembly,
Recalling its resolution 2453 B (XXIII) of 20 December 1968 whereby it established a Working Group of the Committee on the Peaceful Uses of Outer Space to study and report on the technical feasibility of communication by direct broadcast from satellites and the current and foreseeable developments in this field, as well as the implications of such developments in the social, cultural, legal and other fields,
   Taking note with appreciation of the reports prepared by the Working Group during its three sessions,
   Noting that a first satellite-borne instructional television experiment for direct reception into community receivers will be undertaken in India as early as 1973/1974, thereby making it possible to enrich life in isolated communities,
   Noting that the potential benefits of satellite broadcasting have particular significance with regard to better understanding among peoples, the expansion of the flow of information and the wider dissemination of knowledge in the world, and promoting cultural exchanges,
   Recognizing that the use of satellite-borne television for educational and training purposes, particularly in developing countries, can in many instances contribute

towards national programmes of integration and community development and economic, social and cultural development in such areas as formal and adult education, agriculture, health and family planning,

Taking note of the concern of the Committee on the Peaceful Uses of Outer Space in considering the practical interests of all States, in particular the interests of the developing countries, concerning the efficient use of the geostationary orbit and the frequency spectrum,

Recognizing that the effective deployment and use of direct satellite broadcasting requires large-scale international and regional co-operation and that further consideration may have to be given to the legal principles applicable in this field,

Endorsing the Working Group's conclusions on the applicability to such broadcasting of certain existing international legal instruments, including the Charter of the United Nations, the Treaty on Principles Governing the Activities of States in the Exploration and Use of Outer Space, including the Moon and Other Celestial Bodies, and the applicable provisions of the International Telecommunication Convention and Radio Regulations,

1. *Recommends,* on the basis of the probable patterns of use of satellite broadcasting systems outlined by the Working Group of the Committee on the Peaceful Uses of Outer Space, that Member States, regional and international organizations, including broadcasting associations, should promote and encourage international co-operation on regional and other levels in order, *inter alia,* to allow all participating parties to share in the establishment and operation of regional satellite broadcasting services and/or in programme planning and production;

2. *Draws the attention* of Member States, specialized agencies and other interested international organizations to the potential benefits to be derived from direct broadcast satellite services, especially in developing countries, for improving their telecommunications infrastructure, thereby contributing to general economic and social development;

3. *Recommends,* with a view to making available the benefits of this new technology to countries, regardless of the degree of their social and economic development, that Member States, the United Nations Development Programme and other international agencies should promote international co-operation in this field in order to assist interested countries to develop the skills and techniques that may be necessary for its application;

4. *Requests* the Committee on the Peaceful Uses of Outer Space to keep under review the question of reconvening the Working Group at such time as additional material of substance on which further useful studies might be based may have become available;

5. *Recommends* that the Committee on the Peaceful Uses of Outer Space should study through its Legal Sub-Committee, giving priority to the liability convention, the work carried out by the Working Group on Direct Broadcast Satellites, under the item on the implications of space communications;

6. *Invites* the International Telecommunications Union to continue to take the necessary steps to promote the use of satellite broadcasting services by Member States and to consider at the 1971 World Administrative Radio Conference for Space Telecommunications the appropriate provisions under which satellite broadcasting services may be established;

7. *Requests* the International Telecommunication Union to transmit, when available, to the Committee on the Peaceful Uses of Outer Space all information about the use of the geostationary orbit and the frequency spectrum;

8. *Invites* the United Nations Educational, Scientific and Cultural Organization to continue to promote the use of satellite broadcasting for the advancement of education and training, science and culture and, in consultation with appropriate intergovernmental and non-governmental organizations and broadcasting associa-

tions, to direct its efforts towards the solution of problems falling within its mandate.

* * *

PREPARATION OF AN INTERNATIONAL CONVENTION ON PRINCIPLES GOVERNING THE USE BY STATES OF ARTIFICIAL EARTH SATELLITES FOR DIRECT TELEVISION BROADCASTING

United Nations General Assembly Resolution 2916 (XXVIII), 1972

The General Assembly,

Recalling its resolution 2222 (XXI) of 19 December 1966, in which its stressed the importance of international co-operation in the field of activities in the peaceful exploration and use of outer space and the importance of developing the rule of law in this area of human endeavour,

Recalling further its resolution 2453 B (XXIII) of 20 December 1968, in which it stated that the benefits of space exploration can be extended to States at all stages of economic and scientific development,

Reaffirming the common interest of all mankind in furthering the peaceful exploration and use of outer space for the benefit of all States and for the development of friendly relations and mutual understanding among them,

Bearing in mind that direct television broadcasting should help to draw the peoples of the world closer together, to widen the exchange of information and cultural values and to enhance the educational level of people in various countries,

Considering at the same time that direct television broadcasting by means of satellites should take place under conditions in which this new form of space technology will serve only the lofty goals of peace and friendship among peoples,

Mindful of the need to prevent the conversion of direct television broadcasting into a source of international conflict and of aggravation of the relations among States and to protect the sovereignty of States from any external interference,

Noting the draft convention on principles governing the use by States of artificial earth satellites for direct television broadcasting, submitted to the General Assembly by the Union of Soviet Socialist Republics,

Desiring to further the elaboration of specific rules of international law governing the activities of States in this field on the basis of the Charter of the United Nations, the Treaty on Principles Governing the Activities of States in the Exploration and Use of Outer Space, including the Moon and Other Celestial Bodies and the Declaration on Principles of International Law concerning Friendly Relations and Co-operation among States in accordance with the Charter of the United Nations,

Believing that the activity of States in the field of direct television broadcasting must be based on the principles of mutual respect for sovereignty, non-interference in domestic affairs, equality, co-operation and mutual benefit,

Considering at the same time that the introduction of direct television broadcasting by means of satellites could raise significant problems connected with the need to ensure the free flow of communications on a basis of strict respect for the sovereign rights of States,

1. *Considers* it necessary to elaborate principles governing the use by States of artificial earth satellites for direct television broadcasting with a view to concluding an international agreement or agreements;

2. *Requests* the Committee on the Peaceful Uses of Outer Space to undertake the elaboration of such principles as soon as possible;

3. *Requests* the Secretary-General to transmit to the Committee on the Peaceful Uses of Outer Space all documentation relating to the discussion, at the Twenty-seventh session of the General Assembly, of the item entitled "Preparation of an international convention on principles governing the use by States of artificial earth satellites for direct television broadcasting".

DRAFT PRINCIPLES GOVERNING THE USE BY STATES OF
ARTIFICIAL EARTH SATELLITES FOR INTERNATIONAL
DIRECT TELEVISION BROADCASTING

Negotiating text (UN document A/36/20, supplement no. 20 1981)

The General Assembly,

1. *In view* of the benefits of international direct television broadcasting by means of artificial earth satellites for individuals, peoples, countries, and all mankind,

2. *Desiring* to safeguard the legitimate rights and interests of all States and to encourage orderly development on an equitable basis of this new and promising means of television broadcasting,

3. *Recognizing* the unique characteristics of such satellite broadcasting not encountered in other forms of broadcasting which necessitate besides relevant technical regulations also principles solely applicable in this field,

4. *Considering* that States, as well as international governmental and non-governmental organizations, including broadcasting associations, should base their activities in this field upon and encourage international co-operation,

Declares that in their activities in the field of direct television broadcasting by means of artificial earth satellites specifically directed at a foreign State, hereinafter referred to as "international direct television broadcasting by satellite", States should be guided by the following principles:

Purposes and objectives

1. Activities in the field of international direct television broadcasting by satellite should be carried out in a manner compatible with the sovereign rights of States, including the principle of non-intervention as well as with the right of everyone to seek, receive and impart information and ideas as enshrined in the relevant United Nations instruments.

2. Such activities should promote the free dissemination and mutual exchange of information and knowledge in cultural and scientific fields, assist in educational, social and economic development particularly in the developing countries, enhance the qualities of life of all peoples and provide recreation with due respect to the political and cultural integrity of States.

3. These activities should accordingly be carried out in a manner compatible with the development of mutual understanding and the strengthening of friendly relations and co-operation among all States and peoples in the interest of maintaining international peace and security.

Applicability of international law

Activities in the field of international direct television broadcasting by satellite should be conducted in accordance with international law, including the Charter of the United Nations, the Treaty on Principles Governing the Activities of States in the Exploration and Use of Outer Space, including the Moon and Other Celestial Bodies of 27 January 1967, the relevant provisions of the International Telecommunication Convention and its Radio Regulations and of international instruments relating to friendly relations and co-operation among States and to human rights.

Rights and benefits

Every State has an equal right to conduct activities in the field of international direct television broadcasting by satellite and to authorize such activities by persons and entities under its jurisdiction. All States and peoples are entitled to and should enjoy the benefits from such activities. Access to the technology in this field should be available to all States without discrimination on terms mutually agreed by all concerned.

International co-operation

Activities in the field of international direct television broadcasting by satellite should be based upon and encourage international co-operation. Such co-operation should be the subject of appropriate arrangements. Special consideration should be given the needs of the developing countries in the use of international direct television broadcasting by satellite for the purpose of accelerating their national development.

Peaceful settlement of disputes

Any international dispute that may arise from activities covered by these principles should be settled through established procedures for the peaceful settlement of disputes agreed upon by the parties to the dispute in accordance with the provisions of the Charter of the United Nations.

State responsibility

States should bear international responsibility for activities in the field of international direct television broadcasting by satellite carried out by them or under their jurisdiction and for the conformity of any such activities with the principles set forth in this document.

When international direct television broadcasting by satellite is carried out by an international intergovernmental organization, the responsibility referred to in the above paragraph should be borne both by that organization and by the States participating in it.

Duty and right to consult

Any broadcasting or receiving State within an international direct television broadcasting satellite service established between them requested to do so by any other broadcasting or receiving State within the same service should promptly enter into consultations with the requesting State regarding its activities in the field of international direct television broadcasting by satellite, without prejudice to other consultations which these States may undertake with any other State on that subject.

Copyright and neighbouring rights

Without prejudice to the relevant provisions of international law States should co-operate on a bilateral and multilateral basis for protection of copyright and neighbouring rights by means of appropriate agreements between the interested States or the competent legal entities acting under their jurisdiction. In such co-operation they should give special consideration to the interests of developing countries in the use of direct television broadcasting for the purpose of accelerating their national development.

Notification to the United Nations

In order to promote international co-operation in the peaceful exploration and use of outer space, States conducting or authorizing activities in the field of international direct television broadcasting by satellite should inform the Secretary-General of the United Nations to the greatest extent possible of the nature of such activities. On receiving this information, the Secretary-General of the United Nations should disseminate it immediately and effectively to the relevant United Nations specialized agencies, as well as to the public and the international scientific community.

Consultation and agreements between States

1. A State which intends to establish or authorize the establishment of an international direct television broadcasting satellite service shall without delay notify the proposed receiving State or States of such intention and shall promptly enter into consultation with any of those States which so requests.

2. An international direct television broadcasting satellite service shall only be established after the conditions set forth in paragraph 1 above have been met and on the basis of agreements and/or arrangements in conformity with the relevant instruments of the International Telecommunication Union and in accordance with these principles.

3. With respect to the unavoidable overspill of the radiation of the satellite signal the relevant instruments of the International Telecommunication Union shall be exclusively applicable.

REMOTE SENSING

TEXTS OF DRAFT PRINCIPLES AS CONTAINED IN THE REPORT OF THE
LEGAL SUB-COMMITTEE ON THE WORK OF ITS NINETEENTH SESSION
(UN DOC. A/AC.105/271 1981), ANNEX I, APPENDIX

Principle I[1]

For the purpose of these principles with respect to remote sensing of the natural resources of the earth and its environment:[2]

(a) The term "remote sensing of the earth" means "remote sensing of the natural resources of the earth and its environment".[3]

(b) The term "primary data" means those primary data which are acquired by satellite-borne remote sensors and transmitted from a satellite either by telemetry in the form of electromagnetic signals or physically in any form such as photographic film or magnetic tape, as well as preprocessed products derived from those data which may be used for later analysis.

(c) The term "analysed information"** means the end-product resulting from the analytical process performed on the primary data as defined in paragraph (b) above combined with data and/or knowledge obtained from sources other than satellite-borne remote sensors.

Principle II

Remote sensing of the earth from outer space and international co-operation in that field [shall][should] be carried out for the benefit and in the interest of all countries, irrespective of their degree of economic or scientific development, and taking into consideration, in international co-operation, the particular needs of the developing countries.

*Or "as required under the relevant instruments of the International Telecommunication Union and in accordance with those instruments."

[1]The question of the application of these principles to international intergovernmental organizations will be considered later.

[2]The formulation "with respect to remote sensing of the natural resources of the earth and its environment" will be reviewed in light of the title to be given to the principles.

[3]This term is still subject to further discussion. In the view of some delegations, it would be necessary in the future work to further define the meaning of the words "remote sensing of the earth and its environment".

**The content, definition and necessity of the term "analysed information" is still to be clarified.

Principle III

Remote sensing of the earth from outer space [shall][should] be conducted in accordance with international law, including the Charter of the United Nations and the Treaty on Principles Governing the Activities of States in the Exploration and Use of Outer Space, including the Moon and Other Celestial Bodies, and the relevant instruments of ITU.

Principle IV

1. States carrying out programmes for remote sensing of the earth from outer space [should][shall] promote international co-operation in these programmes. To this end, sensing States [should][shall] make available to other States opportunities for participation in these programmes. Such participation should be based in each case on equitable and mutually acceptable terms due regard being paid to principles . . .

2. In order to maximize the availability of benefits from such remote sensing data, States are encouraged to consider agreements for the establishment of shared regional facilities.

Principle V

Remote sensing of the earth from outer space [should][shall] promote the protection of the natural environment of the earth. To this end States participating in remote sensing [should][shall] identify and make available information useful for the prevention of phenomena detrimental to the natural environment of the earth.

Principle VI

States participating in remote sensing of the earth from outer space [should][shall] make available technical assistance to other interested States on mutually agreed terms.

Principle VII

1. The United Nations and the relevant agencies within the United Nations system should promote international co-operation, including technical assistance, and play a role of co-ordination in the area of remote sensing of the earth.

2. States conducting activities in the field of remote sensing of the earth [shall][should] notify the Secretary-General thereof, in compliance with article XI of the Treaty on Principles Governing the Activities of States in the Exploration and Use of Outer Space, including the Moon and Other Celestial Bodies.

Principle VIII

Remote sensing of the earth from outer space should promote the protection of mankind from natural disaster.*** To this end, States which have identified primary data from remote sensing of the earth and/or analysed information in their possession which would be useful in helping to alert States to impending natural disasters, or in assisting States to deal with natural disasters should, as promptly as possible, notify those States affected or likely to be affected of the existence and availability of such data and/or information. Such data and/or information should, upon request, be disseminated as promptly as possible.

Principle IX[1]

Taking into account the principles II and III above, remote sensing data or informa-

***The meaning of this term is subject to further discussion.

[1]Should be considered in connexion with the formulation of a principle on dissemination of data or information and subject to later discussion of the terms "information" and "data".

tion derived therefrom [shall][should] be used by States in a manner compatible with the legitimate rights and interests of other States.* **

Principle X

States participating in remote sensing of the earth either directly or through relevant international organization [shall][should] be prepared to make available to the United Nations and other interested States, particularly the developing countries, upon their request, any relevant technical information involving possible operational systems which they are free to disclose.

Principle XI

[States [shall][should] bear international responsibility for [national] activities of remote sensing of the earth [irrespective of whether] [where] such activities are carried out by governmental [or non-governmental] entities, and [shall][should] [guarantee that such activities will] comply with the provisions of these principles.]

Principle XII

A sensed State [shall][should] have timely and non-discriminatory access to primary data obtained by remote sensing of the earth from outer space, concerning its territory, on [agreed] reasonable terms and [no later than] [before] access is granted to any third State.[1, 2] [[To the greatest extent feasible and practicable,] this principle shall also apply to analysed information.]

Principle XIII

[A State [intending to conduct] [conducting] remote sensing activities of the earth from outer space shall notify the Secretary-General of the United Nations and [upon request] the States whose territory is intended to be covered by such activities [to the fullest extent feasible and as soon as practicable] of the intended launch, [nature of the] mission, duration and coverage of such activities. The Secretary-General shall publish information thus received.]

Principle XIV

[A State carrying out remote sensing of the earth [shall][should] without delay consult with a State whose territory is sensed upon request of the latter in regard to such activity, [in particular dissemination of data and information,] in order to promote international co-operation, friendly relations among States and to enhance the mutual benefits to be derived from this activity.]

Principle XV

[States carrying out remote sensing of the earth shall not, without the approval of the States whose territories are affected by these activities, disseminate or dispose of any data or information on the natural resources of these States to third States, international organizations, public or private entities.]

*Some delegations were of the view that, for the sake of consistency it was necessary to consider this principle in the light of draft principles II and III.

**A delegation reserved its position on removing the square brackets around the words "in a manner compatible with" and on the deletion of the words "not" and "to the detriment of".

[1]The question of from which States access to and provision of data should be obtained, needs further consideration.

[2]Subject to review in the light of the discussion on access by third States.

Principle XVI

[Without prejudice to the principle of the freedom of exploration and use of outer space, as set forth in article I of the Treaty on Principles Governing the Activities of States in the Exploration and Use of Outer Space, including the Moon and Other Celestial Bodies, remote sensing of the earth [should][shall] be conducted with respect for the principle of full and permanent sovereignty of all States and peoples over their own wealth and natural resources [with due regard to the rights and interests of other States and their natural and juridical persons in accordance with international law][as well as their inalienable right to dispose of their natural resources] [and of information concerning those resources].]

Principle XVII

[Any dispute that may arise with respect to the application of [activities covered by] these principles [shall][should] be resolved by prompt consultations among the parties to the dispute. Where a mutually acceptable solution cannot be found by such consultations it [shall][should] be sought through other [established][existing] procedures for the peaceful means of settlement of disputes mutually agreed upon by the parties concerned.]

DECLARATION OF GUIDING PRINCIPLES ON THE USE OF SATELLITE BROADCASTING FOR THE FREE FLOW OF INFORMATION THE SPREAD OF EDUCATION AND GREATER CULTURAL EXCHANGES, UNESCO GENERAL CONFERENCE RESOLUTION, 1972

The General Conference of the United Nations Educational, Scientific and Cultural Organization meeting in Paris at its seventeenth session in 1972,

Recognizing that the development of communication satellites capable of broadcasting programmes for community or individual reception establishes a new dimension in international communication,

Recalling that under its constitution the purpose of Unesco is to contribute to peace and security by promoting collaboration among the nations through education, science and culture, and that, to realize this purpose, the Organization will collaborate in the work of advancing the mutual knowledge and understanding of peoples through all means of mass communication and to that end recommend such international agreements as may be necessary to promote the free flow of ideas by word and image,

Recalling that the Charter of the United Nations specifies, among the purposes and principles of the United Nations, the development of friendly relations among nations based on respect for the principle of equal rights, the non-interference in matters within the domestic jurisdiction of any State, the achievement of international co-operation and the respect for human rights and fundamental freedoms,

Bearing in mind that the Universal Declaration of Human Rights proclaims that everyone has the right to seek, receive and impart information and ideas through any media and regardless of frontiers, that everyone has the right to education and that everyone has the right freely to participate in the cultural life of the community, as well as the right to the protection of the moral and material interests resulting from any scientific, literary or artistic production of which he is the author,

Recalling the Declaration of Legal Principles Governing the Activities of States in the Exploration and Use of Outer Space (resolution 1962 (XVIII) of 13 December 1963), and the Treaty on Principles Governing the Activities of States in the Exploration and Use of Outer Space, including the Moon and Other Celestial Bodies, of 1967 (hereinafter referred to as the Outer Space Treaty),

Taking account of United Nations General Assembly resolution 110 (II) of 3 November 1947, condemning propaganda designed or likely to provoke or encourage any threat to the peace, breach of the peace or act of aggression, which resolution as stated in the preamble to the Outer Space Treaty is applicable to outer space; and the United Nations General Assembly resolution 1721 D (XVI) of 20 December 1961 declaring that communication by means of satellites should be available as soon as practicable on a global and non-discriminatory basis,

Bearing in mind the Declaration of the Principles of International Cultural Co-operation adopted by the General Conference of Unesco, at its fourteenth session,

Considering that radio frequencies are a limited natural resource belonging to all nations, that their use is regulated by the International Telecommunications Convention and its Radio Regulations and that the assignment of adequate frequencies is essential to the use of satellite broadcasting for education, science, culture and information,

Noting the United Nations General Assembly resolution 2733 (XXV) of 16 December 1970 recommending that Member States, regional and international organizations, including broadcasting associations, should promote and encourage international co-operation at regional and other levels in order to allow all participating parties to share in the establishment and operation of regional satellite broadcasting services,

Noting further that the same resolution invites Unesco to continue to promote the use of satellite broadcasting for the advancement of education and training, science and culture, and in consultation with appropriate intergovernmental and non-governmental organizations and broadcasting associations, to direct its efforts towards the solution of problems falling within its mandate,

Proclaims on the 15th day of November 1972, this Declaration of Guiding Principles on the Use of Satellite Broadcasting for the Free Flow of Information, the Spread of Education and Greater Cultural Exchange:

Article I

The use of Outer Space being governed by international law, the development of satellite broadcasting shall be guided by the principles and rules of international law, in particular the Charter of the United Nations and the Outer Space Treaty.

Article II

1. Satellite broadcasting shall respect the sovereignty and equality of all States.

2. Satellite broadcasting shall be apolitical and conducted with due regard for the rights of individual persons and non-governmental entities, as recognized by States and international law.

Article III

1. The benefits of satellite broadcasting should be available to all countries without discrimination and regardless of their degree of development.

2. The use of satellites for broadcasting should be based on international co-operation, world-wide and regional, intergovernmental and professional.

Article IV

1. Satellite broadcasting provides a new means of disseminating knowledge and promoting better understanding among peoples.

2. The fulfilment of these potentialities requires that account be taken of the needs and rights of audiences, as well as the objectives of peace, friendship and co-operation between peoples, and of economic, social and cultural progress.

Article V

1. The objective of satellite broadcasting for the free flow of information is to ensure the widest possible dissemination, among the peoples of the world, of news of all countries, developed and developing alike.

2. Satellite broadcasting, making possible instantaneous world-wide dissemination of news, requires that every effort be made to ensure the factual accuracy of the information reaching the public. News broadcasts shall identify the body which assumes responsibility for the news programme as a whole, attributing where appropriate particular news items to their source.

Article VI

1. The objectives of satellite broadcasting for the spread of education are to accelerate the expansion of education, extend educational opportunities, improve the content of school curricula, further the training of educators, assist in the struggle against illiteracy, and help ensure life-long education.

2. Each country has the right to decide on the content of the educational programmes broadcast by satellite to its people and, in cases where such programmes are produced in co-operation with other countries, to take part in their planning and production, on a free and equal footing.

Article VII

1. The objective of satellite broadcasting for the promotion of cultural exchange is to foster greater contact and mutual understanding between peoples by permitting audiences to enjoy, on an unprecedented scale, programmes on each other's social and cultural life including artistic performances and sporting and other events.

2. Cultural programmes, while promoting the enrichment of all cultures, should respect the distinctive character, the value and the dignity of each, and the right of all countries and peoples to preserve their cultures as part of the common heritage of mankind.

Article VIII

Broadcasters and their national, regional and international associations should be encouraged to co-operate in the production and exchange of programmes and in all other aspects of satellite broadcasting including the training of technical and programme personnel.

Article IX

1. In order to further the objectives set out in the preceding articles, it is necessary that States, taking into account the principle of freedom of information, reach or promote prior agreements concerning direct satellite broadcasting to the population of countries other than the country of origin of the transmission.

2. With respect to commercial advertising, its transmission shall be subject to specific agreement between the originating and receiving countries.

Article X

In the preparation of programmes for direct broadcasting to other countries, account shall be taken of differences in the national laws of the countries of reception.

Article XI

The principles of this Declaration shall be applied with due regard for human rights and fundamental freedoms.

AGREEMENT RELATING TO THE INTERNATIONAL
TELCOMMUNICATIONS SATELLITE ORGANISATION
"INTELSAT", 1971

Preamble

The States Parties to this Agreement,
Considering the principle set forth in Resolution 1721 (XVI) of the General Assembly of the United Nations that communication by means of satellites should be available to the nations of the world as soon as practicable on a global and non-discriminatory basis,

Considering the relevant provisions of the Treaty on Principles Governing the Activities of States in the Exploration and Use of Outer Space, Including the Moon and Other Celestial Bodies, and in particular Article I, which states that outer space shall be used for the benefit and in the interest of all countries,

Noting that pursuant to the Agreement Establishing Interim Arrangements for a Global Commercial Communications Satellite System and the related Special Agreement, a global commercial telecommunications satellite system has been established,

Desiring to continue the development of this telecommunications satellite system with the aim of achieving a single global commercial telecommunications satellite system as part of an improved global telecommunications network which will provide expanded telecommunications services to all areas of the world and which will contribute to world peace and understanding,

Determined, to this end, to provide, for the benefit of all mankind, through the most advanced technology available, the most efficient and economic facilities possible consistent with the best and most equitable use of the radio frequency spectrum and of orbital space,

Believing that satellite telecommunications should be organized in such a way as to permit all peoples to have access to the global satellite system and those States members of the International Telecommunication Union so wishing to invest in the system with consequent participation in the design, development, construction, including the provision of equipment, establishment, operation, maintenance and ownership of the system,

Pursuant to the Agreement Establishing Interim Arrangements for a Global Commercial Communications Satellite System,

Agree as follows:

Article I *(Definitions)*

For the purposes of this Agreement:
(a) "Agreement" means the present agreement, including its Annexes but excluding all titles of Articles, opened for signature by Governments at Washington on 20 August, 1971, by which the international telecommunications satellite organization "INTELSAT" is established;
(b) "Operating Agreement" means the agreement, including its Annex but excluding all titles of Articles, opened for signature at Washington on 20 August, 1971, by Governments or telecommunications entities designated by Governments in accordance with the provisions of this Agreement;
(c) "Interim Agreement" means the Agreement Establishing Interim Arrangements for a Global Commercial Communications Satellite System signed by Governments at Washington on August 20, 1964;
(d) "Special Agreement" means the agreement signed on August 20, 1964, by Governments or telecommunications entities designated by Governments, pursuant to the provisions of the Interim Agreement;
(e) "Interim Communications Satellite Committee" means the Committee established by Article IV of the Interim Agreement;

(f) "Party" means a State for which the Agreement has entered into force or been provisionally applied;

(g) "Signatory" means a Party, or the telecommunications entity designated by a Party, which has signed the Operating Agreement and for which it has entered into force or been provisionally applied;

(h) "Space segment" means the telecommunications satellites, and the tracking, telemetry, command, control, monitoring and related facilities and equipment required to support the operation of these satellites;

(i) "INTELSAT space segment" means the space segment owned by INTELSAT;

(j) "Telecommunications" means any transmission, emission or reception of signs, signals, writing, images and sounds or intelligence of any nature, by wire, radio, optical or other electromagnetic systems;

(k) "Public telecommunications services" means fixed or mobile telecommunications services which can be provided by satellite and which are available for use by the public, such as telephony, telegraphy, telex, facsimile, data transmission, transmission of radio and television programs between approved earth stations having access to the INTELSAT space segment for further transmission to the public, and leased circuits for any of these purposes; but excluding those mobile services of a type not provided under the Interim Agreement and the Special Agreement prior to the opening for signature of this Agreement, which are provided through mobile stations operating directly to a satellite which is designed, in whole or in part, to provide services relating to the safety or flight control of aircraft or to aviation or maritime radio navigation;

(l) "Specialized telecommunications services" means telecommunications services which can be provided by satellite, other than those defined in paragraph (k) of this Article, including, but not limited to, radio navigation services, broadcasting satellite services for reception by the general public, space research services, meteorological services, and earth resources services;

(m) "Property" includes every subject of whatever nature to which a right of ownership can attach, as well as contractual rights; and

(n) "Design" and "development" include research directly related to the purposes of INTELSAT.

Article II (Establishment of INTELSAT)

(a) With full regard for the principles set forth in the Preamble to this Agreement, the Parties hereby establish the international telecommunications satellite organization "INTELSAT", the main purpose of which is to continue and carry forward on a definitive basis the design, development, construction, establishment, operation and maintenance of the space segment of the global commercial telecommunications satellite system as established under the provisions of the Interim Agreement and the Special Agreement.

(b) Each State Party shall sign, or shall designate a telecommunications entity, public or private, to sign, the Operating Agreement which shall be concluded in conformity with the provisions of this Agreement and which shall be opened for signature at the same time as this Agreement. Relations between any telecommunications entity, acting as Signatory, and the Party which has designated it shall be governed by applicable domestic law.

(c) Telecommunications administrations and entities may, subject to applicable domestic law, negotiate and enter directly into appropriate traffic agreements with respect to their use of channels of telecommunications provided pursuant to this Agreement and the Operating Agreement, as well as services to be furnished to the public, facilities, divisions of revenue and related business arrangements.

Article III (Scope of INTELSAT Activities)

(a) In continuing and carrying forward on a definitive basis activities concerning the space segment of the global commercial telecommunications satellite system referred to in paragraph (*a*) of Article II of this Agreement, INTELSAT shall have as its prime objective the provision, on a commercial basis, of the space segment required for international public telecommunications services of high quality and reliability to be available on a non-discriminatory basis to all areas of the world.

(*b*) The following shall be considered on the same basis as international public telecommunications services:

    i. domestic public telecommunications services between areas separated by areas not under the jurisdiction of the State concerned, or between areas separated by the high seas; and

    ii. domestic public telecommunications services between areas which are not linked by any terrestrial wideband facilities and which are separated by natural barriers of such an exceptional nature that they impede the viable establishment of terrestrial wideband facilities between such areas, provided that the Meeting of Signatories, having regard to advice tendered by the Board of Governors, has given the appropriate approval in advance.

(*c*) The INTELSAT space segment established to meet the prime objective shall also be made available for other domestic public telecommunications services on a non-discriminatory basis to the extent that the ability of INTELSAT to achieve its prime objective is not impaired.

(*d*) The INTELSAT space segment may also, on request and under appropriate terms and conditions, be utilized for the purpose of specialized telecommunications services, either international or domestic, other than for military purposes, provided that:

    i. the provision of public telecommunications services is not unfavorably affected thereby; and

    ii. the arrangements are otherwise acceptable from a technical and economic point of view.

(*e*) INTELSAT may, on request and under appropriate terms and conditions, provide satellites or associated facilities separate from the INTELSAT space segment for:

    i. domestic public telecommunications services in territories under the jurisdiction of one or more Parties;

    ii. international public telecommunications services between or among territories under the jurisdiction of two or more Parties;

    iii. specialized telecommunications services, other than for military purposes;

provided that the efficient and economic operation of the INTELSAT space segment is not unfavorably affected in any way.

(*f*) The utilization of the INTELSAT space segment for specialized telecommunications services pursuant to paragraph (*d*) of this Article, and the provision of satellites or associated facilities separate from the INTELSAT space segment pursuant to paragraph (*e*) of this Article, shall be covered by contracts entered into between IN-TELSAT and the applicants concerned. The utilization of INTELSAT space segment facilities for specialized telecommunications services pursuant to paragraph (*d*) of this Article, and the provision of satellites or associated facilities separate from the INTELSAT space segment for specialized telecommunications services pursuant to subparagraph (*e*)(iii) of this Article, shall be in accordance with appropriate authorizations, at the planning stage, of the Assembly of Parties pursuant to subparagraph (*c*)(iv) of Article VII of this Agreement. Where the utilization of IN-TELSAT space segment facilities for specialized telecommunications services would involve additional costs which result from required modifications to existing or planned INTELSAT space segment facilities, or where the provision of satellites or associated facilities separate from the INTELSAT space segment is sought for specialized telecommunications services as provided for in subparagraph (*e*)(iii) of this Article, authorization pursuant to subparagraph (*c*)(iv) of Article VII of this

Agreement shall be sought from the Assembly of Parties as soon as the Board of Governors is in a position to advise the Assembly of Parties in detail regarding the estimated cost of the proposal, the benefits to be derived, the technical or other problems involved and the probable effects on present or foreseeable INTELSAT services. Such authorization shall be obtained before the procurement process for the facility or facilities involved is initiated. Before making such authorizations, the Assembly of Parties, in appropriate cases, shall consult or ensure that there has been consultation by INTELSAT with Specialized Agencies of the United Nations directly concerned with the provision of specialized telecommunications services in question.

* * *

Article V (Financial Principles)

(a) INTELSAT shall be the owner of the INTELSAT space segment and of all other property acquired by INTELSAT. The financial interest in INTELSAT of each Signatory shall be equal to the amount arrived at by the application of its investment share to the valuation effected pursuant to Article 7 of the Operating Agreement.

(b) Each Signatory shall have an investment share corresponding to its percentage of all utilization of the INTELSAT space segment by all Signatories as determined in accordance with the provisions of the Operating Agreement. However, no Signatory, even if its utilization of the INTELSAT space segment is nil, shall have an investment share less than the minimum established in the Operating Agreement.

(c) Each Signatory shall contribute to the capital requirements of INTELSAT, and shall receive capital repayment and compensation for use of capital in accordance with the provisions of the Operating Agreement.

(d) All users of the INTELSAT space segment shall pay utilization charges determined in accordance with the provisions of this Agreement and the Operating Agreement. The rates of space segment utilization charge for each type of utilization shall be the same for all applicants for space segment capacity for that type of utilization.

Article VI (Structure of INTELSAT)

(a) INTELSAT shall have the following organs:
   i.   the Assembly of Parties;
   ii. the Meeting of Signatories;
   iii. the Board of Governors; and
   iv. an executive organ, responsible to the Board of Governors.

(b) Except to the extent that this Agreement or the Operating Agreement specifically provides otherwise, no organ shall make determinations or otherwise act in such a way as to alter, nullify, delay or in any other manner interfere with the exercise of a power or the discharge of a responsibility or a function attributed to another organ by this Agreement or the Operating Agreement.

(c) Subject to paragraph (b) of this Article, the Assembly of Parties, the Meeting of Signatories and the Board of Governors shall each take note of and give due and proper consideration to any resolution, recommendation or view made or expressed by another of these organs acting in the exercise of the responsibilities and functions attributed to it by this Agreement or the Operating Agreement.

Article VII (Assembly of Parties)

(a) The Assembly of Parties shall be composed of all the Parties and shall be the principal organ of INTELSAT.

(b) The Assembly of Parties shall give consideration to those aspects of INTELSAT which are primarily of interest to the Parties as sovereign States. It shall have the power to give consideration to general policy and long-term objectives of INTELSAT consistent with the principles, purposes and scope of activities of INTELSAT, as provided for in this Agreement. In accordance with paragraphs (b) and (c) of Article VI of this Agreement, the Assembly of Parties shall give due and proper consideration to resolutions, recommendations and views addressed to it by the Meeting of Signatories or the Board of Governors.

(c) The Assembly of Parties shall have the following functions and powers:

  i.   in the exercise of its power of considering general policy and long-term objectives of INTELSAT, to formulate its views or make recommendations, as it may deem appropriate, to the other organs of INTELSAT;

  ii. to determine that measures should be taken to prevent the activities of INTELSAT from conflicting with any general multilateral convention which is consistent with this Agreement and which is adhered to by at least two-thirds of the Parties;

  iii. to consider and take decisions on proposals for amending this Agreement in accordance with Article XVII of this Agreement and to propose, express its views and make recommendations on amendments to the Operating Agreement;

  iv. to authorize, through general rules or by specific determinations, the utilization of the INTELSAT space segment and the provision of satellites and associated facilities separate from the INTELSAT space segment for specialized telecommunications services within the scope of activities referred to in paragraph (d) and subparagraph (e)(iii) of Article III of this Agreement;

*   *   *

Article VIII (Meeting of Signatories)

(a) The Meeting of Signatories shall be composed of all the Signatories. In accordance with paragraphs (b) and (c) of Article VI of this Agreement, the Meeting of Signatories shall give due and proper consideration to resolutions, recommendations and views addressed to it by the Assembly of Parties or the Board of Governors.

(b) The Meeting of Signatories shall have the following functions and powers:

  i.   to consider and express its views to the Board of Governors on the annual report and annual financial statements submitted to it by the Board of Governors;

  ii. to express its views and make recommendations on proposed amendments to this Agreement pursuant to Article XVII of this Agreement and to consider and take decisions, in accordance with Article 22 of the Operating Agreement and taking into account any views and recommendations received from the Assembly of Parties or the Board of Governors, on proposed amendments to the Operating Agreement which are consistent with this Agreement;

  iii. to consider and express its views regarding reports on future programs, including the estimated financial implications of such programs, submitted by the Board of Governors;

  iv. to consider and decide on any recommendation made by the Board of Governors concerning an increase in the ceiling provided for in Article 5 of the Operating Agreement;

  v.   to establish general rules, upon the recommendation of and for the guidance of the Board of Governors, concerning:

    (A) the approval of earth stations for access to the INTELSAT space segment,
    (B) the allotment of INTELSAT space segment capacity, and
    (C) the establishment and adjustment of the rates of charge for utilization of the INTELSAT space segment on a non-discriminatory basis;

*   *   *

Article IX (Board of Governors: Composition and Voting)

(a) The Board of Governors shall be composed of:

  i.   one Governor representing each Signatory whose investment share is not less than the minimum investment share as determined in accordance with paragraph (*b*) of this Article;

ii. one Governor representing each group of any two or more Signatories not represented pursuant to subparagraph (i) of this paragraph whose combined investment share is not less than the minimum investment share as determined in accordance with paragraph (*b*) of this Article and which have agreed to be so represented;

iii. one Governor representing any group of at least five Signatories not represented pursuant to subparagraph (i) or (ii) of this paragraph from any one of the regions defined by the Plenipotentiary Conference of the International Telecommunication Union, held at Montreux in 1965, regardless of the total investment shares held by the Signatories comprising the group. However, the number of Governors under this category shall not exceed two for any region defined by the Union or five for all such regions.

*   *   *

Article X (Board of Governors: Functions)

(a) The Board of Governors shall have the responsibility for the design, development, construction, establishment, operation and maintenance of the INTELSAT space segment and, pursuant to this Agreement, the Operating Agreement and such determinations that in this respect may have been made by the Assembly of Parties pursuant to Article VII of this Agreement, for carrying out any other activities which are undertaken by INTELSAT. To discharge the foregoing responsibilities, the Board of Governors shall have the powers and shall exercise the functions coming within its purview according to the provisions of this Agreement and the Operating Agreement, including:

i. adoption of policies, plans and programs in connection with the design, development, construction, establishment, operation and maintenance of the INTELSAT space segment and, as appropriate, in connection with any other activities which INTELSAT is authorized to undertake;

ii. adoption of procurement procedures, regulations, terms and conditions, consistent with Article XIII of this Agreement, and approval of procurement contracts;

iii. adoption of financial policies and annual financial statements, and approval of budgets;

iv. adoption of policies and procedures for the acquisition, protection and distribution of rights in inventions and technical information, consistent with Article 17 of the Operating Agreement;

v. formulation of recommendations to the Meeting of Signatories in relation to the establishment of the general rules referred to in subparagraph (*b*)(v) of Article VIII of this Agreement;

vi. adoption of criteria and procedures, in accordance with such general rules as may have been established by the Meeting of Signatories, for approval of earth stations for access to the INTELSAT space segment, for verification and monitoring of performance characteristics of earth stations having access, and for coordination of earth station access to and utilization of the INTELSAT space segment;

vii. adoption of terms and conditions governing the allotment of INTELSAT space segment capacity, in accordance with such general rules as may have been established by the Meeting of Signatories;

viii. periodic establishment of the rates of charge for utilization of the INTELSAT space segment, in accordance with such general rules as may have been established by the Meeting of Signatories.

*   *   *

AGREEMENT ON THE ESTABLISHMENT OF THE "INTERSPUTNIK"
INTERNATIONAL SYSTEM AND ORGANIZATION
OF SPACE COMMUNICATIONS, 1971

The Contracting Parties,
recognizing the need to contribute to the strengthening and development of comprehensive economic, scientific, technical, cultural and other relations by communications as well as by radio and television broadcasting via satellites;

recognizing the utility of co-operation in theoretical and experimental research as well as in designing, establishing, operating and developing an international communications system via satellites;

in the interests of the development of international co-operation based on respect for the sovereignty and independence of states, quality and non-interference in the internal affairs as well as mutual assistance and mutual benefit;

in pursuance of the provisions of Resolution 1721 (XVI) of the United Nations General Assembly and the Treaty on Principles governing the Activities of States in the Exploration and Use of Outer Space, including the Moon and other Celestial Bodies, of January 27, 1967;

have agreed on the following:

Article 1

1. There shall be established an international system of communications via satellites.

2. To ensure co-operation and co-ordination of efforts in the design, establishment, operation and development of the communications system the Contracting Parties set up the "Intersputnik" international organization, hereinafter referred to as the Organization.

Article 2

1. The "Intersputnik" is an open international organization.

2. The Members of the Organization shall be the governments that have signed this Agreement and have deposited their instruments of ratification in accordance with Article 20 as well as the governments of other states that have acceded to this Agreement pursuant to Article 22.

Article 3

The seat of the Organization shall be in Moscow.

Article 4

1. The international system of communications via satellites shall include as its components:
   - a space segment comprising communications satellites with transponders, satellite-borne facilities and ground systems of control to ensure the normal functioning of the satellites;
   - earth stations mutually communicating via satellites.

2. The space segment shall be the property of the Organization or is leased from Members possessing such systems.

3. The earth stations shall be the property of states or recognized operating agencies.

4. The Members of the Organizations shall have the right to include the earth stations which they have built into the communications system of the Organization, provided those stations meet the Organization's specifications.

Article 5

The international communications system shall be established by the following stages:
- The stage of experimental work done by Members at their earth stations with the use of satellite communications channels made available to the Organization free of charge by the Union of Soviet Socialist Republics on its communications satellites. This stage shall cover the period until the end of 1973.
- The stage of work, involving the use of communications channels on Members' communications satellites on the basis of lease.
- The stage of commercial operation of the communications system through the use of the space segment owned by the Organization or rented by its Members. Transition to this stage will be effected when the establishment of the space segment owned by the Organization or its Members are considered economically advisable by the Contracting Parties.

Article 6

Communication satellites owned by the Organization shall be developed, put into orbit and operated in orbit by Members which possess appropriate facilities for this purpose on the basis of agreement between the Organization and such Members.

Article 7

The Organization shall coordinate its activities with the International Telecommunication Union and co-operate with other organizations concerned with the use of communications satellites both in technology and the use of the frequency spectrum, the application of technical standards for communications channels and of equipment standards through international reglamentation.

*   *   *

Article 11

1. The following bodies shall be established to govern the activities of the Organization:
- the Board–a governing body;
- the Directorate–a permanent executive and administrative body–headed by the Director-General.

The time for the establishment of the Directorate and the beginning of its activities shall be determined by the Board.

2. Prior to the beginning of the Directorate's activities the functions of the Director-General in representing the Organization set forth in paragraph 2 of Article 13 shall be performed by the Chairman of the Board.

3. The Auditing Commission shall be established to supervise the financial activities of the Organization.

4. The Board may also set up auxiliary bodies required for the attainment of the goals of this Agreement.

Article 12

1. The Board shall be composed of one representative from each Member of the Organization.

2. Each Member of the Organization shall have one vote in the Board.

3. The Board shall hold its regular sessions at least once a year. An extraordinary session may be held on the request of any Member of the Organization or the

Director-General if no less than one third of the Members of the Organization favour its convocation.

*   *   *

6. The Board shall be competent to deal with matters covered by this Agreement. The Board shall:

(1) examine and approve measures for establishing, acquiring or basing and operating the space segment;
(2) approve plans for the development and improvement of the Organization's communications system;
(3) determine specifications for the Organization's communications satellites;
(4) examine and approve the programme of putting into orbit the organization's communications satellites;
(5) approve the plan for the distribution of the communications' channels among the Members of the Organization as well as the procedure and conditions for the utilization of the communications channels by other users;
(6) determine specifications for the earth stations;
(7) determine whether the earth stations offered for inclusion into the communications system of the Organization meet the specifications;
(8) elect the Director-General and his deputy and supervise the activities of the Directorate;

*   *   *

(17) set the rates for transmitting a unit of information or the lease cost of the Organization's satellite communications channel;

*   *   *

Article 16

1. The Organization shall operate the space segment making communications channels available to its Members and other users in accordance with the provisions of this Agreement.

2. The communications channels at the disposal of the Organization shall be distributed among the Members of the Organization on the basis of their needs for channels. Communications channels which are in excess of aggregate requirements of all Members of the Organization may be leased to other users.

3. Payment for the communications channels made available shall be charged according to rates established by the Board. The rates shall be fixed at the average world level calculated in gold francs.

The payment for communications services shall be made in a manner determined by the Board.

*   *   *

CONVENTION ON THE INTERNATIONAL MARITIME SATELLITE ORGANIZATION (INMARSAT), 1978

The States Parties to this Convention:
Considering the principle set forth in Resolution 1721 (XVI) of the General Assembly of the United Nations that communication by means of satellites should be available to the nations of the world as soon as practicable on a global and non-discriminatory basis,
Considering the relevant provisions of the Treaty on Principles Governing the Activities of States in the Exploration and Use of Outer Space, Including the Moon and Other Celestial Bodies, concluded on 27 January 1967, and in particular Article 1,

which states that outer space shall be used for the benefit and in the interests of all countries,

Taking into account that a very high proportion of world trade is dependent upon ships,

Being aware that considerable improvements to the maritime distress and safety systems and to the communication link between ships and between ships and their management as well as between crew or passengers on board and persons on shore can be made by using satellites,

Determined, to this end, to make provision for the benefit of ships of all nations through the most advanced suitable space technology available, for the most efficient and economic facilities possible consistent with the most efficient and equitable use of the radio frequency spectrum and of satellite orbits,

Recognizing that a maritime satellite system comprises mobile earth stations and land earth stations, as well as the space segment,

Agree as follows:

Article 1 Definitions

For the purposes of this Convention:

(a) "Operating Agreement" means the Operating Agreement on the International Maritime Satellite Organization (INMARSAT), including its Annex.
(b) "Party" means a State for which this Convention has entered into force.
(c) "Signatory" means either a Party or an entity designated in accordance with Article 2(3), for which the Operating Agreement has entered into force.
(d) "Space segment" means the satellites, and the tracking, telemetry, command, control, monitoring and related facilities and equipment required to support the operation of these satellites.
(e) "INMARSAT space segment" means the space segment owned or leased by IN-MARSAT.
(f) "Ship" means a vessel of any type operating in the marine environment. It includes inter alia hydrofoil boats, air-cushion vehicles, submersibles, floating craft and platforms not permanently moored.
(g) "Property" means anything that can be the subject of a right of ownership, including contractual rights.

Article 2 Establishment of INMARSAT

1. The International Maritime Satellite Organization (INMARSAT), herein referred to as "the Organization", is hereby established.

2. The Operating Agreement shall be concluded in conformity with the provisions of this Convention and shall be opened for signature at the same time as this Convention.

3. Each Party shall sign the Operating Agreement or shall designate a competent entity, public or private, subject to the jurisdiction of that Party, which shall sign the Operating Agreement.

4. Telecommunications administrations and entities may, subject to applicable domestic law, negotiate and enter directly into appropriate traffic agreements with respect to their use of telecommunications facilities provided pursuant to this Convention and the Operating Agreement, as well as with respect to services to be furnished to the public, facilities, division of revenues and related business arrangements.

Article 3 Purpose

1. The purpose of the Organization is to make provision for the space segment necessary for improving maritime communications, thereby assisting in improving

distress and safety of life at sea communications, efficiency and management of ships, maritime public correspondence services and radio determination capabilities.

2. The Organization shall seek to serve all areas where there is need for maritime communications.

3. The Organization shall act exclusively for peaceful purposes.

Article 4 Relations between a Party and its Designated Entity

Where a Signatory is an entity designated by a Party:

(a) Relations between the Party and the Signatory shall be governed by applicable domestic law,

(b) The Party shall provide such guidance and instructions as are appropriate and consistent with its domestic law to ensure that the Signatory fulfils its responsibilities.

(c) The Party shall not be liable for obligations arising under the Operating Agreement. The Party shall, however, ensure that the Signatory, in carrying out its obligations within the Organization, will not act in a manner which violates obligations which the Party has accepted under this Convention or under related international agreements.

(d) If the Signatory withdraws or its membership is terminated the Party shall act in accordance with Article 29(3) or 30(6).

Article 5 Operational and Financial Principles of the Organization

1. The Organization shall be financed by the contributions of Signatories. Each Signatory shall have a financial interest in the Organization in proportion to its investment share which shall be determined in accordance with the Operating Agreement.

2. Each Signatory shall contribute to the capital requirements of the Organization and shall receive capital repayment and compensation for use of capital in accordance with the Operating Agreement.

3. The Organization shall operate on a sound economic and financial basis having regard to accepted commercial principles.

Article 6 Provision of Space Segment

The Organization may own or lease the space segment.

Article 7 Access to Space Segment

1. The INMARSAT space segment shall be open for use by ships of all nations on conditions, to be determined by the Council. In determining such conditions, the Council shall not discriminate among ships on the basis of nationality.

2. The Council may, on a case-by-case basis, permit access to the INMARSAT space segment by earth stations located on structures operating in the marine environment other than ships, if and as long as the operation of such earth stations will not significantly affect the provision of service to ships.

*　*　*

PART SIX
INTELLECTUAL PROPERTY RIGHTS

International agreements designed to regulate communications and the flow of information belong to the oldest branches of modern functional international law. Following the early development of international telecommunications and postal law, the first conventions on intellectual property rights were concluded in the 1880s. They still form the basis for international agreement in this field.

Reference to intellectual property rights is included in all major human rights instruments in the form of provisions protecting the rights of creators to control the use of their work. (*See* Universal Declaration on Human Rights, Article 26; International Covenant on Economic, Social and Cultural Rights, Article 15). References to intellectual property rights are also found in other international agreements such as the Conventions Relating to the Status of Refugees (1951) and to the Status of Stateless Persons (1954).

Intellectual property legislation is divided into two main branches:

i. Industrial property law which principally deals with the protection of inventions, trademarks, industrial designs and the suppression of unfair competition. The major international treaty in this field is the Paris Convention for the Protection of Industrial Property of 1885.

ii. Copyright and neighbouring rights: copyright covers all forms of literary and artistic expression and performance while neighbouring rights concern the protection of performing artists, phonograph producers and broadcasting organizations.

The international system of protection of intellectual property rights presents a somewhat bewildering picture. The relevant international agreements provide varying degrees of protection, and have attracted different but partly overlapping constituencies in the form of adhering states. The organizational structure is complex: in many cases states adhering to a convention form a union most of which are administered by the World Intellectual Property Organization (WIPO). In the copyright field WIPO shares with Unesco responsibility for the administration of some international agreements with the addition of the International Labour Organization in the case of the protection of performing artists.

In view of the great number of international instruments in this area and their easy availability this part has been structured in a different manner from the previous sections. The full texts of the international agreements have not been included; only short excerpts showing the general purpose and objectives of some major conventions. These excerpts will be preceded by a list of all currently valid international agreements.

In terms of future development of intellectual property rights it should be noted that work is proceeding on:
– special protection for the work of translators
– preservation of moving images
– definition and protection of folklore.

I. LIST OF CURRENTLY VALID INTERNATIONAL INSTRUMENTS

1. Organizational structure

(a) Convention Establishing the World Intellectual Property Organization (WIPO), 1967

(b) Other concerned organizations *See* Constitution of Unesco, Constitution of the International Labour Organization (ILO)

2. Copyright and neighbouring rights

Copyright

(a) Berne Convention for the Protection of Literary and Artistic Works, 1885; revised at:
  i.   Paris   1896
  ii. Berlin   1908
  iii. Berne   1914
  iv. Rome   1928
  v.   Brussels   1948
  vi. Stockholm   1967
  vii. Paris   1971

(b) Inter-American Copyright Conventions
  i.   Montevideo   1898
  ii. Mexico City   1902
  iii. Rio de Janeiro   1906
  iv. Buenos Aires   1910
  v.   Havana   1928
  vi. Washington   1946

(c) Universal Copyright Convention 1952; revised at:
  i.   Paris   1971

(d) International Convention for the Protection of Performers, Producers of Phonograms and Broadcasting Organizations, Rome Convention, 1961

(e) Convention for the Protection of Producers of Phonograms Against Unauthorised Duplication of their Phonograms, Geneva Phonogram Convention, 1971

(f) Convention relating to the distribution of programme-carrying signals transmitted by satellite, Brussels Satellite Convention 1974.

(g) Multilateral Convention for the Avoidance of Double Taxation of Copyright Royalties, Madrid, 1979 (not yet in force)

(h) European Agreement Concerning Programme Exchanges by means of Television Films, 1958

(i) European Agreement on the Protection of Television Broadcasts, 1960. Additional Protocol, 1965.

3. Industrial property rights

(a) Paris Convention for the Protection of Industrial Property, 1883; revised at:

      i. Brussels   1900
     ii. Washington   1911
   iii. The Hague   1925
    iv. London   1934
     v. Lisbon   1958
    vi. Stockholm   1967

(b) Madrid Agreement for the Repression of False or Deceptive Indications of Source on Goods, 1891; revised at:
      i. Washington   1911
     ii. The Hague   1925
   iii. London   1934
    iv. Lisbon   1958
     v. Additional Act,
        Stockholm   1967

(c) Madrid Agreement Concerning the International Registration of Marks, 1891; revised at:
      i. Brussels   1900
     ii. Washington   1911
   iii. The Hague   1925
    iv. London   1934
     v. Nice   1957
    vi. Stockholm   1967

(d) The Hague Agreement Concerning the International Deposit of Industrial Designs, 1925; revised at:
      i. London   1934
     ii. The Hague   1960
   iii. Additional Act,
        Monaco   1961
    iv. Complementary
        Act, Stockholm 1967
     v. Protocol,
        Geneva   1975

(e) Nice Agreement Concerning the International Classification of Goods and Services for the Purposes of the Registration of Marks, 1957; revised at:
      i. Stockholm   1967
     ii. Geneva   1977

(f) Lisbon Agreement for the Protection of Appellations of Origin and their International Registration, 1958; revised at:
      i. Stockholm   1967

(g) International Convention for the Protection of New Varieties of Plants, 1961; revised at:
      i. Geneva   1972
     ii. Geneva   1978

(h) Locarno Agreement Establishing an International Classification for Industrial Designs, 1968

(i) Patent Cooperation Treaty, Washington, 1970

(j) Strasbourg Agreement Concerning the International Patent Classification, 1971

(k) Convention on the Grant of European Patents, 1973

(l) Trademark Registration Treaty, Vienna, 1973

(m) Vienna Agreement Establishing an International Classification of the Figurative Elements of Marks, 1973 (not yet in force)

(n) Vienna Agreement for the Protection of Type Faces and their International Deposit, 1973 (not yet in force)

(o) Budapest Treaty on the International Recognition of the Deposit of Microorganisms for the Purposes of Patent Procedure, 1977

(p) Geneva Treaty on the International Recording of Scientific Discoveries, 1978 (not yet in force)

4. Rules concerning industrial property rights may also be found in agreements in other areas: examples

(a) Treaty Establishing the European Atomic Energy Community, 1957

(b) Operating Agreement Relating to the International Telecommunications Satellite Organization 'Intelsat', 1971.

II. DOCUMENTS: EXCERPTS FROM MAJOR CONVENTIONS

Convention Establishing the World Intellectual Property Organization, 1967
- Preamble
- Articles 1–4

Berne Convention for the Protection of Literary and Artistic Works, revised version of 1971
- Preamble
- Articles 1–4
- Appendix, Article I

Universal Copyright Convention, revised version of 1971
- Preamble
- Articles I–II

International Convention for the Protection of Performers, Producers of Phonograms and Broadcasting Organizations (Rome Convention), 1961
- Preamble
- Articles 1–3

Convention for the Protection of Producers of Phonograms Against the Unauthorised Duplication of their Phonograms (Geneva Phonogram Convention), 1971
- Preamble
- Articles 1–3

Convention Relating to the Distribution of Programme-Carrying Signals Transmitted by Satellite (Brussels Satellite Convention), 1974
- Preamble
- Articles 1–3

European Agreement on the Protection of Television Broadcasts, 1960
- Preamble
- Articles 1–2

Paris Convention for the Protection of Industrial Property, revised version 1967
- Preamble
- Articles 1–4

CONVENTION ESTABLISHING THE
WORLD INTELLECTUAL PROPERTY ORGANIZATION, 1967

The Contracting Parties,

Desiring to contribute to better understanding and co-operation among States for their mutual benefit on the basis of respect for their sovereignty and equality,

Desiring, in order to encourage creative activity, to promote the protection of intellectual property throughout the world,

Desiring to modernize and render more efficient the administration of the Unions established in the fields of the protection of industrial property and the protection of literary and artistic works, while fully respecting the independence of each of the Unions,

Agree as follows:

Article 1 Establishment of the Organization

The World Intellectual Property Organization is hereby established.

Article 2 Definitions

For the purposes of this Convention:

   i. "Organization" shall mean the World Intellectual Property Organization (WIPO);
   ii. "International Bureau" shall mean the International Bureau of Intellectual Property;
   iii. "Paris Convention" shall mean the Convention for the Protection of Industrial Property signed on March 20, 1883, including any of its revisions;
   iv. "Berne Convention" shall mean the Convention for the Protection of Literary and Artistic Works signed on September 9, 1886, including any of its revisions;
   v. "Paris Union" shall mean the International Union established by the Paris Convention;
   vi. "Berne Union" shall mean the International Union established by the Berne Convention;
   vii. "Unions" shall mean the Paris Union, the Special Unions and Agreements established in relation with that Union, the Berne Union, and any other international agreement designed to promote the protection of intellectual property whose administration is assumed by the Organization according to Article 4 (iii);
   viii. "Intellectual property" shall include the rights relating to:
   – literary, artistic and scientific works,
   – performances of performing artists, phonograms, and broadcasts,
   – inventions in all fields of human endeavour,
   – scientific discoveries,
   – industrial designs,
   – trademarks, service marks, and commercial names and designations,
   – protection against unfair competition,

and all other rights resulting from intellectual activity in the industrial, scientific, literary or artistic fields.

Article 3 Objectives of the Organization

The objectives of the Organization are:

   i. to promote the protection of intellectual property throughout the world through co-operation among States and, where appropriate, in collaboration

with any other international organization,
ii. to ensure administrative co-operation among the Unions.

Article 4 Functions

In order to attain the objectives described in Article 3, the Organization, through its appropriate organs, and subject to the competence of each of the Unions:

  i. shall promote the development of measures designed to facilitate the efficient protection of intellectual property throughout the world and to harmonize national legislation in this field;
 ii. shall perform the administrative tasks of the Paris Union, the Special Unions established in relation with that Union, and the Berne Union;
iii. may agree to assume, or participate in, the administration of any other international agreement designed to promote the protection of intellectual property;
 iv. shall encourage the conclusion of international agreements designed to promote the protection of intellectual property;
  v. shall offer its co-operation to States requesting legal-technical assistance in the fields of intellectual property;

BERNE CONVENTION FOR THE PROTECTION OF LITERARY AND ARTISTIC WORKS

of September 9, 1886, completed at Paris on May 4, 1896,
revised at Berlin on November 13, 1908, completed at Berne on March 20, 1914,
and revised at Rome on June 2, 1928, at Brussels on June 26, 1948,
at Stockholm on July 14, 1967, and at Paris on July 24, 1971

The Countries of the Union, being equally animated by the desire to protect, in as effective and uniform a manner as possible, the rights of authors in their literary and artistic works,

Recognizing the importance of the work of the Revision Conference held at Stockholm in 1967,

Have resolved to revise the Act adopted by the Stockholm Conference, while maintaining without change Articles 1 to 20 and 22 to 26 of that Act.

Consequently, the undersigned Plenipotentiaries, having presented their full powers, recognized as in good and due form, have agreed as follows:

Article 1

The countries to which this Convention applies constitute a Union for the protection of the rights of authors in their literary and artistic works.

Article 2

1. The expression "literary and artistic works" shall include every production in the literary, scientific and artistic domain, whatever may be the mode or form of its expression, such as books, pamphlets and other writings; lectures, addresses, sermons and other works of the same nature; dramatic or dramatico-musical works; choreographic works and entertainments in dumb show; musical compositions with or without words; cinematographic works to which are assimilated works expressed by a process analogous to cinematography; works of drawing, painting, architecture, sculpture, engraving and lithography; photographic works to which are assimilated works by a process analogous to photography; works of applied art; illustrations, maps, plans, sketches and three-dimensional works relative to geography, topography, architecture or science.

2. It shall, however, be a matter for legislation in the countries of the Union to prescribe that works in general or any specified categories of works shall not be protected unless they have been fixed in some material form.

3. Translations, adaptations, arrangements of music and other alterations of a literary or artistic work shall be protected as original works without prejudice to the copyright in the original work.

4. It shall be a matter for legislation in the countries of the Union to determine the protection to be granted to official texts of a legislative, administrative and legal nature, and to official translations of such texts.

5. Collections of literary or artistic works such as encyclopaedias and anthologies which, by reason of the selection and arrangement of their contents, constitute intellectual creations shall be protected as such, without prejudice to the copyright in each of the works forming part of such collections.

6. The works mentioned in this Article shall enjoy protection in all countries of the Union. This protection shall operate for the benefit of the author and his successors in title.

7. Subject to the provisions of Article 7(4) of this Convention, it shall be a matter for legislation in the countries of the Union to determine the extent of the application of their laws to works of applied art and industrial designs and models, as well as the conditions under which such works, designs and models shall be protected. Works protected in the country of origin solely as designs and models shall be entitled in another country of the Union only to such special protection as is granted in that country to designs and models; however, if no such special protection is granted in that country, such works shall be protected as artistic works.

8. The protection of this Convention shall not apply to news of the day or to miscellaneous facts having the character of mere items of press information.

Article 2bis

1. It shall be a matter for legislation in the countries of the Union to exclude, wholly or in part, from the protection provided by the preceding Article political speeches and speeches delivered in the course of legal proceedings.

2. It shall also be a matter for legislation in the countries of the Union to determine the conditions under which lectures, addresses and other works of the same nature which are delivered in public may be reproduced by the press, broadcast, communicated to the public by wire and made the subject of public communication as envisaged in Article 11bis (1) of this Convention, when such use is justified by the informatory purpose.

3. Nevertheless, the author shall enjoy the exclusive right of making a collection of his works mentioned in the preceding paragraphs.

Article 3

1. The protection of this Convention shall apply to:

(a)   authors who are nationals of one of the countries of the Union, for their works, whether published or not;

(b)   authors who are not nationals of one of the countries of the Union, for their works first published in one of those countries, or simultaneously in a country outside the Union and in a country of the Union.

2. Authors who are not nationals of one of the countries of the Union but who have their habitual residence in one of them shall, for the purposes of this Convention, be assimilated to nationals of that country.

3. The expression "published works" means works published with the consent of their authors, whatever may be the means of manufacture of the copies, provided

that the availability of such copies has been such as to satisfy the reasonable requirements of the public, having regard to the nature of the work. The performance of a dramatic, dramatico-musical, cinematographic or musical work, the public recitation of a literary work, the communication by wire or the broadcasting of literary or artistic works, the exhibition of a work of art and the construction of a work of architecture shall not constitute publication.

4. A work shall be considered as having been published simultaneously in several countries if it has been published in two or more countries within thirty days of its first publication.

Article 4

The protection of this Convention shall apply, even if the conditions of Article 3 are not fulfilled, to:

(a)   authors of cinematographic works the maker of which has his headquarters or habitual residence in one of the countries of the Union;

(b)   authors of works of architecture erected in a country of the Union or of other artistic works incorporated in a building or other structure located in a country of the Union.

*   *   *

APPENDIX

Article I

1. Any country regarded as a developing country in conformity with the established practice of the General Assembly of the United Nations which ratifies or accedes to this Act, of which this Appendix forms an integral part, and which, having regard to its economic situation and its social or cultural needs, does not consider itself immediately in a position to make provision for the protection of all the rights as provided for in this Act, may, by a notification deposited with the Director General at the time of depositing its instrument of ratification or accession or, subject to Article V(1)(c), at any time thereafter, declare that it will avail itself of the faculty provided for in Article II, or of the faculty provided for in Article III, or of both of those faculties. It may, instead of availing itself of the faculty provided for in Article II, make a declaration according to Article V(1)(a).

2. (a)   Any declaration under paragraph (1) notified before the expiration of the period of ten years from the entry into force of Articles 1 to 21 and this Appendix according to Article 28(2) shall be effective until the expiration of the said period. Any such declaration may be renewed in whole or in part for periods of ten years each by a notification deposited with the Director General not more than fifteen months and not less than three months before the expiration of the ten-year period then running.

(b)   Any declaration under paragraph (1) notified after the expiration of the period of ten years from the entry into force of Articles 1 to 21 and this Appendix according to Article 28(2) shall be effective until the expiration of the ten-year period then running. Any such declaration may be renewed as provided for in the second sentence of subparagraph(a).

3. Any country of the Union which has ceased to be regarded as a developing country as referred to in paragraph (1) shall no longer be entitled to renew its declaration as provided in paragraph (2), and, whether or not it formally withdraws its declaration, such country shall be precluded from availing itself of the faculties referred to in paragraph (1) from the expiration of the ten-year period then running or from the expiration of a period of three years after it has ceased to be regarded as a developing country, whichever period expires later.

4. Where, at the time when the declaration made under paragraph (1) or (2) ceases to be effective, there are copies in stock which were made under a license granted by virtue of this Appendix, such copies may continue to be distributed until their stock is exhausted.

5. Any country which is bound by the provisions of this Act and which has deposited a declaration or a notification in accordance with Article 31(1) with respect to the application of this Act to a particular territory, the situation of which can be regarded as analogous to that of the countries referred to in paragraph (1), may, in respect of such territory, make the declaration referred to in paragraph (1) and the notification of renewal referred to in paragraph (2). As long as such declaration or notification remains in effect, the provisions of this Appendix shall be applicable to the territory in respect of which it was made.

6. (a)   The fact that a country avails itself of any of the faculties referred to in paragraph (1) does not permit another country to give less protection to works of which the country of origin is the former country than it is obliged to grant under Articles 1 to 20.

   (b)   The right to apply reciprocal treatment provided for in Article 30(2)(b), second sentence, shall not, until the date on which the period applicable under Article I(3), expires, be exercised in respect of works the country of origin of which is a country which has made a declaration according to Article V(1)(a).

* * *

UNIVERSAL COPYRIGHT CONVENTION AS REVISED
AT PARIS ON 24 JULY 1971

The Contracting States,
Moved by the desire to ensure in all countries copyright protection of literary, scientific and artistic works,
    Convinced that a system of copyright protection appropriate to all nations of the world and expressed in a universal convention, additional to, and without impairing international systems already in force, will ensure respect for the rights of the individual and encourage the development of literature, the sciences and the arts,
    Persuaded that such a universal copyright system will facilitate a wider dissemination of works of the human mind and increase international understanding,
    Have resolved to revise the Universal Copyright Convention as signed at Geneva on 6 September 1952 (hereinafter called "the 1952 Convention"), and consequently,
    Have agreed as follows:

Article I

Each Contracting State undertakes to provide for the adequate and effective protection of the rights of authors and other copyright proprietors in literary, scientific and artistic works, including writings, musical, dramatic and cinematographic works, and paintings, engravings and sculpture.

Article II

1. Published works of nationals of any Contracting State and works first published in that State shall enjoy in each other Contracting State the same protection as that other State accords to works of its nationals first published in its own territory, as well as the protection specially granted by this Convention.

2. Unpublished works of nationals of each Contracting State shall enjoy in each other Contracting State the same protection as that other State accords to unpublished works of its own nations, as well as the protection specially granted by this Convention.

3. For the purpose of this Convention any Contracting State may, by domestic legislation, assimilate to its own nationals any person domiciled in that State.

* * *

INTERNATIONAL CONVENTION
FOR THE PROTECTION OF PERFORMERS, PRODUCERS OF PHONOGRAMS AND BROADCASTING ORGANIZATIONS, 1961

The Contracting States, moved by the desire to protect the rights of performers, producers of phonograms, and broadcasting organizations,
Have agreed as follows:

Article 1

Protection granted under this Convention shall leave intact and shall in no way affect the protection of copyright in literary and artistic works. Consequently, no provision of this Convention may be interpreted as prejudicing such protection.

Article 2

1. For the purposes of this Convention, national treatment shall mean the treatment accorded by the domestic law of the Contracting State in which protection is claimed:
(a) to performers who are its nationals, as regards performances taking place, broadcast, or first fixed, on its territory;
(b) to producers of phonograms who are its national's, as regards phonograms first fixed or first published on its territory;
(c) to broadcasting organizations which have their headquarters on its territory, as regards broadcasts transmitted from transmitters situated on its territory.

2. National treatment shall be subject to the protection specifically guaranteed, and the limitations specifically provided for, in this Convention.

Article 3

For the purposes of this Convention:
(a) «Performs» means actors, singers, musicians, dancers, and other persons who act, sing, deliver, declaim, play in, or otherwise perform literary or artistic works;
(b) «Phonogram» means any exclusively aural fixation of sounds of a performance or of other sounds;
(c) «Producer of phonograms» means the person who, or the legal entity which, first fixes the sounds of a performance or other sounds;
(d) «Publication» means the offering of copies of a phonogram to the public in reasonable quantity;
(e) «Reproduction» means the making of a copy or copies of a fixation;
(f) «Broadcasting» means the transmission by wireless means for public reception of sounds or of images and sounds;
(g) «Rebroadcasting» means the simultaneous broadcasting by one broadcasting organization of the broadcast of another broadcasting organization.

* * *

CONVENTION FOR THE PROTECTION OF PRODUCERS OF PHONOGRAMS AGAINST UNAUTHORIZED DUPLICATION OF THEIR PHONOGRAMS, 1971

The Contracting States,
Concerned at the widespread and increasing unauthorized duplication of

phonograms and the damage this is occasioning to the interests of authors, performers and producers of phonograms;

Convinced that the protection of producers of phonograms against such acts will also benefit the performers whose performances, and the authors whose works, are recorded on the said phonograms;

Recognizing the value of the work undertaken in this field by the United Nations Educational, Scientific and Cultural Organization and the World Intellectual Property Organization;

Anxious not to impair in any way international agreements already in force and in particular in no way to prejudice wider acceptance of the Rome Convention of October 26, 1961, which affords protection to performers and to broadcasting organizations as well as to producers of phonograms;

Have agreed as follows:

Article 1

For the purposes of this Convention:

(a) "phonogram" means any exclusively aural fixation of sounds of a performance or of other sounds;
(b) "Producer of phonograms" means the person who, or the legal entity which, first fixes the sounds of a performance or other sounds;
(c) "duplicate" means an article which contains sounds taken directly or indirectly from a phonogram and which embodies all or a substantial part of the sounds fixed in that phonogram;
(d) "distribution to the public" means any act by which duplicates of a phonogram are offered, directly or indirectly, to the general public or any section thereof.

Article 2

Each Contracting State shall protect producers of phonograms who are nationals of other Contracting States against the making of duplicates without the consent of the producer and against the importation of such duplicates, provided that any such making or importation is for the purpose of distribution to the public, and against the distribution of such duplicates to the public.

Article 3

The means by which this Convention is implemented shall be a matter for the domestic law of each Contracting State and shall include one or more of the following: protection by means of the grant of a copyright or other specific right; protection by means of the law relating to unfair competition; protection by means of penal sanctions.

* * *

CONVENTION RELATING TO THE DISTRIBUTION OF PROGRAMME-CARRYING SIGNALS TRANSMITTED BY SATELLITE, 1974

The Contracting States,

Aware that the use of satellites for the distribution of programme-carrying signals is rapidly growing both in volume and geographical coverage;

Concerned that there is no world-wide system to prevent distributors from distributing programme-carrying signals transmitted by satellite which were not intended for those distributors, and that this lack is likely to hamper the use of satellite communications;

Recognizing, in this respect, the importance of the interests of authors, performers, producers of phonograms and broadcasting organizations;

Convinced that an international system should be established under which measures would be provided to prevent distributors from distributing programme-carrying signals transmitted by satellite which were not intended for those distributors;

Conscious of the need not to impair in any way international agreements already in force, including the International Telecommunication Convention and the Radio Regulations annexed to that Convention, and in particular in no way to prejudice wider acceptance of the Rome Convention of October 26, 1961, which affords protection to performers, producers of phonograms and broadcasting organizations, Have agreed as follows:

Article 1

For the purposes of this Convention:

i.   "signal" is an electronically-generated carrier capable of transmitting programmes;
ii. "programme" is a body of live or recorded material consisting of images, sounds or both, embodied in signals emitted for the purpose of ultimate distribution;
iii. "satellite" is any device in extraterrestrial space capable of transmitting signals;
iv. "emitted signal" or "signal emitted" is any programme-carrying signal that goes to or passes through a satellite;
v.   "derived signal" is a signal obtained by modifying the technical characteristics of the emitted signal, whether or not there have been one or more intervening fixations;
vi. "originating organization" is the person or legal entity that decides what programme the emitted signals will carry;
vii. "distributor" is the person or legal entity that decides that the transmission of the derived signals to the general public or any section thereof should take place;
viii. "distribution" is the operation by which a distributor transmits derived signals to the general public or any section thereof.

Article 2

1. Each Contracting State undertakes to take adequate measures to prevent the distribution on or from its territory of any programme-carrying signal by any distributor for whom the signal emitted to or passing through the satellite is not intended. This obligation shall apply where the originating organization is a national of another Contracting State and where the signal distributed is a derived signal.

2. In any Contracting State in which the application of the measures referred to in paragraph (1) is limited in time, the duration thereof shall be fixed by its domestic law. The Secretary-General of the United Nations shall be notified in writing of such duration at the time of ratification, acceptance or accession, or if the domestic law comes into force or is changed thereafter, within six months of the coming into force of that law or of its modification.

3. The obligation provided for in paragraph (1) shall not apply to the distribution of derived signals taken from signals which have already been distributed by a distributor for whom the emitted signals were intended.

Article 3

This Convention shall not apply where the signals emitted by or on behalf of the originating organization are intended for direct reception from the satellite by the general public.

*   *   *

EUROPEAN AGREEMENT ON THE
PROTECTION OF TELEVISION BROADCASTS, 1960

The Governments signatory hereto, being Members of the Council of Europe,
Considering that the object of the Council is to achieve a greater unity between its Members;

Considering that exchanges of television programmes between the countries of Europe are calculated to further the achievement of that object;

Considering that these exchanges are hampered by the fact that the majority of television organizations are at present powerless to restrain the re-broadcasting, fixation or public performance of their broadcasts, whereas the organizers of musical or dramatic performances or the like, and the promoters of sports meetings, make their consent to broadcasting to other countries conditional upon an undertaking that the relays will not be used for purposes other than private viewing;

Considering that the international protection of television broadcasts will in no way affect any rights of third parties in these broadcasts;

Considering that the problem is one of some urgency, in view of the installations and links now being brought into service throughout Europe, which are such as to make it easy from the technical point of view for European television organizations to exchange their programmes;

Considering that, pending the conclusion of a potentially universal Convention on "neighbouring rights" at present in contemplation, it is fitting to conclude a regional Agreement restricted in scope to television broadcasts and of limited duration,
Have agreed as follows:

Article 1

Broadcasting organizations constituted in the territory and under the laws of a Party to this Agreement or transmitting from such territory shall enjoy, in respect of all their television broadcasts:

1. In the territory of all Parties to this Agreement, the right to authorize or prohibit:

(a) the re-broadcasting of such broadcasts;
(b) the diffusion of such broadcasts to the public by wire;
(c) the communication of such broadcasts to the public by means of any instrument for the transmission of signs, sounds or images;
(d) any fixation of such broadcasts or still photographs thereof, and any reproduction of such a fixation; and
(e) re-broadcasting, wire diffusion or public performance with the aid of the fixations or reproductions referred to in subparagraph (d) of this paragraph, except where the organization in which the right vests has authorized the sale of the said fixations or reproductions to the public;

2. In the territory of any other Party to this Agreement, the same protection as that other Party may extend to organizations constituted in its territory and under its laws or transmitting from its territory, where such protection is greater than that provided for in paragraph 1 above.

Article 2

1. Subject to paragraph 2 of Article 1, and Articles 13 and 14, the protection provided for in paragraph 1 of Article 1 shall continue until the end of the tenth calendar year following the year in which the first broadcast was made from the territory of a Party to this Agreement.

2. No Party to this Agreement shall be required, in pursuance of paragraph 2 of Article 1, to accord to the broadcasts of any broadcasting organizations constituted in the territory and under the laws of another Party to this Agreement or transmitting from

the territory of another Party longer protection than that granted by the said other Party.

* * *

PARIS CONVENTION FOR THE PROTECTION OF INDUSTRIAL PROPERTY OF MARCH 20, 1883, AS REVISED AT BRUSSELS ON DECEMBER 14, 1900, AT WASHINGTON ON JUNE 2, 1911, AT THE HAGUE ON NOVEMBER 6, 1925, AT LONDON ON JUNE 2,1934, AT LISBON ON OCTOBER 31, 1958, AND AT STOCKHOLM ON JULY 14, 1967

Article 1 Establishment of the Union; Scope of Industrial Property

1. The countries to which this Convention applies constitute a Union for the protection of industrial property.

2. The protection of industrial property has as its object patents, utility models, industrial designs, trademarks, service marks, trade names, indications of source or appellations of origin, and the repression of unfair competition.

3. Industrial property shall be understood in the broadest sense and shall apply not only to industry and commerce proper, but likewise to agricultural and extractive industries and to all manufactured or natural products, for example, wines, grain, tobacco leaf, fruit, cattle, minerals, mineral waters, beer, flowers, and flour.

4. Patents shall include the various kinds of industrial patents recognized by the laws of the countries of the Union, such as patents of importation, patents of improvement, patents and certificates of addition, etc.

Article 2 National Treatment for Nationals of Countries of the Union

1. Nationals of any country of the Union shall, as regards the protection of industrial property, enjoy in all the other countries of the Union the advantages that their respective laws now grant, or may hereafter grant, to nationals; all without prejudice to the rights specially provided for by this Convention. Consequently, they shall have the same protection as the latter, and the same legal remedy against any infringement of their rights, provided that the conditions and formalities imposed upon nationals are complied with.

2. However, no requirement as to domicile or establishment in the country where protection is claimed may be imposed upon nationals of countries of the Union for the enjoyment of any industrial property rights.

3. The provisions of the laws of each of the countries of the Union relating to judicial and administrative procedure and to jurisdiction, and to the designation of an address for service or the appointment of an agent, which may be required by the laws on industrial property are expressly reserved.

Article 3 Same Treatment for Certain Categories of Persons as for Nationals of Countries of the Union

Nationals of countries outside the Union who are domiciled or who have real and effective industrial or commercial establishments in the territory of one of the countries of the Union shall be treated in the same manner as nationals of the countries of the Union.

Article 4 A to F. Patents, Utility Models, Industrial Designs, Marks, Inventors' Certificates: Right of Priority. — G. Patents: Division of the Application

A. — 1. Any person who has duly filed an application for a patent, or for the registration of a utility model, or of an industrial design, or of a trademark, in one of the countries of the Union, or his successor in title, shall enjoy, for the purpose of filing in the other countries, a right of priority during the periods hereinafter fixed.

2. Any filing that is equivalent to a regular national filing under the domestic legislation of any country of the Union or under bilateral or multilateral treaties concluded between countries of the Union shall be recognized as giving rise to the right of priority.

3. By a regular national filing is meant any filing that is adequate to establish the date on which the application was filed in the country concerned, whatever may be the subsequent fate of the application.

B. – Consequently, any subsequent filing in any of the other countries of the Union before the expiration of the periods referred to above shall not be invalidated by reason of any acts accomplished in the interval, in particular, another filing, the publication or exploitation of the invention, the putting on sale of copies of the design, or the use of the mark, and such acts cannot give rise to any third-party right or any right of personal possession. Rights acquired by third parties before the date of the first application that serves as the basis for the right of priority are reserved in accordance with the domestic legislation of each country of the Union.

C. – 1. The periods of priority referred to above shall be twelve months for patents and utility models, and six months for industrial designs and trademarks.

2. These periods shall start from the date of filing of the first application; the day of filing shall not be included in the period.

3. If the last day of the period is an official holiday, or a day when the office is not open for the filing of applications in the country where the protection is claimed, the period shall be extended until the first following working day.

4. A subsequent application concerning the same subject as a previous first application within the meaning of paragraph (2), above, filed in the same country of the Union, shall be considered as the first application, of which the filing date shall be the starting point of the period of priority, if, at the time of filing the subsequent application, the said previous application has been withdrawn, abandoned, or refused, without having been laid open to public inspection and without leaving any rights outstanding, and if it has not yet served as a basis for claiming a right of priority. The previous application may not thereafter serve as a basis for claiming a right of priority.

D. – 1. Any person desiring to take advantage of the priority of a previous filing shall be required to make a declaration indicating the date of such filing and the country in which it was made. Each country shall determine the latest date on which such declaration must be made.

2. These particulars shall be mentioned in the publications issued by the competent authority, and in particular in the patents and the specifications relating thereto.

3. The countries of the Union may require any person making a declaration of priority to produce a copy of the application (description, drawings, etc.) previously filed. The copy, certified as correct by the authority which received such application, shall not require any authentication, and may in any case be filed, without fee, at any time within three months of the filing of the subsequent application. They may require it to be accompanied by a certificate from the same authority showing the date of filing, and by a translation.

4. No other formalities may be required for the declaration of priority at the time of filing the application. Each country of the Union shall determine the consequences of failure to comply with the formalities prescribed by this Article, but such consequences shall in no case go beyond the loss of the right of priority.

5. Subsequently, further proof may be required.

Any person who avails himself of the priority of a previous application shall be required to specify the number of that application; this number shall be published as provided for by paragraph (2), above.

E.–1. Where an industrial design is filed in a country by virtue of a right of priority based on the filing of a utility model, the period of priority shall be the same as that fixed for industrial designs.

2. Furthermore, it is permissible to file a utility model in a country by virtue of a right of priority based on the filing of a patent application, and vice versa.

F.–No country of the Union may refuse a priority or a patent application on the ground that the applicant claims multiple priorities, even if they originate in different countries, or on the ground that an application claiming one or more priorities contains one or more elements that were not included in the application or applications whose priority is claimed, provided that, in both cases, there is unity of invention within the meaning of the law of the country.

*   *   *

PART SEVEN
INFORMATICS LAW

The notion of informatics law is here used referring to international law and regulation governing automated information services and data systems as well as transborder data flows.

It should be noted that many other branches of communications and information law included in this collection are applicable to informatics, directly or implicitly. Thus, informatics is subject to relevant aspects of: information law as most obviously reflected in the evolving rules for the protection of privacy; telecommunications law as applicable to all users of telecommunications facilities; space law as it refers to the use of satellite communication and data transmission; intellectual property law where particular attention is focused on the application of copyright rules to computer programmes, computer-originated works and protected works stored in computerized data banks; customs law in so far as computer output is transported on physical support across national frontiers and, in a more general sense, trade regulations and agreements.

At the international level, discussion of action towards the adoption of international legal rules specifically regulating the use of computerized data systems and data transmission mainly concerns the following issue areas:

(a) As mentioned in Part Two Section 7, attention has been focussed on the promotion of technological progress for the welfare of man and on the consequences of technical developments for the exercise of human rights and fundamental freedoms; these issues have been the subject of action within the UN and within a number of the specialized agencies; thus the International Labour Organization has focussed attention on the effects of computerized data systems on employment and labour conditions.

(b) At the regional level, efforts in Western Europe to achieve harmonization of national policy and legislation concerning the protection of privacy have already resulted in the adoption of a convention sponsored by the Council of Europe. Furthermore, the Organization for Economic Co-operation and Development (OECD) has adopted a set of guidelines governing the protection of privacy and transborder data flows and the European Parliament has adopted recommendations concerning EEC principles for the protection of the rights of the individual with regard to data processing. In the UN context, the Economic and Social Council has proposed points for possible inclusion in draft international standards for the protection of individual rights against threats arising from the use of computerized personal data systems.

(c) There are also proposals to provide more general international regulation of transborder data flows. However, these aspects have not yet been clearly formulated to the same extent as the privacy rules and represent a new, still emerging legal area. In this respect, distinctions are being made between different kinds of information (personal, economic, security etc.) and between the purposes of possible regulation (protection of individuals, protection of national economic, security and other interests).

Documents

1. Protection of individual rights, in particular privacy

Treaties
  i. Convention for the Protection of Individuals with regard to Automatic Processing of Personal Data, Council of Europe, 1980
    − Full text

Resolutions and other texts
  ii. Human rights and scientific and technological development: additional points suggested for possible inclusion in the drafting of international standards, Report of the Secretary General, UN document E/CN 4/1233, 1976
    − Full text
  iii. Guidelines Governing the Protection of Privacy and Transborder Data Flows of Personal Data, Organisation for Economic Co-operation and Development, 1980
    − Full text
  iv. Recommendations concerning the principles which should form the basis of Community norms on the protection of the rights of the individual in the face of developing technical progress in the field of data processing, recommendations from Parliament to the Commission and Council, European Economic Community, 1979
    − Full text

2. Organisational structure

  v. Convention of the Intergovernmental Bureau of Informatics, 1951 amended 1974 and 1978
    − Preamble
    − Articles I-V

CONVENTION FOR THE PROTECTION OF INDIVIDUALS
WITH REGARD TO AUTOMATIC PROCESSING OF PERSONAL DATA,
COUNCIL OF EUROPE, 1980

Preamble

The Member States of the Council of Europe, signatory hereto,
Considering that the aim of the Council of Europe is to achieve greater unity between its Members, based in particular on respect for the rule of law, as well as human rights and fundamental freedoms,
  Considering that it is desirable to extend the safeguards for everyone's rights and fundamental freedoms, and in particular the right to respect for privacy, taking account of the increasing flow across frontiers of personal data undergoing automatic processing,
  Reaffirming at the same time their commitment to freedom of information regardless of frontiers,
  Recognizing that it is necessary to reconcile the fundamental values of the respect for privacy and the free flow of information between peoples,
Have agreed as follows:

Chapter I – General Provisions

Article 1–Object and purpose

The purpose of this Convention is to secure in the territory of each Party for every individual, whatever his nationality or residence, respect for his rights and fundamental freedoms, and in particular his right to privacy, with regard to automatic processing of personal data relating to him ('data protection').

Article 2–Definitions

For the purpose of this Convention:

(a) 'personal data' means any information relating to an identified or identifiable individual ('data subject');

(b) 'automated data file' means any set of data undergoing automatic processing;

(c) 'automatic processing' includes the following operations if carried out in whole or in part by automated means: storage of data; carrying out of logical and/or arithmetical operations on those data; their alteration, erasure, retrieval or dissemination;

(d) 'controller of the file' means the natural or legal person, public authority, agency or any other body who is competent according to his national law to decide what should be the purpose of the automated data file, which categories of personal data should be stored and which processes should be applied to them.

Article 3–Scope

1. The Parties undertake to apply this Convention to automated personal data files and automatic processing of personal data in the public and private sectors.

2. Any State may, at the time of signature or when depositing its instrument of ratification, acceptance, approval or concession, or at any later time, give notice by a declaration addressed to the Secretary General of the Council of Europe:

(a) that it will not apply this Convention to certain categories of automated personal data files, a list of which will be deposited. In this list it shall not include, however, categories of automated data files subject in its domestic law to data protection provisions. Consequently, it shall amend this list by a new declaration whenever additional categories of automated personal data files are subjected to data protection provisions in its domestic law;

(b) that it will apply this Convention also to information relating to groups of persons, associations, foundations, companies, corporations and any other bodies consisting directly or indirectly of individuals, whether or not such bodies possess legal personality;

(c) that it will apply this Convention also to personal data files which are not processed automatically.

3. Any State which has extended the scope of the Convention by any of the declarations provided for in sub-paragraph (b) or (c) above may give notice in the said declaration that such extensions shall apply only to certain categories of personal data files, a list of which will be deposited.

4. Any Party which has excluded certain categories of automated personal data files by a declaration provided for in sub-paragraph 2(a) above may not claim the application of the Convention to such categories by a Party which has not included them.

5. Likewise, a Party which has not made one or other of the extensions provided for in sub-paragraph 2(b) and (c) may not claim the application of this Convention on the points with respect to a Party which has made such extensions.

6. The declarations provided for in paragraph 2 above to take effect from the mo-

ment of the entry into force of the Convention with regard to the State which has made them at the time of signature or deposit of its instrument of ratification, acceptance, approval or accession, or three months after receipt by the Secretary General of the Council of Europe if they have been formulated at any later time. These declarations may be withdrawn, in whole or in part, by a notification addressed to the Secretary General of the Council of Europe. Such withdrawals shall take effect three months after the date of receipt of such notification.

Chapter II – Basic Principles for Data Protection

Article 4–Duties of the Parties

1. Each Party shall take the necessary measures in its domestic law to give effect to the basic principles for data protection set out in this chapter.

2. These measures shall be taken at the latest at the time of entry into force of this Convention in respect of that Party.

Article 5–Quality of data

Personal data undergoing automatic processing shall be:

(a) obtained and processed fairly and lawfully;
(b) stored for specified and legitimate purposes and not used in a way incompatible with those purposes;
(c) adequate, relevant and not excessive in relation to the purpose for which they are stored;
(d) accurate and, where necessary, kept up-to-date;
(e) preserved in a form which permits identification of the data subjects for no longer than is required for the purpose for which those data are stored.

Article 6–Special categories of data

Personal data revealing racial origin, political opinions or religious or other beliefs, as well as personal data concerning health or sexual life, may not be processed automatically unless domestic law provides appropriate safeguards. The same shall apply to personal data relating to criminal convictions.

Article 7–Data security

Appropriate security measures shall be taken for the protection of personal data stored in automated data files against accidental or unauthorized destruction or accidental loss as well as against unauthorized access, alteration or dissemination.

Article 8–Additional safeguards for the data subject

Any person shall be enabled:

(a) to establish the existence of an automated personal data file, its main purposes, as well as the identity and habitual residence or principal place of business of the controller of the file;
(b) to obtain at reasonable intervals and without excessive delay or expense confirmation of whether personal data relating to him are stored in the automated data file as well as communication to him of such data in an intelligible form;
(c) to obtain, as the case may be, rectification or erasure of such data if these have been processed contrary to the provisions of domestic law giving effect to the basic principles set out in Articles 5 and 6 of this Convention;
(d) to have a remedy if a request for confirmation or, as the case may be, communication, rectification or erasure as referred to in paragraphs (b) and (c) of this article is not complied with.

Article 9–Exceptions and restrictions

1. No exception to the provisions of Articles 5, 6, and 8 of this Convention shall be allowed except within the limits defined in this article.

2. Derogation from the provisions of Articles 5, 6 and 8 of this Convention shall be allowed where such derogation provided for by the law of the Party constitutes a necessary measure in a democratic society in the interests of:

(a) protecting state security, public safety, the monetary interests of the State or the suppression of criminal offences;
(b) protecting the data subject or the rights and freedoms of others.

3. Restrictions on the exercise of the rights specified in Article 8, paragraphs (b), (c) and (d) may be provided by law with respect to automated personal data files used for statistics or for scientific research purposes when there is obviously no risk of an infringement of the privacy of the data subjects.

Article 10–Sanctions and remedies

Each Party undertakes to establish appropriate sanctions and remedies for violations of provisions of domestic law giving effect to the basic principles for data protection set out in this chapter.

Article 11–Extended protection

None of the provisions of this chapter shall be interpreted as limiting or otherwise affecting the possibility for a Party to grant data subjects a wider measure of protection than that stipulated in this Convention.

Chapter III – Transborder Data Flows

Article 12–Transborder flows of personal data and domestic law

1. The following provisions shall apply to the transfer across national borders, by whatever medium, of personal data undergoing automatic processing or collected with a view to their being automatically processed.

2. A Party shall not, for the sole purpose of the protection of privacy, prohibit or subject to special authorization transborder flows of personal data going to the territory of another Party.

3. Nevertheless, each Party shall be entitled to derogate from the provisions of paragraph 2:

(a) in so far as its legislation includes specific regulations for certain categories of personal data or of automated personal data files, because of the nature of those data or those files, except where the regulations of the other Party provide an equivalent protection;
(b) when the transfer is made from its territory to the territory of a non-Contracting State through the intermediary of the territory of another Party, in order to avoid such transfers resulting in circumvention of the legislation of the Party referred to at the beginning of this paragraph.

Chapter IV – Mutual Assistance

Article 13–Cooperation between Parties

1. The Parties agree to render each other mutual assistance in order to implement this Convention.

2. For that purpose:

(a) each Party shall designate one or more authorities the name and address of each of which it shall communicate to the Secretary General of the Council of Europe;

(b) each Party which has designated more than one authority shall specify in its communication referred to in the previous sub-paragraph the competence of each authority.

3. An authority designated by a Party shall at the request of an authority designated by another Party:

(a) furnish information on its law and administrative practice in the field of data protection;

(b) for the sole purpose of protection of privacy, take all appropriate measures, in conformity with its domestic law, for furnishing factual information relating to specific automatic processing carried out in its territory, with the exception however of the personal data being processed.

Article 14–Assistance to data subjects resident abroad

1. Each Party shall assist any person resident abroad to exercise the rights conferred by its domestic law giving effect to the principles set out in Article 8 of this Convention.

2. When such a person resides in the territory of another Party he shall be given the option of submitting his request through the intermediary of the authority designated by that Party.

3. The request for assistance shall contain all the necessary particulars, relating inter alia to:

(a) the name, address and any other relevant particulars identifying the person making the request;

(b) the automated personal data file to which the request pertains, or its controller;

(c) the nature of the request.

Article 15–Safeguards concerning assistance rendered by designated authorities

1. An authority designated by a Party which has received information from an authority designated by another Party either accompanying a request for assistance or in reply to its own request for assistance shall not use that information for purposes other than those specified in the request for assistance.

2. Each Party shall see to it that the persons belonging to or acting on behalf of the designated authority shall be bound by appropriate restrictions of secrecy or confidentiality with regard to that information.

3. In no case may a designated authority be allowed to make a request for assistance on behalf of a data subject resident abroad, as referred to in Article 14, paragraph 2 of its own accord and without the express consent of the person concerned.

Article 16–Refusal of requests for assistance

A designated authority to which a request for assistance is addressed under Articles 13 or 14 of this Convention may not refuse to comply with it unless:

(a) the request is not compatible with the powers in the fields of data protection of the authorities responsible for replying;

(b) the request does not comply with the provisions of this Convention;

(c) compliance with the request would be incompatible with the sovereignty, security or public policy (ordre public) of the Party by which it was designated, or with the rights and fundamental freedoms of persons under the jurisdiction of that Party.

Article 17–Costs and procedures of assistance

1. Mutual assistance which the Parties render each other under Article 13, and assistance they render to data subjects abroad under Article 14 shall not give rise to the payment of any costs or fees other than those incurred for experts and interpreters. The latter costs or fees shall be borne by the party which has designated the authority making the request for assistance.

2. The data subject may be charged no costs or fees in connection with the steps taken on his behalf in the territory of another Party other than those lawfully payable by residents of that Party.

3. Other details concerning the assistance relating in particular to the forms and procedures and the languages to be used, shall be established directly between the Parties concerned.

Chapter V – Consultative Committee

Article 18–Composition of the Committee

1. A Consultative Committee shall be set up after the entry into force of this Convention.

2. Each Party shall appoint a representative to the Committee and a deputy representative. Any Member State of the Council of Europe which is not a Party to the Convention shall have the right to be represented on the Committee by an observer.

3. The Consultative Committee may, by unanimous decision, invite any non-Member State of the Council of Europe which is not a Party to the Convention to be represented by an observer at any of its meetings.

Article 19–Functions of the Committee

The Consultative Committee:

(a) may make proposals with a view to facilitating or improving the application of the Convention;
(b) may make proposals for amendment of this Convention in conformity with Article 21;
(c) shall formulate its opinion on any proposal for amendment of this Convention which is referred to it in conformity with Article 21, paragraph 3;
(d) may, at the request of a Party, express an opinion on any question concerning the application of this Convention.

Article 20–Procedure

1. The Consultative Committee shall be convened by the Secretary General of the Council of Europe. Its first meeting shall be held within twelve months of the entry into force of this Convention. It shall subsequently meet at least once every two years and in any case when one third of the representatives of the Parties request its convocation.

2. A majority of representatives of the Parties shall constitute a quorum for a meeting of the Consultative Committee.

3. After each of its meetings, the Consultative Committee shall submit to the Committee of Ministers of the Council of Europe a report on its work and on the functioning of the Convention.

4. Subject to the provisions of this Convention, the Consultative Committee shall draw up its own Rules of Procedure.

Chapter VI – Amendments

Article 21-Amendments

1. Amendments to this Convention may be proposed by a Party, the Committee of Ministers of the Council of Europe or the Consultative Committee.

2. Any proposal for amendment shall be communicated by the Secretary General of the Council of Europe to the Member States of the Council of Europe and to every non-Member State which has acceded to or has been invited to accede to this Convention in accordance with the provision of Article 23.

3. Moreover, any amendment proposed by a Party or the Committee of Ministers shall be communicated to the Consultative Committee which shall submit to the Committee of Ministers its opinion on that proposed amendment.

4. The Committee of Ministers shall consider the proposed amendment and any opinion submitted by the Consultative Committee and may approve the amendment.

5. The text of any amendment approved by the Committee of Ministers in accordance with paragraph 4 of this article shall be forwarded to the Parties for acceptance.

6. Any amendment approved in accordance with paragraph 4 of this article shall come into force on the thirtieth day after all Parties have informed the Secretary General of their acceptance thereof.

Chapter VII – Final Clauses

Article 22-Entry into force

1. This convention shall be open for signature by the Member States of the Council of Europe. It is subject to ratification, acceptance or approval. Instruments of ratification, acceptance or approval shall be deposited with the Secretary General of the Council of Europe.

2. This Convention shall enter into force on the first day of the month following the expiration of a period of three months after the date on which five Member States of the Council of Europe have expressed their consent to be bound by the Convention in accordance with the provisions of the preceding paragraph.

3. In respect of any Member State which subsequently expresses its consent to be bound by it, the Convention shall enter into force on the first day of the month following the expiration of a period of three months after the date of the deposit of the instrument of ratification, acceptance or approval.

Article 23-Accession by non-Member States

1. After the entry into force of this Convention, the Committee of Ministers of the Council of Europe may invite any State not a member of the Council of Europe to accede to this Convention by a decision taken by the majority provided by Article 20(d) of the Statute of the Council of Europe and by the unanimous vote of the representatives of the Contracting States entitled to sit on the Committee.

2. In respect of any acceding State, the Convention shall enter into force on the first day of the month following the expiration of a period of three months after the date of deposit of the instrument of ratification with the Secretary General of the Council of Europe.

Article 24-Territorial clause

1. Any State may at the time of signature or when depositing its instrument of

ratification, acceptance, approval or accession, specify the territory or territories to which this Convention shall apply.

2. Any State may at any later date, by a declaration addressed to the Secretary General of the Council of Europe, extend the application of this Convention to any other territory specified in the declaration. In respect of such territory the Convention shall enter into force on the first day of the month following the expiration of a period of three months after the date of receipt by the Secretary General of such declaration.

3. Any declaration made under the two preceding paragraphs may, in respect of any territory specified in such declaration, be withdrawn by a notification addressed to the Secretary General. The withdrawal shall become effective on the first day of the month following the expiration of a period of six months after the date of receipt of such notification by the Secretary General.

Article 25-Reservations

No reservation may be made in respect of the provisions of this Convention.

Article 26-Denunciation

1. Any Party may at any time denounce this Convention by means of a notification addressed to the Secretary General of the Council of Europe.

2. Such denunciation shall become effective on the first day of the month following the expiration of a period of six months after the date of receipt of the notification by the Secretary General.

Article 27-Notifications

The Secretary General of the Council of Europe shall notify the Member States of the Council and any State which has acceded to this Convention of:

(a) any signature;
(b) the deposit of any instrument of ratification, acceptance, approval or accession;
(c) any date of entry into force of this Convention in accordance with Articles 22, 23, and 24;
(d) any other act, notification or communication relating to this Convention.

POINTS FOR POSSIBLE INCLUSION IN DRAFT INTERNATIONAL STANDARDS
FOR THE PROTECTION OF THE RIGHTS OF THE INDIVIDUAL
AGAINST THREATS ARISING FROM THE USE OF
COMPUTERIZED PERSONAL DATA SYSTEMS

Report by the Secretary General, United Nations document E/CN.4/1233, 1976

320. In the light of the existing and proposed safeguards dealt with in this present report, it is suggested that the following points be taken into account in the drafting of international standards relating to the protection of the rights of the individual against threats arising from the use of computerized personal data systems:

   i. The States which have not yet done so should adopt appropriate legislation containing rules relating to computerized personal data systems in both the public and the private sectors. As far as possible, legislation should be adopted concerning all types of computerized personal data systems (statistical and research systems, administrative systems and intelligence systems), but may vary according to the nature of those types of systems.
   ii. The following minimum standards should be followed in drawing up national legislation:

(a) only the personal information strictly necessary for the purposes of the respective system should be collected;

(b) the individual should be notified that information is being gathered about him and his agreement should be obtained before the information is stored, provided that information may be gathered without such knowledge and agreement in areas related to national security, law enforcement and criminal justice, and in other areas for which the law has established that such knowledge and agreement are not required due to the purpose of the gathering of information, subject to appropriate safeguards for human rights which should include those suggested in points 3 (a)(i) and (iii) and 3 (b) appearing in paragraph 177 of document E/CN.4/1116.

(c) the collection and storage of hearsay and other subjective material should be avoided;

(d) data concerning political and religious views, race and ethnic origin and intimate life should not be collected and stored, except under conditions explicitly provided by the law;

(e) all necessary measures, including technical procedures, should be taken to maintain the accuracy, completeness and pertinence of the stored information, and to remove or update obsolete information;

(f) legal responsibility should rest upon computer manufacturers and/or software developers, who with knowledge or through gross negligence fail to install basic safeguards for confidentiality and security of information;

(g) the individual should have the right, through special procedures laid down by the law, to receive a copy, intelligible to him, of stored information relating to him, to challenge it, to add explanations to it, and to obtain the correction or removal of inaccurate, obsolete or unverifiable data about him;

(h) the stored information should be disclosed or otherwise used only for the purposes for which it has been collected and disclosed only to legally authorized authorities or persons;

(i) all necessary measures, including technical procedures, to protect the confidentiality of the data and prevent their unauthorized disclosure and dissemination should be taken;

(j) any damage suffered by the individual in his rights, by the misuse of computerized data concerning him, should be compensated;

(k) violations of laws aiming at protecting the rights of the person to whom the stored information relates should be made punishable;

(l) the legality of decisions about individuals based on computerized personal data systems and their judicial control should be ensured;

iii. The use as evidence of information stored in computerized systems should be regulated by special legislation.

iv. Rules should protect the rights of the person whenever information about him is stored in computerized systems operating in countries other than his own.

v. The establishment of a supervisory body in the field of operation of computerized personal data systems should be considered. Its functions might include:

(a) registering existing computerized personal data systems;

(b) supervising the observance of existing laws protecting human rights against the abuse of such systems;

(c) following developments in the field affecting human rights and drawing the attention of the legislature, the executive and the public to the effects of such developments upon human rights and to possible further required safeguards.

vi. The establishment of professional associations for computer personnel should be promoted and such associations should be encouraged to adopt codes of ethics which should contain minimum rules aiming at regulating the professional conduct of such personnel in such a manner as to prevent infringements of human rights.

vii. Professional associations for computer personnel might be given some jurisdiction over the professional education and the selection of such personnel and the power to apply disciplinary measures for non-compliance with the code of ethics mentioned above."

GUIDELINES GOVERNING THE PROTECTION OF PRIVACY AND TRANSBORDER FLOWS OF PERSONAL DATA

Organisation for Economic Co-operation and Development, 1980

The Council
Having regard to articles 1(c), 3(a) and 5(b) of the Convention on the Organisation for Economic Co-operation and Development of 14th December, 1960,
Recognizing:
that, although national laws and policies may differ, Member countries have a common interest in protecting private and individual liberties, and in reconciling fundamental but competing values such as privacy and the free flow of information;
that transborder flows of personal data contribute to economic and social development;
that domestic legislation concerning privacy protection and transborder flows of personal data may unduly burden such transborder flows.

Determined to advance the free flow of information between Member countries and to avoid the creation of unjustified obstacles to the development of economic and social relations among Member countries;
Recommends
1. That Member countries take into account in their domestic legislation the principles concerning the protection of privacy and individual liberties set forth in the Guidelines contained in the Annex to this Recommendation which is an integral part thereof.

2. That Member countries undertake to remove or avoid creating unjustified obstacles to transborder flows of personal data;

3. That Member countries co-operate in the implementation of the Guidelines set forth in Annex;

4. That Member countries agree as soon as possible on a specific mechanism of consultation and co-operation for the application of these Guidelines.

Part One. General

Definitions

1. For the purposes of these Guidelines:
(a) "data controller" means a party who, according to domestic law, is competent to decide about the contents and use of personal data regardless of whether or not such data are collected, stored, processed or disseminated by that party or by an agent on its behalf;
(b) "personal data" means any information relating to an identified or identifiable individual (data subject);
(c) "transborder flows of personal data" means movements of personal data across national borders.

Scope of Guidelines

2. These Guidelines apply to personal data, whether in the public or private sectors, which, because of the manner in which they are processed, or because of their nature or context, pose a danger to privacy and individual liberties.

3. These Guidelines should not be interpreted as preventing:

(a) the application of different protective measures to different categories of personal data, depending upon their nature and the context in which they are collected, stored, processed or disseminated;

(b) the exclusion from the application of the Guidelines of personal data which obviously do not contain any risk to privacy and individual liberties; or

(c) the application of the Guidelines only to automatic processing of personal data. "Automatic processing" means the processing of data performed in whole or in part by data processing equipment which can perform substantial computation without intervention by a human operator.

4. Exceptions to these Principles contained in Parts Two and Three of these Guidelines should be:

(a) as few as possible, and

(b) made known to the public

5. In the particular case of Federal countries the observance of these Guidelines may be affected by the division of powers in the Federation.

6. These Guidelines should be regarded as minimum standards which are capable of being supplemented by additional measures for the protection of privacy and individual liberties.

Part Two. Basic Principles of National Application

Collection Limitation Principle

7. There should be limits to the collection of personal data and any such data should be obtained by lawful and fair means and, where appropriate, with the knowledge or consent of the data subject.

Data Quality Principle

8. Personal data should be relevant to the purposes for which they are to be used, and, to the extent necessary for those purposes, should be accurate, complete and kept up-to-date.

Purpose Specification Principle

9. The purpose for which personal data are collected should be specified at the time of data collection and the subsequent use limited to the fulfilment of those purposes or such others as are not incompatible with those purposes and as are specified on each occasion.

Use Limitation Principle

10. Personal data should not be disclosed, made available or otherwise used for purposes other than those specified in accordance with Paragraph 9 except:

(a)   with the consent of the data subject; or

(b)   by the authority of law.

Security Safeguards Principle

11. Personal data should be protected by reasonable security safeguards against

such risks as loss or unauthorized access, destruction, use, modification or disclosure of data.

Openness Principle

12. There should be a general policy of openness about developments, practices and policies with respect to personal data. Means should be readily available of establishing the existence and nature of personal data, and the main purposes of their use, as well as the identity and usual residence of the data controller.

*   *   *

Individual Participation Principle

13. An individual should have the right:

(a) to obtain from a data controller, or otherwise, confirmation of whether or not the data controller has data relating to him:
(b) to have communicated to him, data relating to him
  i. within a reasonable time;
  ii. at a charge, if any, that is not excessive;
  iii. in a reasonable manner; and
  iv. in a form that is readily intelligible to him;
(c) to be given reasons if a request made under sub paragraphs (a) and (b) is denied, and to be able to challenge such denial; and
(d) to challenge data relating to him and, if the challenge is successful, to have the data erased, rectified, completed or amended.

Accountability Principle

14. A data controller should be accountable for complying with measures which give effect to the principles stated above.

Part Three. Basic Principles of International Application
Free Flow and Legitimate Restrictions

15. Member countries should take into consideration the implications for other Member countries of domestic processing and re-export of personal data, particularly where processing in one Member country would result in a circumvention or violation of the domestic legislation of other Member countries.

16. Member countries should take all reasonable and appropriate steps to ensure that transborder flows of personal data, including transit through a Member country are uninterrupted and secure.

17. A Member country should refrain from restricting transborder flows of personal data between itself and another Member country except where the latter does not yet substantially observe these Guidelines.

18. Member countries should refrain from developing laws, policies and practices in the name of the protection of privacy and individual liberties which, by exceeding requirements for the protection of privacy and individual liberties are inconsistent with the free transborder flow of personal data.

Part Four. National Implementation

19. In implementing domestically the principles set forth in Parts Two and Three, Member countries should in particular:

(a) provide for reasonable means for individuals to exercise their rights;
(b) encourage and support self-regulation, whether in the form of codes of conduct or otherwise;

(c) provide for adequate sanctions and remedies in case of failures to comply with measures which implement the principles set forth in Parts Two and Three;

(d) establish legal, administrative or other procedures or institutions for the protection of privacy and individual liberties in respect of personal data; and

(e) ensure that there is no unfair discrimination against data subjects.

Part Five. International Co-operation

20. Member countries should, where requested, make known to other Member countries details of the observance of the principles set forth in these Guidelines. Member countries should also ensure that procedures for transborder flows of personal data and for the protection of privacy and individual liberties are simple and compatible with those of other Member countries.

21. Member countries should establish procedures to facilitate:

i. information exchange related to these Guidelines, and

ii. mutual assistance in the procedural and investigative matters involved.

22. Member countries should work towards the development of principles, domestic and international, to govern the applicable law in the case of transborder flows of personal data.

RECOMMENDATIONS FROM PARLIAMENT TO THE COMMISSION AND
COUNCIL PURSUANT TO PARAGRAPH 10 OF THE MOTION FOR
A RESOLUTION CONCERNING THE PRINCIPLES WHICH SHOULD FORM
THE BASIS OF COMMUNITY NORMS ON THE PROTECTION OF THE
RIGHTS OF THE INDIVIDUAL IN THE FACE OF DEVELOPING
TECHNICAL PROGRESS IN THE FIELD OF DATA PROCESSING

European Economic Community, 1979

The Community norms to be adopted in the field covered by this resolution should embody the following principles:

I

1. Computerized or manual personal data banks shall be subject to prior registration or authorization. The data protection body may permit individual and general exceptions.

2. Personal data to be processed shall be
- obtained by lawful means; the acquisition of especially sensitive data shall be subject to the consent of the person concerned or to special legal authorization;
- recorded and transmitted for the designated purposes and in conformity with the declaration made by, or the authorization granted to, the data controller; the data protection body may permit exception;
- accurate and necessary for the purpose for which the data bank has been established;
- erased whenever they have been obtained by unlawful means, are inaccurate or out of date, or as soon as the purpose for which they were recorded has been achieved.

3. The data controller shall be liable for material and non-material damage caused by the misuse of data, whether or not there was any negligence on his part.

4. Data controllers shall inform the person concerned when personal data are first stored.

5. Public and private agencies shall at the earliest opportunity inform the data protection body of data processing plans which may involve personal data.

6. The amalgamation, in whatever form, of separate data banks shall require the consent of the data protection body.

7. Data from medical, police or intelligence service data banks and from the social security sector may be amalgamated or combined with other data banks only with the consent of the person concerned. Exceptions shall require the consent of the data control body.

II

8. All persons whose usual residence is in the territory of a Member State shall have the right:

(a) to information on all measures involving the recording, storage or transmission to third parties of the data relating to them . . . and on the content, purpose and recipient thereof;

(b) to have personal data erased where the conditions set out in point 2 above are not fulfilled, unless the data controller can prove the opposite;

(c) to have inaccurate or incorrect data relating to them corrected and third parties to whom such data have been transmitted informed accordingly;

(d) to require the data control body to check the legality of any data relating to them and stored in data banks which, for reasons of national security, are not by law subject to the exercise of the rights referred to above.

9. The Member States shall guarantee that the persons concerned may exercise their rights in an appropriate manner in respect of the protection of personal data within a reasonable period and free of charge.

III

10. Each Member State shall appoint an independent body with the appropriate staff and funds to monitor the application in its territory of the Community norms and the national norms introduced in implementation thereof. This body shall submit an annual report to the data control body of the European Community.

11. The body set up by each Member State shall publish the names of registered data banks in apropriate form, inform citizens of their rights to the protection of personal data, and assist them in exercising these rights.

12. In the cases referred to in I, paragraphs 4 and 5, the data protection body shall keep a register, which may be inspected where proof of a legitimate interest is established.

13. Cross-frontier transmissions of personal data intended for a recipient in another Member State or originating in another Member State shall not be subject to special arrangements within the Community. They shall be reported to the control body of the European Community.

14. The authorization of the data protection body of the European Community will be required for the export of data from the territory of the Member States.

15. The data protection body of the European Community shall submit an annual report to the European Parliament.

16. Infringements of these minimum norms for the protection of personal data shall be punishable by appropriate penalties.

17. Data relating to groups of individuals and the rights of such groups within the ambit of these principles shall be accorded the same protection as personal data and the rights of individuals within the meaning of the above-mentioned principles.

CONVENTION OF THE INTERGOVERNMENTAL BUREAU
OF INFORMATICS, 1951 (amended 1974 and 1978)

Article I Establishment of the IBI

An international organization is hereby established, hereinafter referred to as Inter-governmental Bureau for Informatics (IBI). The seat of this international organisation is in Rome. It may be changed by decision of the General Assembly. Such decision shall become effective only if the votes in favour are at least two thirds of the votes cast and provided however that the number of votes is higher than half the total of IBI Member States.

Article II Scope and Functions

The scope of the IBI is to permanently assist people, in the field of informatics, to help them live in the context created by this discipline, to understand better its impact on society and to derive the maximum benefit from its possibilities.

In general terms the IBI shall undertake all action promoting the development and diffusion of informatics, which will allow it to achieve its objective in conformity with the spirit of the Convention and as set forth above; In particular it shall:
- promote the development and application of informatics disciplines;
- collect, analyze and evaluate knowledge and information relating to informatics;
- promote the exchange and the transfer of techniques in the field of informatics;
- furnish, within the limits of its possibilities, such assistance in the field of informatics as may be requested by governments and intergovernmental organizations;
- disseminate knowledge, information and experience achieved in the field of informatics;
- advise, promote and, where required, recommend action of a national or international nature concerning, inter alia:
(a) the adoption of national and international policies for informatics;
(b) the adoption of improved methods of administration by means of informatics;
(c) the improvement of education in and through informatics;
(d) research, studies and development programmes contributing to the scope of the IBI;
- put at the disposal of the Member States the studies and the general programmes acquired or achieved by IBI or by one or more of its Members;
- supply its Member States with facilities for training and education in informatics.

In carrying out the functions set out above the IBI shall endeavour primarily to meet the needs of its Member States, and especially the needs of those which may have limited resources.

It shall, at all times, act in conformity with the objectives of international peace and the common welfare of mankind, for which the United Nations Organization was established, and which its Charter proclaims.

Article III Membership

States which are members either of the United Nations, or of the United Nations Educational, Scientific and Cultural Organization, or of one of the other Specialized Agencies of the United Nations and which become parties to the present Convention under the terms of Article XXII, shall be members of the IBI.

Article IV Organs

The IBI shall comprise:

1. A General Assembly

2. An Executive Council

3. A scientific, professional and administrative staff, headed by a Director General.

Article V General Assembly

1. The General Assembly shall consist of one representative, preferably with qualifications in the field of informatics, of each Member State of the IBI and of a representative of the United Nations Educational, Scientific and Cultural Organization. The representatives may be assisted by deputies and advisers: each member of the General Assembly has the right to one vote.

2. The General Assembly is the supreme organ of the IBI. It shall determine the policy of the Organization and settle at each of its ordinary sessions the programme, and in conformity with the Financial Regulations, the budget of the IBI for the two succeeding years. It shall examine the biennial report of activities presented by the Director General, which shall be accompanied by the comments of the Executive Council; it shall elect, in accordance with Article VI, the States which will sit on the Executive Council. It shall appoint the Director General of the IBI, in accordance with Article VII, and shall determine the terms and conditions of appointment including the salary and other emoluments attached to the office. It shall establish the regulations and adopt all decisions relative to the functioning of the IBI.

3. The General Assembly shall elect its officers and make its own rules of procedure. Its decisions shall be made by a majority of members present and voting, unless otherwise provided in this Convention.

4. The General Assembly shall meet in ordinary session every two years. It shall meet in extraordinary session on the summons of the Chairman of the Executive Council at the request of a majority of Member States, or upon the decision of the Executive Council.

5. A Member State which is in arrears in the payment of its financial contributions to the IBI shall have no vote in the General Assembly if the amount of its arrears equals or exceeds the amount of the contributions due from it for the two preceding calendar years. The General Assembly may, nevertheless, permit such a Member State to vote if it is satisfied that the failure to pay is justified.

6. The General Assembly may invite any international organization which has responsibilities related to those of the IBI to be represented at the meetings of the General Assembly, in an observer capacity. No representative of such an organization shall have the right to vote.

7. The General Assembly may make recommendations to Member States concerning questions pertaining to the purpose of the IBI for consideration by them with a view to implementation by national action.

8. The General Assembly may review any decision taken by the Executive Council.

* * *

PART EIGHT
TRADE AND CUSTOMS REGULATIONS

The international movement of information increasingly presents important trade and commercial aspects. Agreements on trade and economic relations can therefore be expected to play a growing role in the international regulation of information and communications. It is significant that the United Nations Conference on Trade and Development (UNCTAD) pays increasing attention to the economic and trade implications of transborder data flows and that similar subject matters have been under negotiation within the Organisation for Economic Co-operation and Development (OECD). In more specific terms it is worth noting that special provisions concerning cinematograph film have been included in the General Agreement on Tariffs and Trade (GATT). The movement of trade information is an important function of the International Trade Center (ITC) operated jointly by GATT and UNCTAD.

A similar trend can be seen in the context of the European Economic Community: recent activities in the cultural and communications field concern such issues as freedom of trade in cultural goods, freedom of movement and establishment for cultural workers, the possible harmonization of copyright and neighbouring rights legislation and rules concerning subsidies to the cinema industry. In the field of informatics, EEC activities have concerned the establishment of a European data network and the protection of privacy in relation to automated data processing.

Information material fixed on a physical support moving across frontiers becomes subject to customs rules and agreements. In recent years, multilateral customs agreements have been concluded within the framework of the Customs Co-operation Council (CCC) established 1950 in Brussels. General customs agreements are supplemented by special agreements covering specific kinds of informational and cultural materials, examples are the Beirut and Florence Agreements and other instruments designed to promote the free flow of information in certain areas.

Documents

1. Economic and Trade Agreements

  i. Establishment of the United Nations Conference on Trade and Development (UNCTAD), UN General Assembly Resolution 1995 (XIX), 1964
     - Preamble
     - Section I, II
 ii. General Agreement on Tariffs and Trade (GATT), as in force 1 March 1969
     - Preamble
     - Articles: I, II: 1, III: 1, 2, IV, V: 1-2, XVIII: 1-2, XX, XXXVI
iii. Treaty Establishing the European Economic Community, Rome, 1957
     - Preamble
     - Articles 1-7, 9, 12, 18, 30, 36-37, 48, 52, 59-60, 85, 92, 110, 117

2. Customs Agreements

    i. Convention Establishing a Customs Co-operation Council, Brussels, 1950
        − Preamble
        − Articles I–VI
   ii. Specific customs agreements (mentioned as examples, texts not included

        (a) International Convention to Facilitate the Importation of Commercial Samples and Advertising Material, Geneva, 1952
        (b) Convention concerning Customs Facilities for Touring, New York, 1954
        (c) Customs Convention on the Temporary Importation of Professional Equipment, Brussels, 1961
        (d) Customs Convention concerning Facilities for the Importation of Goods for Display or Use at Exhibitions, Fairs, Meetings or similar Events, Brussels, 1961
        (e) Customs Convention on the Temporary Importation of Scientific Equipment, Brussels, 1968
        (f) Customs Convention on the Temporary Importation of Pedagogic Material, Brussels, 1970

  iii. *See also* Florence and Beirut Agreements, Part Two, Section 3; Intellectual Property Rights, Part Six; Informatics Law, Part Seven

ESTABLISHMENT OF THE UNITED NATIONS CONFERENCE ON
TRADE AND DEVELOPMENT AS AN ORGAN OF THE GENERAL ASSEMBLY

United Nations General Assembly Resolution 1995 (XIX), 1964

The General Assembly,
Convinced that sustained efforts are necessary to raise the standards of living in all countries and to accelerate the economic growth of the developing countries,

   Considering that international trade is an important instrument for economic development,

   Recognizing that the United Nations Conference on Trade and Development has provided a unique opportunity to make a comprehensive review of the problems of trade and of trade in relation to economic development, particularly those affecting the developing countries,

   Convinced that adequate and effectively functioning organizational arrangements are essential if the full contribution of international trade to the accelerated economic growth of the developing countries is to be successfully realized through the formulation and implementation of the necessary policies,

   Taking into account that the operation of existing international institutions was examined by the United Nations Conference on Trade and Development, which recognized both their contributions and their limitations in dealing with all the problems of trade and related problems of development,

   Believing that all States participating in the United Nations Conference on Trade and Development should make the most effective use of institutions and arrangements to which they are or may become parties,

   Convinced that, at the same time, there should be a further review of both the present and the proposed institutional arrangements, in the light of the experience of their work and activities,

   Taking note of the widespread desire among developing countries for a comprehensive trade organization,

Recognizing that further institutional arrangements are necessary in order to continue the work initiated by the Conference and to implement its recommendations and conclusions,

I

Establishes the United Nations Conference on Trade and Development as an organ of the General Assembly in accordance with the provisions set forth in section II below;

II

1. The members of the United Nations Conference on Trade and Development (hereinafter referred to as the Conference) shall be those States which are Members of the United Nations or members of the specialized agencies or of the International Atomic Energy Agency.

2. The Conference shall be convened at intervals of not more than three years. The General Assembly shall determine the date and location of the session of the Conference taking into account the recommendations of the Conference or of the Trade and Development Board established under paragraph (h) below.

3. The principal functions of the Conference shall be:

(a) To promote international trade, especially with a view to accelerating economic development, particularly trade between countries at different stages of development, between developing countries and between countries with different systems of economic and social organization, taking into account the functions performed by existing international organizations;

(b) To formulate principles and policies on international trade and related problems of economic development;

(c) To make proposals for putting the said principles and policies into effect and to take such other steps within its competence as may be relevant to this end having regard to differences in economic systems and stages of development;

(d) Generally, to review and facilitate the co-ordination of activities of other institutions within the United Nations system in the field of international trade and related problems of economic development and in this regard to co-operate with the General Assembly and the Economic and Social Council with respect to the performance of their responsibilities for co-ordination under the Charter of the United Nations;

(e) To initiate action, where appropriate, in co-operation with the competent organs of the United Nations for the negotiation and adoption of multilateral legal instruments in the field of trade, with due regard to the adequacy of existing organs of negotiation and without duplication of their activities;

(f) To be available as a centre for harmonizing the trade and related development policies of Government and regional economic groupings in pursuance of Article 1 of the Charter;

(g) To deal with any other matters within the scope of its competence.

* * *

THE GENERAL AGREEMENT ON TARIFFS AND TRADE, 1969

The Governments of the Commonwealth of Australia, the Kingdom of Belgium, the United States of Brazil, Burma, Canada, Ceylon, the Republic of Chile, the Republic of China, the Republic of Cuba, the Czechoslovak Republic, the French Republic, India, Lebanon, the Grand-Duchy of Luxemburg, the Kingdom of the Netherlands, New Zealand, the Kingdom of Norway, Pakistan, Southern Rhodesia, Syria, the

Union of South Africa, the United Kingdom of Great Britain and Northern Ireland, and the United States of America:

Recognizing that their relations in the field of trade and economic endeavour should be conducted with a view to raising standards of living, ensuring full employment and a large and steadily growing volume of real income and effective demand, developing the full use of the resources of the world and expanding the production and exchange of goods,

Being desirous of contributing to these objectives by entering into reciprocal and mutually advantageous arrangements directed to the substantial reduction of tariffs and other barriers to trade and to the elimination of discriminatory treatment in international commerce,

Have through their Representatives agreed as follows:

Part I

Article I General Most-Favoured-Nation Treatment

1. With respect to customs duties and charges of any kind imposed on or in connection with importation or exportation or imposed on the international transfer of payments for imports or exports, and with respect to the method of levying such duties and charges, and with respect to all rules and formalities in connection with importation and exportation, and with respect to all matters referred to in paragraphs 2 and 4 of Article III, any advantage, favour, privilege or immunity granted by any contracting party to any product originating in or destined for any other country shall be accorded immediately and unconditionally to the like product originating in or destined for the territories of all other contracting parties.

*   *   *

Article II Schedules of Concessions

1. (a) Each contracting party shall accord to the commerce of the other contracting parties treatment no less favourable than that provided for in the appropriate Part of the appropriate Schedule annexed to this Agreement.

(b) The products described in Part I of the Schedule relating to any contracting party, which are the products of territories of other contracting parties, shall, on their importation into the territory to which the Schedule relates, and subject to the terms, conditions or qualifications set forth in that Schedule, be exempt from ordinary customs duties in excess of those set forth and provided for therein. Such products shall also be exempt from all other duties or charges of any kind imposed on or in connection with importation in excess of those imposed on the date of this Agreement or those directly and mandatorily required to be imposed thereafter by legislation in force in the importing territory on that date.

*   *   *

Part II

Article III National Treatment on Internal Taxation and Regulation

1. The contracting parties recognize that internal taxes and other internal charges, and laws, regulations and requirements affecting the internal sale, offering for sale, purchase, transportation, distribution or use of products, and internal quantitative regulations requiring the mixture, processing or use of products in specified amounts or proportions, should not be applied to imported or domestic products so as to afford protection to domestic production.

2. The products of the territory of any contracting party imported into the territory of any other contracting party shall not be subject, directly or indirectly, to internal taxes or other internal charges of any kind in excess of those applied, directly or indirectly, to like domestic products. Moreover, no contracting party shall otherwise apply internal taxes or other internal charges to imported or domestic products in a manner contrary to the principles set forth in paragraph 1.

* * *

Article IV Special Provisions relating to Cinematograph Films

If any contracting party establishes or maintains internal quantitative regulations relating to exposed cinematograph films, such regulations shall take the form of screen quotas which shall conform to the following requirements:

(a) Screen quotas may require the exhibition of cinematograph films of national origin during a specified minimum proportion of the total screen time actually utilized, over a specified period of not less than one year, in the commercial exhibition of all films of whatever origin, and shall be computed on the basis of screen time per theatre per year or the equivalent thereof;

(b) With the exception of screen time reserved for films of national origin under a screen quota, screen time including that released by administrative action from screen time reserved for films of national origin, shall not be allocated formally or in effect among sources of supply;

(c) Notwithstanding the provisions of sub-paragraph (b) of this Article, any contracting party may maintain screen quotas conforming to the requirements of sub-paragraph (a) of this Article which reserve a minimum proportion of screen time for films of a specified origin other than that of the contracting party imposing such screen quotas; *Provided* that no such minimum proportion of screentime shall be increased above the level in effect on April 10, 1947;

(d) Screen quotas shall be subject to negotiation for their limitation, liberalization or elimination.

Article V Freedom of Transit

1. Goods (including baggage), and also vessels and other means of transport, shall be deemed to be in transit across the territory of a contracting party when the passage across such territory, with or without trans-shipment, warehousing, breaking bulk, or change in the mode of transport, is only a portion of a complete journey beginning and terminating beyond the frontier of the contracting party across whose territory the traffic passes. Traffic of this nature is termed in this Article "traffic in transit".

2. There shall be freedom of transit through the territory of each contracting party, via the routes most convenient for international transit, for traffic in transit to or from the territory of other contracting parties. No distinction shall be made which is based on the flag of vessels, the place of origin, departure, entry, exit, or destination, or on any circumstances relating to the ownership of goods, of vessels or of other means of transport.

* * *

Article XVIII Governmental Assistance to Economic Development

1. The contracting parties recognize that the attainment of the objectives of this Agreement will be facilitated by the progressive development of their economies, particularly of those contracting parties the economies of which can only support low standards of living and are in the early stages of development.

2. The contracting parties recognize further that it may be necessary for those contracting parties, in order to implement programmes and policies of economic development designed to raise the general standard of living of their people, to take

protective or other measures affecting imports, and that such measures are justified in so far as they facilitate the attainment of the objectives of this Agreement. They agree, therefore, that those contracting parties should enjoy additional facilities to enable them (a) to maintain sufficient flexibility in their tariff structure to be able to grant the tariff protection required for the establishment of a particular industry and (b) to apply quantitative restrictions for balance of payments purposes in a manner which takes full account of the continued high level of demand for imports likely to be generated by their programmes of economic development.

*   *   *

Article XX General Exceptions

Subject to the requirement that such measures are not applied in a manner which would constitute a means of arbitrary or unjustifiable discrimination between countries where the same conditions prevail, or a disguised restriction on international trade, nothing in this Agreement shall be construed to prevent the adoption or enforcement by any contracting party of measures:

(a) necessary to protect public morals;
(b) necessary to protect human, animal or plant life or health;
(c) relating to the importation or exportation of gold or silver;
(d) necessary to secure compliance with laws or regulations which are not inconsistent with the provisions of this Agreement, including those relating to customs enforcement, the enforcement of monopolies operated under paragraph 4 of Article II and Article XVII, the protection of patents, trade marks and copyrights, and the prevention of deceptive practices;
(e) relating to the products of prison labour;
(f) imposed for the protection of national treasures of artistic, historic or archaeological value;
(g) relating to the conservation of exhaustible natural resources if such measures are made effective in conjunction with restrictions on domestic production or consumption;
(h) undertaken in pursuance of obligations under any intergovernmental commodity agreement which conforms to criteria submitted to the *Contracting parties* and not disapproved by them or which is itself so submitted and not so disapproved;
(i) involving restrictions on exports of domestic materials necessary to ensure essential quantities of such materials to a domestic processing industry during periods when the domestic price of such materials is held below the world price as part of a governmental stabilization plan; *Provided* that such restrictions shall not operate to increase the exports of or the protection afforded to such domestic industry, and shall not depart from the provisions of this Agreement relating to non-discrimination;
(j) essential to the acquisition or distribution of products in general or local short supply; *Provided* that any such measures shall be consistent with the principle that all contracting parties are entitled to an equitable share of the international supply of such products, and that any such measures, which are inconsistent with the other provisions of this Agreement shall be discontinued as soon as the conditions giving rise to them have ceased to exist. The *Contracting parties* shall review the need for this sub-paragraph not later than 30 June 1960.

*   *   *

Part IV Trade and Development

Article XXXVI Principles and Objectives

1. The contracting parties,

(a) recalling that the basic objectives of this Agreement include the raising of standards of living and the progressive development of the economies of all contracting parties, and considering that the attainment of these objectives is particularly urgent for less-developed contracting parties;

(b) considering that export earnings of the less-developed contracting parties can play a vital part in their economic development and that the extent of this contribution depends on the prices paid by the less-developed contracting parties for essential imports, the volume of their exports, and the prices received for these exports;

(c) noting, that there is a wide gap between standards of living in less-developed countries and in other countries;

(d) recognizing that individual and joint action is essential to further the development of the economies of less-developed contracting parties and to bring about a rapid advance in the standards of living in these countries;

(e) recognizing that international trade as a means of achieving economic and social advancement should be governed by such rules and procedures – and measures in conformity with such rules and procedures – as are consistent with the objectives set forth in this Article;

(f) noting that the *Contracting Parties* may enable less-developed contracting parties to use special measures to promote their trade and development;

agree as follows.

2. There is need for a rapid and sustained expansion of the export earnings of the less-developed contracting parties.

3. There is need for positive efforts designed to ensure that less-developed contracting parties secure a share in the growth in international trade commensurate with the needs of their economic development.

* * *

TREATY ESTABLISHING
THE EUROPEAN ECONOMIC COMMUNITY, ROME, 1957

PART ONE PRINCIPLES

Article 1

By this Treaty, the High Contracting Parties establish among themselves a EUROPEAN ECONOMIC COMMUNITY.

Article 2

The Community shall have as its task, by establishing a common market and progressively approximating the economic policies of Member States, to promote throughout the Community a harmonious development of economic activities, a continuous and balanced expansion, an increase in stability, an accelerated raising of the standard of living and closer relations between the States belonging to it.

Article 3

For the purposes set out in Article 2, the activities of the Community shall include, as provided in this Treaty and in accordance with the timetable set out therein

(a) the elimination, as between Member States, of customs duties and of quantitative restrictions on the import and export of goods, and of all other measures having equivalent effect;

(b) the establishment of a common customs tariff and of a common commercial policy towards third countries;

(c) the abolition, as between Member States, of obstacles to freedom of movement for persons, services and capital;

(*d*) the adoption of a common policy in the sphere of agriculture;

(*e*) the adoption of a common policy in the sphere of transport;

(*f*) the institution of a system ensuring that competition in the common market is not distorted;

(*g*) the application of procedures by which the economic policies of Member States can be coordinated and disequilibria in their balances of payments remedied;

(*h*) the approximation of the laws of Member States to the extent required for the proper functioning of the common market;

(*i*) the creation of a European Social Fund in order to improve employment opportunities for workers and to contribute to the raising of their standard of living;

(*j*) the establishment of a European Investment Bank to facilitate the economic expansion of the Community by opening up fresh resources;

(*k*) the association of the overseas countries and territories in order to increase trade and to promote jointly economic and social development.

Article 4

1. The tasks entrusted to the Community shall be carried out by the following institutions:

an Assembly,
a Council,
a Commission,
a Court of Justice.

Each institution shall act within the limits of the powers conferred upon it by this Treaty.

2. The Council and the Commission shall be assisted by an Economic and Social Committee acting in an advisory capacity.

3. The audit shall be carried out by a Court of Auditors acting within the limits of the powers conferred upon it by this Treaty.

Article 5

Member States shall take all appropriate measures, whether general or particular, to ensure fulfilment of the obligations arising out of this Treaty or resulting from action taken by the institutions of the Community. They shall facilitate the achievement of the Community's tasks.

They shall abstain from any measure which could jeopardise the attainment of the objectives of this Treaty.

Article 6

1. Member States shall, in close cooperation with the institutions of the Community, coordinate their respective economic policies to the extent necessary to attain the objectives of this Treaty.

2. The institutions of the Community shall take care not to prejudice the internal and external financial stability of the Member States.

Article 7

Within the scope of application of this Treaty, and without prejudice to any special provisions contained therein, any discrimination on grounds of nationality shall be prohibited.

The Council may, on a proposal from the Commission and after consulting the Assembly, adopt, by a qualified majority, rules designed to prohibit such discrimination.

*   *   *

PART TWO FOUNDATIONS OF THE COMMUNITY

Title I Free movement of goods

Article 9

1. The Community shall be based upon a customs union which shall cover all trade in goods and which shall involve the prohibition between Member States of customs duties on imports and exports and of all charges having equivalent effect, and the adoption of a common customs tariff in their relations with third countries.

2. The provisions of Chapter 1, Section 1, and of Chapter 2 of this Title shall apply to products originating in Member States and to products coming from third countries which are in free circulation in Member States.

* * *

Chapter 1 The Customs Union

Section 1 Elimination of customs duties between Member States

Article 12

Member States shall refrain from introducing between themselves any new customs duties on imports or exports or any charges having equivalent effect, and from increasing those which they already apply in their trade with each other.

* * *

Section 2 Setting up of the common customs tariff

Article 18

The Member States declare their readiness to contribute to the development of international trade and the lowering of barriers to trade by entering into agreement designed, on a basis of reciprocity and mutual advantage, to reduce customs duties below the general level of which they could avail themselves as a result of the establishment of a customs union between them.

* * *

Chapter 2 Elimination of Quantitative Restrictions Between Member States

Article 30

Quantitative restrictions on imports and all measures having equivalent effect shall, without prejudice to the following provisions, be prohibited between Member States.

* * *

Article 36

The provisions of Articles 30 to 34 shall not preclude prohibitions or restrictions on imports, exports or goods in transit justified on grounds of public morality, public policy or public security; the protection of health and life of humans, animals or plants; the protection of national treasures possessing artistic, historic or archaeological value; or the protection of industrial and commercial property. Such prohibitions or restrictions shall not, however, constitute a means of arbitrary discrimination or a disguised restriction on trade between Member States.

Article 37

1. Member States shall progressively adjust any State monopolies of a commercial character so as to ensure that when the transitional period has ended no discrimination regarding the conditions under which goods are procured and marketed exists between nationals of Member States.

The provisions of this Article shall apply to any body through which a Member State, in law or in fact, either directly or indirectly supervises, determines or appreciably influences imports or exports between Member States. These provisions shall likewise apply to monopolies delegated by the States to others.

* * *

Title III Freedom of Movement of Persons, Services and Capital

Chapter 1 Workers

Article 48

1. Freedom of movement for workers shall be secured within the Community by the end of the transitional period at the latest.

2. Such freedom of movement shall entail the abolition of any discrimination based on nationality between workers of the Member States as regards employment, remuneration and other conditions of work and employment.

3. It shall entail the right, subject to limitations justified on grounds of public policy, public security or public health:

(a) to accept offers of employment actually made;
(b) to move freely within the territory of Member States for this purpose;
(c) to stay in a Member State for the purpose of employment in accordance with the provisions governing the employment of nationals of that State laid down by law, regulation or administrative action;
(d) to remain in the territory of a Member State after having been employed in that State, subject to conditions which shall be embodied in implementing regulations to be drawn up by the Commission.

4. The provisions of this Article shall not apply to employment in the public service.

* * *

Chapter 2 Right of Establishment

Article 52

Within the framework of the provisions set out below, restrictions on the freedom of establishment of nationals of a Member State in the territory of another Member State shall be abolished by progressive stages in the course of the transitional period. Such progressive abolition shall also apply to restrictions on the setting up of agencies, branches or subsidiaries by nationals of any Member States established in the territory of any Member State.

Freedom of establishment shall include the right to take up and pursue activities as self-employed persons and to set up and manage undertakings, in particular companies or firms within the meaning of the second paragraph of Article 58, under the conditions laid down for its own nationals by the law of the country where such establishment is effected, subject to the provisions of the Chapter relating to capital.

* * *

Chapter 3 Services

Article 59

Within the framework of the provisions set out below, restrictions on freedom to provide services within the Community shall be progressively abolished during the transitional period in respect of nationals of Member States who are established in a State of the Community other than that of the person for whom the services are intended.

The Council may, acting unanimously on a proposal from the Commission, extend the provisions of this Chapter to nationals of a third country who provide services and who are established within the Community.

Article 60

Services shall be considered to be "services" within the meaning of this Treaty where they are normally provided for remuneration, in so far as they are not governed by the provisions relating to freedom of movement of goods, capital and persons.

"Services" shall in particular include:
(a) activities of an industrial character;
(b) activities of a commercial character;
(c) activities of craftsmen;
(d) activities of the professions.

Without prejudice to the provisions of the Chapter relating to the right of establishment, the person providing a service may, in order to do so, temporarily pursue his activity in the State where the service is provided, under the same conditions as are imposed by that State on its own nationals.

*   *   *

PART THREE   POLICY OF THE COMMUNITY

Title I Common Rules

Chapter 1 Rules on competition

Section 1 Rules applying to undertakings

Article 85

1. The following shall be prohibited as incompatible with the common market: all agreements between undertakings, decisions by associations of undertakings and concerted practices which may affect trade between Member States and which have as their object or effect the prevention, restriction or distortion of competition within the common market, and in particular those which:
(a) directly or indirectly fix purchase or selling prices or any other trading conditions;
(b) limit or control production, markets, technical development, or investment;
(c) share markets or courses of supply;
(d) apply dissimilar conditions to equivalent transactions with other trading parties, thereby placing them at a competitive disadvantage;
(e) make the conclusion of contracts subject to acceptance by the other parties of supplementary obligations which, by their nature or according to commercial usage, have no connection with the subject of such contracts.

*   *   *

Section 3 Aids granted by States

Article 92

1. Save as otherwise provided in this Treaty, any aid granted by a Member State or through State resources in any form whatsoever which distorts or threatens to distort competition by favouring certain undertakings or the production of certain goods shall, in so far as it affects trade between Member States, be incompatible with the common market.

2. The following shall be compatible with the common market:

(a)   aid having a social character, granted to individual consumers, provided that such aid is granted without discrimination related to the origin of the products concerned;

(b)   aid to make good the damage caused by natural disasters or exceptional occurrences;

(c)   aid granted to the economy of certain areas of the Federal Republic of Germany affected by the division of Germany, in so far as such aid is required in order to compensate for the economic disadvantages caused by that division.

3. The following may be considered to be compatible with the common market:

(a)   aid to promote the economic development of areas where the standard of living is abnormally low or where there is serious under-employment;

(b)   aid to promote the execution of an important project of common European interest or to remedy a serious disturbance in the economy of a Member State;

(c)   aid to facilitate the development of certain economic activities or of certain economic areas, where such aid does not adversely affect trading conditions to an extent contrary to the common interest. However, the aids granted to ship-building as of 1 January 1957 shall, in so far as they serve only to compensate for the absence of customs protection, be progressively reduced under the same conditions as apply to the elimination of customs duties, subject to the provisons of the Treaty concerning common commercial policy towards third countries;

(d)   such other categories of aid as may be specified by decision of the Council acting by a qualified majority on a proposal from the Commission.

*   *   *

Title II Economic Policy

Chapter 3 Commercial Policy

Article 110

By establishing a customs union between themselves Member States aim to contribute, in the common interest, to the harmonious development of world trade, the progressive abolition of restrictions on international trade and the lowering of customs barriers.

The common commercial policy shall take into account the favourable effect which the abolition of customs duties between Member States may have on the increase in the competitive strength of undertakings in those States.

*   *   *

Title III Social Policy

Chapter 1 Social Provisions

Article 117

Member States agree upon the need to promote improved working conditions and an improved standard of living for workers, so as to make possible their harmonisation while the improvement is being maintained.

They believe that such a development will ensue not only from the functioning of the common market, which will favour the harmonisation of social systems, but also from the procedures provided for in this Treaty and from the approximation of provisions laid down by law, regulation or administrative action.

* * *

CONVENTION ESTABLISHING A CUSTOMS CO-OPERATION COUNCIL

Brussels, December 15, 1950

The Governments signatory to the present Convention,

Considering it advisable to secure the highest degree of harmony and uniformity in their customs systems and especially to study the problems inherent in the development and improvement of customs techniques and customs legislation in connexion therewith.

Convinced that it will be in the interests of international trade to promote co-operation between Governments in these matters, bearing in mind the economic and technical factors involved therein.

Have agreed as follows:

Article I

A Customs Co-operation Council (hereinafter referred to as "the Council") is hereby set up.

Article II

(a) The Members of the Council shall be –
    i. the Contracting Parties to the present Convention;
    ii. the Government of any separate customs territory which is proposed by a Contracting Party having responsibility for the formal conduct of its diplomatic relations, which is autonomous in the conduct of its external commercial relations and whose admission as a separate Member is approved by the Council.

(b) Any Government of a separate customs territory, which is a Member of the Council under paragraph (a)(ii) above, shall cease to be a Member on notification to the Council of the withdrawal of its membership by the Contracting Party having responsibility for the formal conduct of its diplomatic relations.

(c) Each Member shall nominate one delegate and one or more alternates to be its representatives on the Council. These representatives may be assisted by advisers.

(d) The Council may admit representatives of non-member Governments or of international organizations in the capacity of observers.

Article III

The functions of the Council shall be –

(a) to study all questions relating to co-operation in customs matters which the Contracting Parties agree to promote in conformity with the general purposes of the present Convention;

(b) to examine the technical aspects, as well as the economic facts related thereto, of customs systems with a view to proposing to Member States practical means of attaining the highest possible degree of harmony and uniformity;

(c) to prepare draft Conventions and amendments to Conventions, to recommend their adoption by interested Governments:

(d)   to make recommendations to ensure the uniform interpretation and application of the Conventions concluded as a result of its work as well as those concerning the Nomenclature for the Classification of Goods in Customs Tariffs and the Valuation of Goods for Customs Purposes prepared by the European Customs Union Study Group and, to this end, to perform such functions as may be expressly assigned to it in these Conventions in accordance with the provisions thereof;

(e)   to make recommendations, in a conciliatory capacity, for the settlement of disputes concerning the interpretation or application of the Conventions referred to in paragraph (d) above in accordance with the provisions of those Conventions; the parties in dispute may agree in advance to accept the recommendations of the Council as binding;

(f)   to ensure the circulation of information regarding customs regulations and procedures;

(g)   on its own initiative or on request, to furnish to interested Governments information or advice on customs matters within the general purposes of the present Convention and to make recommendations thereon;

(h)   to co-operate with other intergovernmental organizations as regards matters within its competence.

Article IV

The Members of the Council shall supply to the Council any information and documentation requested by it which is necessary for the execution of its functions provided that no Member shall be required to divulge confidential information, the disclosure of which would impede the enforcement of its laws, or which would otherwise be contrary to the public interest or prejudice the legitimate commercial interests of any enterprise, public or private.

Article V

The Council shall be assisted by a Permanent Technical Committee and a General Secretariat.

Article VI

(a)   The Council shall elect annually, from among the delegates of Members, a Chairman and not less than two Vice-Chairmen.

(b)   It shall establish its own Rules of Procedure by a majority of no less than two-thirds of its Members.

(c)   It shall establish a Nomenclature Committee as provided in the Convention on Nomenclature for the Classification of Goods in Customs Tariffs and a Valuation Committee as provided in the Convention on the Valuation of Goods for Customs Purposes. It shall also establish such other committees as may be desirable for the purposes of the Conventions referred to in Article III(d) or for any other purpose within its competence.

(d)   It shall determine the tasks to be assigned to the Permanent Technical Committee and the powers to be delegated to it.

(e)   It shall approve its annual budget, control its expenditure and give such directions as it may consider desirable regarding its finances to the General Secretariat.

*   *   *

PART NINE
CULTURE AND EDUCATION

The areas of culture and education are closely related to those of communications and information: agreements and rules in one of these areas will often include provisions related to those in the other areas.

The basic provisions in international law applicable to culture and to education are laid down in all major human rights instruments with regard to the right to culture and education. These standard-setting provisions have been supplemented by more specific international legal texts, most of which are of a non-binding character.

In the field of culture international agreements are mainly of two kinds
- general agreements providing for culture co-operation and measures in support of cultural development
- agreements of a more specific nature on such issues as the protection of cultural property and the preservation of cultural heritage, and the control of illicit traffic in cultural property.

In the field of education, international legal texts mainly deal with the principles and promotion of education.

In both areas the international instruments are supplemented by regional agreements and by numerous bilateral agreements.

Documents

1. Culture

United Nations
(a) Human Rights Instruments
  i. International Covenant on Economic, Social and Cultural Rights, 1966 (text included in Part One)
     - Article 15
  ii. International Convention on the Elimination of All Forms of Racial Discrimination, 1966 (text included in Part One)
     - Preamble, Articles 5, 7
  iii. Universal Declaration of Human Rights, 1948 (text included in Part One)
     - Article 27
(b) Other texts
  iv. Preservation and further development of cultural values
     General Assembly Resolution 3148 (XXVIII), 1973
     - Full text

UNESCO
  v. Constitution of Unesco (text included in Part One)
     - Preamble, Article 1
  vi. Convention for the Protection of the World Cultural and Natural Heritage, 1972
     - Preamble, Articles 1–7, 27–28

vii. Declaration of the Principles of International Cultural Co-operation
      General Conference Resolution, 8.1, 1966
      − Full Text
viii. Culture and Communication
      General Conference Resolution 4/0.1, 1978
      − Parts I, II
 ix. *See also* the conventions for the protection of cultural property spon-
      sored by Unesco (not included):
      − Convention for the Protection of Cultural Property in the Event of
         Armed Conflict and additional Protocol, 1954
      − Convention on the Means of Prohibiting and Preventing the Illicit
         Import, Export and Transfer of Ownership of Cultural Property,
         1970

Regional Agreements
The following instruments are mentioned as examples, the texts are not in-
cluded
− Cultural Treaty between the Arab League States, Cairo, 1954
− Convention for the Promotion of Inter-American Cultural Relations,
   Caracas, 1954
− European Cultural Convention, Council of Europe, Paris, 1954
− Arab Cultural Unity Agreement, Baghdad, 1964
− Nordic Agreement for Cultural Co-operation, Helsinki, 1971

2. Education

(a) Human Rights Instruments
   i. International Covenant on Economic, Social and Cultural Rights,
      1966 (text included in Part One)
      − Articles 13, 14
  ii. International Convention on the Elimination of All Forms of Racial
      Discrimination, 1966 (text included in Part One)
      − Articles 5, 7
 iii. Universal Declaration of Human Rights, 1948 (text included in Part
      One)
      − Article 26
  iv. Declaration of the Rights of the Child (text included in Part One)
      − Article 7
(b) Unesco-sponsored Instruments
   v. Convention against Discrimination in Education, 1960
      − Full text
  vi. Recommendation concerning Education for International Under-
      standing Co-operation and Peace and Education relating to Human
      Rights and Fundamental Freedoms
      General Conference Resolution 3.8, 1974
      − Preamble
      − Parts I–III
 vii. Education
      General Conference Resolution 1/0.1, 1978
      − Full text

PRESERVATION AND FURTHER DEVELOPMENT OF CULTURAL VALUES

United Nations General Assembly Resolution 3148 (XXVIII), 1973

The General Assembly,
Recalling its resolution 3026 A (XXVII) of 18 December 1972,
Noting the existence in numerous countries of legislation for the protection of the artistic and cultural heritage,
Taking note with appreciation of the report of the Director-General of the United Nations Educational, Scientific and Cultural Organization on the subject of the preservation and further development of cultural values,
Considering that the preservation of national culture should not lead to a division of the world through the withdrawal of various cultures into themselves,
Affirming the sovereign right of each State to formulate and implement, in accordance with its own conditions and national requirements, the policies and measures conducive to the enhancement of its cultural values and national heritage,
Recognizing that the uniqueness of each culture derives from a multiplicity of influences operating in an extended time-scale,
Considering that the value and dignity of each culture as well as the ability to preserve and develop its distinctive character is a basic right of all countries and peoples,
Taking into account the rapid development of the mass media as one of the most important means of diffusion of scientific and technological progress and the increasing role of the mass media in the cultural and moral life of society,
Convinced that, on the one hand, intensified efforts must be made to prevent the misuse or abuse of scientific and technological developments, which endangers the distinctive character of all cultures, and that, on the other hand, all necessary steps have to be taken toward the preservation, enrichment and further development of national cultures and ways of life,
Convinced further that the preservation, renewal and continous creation of cultural values should be not a static but a dynamic concept, linking the cultural heritage of nations with the present and future programmes of national development,

1. *Urges* Governments to make cultural values, both material and spiritual, an integral part of development efforts by giving attention in particular to the following:

   (a) The fullest possible access of all people to places, buildings, facilities and institutions which serve as media of cultural transmission and form a system of ideas promoting national culture;

   (b) The preservation and/or restoration of sites of special historical importance;

   (c) Involvement of the population in the elaboration and implementation of measures ensuring preservation and further development of cultural and moral values;

   (d) Wide education and information activity with a view to:

      i. Encouraging civic responsibility for the cultural heritage to enable every individual to absorb and use cultural values, both material and spiritual, as a means of advancement and development of his personality;

      ii. Making the public aware of the social and aesthetic significance of the cultural environment;

      iii. Enhancing and developing living values through free creative activity;

   (e) The identification, preservation and development of the varied cultural values of each region in order to maintain and make the widest possible use of local aspirations in the implementation of developmental plans, especially as regards the improvement of living conditions and the general quality of life;

2. *Recognizes* that contacts and exchanges among various cultures, conducted on the basis of equality and with due regard to the principle of sovereignty of States, may

positively contribute to the enrichment and development of national cultures and regional cultural values;

3. *Appeals* to all Member States to respect national legislation for the protection of the artistic heritage;

4. *Requests* the Director-General of the United Nations Educational, Scientific and Cultural Organization, in co-operation with Member States, to study all the legal implications flowing from the existence of legislation for the protection of the national artistic heritage, including problems of exchange and the voluntary return of various cultural works;

5. *Recommends* that the Director-General of the United Nations Educational, Scientific and Cultural Organization, taking due account of the work already done, should initiate, within the existing facilities at his disposal, the preparation of an interdisciplinary programme of research in education, mass communication and developmental planning, designed to preserve and further develop and promote wider knowledge of distinctive cultural values in this era of accelerated scientific and technological development, and, in particular, should:

(a) Assemble information on the above-mentioned problems in various social and cultural contexts;

(b) Promote the international exchange of information concerning the development and application of methods now employed by States for the preservation and further development of cultural values;

(c) Analyse the role of the mass media in the preservation and further development of cultural values, in particular with respect to integration of the mass media into national cultural policies;

6. *Requests* the Director-General of the United Nations Educational, Scientific and Cultural Organization to report to the General Assembly at its thirty-first session on the progress made in the implementation of the present resolution;

7. *Decides* to include in the provisional agenda of its thirty-first session an item entitled "Preservation and further development of cultural values".

CONVENTION FOR THE PROTECTION OF THE WORLD CULTURAL AND NATURAL HERITAGE, 1972

The General Conference of the United Nations Educational, Scientific and Cultural Organization meeting in Paris from 17 October to 21 November 1972, at its seventeenth session,

Noting that the cultural heritage and the natural heritage are increasingly threatened with destruction not only by the traditional causes of decay, but also by changing social and economic conditions which aggravate the situation with even more formidable phenomena of damage or destruction,

Considering that deterioration or disappearance of any item of the cultural or natural heritage constitutes a harmful impoverishment of the heritage of all the nations of the world,

Considering that protection of this heritage at the national level often remains incomplete because of the scale of the resources which it requires and of the insufficient economic, scientific and technical resources of the country where the property to be protected is situated,

Recalling that the Constitution of the Organization provides that it will maintain, increase and diffuse knowledge, by assuring the conservation and protection of the world's heritage, and recommending to the nations concerned the necessary international conventions,

Considering that the existing international conventions, recommendations and resolutions concerning cultural and natural property demonstrate the importance, for all the peoples of the world, of safeguarding this unique and irreplaceable property, to whatever people it may belong,

Considering that parts of the cultural or natural heritage are of outstanding interest and therefore need to be preserved as part of the world heritage of mankind as a whole,

Considering that, in view of the magnitude and gravity of the new dangers threatening them, it is incumbent on the international community as a whole to participate in the protection of the cultural and natural heritage of outstanding universal value, by the granting of collective assistance which, although not taking the place of action by the State concerned, will serve as an effective complement thereto,

Considering that it is essential for this purpose to adopt new provisions in the form of a convention establishing an effective system of collective protection of the cultural and natural heritage of outstanding universal value, organized on a permanent basis and in accordance with modern scientific methods,

Having decided, at its sixteenth session, that this question should be made the subject of an international convention,

Adopts this sixteenth day of November 1972 this Convention.

I. Definitions of the Cultural and the Natural Heritage

Article 1

For the purposes of this Convention, the following shall be considered as 'cultural heritage': Monuments: architectural works, works of monumental sculpture and painting, elements or structures of an archaeological nature, inscriptions, cave dwellings and combinations of features, which are of outstanding universal value from the point of view of history, art or science;

Groups of buildings: groups of separate or connected buildings which, because of their architecture, their homogeneity or their place in the landscape, are of outstanding universal value from the point of view of history, art or science;

Sites: works of man or the combined works of nature and of man, and areas including archaeological sites which are of outstanding universal value from the historical, aesthetic, ethnological or anthropological points of view.

Article 2

For the purposes of this Convention, the following shall be considered as 'natural heritage': Natural features consisting of physical and biological formations or groups of such formations, which are of outstanding universal value from the aesthetic or scientific point of view;

Geological and physiographical formations and precisely delineated areas which constitute the habitat of threatened species of animals and plants of outstanding universal value from the point of view of science or conservation;

Natural sites or precisely delineated natural areas of outstanding universal value from the point of view of science, conservation or natural beauty.

Article 3

It is for each State Party to this Convention to identify and delineate the different properties situated on its territory mentioned in Article 1 and 2 above.

II. National Protection and International Protection of the Cultural and Natural Heritage

Article 4

Each State Party to this Convention recognizes that the duty of ensuring the identification, protection, conservation, presentation and transmission to future generations of the cultural and natural heritage referred to in Articles 1 and 2 and situated on its territory, belongs primarily to that State. It will do all it can to this end, to the utmost of its own resources and, where appropriate, with any international assistance and co-operation, in particular, financial, artistic, scientific and technical, which it may be able to obtain.

Article 5

To ensure that effective and active measures are taken for the protection, conservation and presentation of the cultural and natural heritage situated on its territory, each State Party to this Convention shall endeavour, in so far as possible and as appropriate for each country:

(a)   to adopt a general policy which aims to give the cultural and natural heritage a function in the life of the community and to integrate the protection of that heritage into comprehensive planning programmes;

(b)   to set up within its territories, where such services do not exist, one or more services for the protection, conservation and presentation of the cultural and natural heritage with an appropriate staff and possessing the means to discharge their functions;

(c)   to develop scientific and technical studies and research and to work out such operating methods as will make the State capable of counteracting the dangers that threaten its cultural or natural heritage;

(d)   to take the appropriate legal, scientific, technical, administrative and financial measures necessary for the identification, protection, conservation, presentation and rehabilitation of this heritage; and

(e)   to foster the establishment or development of national or regional centres for training in the protection, conservation and presentation of the cultural and natural heritage and to encourage scientific research in this field.

Article 6

1. Whilst fully respecting the sovereignty of the States on whose territory the cultural and natural heritage mentioned in Articles 1 and 2 is situated, and without prejudice to property rights provided by national legislation, the States Parties to this Convention recognize that such heritage constitutes a world heritage for whose protection it is the duty of the international community as a whole to co-operate.

2. The States Parties undertake, in accordance with the provisions of this Convention, to give their help in the identification, protection, conservation and preservation of the cultural and natural heritage referred to in paragraphs 2 and 4 of Article 11 if the States on whose territory it is situated so request.

3. Each State Party to this Convention undertakes not to take any deliberate measures which might damage directly or indirectly the cultural and natural heritage referred to in Articles 1 and 2 situated on the territory of other States to this Convention.

Article 7

For the purpose of this Convention, international protection of the world cultural and natural heritage shall be understood to mean the establishment of a system of international co-operation and assistance designed to support States Parties to the Convention in their efforts to conserve and identify that heritage.

*   *   *

Article 27

1. The States Parties to this Convention shall endeavour by all appropriate means,

and in particular by educational and information programmes, to strengthen appreciation and respect by their peoples of the cultural and natural heritage defined in Articles 1 and 2 of the Convention.

2. They shall undertake to keep the public broadly informed of the dangers threatening this heritage and of activities carried on in pursuance of this Convention.

Article 28

States Parties to this Convention which receive international assistance under the Convention shall take appropriate measures to make known the importance of the property for which assistance has been received and the role played by such assistance.

* * *

DECLARATION OF THE PRINCIPLES OF
INTERNATIONAL CULTURAL CO-OPERATION

Unesco General Conference Resolution 8.1, 1966

The General Conference of the United Nations Educational, Scientific and Cultural Organization met in Paris for its fourteenth session, this fourth day of November 1966 being the twentieth anniversary of the foundation of the Organization,

Recalling that the Constitution of the Organization declares that 'since wars begin in the minds of men, it is in the minds of men that the defences of peace must be constructed' and that peace must be founded, if it is not to fail, upon the intellectual and moral solidarity of mankind,

Recalling that the Constitution also states that the wide diffusion of culture and the education of humanity for justice and liberty and peace are indispensable to the dignity of man and constitute a sacred duty which all the nations must fulfil in a spirit of mutual assistance and concern,

Considering that the Organization's Member States, believing in the pursuit of truth and the free exchange of ideas and knowledge, have agreed and determined to develop and to increase the means of communication between their peoples,

Considering that, despite the technical advances which facilitate the development and dissemination of knowledge and ideas, ignorance of the way of life and customs of peoples still presents an obstacle to friendship among the nations, to peaceful co-operation and to the progress of mankind,

Taking account of the Universal Declaration of Human Rights, the Declaration of the Rights of the Child, the Declaration of the Granting of Independence to Colonial Countries and Peoples, the United Nations Declaration on the Elimination of all Forms of Racial Discrimination, the Declaration on the Promotion among Youth of the Ideals of Peace, Mutual Respect and Understanding between Peoples, and the Declaration on the Inadmissibility of Intervention in the Domestic Affairs of States and the Protection of their Independence and Sovereignty, proclaimed successively by the General Assembly of the United Nations,

Convinced by the experience of the Organization's first twenty years that, if international cultural co-operation is to be strengthened, its principles require to be affirmed,

Proclaims this Declaration of the principles of international cultural co-operation, to the end that governments, authorities, organizations, associations and institutions responsible for cultural activities may constantly be guided by these principles; and for the purpose, as set out in the Constitution of the Organization, of advancing, through the educational, scientific and cultural relations of the peoples of the world, the objectives of peace and welfare that are defined in the Charter of the United Nations:

Article I

1. Each culture has a dignity and value which must be respected and preserved.

2. Every people has the right and the duty to develop its culture.

3. In their rich variety and diversity, and in the reciprocal influences they exert on one another, all cultures form part of the common heritage belonging to all mankind.

Article II

Nations shall endeavour to develop the various branches of culture side by side and, as far as possible, simultaneously, so as to establish a harmonious balance between technical progress and the intellectual and moral advancement of mankind.

Article III

International cultural co-operation shall cover all aspects of intellectual and creative activities relating to education, science and culture.

Article IV

The aims of international cultural co-operation in its various forms, bilateral or multilateral, regional or universal, shall be:

1. To spread knowledge, to stimulate talent and to enrich cultures;

2. To develop peaceful relations and friendship among the peoples and bring about a better understanding of each other's way of life;

3. To contribute to the application of the principles set out in the United Nations Declarations that are recalled in the Preamble to this Declaration;

4. To enable everyone to have access to knowledge, to enjoy the arts and literature of all peoples, to share in advances made in science in all parts of the world and in the resulting benefits, and to contribute to the enrichment of cultural life;

5. To raise the level of the spiritual and material life of man in all parts of the world.

Article V

Cultural co-operation is a right and a duty for all peoples and all nations, which should share with one another their knowledge and skills.

Article VI

International co-operation, while promoting the enrichment of all cultures through its beneficent action, shall respect the distinctive character of each.

Article VII

1. Broad dissemination of ideas and knowledge, based on the freest exchange and discussion, is essential to creative activity, the pursuit of truth and the development of the personality.

2. In cultural co-operation, stress shall be laid on ideas and values conducive to the creation of a climate of friendship and peace. Any mark of hostility in attitudes and in expression of opinion shall be avoided. Every effort shall be made, in presenting and disseminating information, to ensure its authenticity.

Article VIII

Cultural co-operation shall be carried on for the mutual benefit of all the nations practising it. Exchanges to which it gives rise shall be arranged in a spirit of broad reciprocity.

Article IX

Cultural co-operation shall contribute to the establishment of stable, long-term relations between peoples, which should be subject as little as possible to the strains which may arise in international life.

Article X

Cultural co-operation shall be specially concerned with the moral and intellectual education of young people in a spirit of friendship, international understanding and peace and shall foster awareness among States of the need to stimulate talent and promote the training of the rising generations in the most varied sectors.

Article XI

1. In their cultural relations, States shall bear in mind the principles of the United Nations. In seeking to achieve international co-operation, they shall respect the sovereign equality of States and shall refrain from intervention in matters which are essentially within the domestic jurisdiction of any State.

2. The principles of this Declaration shall be applied with due regard for human rights and fundamental freedoms.

CULTURE AND COMMUNICATION

Unesco General Conference Resolution 4/0.1, 1978

The General Conference,

I

Aware of the crucial role of culture, which constitutes for every human being a foundation of his values and of his identity, just as it is the inspiration and life-blood of every human community, which gives it its identity, maintains its historical continuity and provides the basis for its future,

Also aware of the importance of communication, which is a component, medium and vector of culture and, in its widest sense, a fundamental dimension of the human condition and of the life of every society,

Considering that culture and communication are closely interrelated and that their complementarity must be borne in mind in any effort designed to achieve the self-fulfilment of individuals, the development of societies and the solidarity of mankind as a whole,

1. *Recommends* that the Director-General continue, during the 1979–1980 biennium, the action to ensure the unity of conception of the programme concerning culture and communication and to accentuate the convergence of activities designed to attain the objectives of that programme;

II

Considering that in culture, which encompasses the values inherent in thought artistic expression, traditions and ways of life, one finds combined a number of conditions necessary for the advancement of the individual and of the community,

Recalling that 'the right freely to participate in the cultural life of the community' is written into the Universal Declaration of Human Rights and that the dissemination of culture is one of the purposes which the Constitution of Unesco assigns to the Organization,

Recalling that according to the Declaration of the Principles of International

Cultural Co-operation, adopted by the General Conference of Unesco at its four-teenth session, 'each culture has a dignity and value which must be respected and preserved',

Recalling that the United Nations General Assembly has on three occasions, by resolution 3026 A(XXVII), 3148(XXVIII) and 31/39, asserted the importance of the work which Unesco is carrying out in increasing mankind's awareness of the need for concerted action in the preservation and further development of cultural values,

Considering that respect for and appreciation of cultural values and achievements, as expressions of the identity of diverse societies and as elements of the common heritage of mankind, should go hand in hand with the updating and enrichment, through artistic and intellectual creation, of forms, relations and signs and, more generally, of all that gives life to cultures,

Emphasizing that the assertion of cultural identity, far from calling for an inward-looking society, is, on the contrary, the basis for the mutual appreciation and understanding of cultures and that the universality of culture rests on the specificity and diversity of the contributions made by the various human communities,

Noting with satisfaction that it is now widely acknowledged that a development process implemented by a society in its own way should take account of cultural and historical factors, and in particular of the cultural prerequisites and consequences of transfers of technology and economic growth,

Reaffirming the dynamic role of cultural identity in man-centred development and the importance which the cultural dimension of development assumes in the con-text of the establishment of a new international economic order, the strengthening of peace and international understanding,

Stressing that culture, as an essential aspect of the development of individuals and communities, calls for the participation of individuals and communities, creative ar-tists and their public, and the active assistance of cultural and artistic institutions and associations, organizations and public or private foundations serving a social, cultural, educational or vocational purpose, and that it requires special attention from the State,

2. *Invites* the Director-General:

(a) to foster the growth of awareness in each individual and in each society of the specific values of its culture, thereby strengthening those feelings of respect and appreciation for cultural identity which are essential features of the process of man-centred development;

(b) to seek to highlight the points where cultures meet and converge, so as to reveal their affinities more clearly and to develop their mutual relations for the ad-vancement of the various societies;

(c) to encourage the formulation, adoption and implementation of cultural policies which take account of the various factors involved in cultural development, regarded as an essential dimension of the overall development of societies;

(d) to ensure that the programme helps to foster wider access and participation in cultural life and the further development of intellectual and artistic creation, with special attention to be paid to the specific problems that may be en-countered in this connection by the least privileged sectors of the population;

(e) to help to safeguard and develop the cultural heritage of mankind by ensuring that activities carried out for that purpose are accompanied by measures, especially of an educational nature, which encourage public participation and are designed both to make that heritage an integral part of the life of the com-munity and, at the international level, a factor of understanding among dif-ferent cultures and societies;

*   *   *

CONVENTION AGAINST DISCRIMINATION IN EDUCATION, 1960

The General Conference of the United Nations Educational, Scientific and Cultural

Organization, meeting in Paris from 14 November to 15 December 1960, at its eleventh session,

Recalling that the Universal Declaration of Human Rights asserts the principle of non-discrimination and proclaims that every person has the right to education,

Considering that discrimination in education is a violation of rights enunciated in that declaration,

Considering that, under the terms of its constitution, the United Nations Educational, Scientific and Cultural Organization has the purpose of instituting collaboration among the nations with a view to furthering for all universal respect for human rights and equality of educational opportunity.

Recognizing that, consequently, the United Nations Educational, Scientific and Cultural Organization, while respecting the diversity of national educational systems, has the duty not only to proscribe any form of discrimination in education but also to promote equality of opportunity and treatment for all in education,

Having before it proposals concerning the different aspects of discrimination in education, constituting item 17.I.4 of the agenda of the session,

Having decided at its tenth session that this question should be made the subject of an international convention as well as of recommendations to Member States,

Adopts this convention on the fourteenth day of December 1960.

Article 1

For the purposes of this convention, the term 'discrimination' includes any distinction, exclusion, limitation or preference which, being based on race, colour, sex, language, religion, political or other opinion, national or social origin, economic condition or birth, has the purpose or effect of nullifying or impairing equality of treatment in education and in particular:

(a) Of depriving any person or group of persons of access to education of any type or at any level;

(b) Of limiting any person or group of persons to education of an inferior standard;

(c) Subject to the provisions of article 2 of this convention, of establishing or maintaining separate educational systems or institutions for persons or groups of persons; or

(d) Of inflicting on any person or group of persons conditions which are incompatible with the dignity of man.

For the purposes of this convention, the term 'education' refers to all types and levels of education, and includes access to education, the standards and quality of education, and the conditions under which it is given.

Article 2

When permitted in a State, the following situations shall not be deemed to constitute discrimination, within the meaning of article 1 of this convention:

(a) The establishment or maintenance of separate educational systems or institutions for pupils of the two sexes, if these systems or institutions offer equivalent access to education, provide a teaching staff with qualifications of the same standard as well as school premises and equipment of the same quality, and afford the opportunity to take the same or equivalent courses of study;

(b) The establishment or maintenance, for religious or linguistic reasons, of separate educational systems or institutions offering an education which is in keeping with the wishes of the pupils, parents or legal guardians, if participation in such systems and attendance at such institutions is optional and if the education provided conforms to such standards as may be laid down or approved by the competent authorities, in particular for education of the same level;

(c) The establishment or maintenance of private educational institutions, if the object of the institutions is not to secure the exclusion of any group but to provide educational facilities in addition to those provided by the public authorities, if the institutions are conducted in accordance with that object, and if the education provided conforms with such standards as may be laid down or approved by the competent authorities, in particular for education of the same level.

Article 3

In order to eliminate and prevent discrimination within the meaning of this convention, the States parties thereto undertake:

(a) To abrogate any statutory provisions and any administrative instructions and to discontinue any administrative practices which involve discrimination in education;

(b) To ensure, by legislation where necessary, that there is no discrimination in the admission of pupils to educational institutions

(c) Not to allow any differences of treatment by the public authorities between nationals, except on the basis of merit or need, in the matter of school fees and the grant of scholarships or other forms of assistance to pupils and necessary permits and facilities for the pursuit of studies in foreign countries;

(d) Not to allow, in any form of assistance granted by the public authorities to educational institutions, any restrictions or precedence based solely on the ground that pupils belong to a particular group;

(e) To give foreign nationals resident within their territory the same access to education as that given to their own nationals.

Article 4

The States parties to this convention undertake furthermore to formulate, develop and apply a national policy which, by methods appropriate to the circumstances and to national usage, will tend to promote equality of opportunity and of treatment in the matter of education and in particular:

(a) To make primary education free and compulsory; make secondary education in its different forms generally available and accessible to all; make higher education equally accessible to all on the basis of individual capacity; assure compliance by all with the obligation to attend school prescribed by law;

(b) To ensure that the standards of education are equivalent in all public educational institutions of the same level, and that the conditions relating to the quality of the education provided are also equivalent;

(c) To encourage and intensify by appropriate methods the education of persons who have not received any primary education or who have not completed the entire primary education course and the continuation of their education on the basis of individual capacity;

(d) To provide training for the teaching profession without discrimination.

Article 5

1. The States parties to this convention agree that:

(a) Education shall be directed to the full development of the human personality and to the strengthening of respect for human rights and fundamental freedoms; it shall promote understanding, tolerance and friendship among all nations, racial or religious groups, and shall futher the activities of the United Nations for the maintenance of peace;

(b) It is essential to respect the liberty of parents and, where applicable, of legal guardians, firstly to choose for their children institutions other than those maintained by the public authorities but conforming to such minimum education standards as may be laid down or approved by the competent authorities and, secondly, to ensure in a manner consistent with the procedures followed in the State for the application of its legislation, the religious and moral education of the children in conformity with their own convictions; and no person or group of persons should be compelled to receive religious instruction inconsistent with his or their conviction.

(c) It is essential to recognize the right of members of national minorities to carry on their own educational activities, including the maintenance of schools and, depending on the educational policy of each State, the use or the teaching of their own language, provided however:

    i. that this right is not exercised in a manner which prevents the members of these minorities from understanding the culture and language of the community as a whole and from participating in its activities, or which prejudices national sovereignty;

    ii. That the standard of education is not lower than the general standard laid down or approved by the competent authorities; and

    iii. That attendance at such schools is optional.

2. The States parties to this convention undertake to take all necessary measures to ensure the application of the principles enunciated in paragraph 1 of this article.

Article 6

In the application of this convention, the States parties to it undertake to pay the greatest attention to any recommendations hereafter adopted by the General Conference of the United Nations Educational, Scientific and Cultural Organization defining the measures to be taken against the different forms of discrimination in education and for the purpose of ensuring equality of opportunity and treatment in education.

RECOMMENDATION CONCERNING EDUCATION FOR INTERNATIONAL UNDERSTANDING, CO-OPERATION AND PEACE AND EDUCATION RELATING TO HUMAN RIGHTS AND FUNDAMENTAL FREEDOMS

Unesco General Conference Resolution 3.8, 1974

The General Conference of the United Nations Educational, Scientific and Cultural Organization, meeting in Paris from 17 October to 23 November 1974, at its eighteenth session,

Mindful of the responsibility incumbent on States to achieve through education the aims set forth in the Charter of the United Nations, the Constitution of Unesco, the Universal Declaration of Human Rights and the Geneva Conventions of the Protection of Victims of War of 12 August 1949, in order to promote international understanding, co-operation and peace and respect for human rights and fundamental freedoms,

Reaffirming the responsibility which is incumbent on Unesco to encourage and support in Member States any activity designed to ensure the education of all for the advancement of justice, freedom, human rights and peace,

Noting nevertheless that the activity of Unesco and of its Member States sometimes has an impact only on a small minority of the steadily growing numbers of school children, students, young people and adults continuing their education, and educators, and that the curricula and methods of international education are not always attuned to the needs and aspirations of the participating young people and adults,

Noting moreover that in a number of cases there is still a wide disparity between proclaimed ideals, declared intentions and the actual situation,

Having decided, at its seventeenth session, that this education should be the subject of a recommendation to Member States,

Adopts this nineteenth day of November 1974, the present recommendation,

The General Conference recommends that Member States should apply the following provisions by taking whatever legislative or other steps may be required in conformity with the constitutional practice of each State to give effect within their respective territories to the principles set forth in this recommendation.

The General Conference recommends that Member States bring this recommendation to the attention of the authorities, departments or bodies responsible for school education, higher education and out-of-school education, of the various organizations carrying out educational work among young people and adults such as student and youth movements, associations of pupils' parents, teachers' unions and other interested parties.

The General Conference recommends that Member States submit to it, by dates and in the form to be decided upon by the Conference, reports concerning the action taken by them in pursuance of this recommendation.

I. Significance of terms

1. For the purposes of this recommendation:

(a)   The word 'education' implies the entire process of social life by means of which individuals and social groups learn to develop consciously within, and for the benefit of, the national and international communities, the whole of their personal capacities, attitudes, aptitudes and knowledge. This process is not limited to any specific activities.

(b)   The terms 'international understanding', 'co-operation' and 'peace' are to be considered an indivisible whole based on the principle of friendly relations between peoples and States having different social and political systems and on the respect for human rights and fundamental freedoms. In the text of this recommendation, the different connotations of the terms are sometimes gathered together in a concise expression, 'international education'.

(c)   'Human rights' and 'fundamental freedoms' are those defined in the United Nations Charter, the Universal Declaration of Human Rights and the International Covenants on Economic, Social and Cultural Rights, and on Civil and Political Rights.

II. Scope

2. This recommendation applies to all stages and forms of education.

III. Guiding principles

3. Education should be infused with the aims and purposes set forth in the Charter of the United Nations, the Constitution of Unesco and the Universal Declaration of Human Rights, particularly Article 26, paragraph 2 of the last-named, which states 'Education shall be directed to the full development of the human personality and to the strengthening of respect for human rights and fundamental freedoms. It shall promote understanding, tolerance and friendship among all nations, racial or religious groups, and shall further the activities of the United Nations for the maintenance of peace.'

4. In order to enable every person to contribute actively to the fulfilment of the aims referred to in paragraph 3, and promote international solidarity and co-operation, which are necessary in solving the world problems affecting the individuals' and communities' life and exercise of fundamental rights and freedoms, the following objectives should be regarded as major guiding principles of educational policy:

(a)   an international dimension and a global perspective in education at all levels and in all its forms;

(b)   understanding and respect for all peoples, their cultures, civilizations, values and ways of life, including domestic ethnic cultures and cultures of other nations;

(c) awareness of the increasing global interdependence between peoples and nations;
(d) abilities to communicate with others;
(e) awareness not only of the rights but also of the duties incumbent upon individuals, social groups and nations towards each other;
(f) understanding of the necessity for international solidarity and co-operation;
(g) readiness on the part of the individual to participate in solving the problems of his community, his country, and the world at large;

5. Combining learning, training, information and action, international education should further the appropriate intellectual and emotional development of the individual. It should develop a sense of social responsibility and of solidarity with less privileged groups and should lead to observance of the principles of equality in everyday conduct. It should also help to develop qualities, aptitude and abilities which enable the individual to acquire a critical understanding of problems at the national and international level; to understand and explain facts, opinions and ideas; to work in a group; to accept and participate in free discussions; to observe the elementary rules of procedure applicable to any discussion; and to base value-judgements and decisions on a rational analysis of relevant facts and factors.

6. Education should stress the inadmissibility of recourse to war for purposes of expansion, aggression and domination, or to the use of force and violence for purposes of repression, and should bring every person to understand and assume his or her responsibilities for the maintenance of peace. It should contribute to international understanding and strengthening of world peace and to the activities in the struggle against colonialism and neo-colonialism in all their forms and manifestations, and against all forms and varieties of racialism, fascism, and apartheid as well as other ideologies which breed national and racial hatred and which are contrary to the purposes of this recommendation.

* * *

EDUCATION

Unesco General Conference Resolution 1/0.1, 1978

The General Conference,
Recalling the principles and the spirit of the Constitution and the successive resolutions adopted by the General Conference at its various sessions with a view to promoting equality of educational opportunity for all and enhancing the contribution of education to the advancement of knowledge and culture, national development, understanding and co-operation between peoples, peace, disarmament and the establishment of a new international economic order,

Considering that 'nowhere does Unesco's role as "shaper of the future" appear so clearly as in education' (resolution 9.,1 adopted by the General Conference at its eighteenth session),

Noting that the desire of each individual to participate fully in economic, social, cultural and political activities, the resulting increase in the demand for education, the acceleration socio-economic change in the world, the speed of scientific and technological progress and the application of science and technology to an ever wider variety of fields, confer upon education, for the benefit of mankind and with a view to social progress, a heightened role and increasingly extensive and varied responsibilities toward both societies and individuals, and make it essential that education should be accessible to peoples of all ages, categories and social groups,

Considering that, by the very complexity of the problems which it must help to solve, education should be conceived in an interdisciplinary context as a factor of multidimensional development of which man is both the end and the instrument,

Considering that, in accordance with the approach reflected in the Medium-Term Plan for 1977 the activities in the field of education should be combined with activities undertaken in science, technology, the social sciences, culture and communication,

Recalling the decisions concerning education adopted by the General Conference at its nineteenth session, particularly resolution 100, the General Resolutions and the Guidance Notes containing objectives relating to education in the Medium-Term Plan,

Considering that the principles of renewal and democratization of education within the contents of lifelong education should provide even greater inspiration for the action of Unesco and other Member States in the field of education,

1. *Stresses* that the programme should be aimed particularly at:

(a) making the right of education effective through an intensification of the struggle against all forms of discrimination, the generalization of access to education and the elaboration of flexible and diversified structures, with special regard to the important role of the school, corresponding to the various needs of individuals and society, with special attention to the needs of underprivileged groups and rural communities; and stimulating Member States in their efforts to eliminate the scourge of illiteracy and to promote the education of adults and their full participation in the development of the community;

(b) contributing to the strengthening of peace, disarmament, international understanding and co-operation, the promotion of human rights, the elimination of colonialism, racialism, apartheid, fascism and all other forms of oppression, and continuing and intensifying the support given to national liberation movements;

(c) creating closer links between education systems, cultural, economic and social activities and scientific and technological development;

(d) intensifying efforts to improve the content and methods of education and to ensure its relevance through a broad involvement with life and the problems facing mankind;

(e) developing and improving technical and vocational education and linking it closely to the general education;

(f) strengthening the contribution of education to cultural identity, particularly by promoting mother tongues and national languages as languages of instruction;

(g) taking special measures for the benefit of the developing countries, particularly those which are the least advanced;

(h) contributing to the improvement of the status of women through measures designed to ensure effective equality of opportunity for access to, and success in, education, thus enabling women to participate fully in development and the life of society;

2. *Considers* that the programme proposed for 1979–1980 should place special emphasis on the need to:

(a) strengthen links between education and working life, particularly through the introduction of productive work into the educational process;

(b) promote better links between school and out-of-school education, within the context of lifelong education, as well as closer association between the school and other educational institutions and agents, taking into account the important role of the school;

(c) encourage and stimulate a wide-ranging, forward-looking inquiry regarding education;

3. *Reaffirms* Unesco's special responsibility in the promotion of intellectual co-operation, discussion by the international community and the exchange of ideas, experience and information on education;

4. *Encourages* the Director-General to continue present efforts to use the proposed activities to strengthen the national capacity of Member States with a view to en-

dogenous development, and to give greater importance to training activities as a major function of education, particularly in respect of the training of the various categories of staff participating in educational action;

5. *Stresses* the particular value of the forms of international co-operation which have been devised to enable each society to ensure the advancement of education in terms of its own development requirements and priorities;

6. *Endorses* the Director-General's concern to create closer links between studies, research and standard-setting activities, on the one hand, and operational action, on the other, with a view to contributing to the renewal of education systems and their increased effectiveness;

7. *Emphasizes* in this connection the importance of creating or strengthening regional or subregional innovation networks or mechanisms;

8. *Invites* the Director-General to bear in mind the above-mentioned guidelines and considerations in the implementation of the programme for 1979–1980 in the field of education.

PART TEN
NATIONAL SECURITY AND
LAW ENFORCEMENT

Similar to numerous international agreements in other areas, those concluded in the field of national and collective security include provisions concerning communications: establishment of joint military communications networks, exchange of information and intelligence. Agreements in this area have not been included.

International co-operation in the field of law enforcement has been formalized through the International Criminal Police Organization (Interpol). The legal basis for co-operation in this area which to a large extent concerns exchange and transfer of information is the Constitution of the Organization, of which the general provisions have been documented below.

Document

Constitution of the International Criminal Police Organization (Interpol), 1956
– Articles 1–9, 31–33

INTERNATIONAL CRIMINAL POLICE ORGANIZATION, INTERPOL, 1956

Constitution

General Provisions

Article 1

The Organization called the INTERNATIONAL CRIMINAL POLICE COMMISSION shall henceforth be entitled: THE INTERNATIONAL CRIMINAL POLICE ORGANIZATION (INTERPOL). Its seat shall be in Paris.

Article 2

Its aims are:
(a) To ensure and promote the widest possible mutual assistance between all criminal police authorities within the limits of the laws existing in the different countries and in the spirit of the Universal Declaration of Human Rights;
(b) To establish and develop all institutions likely to contribute effectively to the prevention and suppression of ordinary law crimes.

Article 3

It is strictly forbidden for the Organization to undertake any intervention or activities of a political, military, religious or racial character.

Article 4

Any country may delegate as a Member to the Organization any official police body whose functions come within the framework of activities of the Organization.

The request for membership shall be submitted to the Secretary General by the appropriate governmental authority.

Membership shall be subject to approval by a two-thirds majority of the General Assembly.

Structure and Organization

Article 5

The International Criminal Police Organization (INTERPOL) shall comprise:
- The General Assembly,
- The Executive Committee,
- The General Secretariat,
- The National Central Bureau
- The Advisers.

The General Assembly

Article 6

The General Assembly shall be the body of supreme authority in the Organization. It is composed of delegates appointed by the members of the Organization.

Article 7

Each Member may be represented by one or several delegates; however for each country there shall be only one delegation head, appointed by the competent governmental authority of that country.

Because of the technical nature of the Organization, Members should attempt to include the following in their delegation:

(a) High officials of departments dealing with police affairs,
(b) Officials whose normal duties are connected with the activities of the Organization,
(c) Specialists in the subjects on the agenda.

Article 8

The functions of the General Assembly shall be the following:

(a) To carry out the duties laid down in the Constitution,
(b) to determine principles and lay down the general measures suitable for attaining the objectives of the Organization as given in Article 2 of the Constitution,
(c) To examine and approve the general programme of activities prepared by the Secretary General for the coming year,
(d) to determine any other regulations deemed necessary,
(e) To elect persons to perform the functions mentioned in the Constitution,
(f) To adopt resolutions and make recommendations to Members on matters with which the Organization is competent to deal,
(g) To determine the financial policy of the Organization,
(h) To examine and approve any agreements to be made with other organizations.

Article 9

Members shall do all within their power, in so far as is compatible with their own obligations, to carry out the decisions of the General Assembly.

*   *   *

National Central Bureau

Article 31

In order to further its aims, the Organization needs the constant and active co-operation of its Members, who should do all within their power which is compatible with the legislations of their countries to participate diligently in its activities.

Article 32

In order to ensure the above co-operation, each country shall appoint a body which will serve as the National Central Bureau. It shall ensure liaison with:

(a)   The various departments in the country,
(b)   Those bodies in other countries serving as National Central Bureau,
(c)   the Organization's General Secretariat.

Article 33

In the case of those countries where the provisions of Art. 32 are inapplicable or do not permit of effective, centralized co-operation, the General Secretariat shall decide, with these countries, the most suitable alternative means of co-operation.

*   *   *

INDEX

Advertising material, 149
African states, 109–10
American states, 101–4
  see also USA
Apartheid, 78–9, 172–9
Arab League, see League of Arab States
Arab states, 112–14
Arms race, 84–6
  see also Disarmament
Artistic works, 303–6
ASEAN, see Association of Southeast
  Asian Nations
Association of Southeast Asian Nations,
  110–12
Automated data systems, 315–30

Broadcasting, 169–70, 256, 284–6
  see also Radio communications
Broadcasting organizations, 257–60, 307–8

CCIR, see International Radio Consultative
  Committee
CCITT, see International Telegraph and
  Telephone Consultative Committee
Child, rights of, 45–7
Civil rights, 21–9
Codes of ethics, 181–2
Colonial countries, see Decolonization
Colonialism, see Decolonization
Committee on the peaceful uses of outer
  space, 266
Communications, development, 187–204
  policy, 167, 204–17
  see also New world information and
  communications order; Right to
  communicate; Telecommunications
Conference of Non-Aligned States, see
  Non-Aligned States
Conference on security and co-operation
  in Europe, 119–24
Continental Shelf, see Law of the Sea
Copyright, 280, 303, 306–7
Correction, right of, 108, 129–32, 317,
  323, 328
Correspondence, diplomatic, 239
  secrecy, 238
Council of Europe, 92–4, 314
Cultural heritage, 211, 347–51, 353–4
  property, 347
Culture, 17–21, 82, 103–4, 144–55, 205–6,
  345–61
Customs Co-operation Council, 343–4
Customs regulations, 265, 331–44

Decolonization, 35–8
Development, related to trade, 336–7

technical, 163–7
Development of communications, see
  Communications development
Diplomatic correspondence, see
  Correspondence
Direct broadcast satellites, 278–81
Disarmament, 47–51, 84–6
  see also Arms race
Discrimination, against women, 38–9
  in education, 354–7
  racial, 30–4, 79–84

Economic and Social Council, 7–8
Economic co-operation, 6, 61–9
Economic development, 63
Economic rights and duties, 17–21, 66–9
ECOSOC, see Economic and Social Council
Education, 103–4, 144–55, 345–61
  see also Discrimination in education
EEC, see European Economic Community
European Atomic Energy Community, 301
European Economic Community, 327–8,
  337–43

False reports, see Reports
Folklore, see Cultural heritage
Foreign correspondents, 157–8, 178–81
France, 126–7
Free flow of information, 142–67, 188–9,
  190–4, 212, 284–6
Freedom of information, 125, 127–42,
  189–90
Friendly relations, 123

General Agreement on Tariffs and Trade
  (GATT), 333–7
Geneva, see World Administrative Radio
  Conference, Geneva, 1979
Genocide, 29–30

Havana Declaration, see Non-alignment,
  policy of
Helsinki Conference, see Conference on
  security and co-operation in Europe
Heritage, cultural, see Cultural heritage
High Seas, see Law of the Sea
Human Rights, and scientific and
  technological development, 183–5
  basic instruments, 12–34
  regional instruments, 94–114, 126–7
  UN resolutions, 12–17, 34–47
  Unesco resolutions, 357–61

IBI, see Intergovernmental Bureau of
  Informatics

365